☆, Chapter 1 The Third D Family

Chapter 1: The Third Girl of the Cui Family

"Cui Xiang, look at you, you are being cunning again. If I see you again, you will be in trouble!" A girl in a blue shirt, pink skirt and a heart-shaped bun lowered her voice and poked the forehead of a little girl who was dozing off with a warm pillow outside the warm room. The little girl's eyes were filled with tears after being scolded like this, and she cried, "Miss Lan Xiang, I won't dare to do it again."

Lanxiang thought that she was abducted and sold to a woman at a young age and had a pitiful life. She also thought that she had a good attitude in admitting her mistakes, so she suppressed her anger and asked, "Is the third young lady still asleep?"

Cuixiang quickly shook her head and said, "No, the third lady usually sleeps until the afternoon."

Lanxiang lifted the curtain and peeked inside. Through the green gauze curtain, she saw a small ball in the quilt, rising and falling slightly. It was obvious that she was sleeping soundly. So she tiptoed out and told Cuixiang before leaving, "Be careful. If there is no one to serve you tea or water when the third lady wakes up, you will be in trouble!"

At the time of Shen, Cuixiang heard a slight noise in the warm room and hurried in. Sure enough, Cui Xiuxin, the third daughter of the Cui family, had already woken up. Her hair was slightly disheveled and her cheeks were rosy, showing the unique pink color of a young girl. Perhaps she had just woken up, and her eyes were still dazed.

"Would you like some tea to rinse your mouth?"

Cui Xiuxin nodded.

Cuixiang helped her rinse her mouth and put on her clothes. Qinxiang, who was outside, lifted the curtain and came in to fix Xiuxin's hair. Two quarters of an hour had passed. At this time, Lanxiang was heard outside saying, "Miss, have you finished dressing? Mingxiang, the maid of the first lady, is outside saying that the second lady wants you to come to the main hall."

"All right." Cui Xiang finally tied a white sable fur cape on Cui Xiu Xin before answering from inside, "Miss, all right."

Qinxiang opened the curtain for her, and Cui Xiuxin walked out. A chill hit her face, and she shivered. Lanxiang was about to ask Cuixiang to bring a hand warmer, but Qinxiang had already come out of the door and handed a warm hand warmer to Xiuxin, "Miss, be careful about your cold hands."

Outside, the sky was overcast and it was snowing lightly. A thin layer of snow had accumulated on the ground. Lanxiang was afraid that Cui Xiuxin would slip, so she held out her hand for her to hold on. In this way, they passed through two corridors and a small garden and finally reached the main hall. Before entering the door, a lady in her forties, wearing gold and silver, came out and held Cui Xiuxin's hand while leading her inside. "Oh, my child, are you cold? It's so cold." At the same time, she reminded Lanxiang and others, "You guys should be careful and don't let the girl catch a cold, okay? The winter before last, Xiuxin had a cough, which scared me so much that I couldn't sleep for several days and nights."

"Yes, ma'am." Lanxiang and Qinxiang responded in unison.

The third daughter of the Cui family is the youngest daughter of Mrs. Cui. She has been weak and sickly since childhood, so naturally she is doted on by the second wife of the Cui family. Because she is a daughter who has been raised by her side since childhood, this doting even surpasses her eldest brother Cui Jinghong.

Xiuxin was very relaxed in front of her mother, half leaning against her mother and whispering, "Mom, it's okay. I haven't had a cough for more than a year after taking the prescription prescribed by Doctor Chen. Besides, I'm older now, and Doctor Chen said that as long as I'm properly cared for, it won't recur easily."

Mrs. Cui smiled comfortingly and led Xiuxin

to sit on the low couch. Mingxiang and others in Mrs. Cui's room brought some snacks and hot tea. The mother and daughter talked affectionately for a while, and the topic turned to Cui Yixin, the second daughter of the Cui family. "Now that the girl is promised to the third master of the Xie family, she has become so arrogant that she makes trouble all day long without stopping. Today she beats this and tomorrow she scolds that. Today she complains about the style of the clothes and tomorrow she complains about the weight of the hairpin." Mrs. Cui snorted, "I just thought she was promised to the emperor as a concubine." Cui Yixin is the daughter of the eldest master of the Cui family and the second oldest among the girls.

"Although we are a branch of the Cui family and not as good as the main branch of the Qinghe Cui family, she is a legitimate daughter marrying a illegitimate son and she seems to be proud of it. She really has no sense of propriety." Madam Cui smiled again, "Tomorrow I will ask the master to help my daughter Xiuxin find a best marriage." Madam Cui started looking for this matter several years ago. Her daughter knew her very well, because she was favored by the second master since she was a child and he did not have concubines, so she didn't understand the ins and outs of the house at all. Madam Cui only hoped that she could find a simple single man from a clean family to prevent her daughter from suffering any grievances.

Cui Xiuxin was not as shy as other girls. She swallowed the sweet-scented osmanthus cake in her mouth before saying, "Mother, I want to marry a talented man like my elder sister."

The eldest sister of the Cui family, Cui Jinxin, married a commoner scholar, Zhao Zichen. Although he was from a humble family, he worked hard and won the third place in the imperial examination. Now he is an editor in the Hanlin Academy. He treats Cui Jinxin gently and considerately, and the couple respect each other like guests. Even though Cui Jinxin has been childless for three years after marrying into the Zhao family, Zhao Zichen has never mentioned the idea of taking a concubine, which makes everyone envious.

Speaking of her eldest daughter, Madam Cui could not help but frown again. "Although Jinxin married well, she has been childless for three years, which is always a hidden danger. As a mother, I can only pray to the gods and Buddha every day, hoping that Guanyin, the Goddess of Childbirth, can protect her a little bit."

"Big sister... well, it's strange that you can have a baby." Cui Jin said incoherently with another sweet-scented osmanthus cake stuffed in her heart. Madam Cui Er looked at her daughter's clear and bright eyes, lovingly reached out to wipe the cake crumbs from the corners of her mouth, and sighed deeply in her heart.

Cui Xiuxin had finished her meal at the Second Madam's place. When she passed by the small garden, she saw some red plum blossoms in full bloom. She could not help but stop and go over to smell them. Lanxiang and Qinxiang, two big maids, hurriedly opened an umbrella for her to shield her from the snow. Cui Xiuxin had just finished her meal and did not feel cold. She felt warm all over, so she said, "Let's stay here for a while before going back." Lanxiang said, "You can stay for a while, but don't stand too long. The snow is cold and wet. Be careful not to get your shoes wet and catch a cold."

Cui Xiuxin was just about to ask Lanxiang to pick a few plum blossoms and put them in the bedroom, when she saw Ruixiang and Ruixiang from the second young lady's room not far away coming over with a vase of flowers. When they saw Xiuxin, they bowed their heads and called out, "Third young lady."

Seeing this, Lanxiang knew that Cui Yixin had ordered people to come and pick the flowers, so she said, "Oh, you guys are early. The red plum blossoms have only been in bloom for a few days and you're here so eagerly."

"Sister Lanxiang, you got the wrong idea. It's not that we came early. Our eldest lady said that the second young lady is going to get married, and she ordered the whole mansion to give priority to our second young lady. Our second young lady happens to be a red plum. When the eldest lady saw that a few branches had bloomed today, she told us not to forget to pick some for the second young lady and put them in her bedroom. But if your young lady likes it, it's okay for our second young lady to give way. Anyway, there are so many good things in our young lady's room." Ruixiang said.

Lanxiang was so angry that her face turned red and white. She was about to retort, but when she turned around, she saw Cui Xiuxin picked five or six red plum blossoms while she was talking. The red plums were in full bloom, making her cheeks look rosy.

"Lanxiang and Qinxiang, let's go back." After saying that, she walked towards her own garden, leaving Ruixiang and Ruixiang staring at each other in silence, stunned.

"Girl, why did you pick all the plum blossoms so quickly? You should at least inform the second girl." Qinxiang said.

Cui Xiuxin asked in confusion, "Didn't Ruixiang say that she would give it to us?"

Qin Xiang: "…"

Lan Xiang smiled and said, "You have to be straightforward when talking to our girls. Our girls will take those beating around the bush seriously. But it's okay, they are just some small things, they won't cause any trouble."

Cui Xiuxin didn't pay attention to what they were saying at this time. She happily put the red plums into the blue and white porcelain vase and kept them in water. The room was immediately filled with fragrance. Before going to bed, Xiuxin ate a bowl of sweet lotus seed soup and three sticky cakes before rinsing her mouth and going to bed. Qinxiang and Lanxiang, the two big maids, slept together in the outer room. Before going to bed, Qinxiang asked, "Who do you think will be taken with us if the young lady gets married?"

Lan Xiang said, "I will definitely go with you. From what Madam said, we should take at least four with us."

Qin Xiang was silent for a moment, took off her clothes and lay down with a lot on her mind. Lan Xiang looked at her expression, let go of her hair and said, "Why, you don't want to go?"

Qin Xiang shook her head, "Not really."

Lan Xiang was silent, thinking of her daughter's temperament, she couldn't help but sigh in her heart. She only hoped that her daughter's future husband's family environment would be simpler, otherwise...

Today it was Lianxiang, the second-class maid, who was on duty. At midnight, she had just rested on the small couch in the outer room when she heard a low moan coming from the inner room. Lianxiang was so scared that she threw back the quilt and ran inside, only to see Cui Xiuxin holding her

lower abdomen in pain with sweat on her forehead. Lianxiang was startled and quickly took a white sweat towel to wipe the sweat off Cui Xiuxin's forehead, "Girl, girl, girl, what's wrong with you?"
"I... my stomach hurts... ah..." Cui Xiu was so heartbroken that her brows were tightly furrowed. She bit her lower lip tightly and was almost unable to speak.
Lianxiang quickly ran to the outer room and knocked on the door, "Lanxiang, Qinxiang, get up quickly, the girl is sick!"
Lanxiang was almost asleep, but when she heard that, she got up, put on her clothes and opened the door. "What's wrong?"
"Lanxiang, go and see the girl. She suddenly has a stomachache and is sweating all over." Lianxiang said anxiously.
Lanxiang was also startled. She didn't even bother to put on her clothes and went to the warm room. As she walked, she said, "Go to the front of the lady's room to find Mingxiang and see if the lady is asleep. If she is asleep, don't disturb the lady. Go with Mingxiang to find a capable servant and ask him to invite Doctor Chen who usually treats our girl."
"Okay, I'll go right away." Lianxiang agreed and trotted away.
On this side, Lanxiang served Cui Xiuxin a bowl of warm water and changed her into dry clothes. She felt relieved when she saw that Xiuxin's pain was gradually becoming less severe.

It was past midnight when Doctor Chen came over. After taking the pulse through the curtain, Doctor Chen stroked his graying beard and asked, "What did the third young lady take tonight?"

Lanxiang said, "In the evening, I had a bowl of rice, a few pieces of venison, a bowl of fish fillet soup, five or six pieces of osmanthus cake, four or five pieces of cloud cake, and before going to bed, I drank a bowl of lotus seed soup and three sticky cakes."

Doctor Chen said, "It's nothing serious. You just ate some sticky food at night. It's hard to digest and that's why you have abdominal pain. I'll prescribe some medicine to help digestion. You can take it for three days and it will be fine. But you have to remind Miss San not to eat too much sweets during the day. It's easy to make you fat and it's hard to digest."

Lanxiang took a look at her girl's slightly plump face and round and smooth figure, and sighed deeply again.

☆, Chapter 2: Qionglin Banquet

Chapter 2: The Banquet at Qionglin
Although Cui Xiuxin was not seriously injured, the Second Madam was alarmed. The next morning, she rushed to Cui Xiuxin's courtyard in a hurry and called her with a worried look. She was relieved to see that Xiuxin looked normal. She also blamed the

maids in the courtyard for not taking good care of her and deducted one month's salary from the two maids, Lanxiang and Qinxiang.

A month later, the imperial edict, which was issued every three years, was released, and the Cui family had a happy event. The second son of the second master, Cui Qihong, ranked 14th in the second class and earned the title of Jinshi. The whole family was filled with joy and laughter.

On this side, Mrs. Jiang, the second wife of Cui, was delighted, but she set her sights on the runner-up of the first class. The runner-up was called Li Yuzhi. Her father was the magistrate of Yangzhou County, but her father died early, and she had no brothers or sisters, and only her mother was at home. And because there was a precedent in this dynasty that the three people in the first class could stay in Beijing to serve, so Li Yuzhi would definitely stay in Beijing. This condition hit Jiang's heart, and she was so happy that her eyebrows were about to fly.

"Second Madam, the second master is back." Mingxiang stepped into the main courtyard, her eyes full of joy.

Jiang stopped her embroidery and quickly stood up to greet him. "The master is back. Mingxiang, hurry up and bring the food." At the same time, she ordered the second-class maid Danxiang to heat up the charcoal fire. "Are you cold? It's snowing outside all day."

Cui Zhengkai, the second master of Cui, is now in his prime, with a tall figure. Although his eyebrows and eyes are vicissitudes, he still looks handsome. Cui Zhengkai is now the third-rank left deputy censor, which is an important position, and he is busy with official duties. Although Jiang is the only one in Cui Zhengkai's room, Cui Zhengkai does not come to the main room every day. When he is busy late, he will just rest in the study.

Cui Zhengkai took off his outermost felt and handed it to Mingxiang, then straightened his long-collared jacket before sitting down and taking the tea from Cui. Seeing that he frowned slightly and looked unhappy, Jiang winked at Mingxiang. After Mingxiang and the others left, Cui stood up and stood behind Cui Zhengkai to massage his shoulders, "Master, have you been worried recently?"

Cui Zhengkai sighed, "It's just the things in the court. There are serious divisions among the civil officials. One faction is led by Wang Fusheng of the Wang family, and the other is led by Cui Jinyi, the main branch of our Cui family. I am the left deputy censor, and I am really sitting on pins and needles all the time. I really have to be careful at every step, otherwise, if I make a wrong step, I will be doomed."

Jiang paused, "In theory, the main branch of the Cui family and we are of the same origin, but the power of the Wang family is getting stronger and stronger. What are your plans, sir?" Jiang didn't know much about court affairs, but the reason why Cui Zhengkai talked to Jiang was that he had been suppressing some things in his heart for a long time and wanted to talk to someone.

Cui Zhengkai took another sip of tea and said, "The main branch of the Cui family has always looked down upon us side branches. If we side with them, I'm afraid we won't get much benefit."

"What does the master mean?" Jiang's heart skipped a beat.

Cui Zhengkai squeezed Jiang's hand, and felt it was smooth. Cui Zhengkai's brows relaxed, "We can't rush this matter. We need to plan it slowly."

Cui Zhengkai had two concubines before marrying Jiang. After marrying Jiang, he also had a concubine named Zhang. Concubine Zhang even gave birth to a concubine named Cui Minxin, but she died soon after giving birth to Cui Minxin. Jiang was the eldest daughter of the Jiang family in Jiangnan. She was of noble status, so marrying Cui Zhengkai was considered marrying down. Jiang was also very capable of managing the household. After only a month of entering the mansion, she was praised by everyone in the mansion. Even Mrs. Cui brought her son to tell him that it was his blessing to marry the daughter of the Jiang family and he should treat her well. Jiang was originally very beautiful, full of the gentleness of a Jiangnan woman. In addition, she gave birth to the eldest son Cui Jinghong and the second son Cui Qihong as soon as she married. Therefore, Cui Zhengkai gradually became indifferent to Concubine Zhang. After Concubine Zhang passed away, he never took a concubine again.

After resting, Jiang half leaned on Cui Zhengkai's shoulder and chatted about some things at home. Cui Zhengkai half closed his eyes and responded incoherently. Jiang took the opportunity to tactfully mention the top three people who passed the imperial examination this year. Cui Zhengkai became interested when he mentioned this, and opened his eyes and said:

"This year, we can say that there are many talented people. The number one scholar is from the Sun family in Jiangbei. He is over 40 years old. Originally, Sun Changchun has always been obsessed with calligraphy and painting and had no intention of pursuing a career in politics. In recent years, he has become more focused and won the number one scholar. The emperor is very happy and will definitely make use of him. As for the runner-up, although he was born in poverty, he is a good writer and has a handsome appearance. It is very easy for him to enter the Hanlin Academy or one of the six ministries. The third scholar is the eldest son of Wang Fusheng from the Wang family. He is only sixteen years old now. He is a young prodigy and has inherited his father's style. He is really a person of orchids and jade trees. He is also very humble and does not have the wildness of young people at all. It can only be said that the family tradition of the Wang family is really good, and the children born are all excellent."

Jiang secretly tried to figure out Cui Zhengkai's intention and asked tentatively, "Master, do you mean to..."

Cui Zhengkai glanced at her and shook his head silently, "I have thought about it before, but Wang Fusheng hinted that he intends to marry into the Xie family."

"The Xie family in Jiangzhong?" Jiang's eyes widened and she took a deep breath.

"Yes." Cui Zhengkai nodded.

It is said that the clans in this world are intertwined, among which the Wang family, Xie family, Cui family, and Sun family are the most powerful. The Wang family has always been the leader of the four major clans, but the power of the Xie family should not be underestimated. The royal family often marries princesses or princesses to the Wang family. For example, the wife of the Wang family is the eldest princess of the previous emperor and the aunt of the current emperor. The eldest wife of the Wang family is the daughter of the third prince, Princess Anyang. However, the royal family often marries the daughters of the Xie family as concubines and queens. For example, the current queen mother is a daughter of the Xie family, and the most favored concubine is also a daughter of the Xie family. Therefore, the status of the Xie family among the four major clans is also transcendent.

"So that's the case." Jiang felt a little sorry, but she smiled after thinking about it, "That's fine. But I don't know what the master's plan is for Xiuxin's marriage?"

Cui Zhengkai said, "I have some ideas in mind, but I still need to think carefully. What's more, I have to discuss this matter with my mother."

"That's right." Jiang was worried that Cui Zhengkai would marry Xiuxin into a wealthy family, so she asked, "What does the master think of this year's runner-up, Li Yuzhi?"

Cui Zhengkai was silent for a while and said, "He is a talented person, but his family background is too weak. We already have a Jinxin who married into a poor family. How can our Xiuxin's marriage be so sloppy?"

Jiang Shi held back her words after hearing this, and her heart began to churn. From what the master meant, he was determined not to marry Xiu Xin into a poor family again. She was afraid that Xiu Xin's marriage would be chosen from the Sun family, the Xie family, or other large families. But no matter who was chosen in the end, it would be a large mansion with complicated relationships. How could Xiu Xin, who was confused, handle it well?

I'm afraid it will take some thought, Jiang thought secretly.

It happened that Cui Qihong won the second place and was ranked 14th, so a big banquet was prepared as usual. Although the Cui family was not as good as the Qinghe branch, it was still a first-class wealthy family. The eldest master Cui inherited the title, and the second master Cui was appointed as the third-rank imperial censor. There were many powerful officials and nobles who came to congratulate at the banquet. Even half of the top three winners came, and the runner-up Li Yuzhi was naturally present.

The whole Cui Mansion was busy that day. Even Cui Xiuxin's two second-class maids, Cuixiang and Lianxiang, were called to work. Cui Xiuxin was a young lady who was raised in seclusion. At this time, she had some free time. It was quite lively when she got together with Yixin, Minxin, Yuxin and others in the mansion.

Among the four sisters, the most eye-catching one is Yixin, who wears a pink double-breasted jacket on the upper body, a pomegranate colored silk pleated skirt on the lower body, and several jade hairpins in her hair. Minxin is the daughter of Aunt Zhang. Not to mention that Aunt Zhang has passed away, even if Aunt Zhang is still alive, she, a concubine's daughter, is just a green leaf next to the flowers compared to Xiuxin, the real legitimate daughter who is doted on. Therefore, Minxin has developed a taciturn personality for a long time and is unwilling to speak easily. Yuxin is Yixin's sister. She is only six years old now, which is the most lively age. It's just strange that she doesn't get close to her sister Yixin, but is particularly close to Xiuxin. At this time, she is asking Xiuxin to pick up the mutton from the hot pot for her.

Xiuxin followed her instructions and picked up a piece of thinly cut mutton for her, dipped it in sauce and passed it to her mouth to feed her. Chen Pozi, Yuxin's wet nurse, said, "Hey, Third Miss, please feed my sister less. If she gets sick later, it will be my fault."

Xiuxin put down her chopsticks and was about to speak, but Lanxiang, who was standing beside her, snorted coldly and said, "It seems that our girl fed your sister a few slices of mutton and she got sick. Your sister is wearing a gold carved jade bracelet, and if she gets hurt by accident, it will be our girl's fault. In this case, our girl will not dare to get close to your sister anymore."

Mrs. Chen's face turned red and white. After a long while, she stammered, "Miss Lanxiang, that's not how you say it."

Xiuxin didn't really listen to what they were saying, her attention was focused on the food on the table. Because there was a wedding in the mansion today, the dishes on the table were very rich. In addition to the mutton hot pot, there were also her favorite white braised fish lips, charcoal grilled venison, first-class official bird's nest, etc. In addition, there were several exquisite Suzhou-style pastries on the table. These things made Xiuxin's attention never leave the dishes.

"Although our Cui family is also a wealthy family, we can't compare to the direct line of the Xie family. I heard that the Xie family spends as much as one thousand taels of silver on food every day, and many of the things are directly awarded from the palace. No other family can afford such a luxury." Yi Xin's eyes were full of satisfaction.

"Oh, my aunt, this is incredible." Mrs. Chen said flatteringly.

Xiu Xin raised her head when she heard this, her eyes slightly shining, "Wouldn't that mean there would be a lot of delicious food?"

"Of course." When Yixin saw Xiuxin's look, the pride between her eyebrows became more obvious.

"My sister married well." There are lots of delicious food every day.

Yi Xin raised her eyebrows when she heard Xiu Xin complimenting her. "Third sister, you will definitely find a good husband in the future. But if you want to marry into a big family like the Xie family, you may need some luck."

Xiu Xin lowered her head and stuffed a piece of mutton into her mouth, "Second sister is right."

At this time, Lianxiang came over and called Lanxiang over to whisper something. Lanxiang was surprised after hearing what she said. She turned back and went back to the pavilion and said to Xiuxin, "Third Miss, the second lady in front said that she just got a piece of top-quality Su brocade. Please come over and take a look."

☆, Chapter 3: There is no coincidence in the world

Chapter 3: There is no coincidence in the world

Cui Xiuxin heard Lanxiang say this, but she did not doubt it. She said to her sisters, "I'll be back soon." Then she followed Lianxiang to the front. Before leaving, Xiuxin did not forget to pick up a few pieces of candied fruit with her handkerchief and eat them on the road. When they reached the small garden, Lianxiang saw Xiuxin like this and could not help but persuade her, "Miss, you should eat less sweets. You had a stomachache because you ate too much the other day. Besides, if someone sees you eating on the road and tells the master, the master will punish you."

Originally, Xiuxin didn't take Lianxiang's words to heart, but Lianxiang's last sentence played a decisive role. However, she was reluctant to part with the candied fruits wrapped in her handkerchief. After weighing the pros and cons, Xiuxin stuffed all the candied fruits in her hand into her mouth, making her cheeks plump and making her eyes look even rounder.

Lianxiang was at a loss whether to laugh or cry. "Miss, why are you going through so much trouble just for a few candied fruits? If you want to eat some, you can just ask the kitchen staff to prepare them for you at any time."

"Isn't that different..." Cui Xiuxin bit the candied fruit in her mouth with difficulty, and spoke vaguely, "Today is a rare day for my brother to pass the imperial examination and host a banquet for guests, and no one is watching over me. On ordinary days, I would never be allowed to do this."

Lianxiang smiled and said, "That's true."

When Xiuxin passed by the small garden, she saw that the red plums she had picked the day before had bloomed again. She could not help but linger among them for a while and said, "Next time we come back, we can get a small bottle and put the snow on the red plums in it. It will be perfect for making tea in the spring next year."

"But there are only a few hundred red plum blossoms, and even less snow on them. How can there be so many to make tea?" Lianxiang said.

"How many do you think there are? It's great to be able to collect a few small ones in a winter. Is it possible that there are several large jars of them?"

"Miss, look, there seems to be someone in front." Lianxiang said anxiously, "From the way he is dressed, he doesn't seem to be from our house."

Cui Xiuxin leaned over to look over there through the thick flowers and trees, and only vaguely saw a tall man walking towards this side. He was tall and slender, with an extraordinary demeanor, and the cloud-patterned brocade boots on his feet made a squeaking sound as he stepped on the snow.

"Oh, I'm afraid it's the guests in front." Cui Xiuxin immediately lowered her head, feeling a little panicked. The Cui family had very strict family education. Unmarried young ladies would avoid meeting outsiders, not to mention their own uncles and brothers. "Lianxiang, let's go quickly."

It had just snowed, the ground was slippery, and Xiuxin was walking in a hurry. She accidentally stepped on a piece of ice and fell backwards. Lianxiang was so frightened that she cried out in a low voice, "Girl!"

Xiuxin was not thin to begin with, and she looked even more plump today. She was not seriously injured after the fall, except that her outer cape and trouser legs were soaked. Xiuxin struggled to get up with

Lianxiang's hand, but saw that the man over there was already three meters away. Perhaps he knew that there was an unmarried girl over here, so he stood still.

Xiuxin glanced over there and was shocked. This man had such an aura that was hard to find in the entire Cui Mansion. At this moment, he was looking at Xiuxin with interest, his lips slightly raised, and a hint of mischief flashed in his narrow eyes. Xiuxin's face suddenly turned red, and she lowered her head and cursed in a low voice, "Lecher." She turned around and took Lianxiang away in a hurry.

The man watched Cui Xiuxin's hurriedly running back and then he noticed a handkerchief left on the ground. He bent down to pick it up and saw a very beautiful word embroidered on the lower right corner of the white brocade handkerchief. The center was mottled with honey color, as if it had been wrapped with candied fruit or something. The man chuckled and said, "Interesting."

Xiuxin hurried to the main room, but she didn't see Jiang. She was surprised. Then she saw Mingxiang coming in with a plate of snacks "Miss San, the Madam is still entertaining guests in front. Please sit down. The Madam will be here soon." Xiuxin was relieved. She sat down and picked up a fried five-spice soybean and put it in her mouth. Mingxiang winked at Lianxiang and said, "There are more people in the front.

Lianxiang, come with me to help."

Lianxiang hurriedly took her leave, lifted the curtain and went out.

Although Xiuxin was puzzled, she did not think too much about it. She just thought that there were not enough guests for today's banquet and the front was short of manpower. After waiting for a while, Xiuxin saw that there seemed to be no one in the main room. It was so quiet and strange. She was about to lift the curtain to go out, but she saw a man walking in. The man was about twenty years old, dressed in green, with fair skin, delicate eyebrows and eyes, and quite a romantic taste. But his cheeks were slightly red, and his eyes were slightly blurred, as if he was slightly drunk.

Xiu Xin was startled and wondered what day it was that she met men from outside one after another. However, compared to the quick glance in the garden just now, this time a man and a woman were alone in the same room, which was really embarrassing.

This man is undoubtedly Li Yuzhi.

During the banquet, Cui Jinghong and Cui Qihong forced him to drink three or four glasses of wine. He was not good at drinking, so after three or four glasses, he immediately felt dizzy. Cui Qihong sent a servant to take him to the inner room to rest. The servant led him into the room, and he didn't pay much attention to it, thinking that it was a guest room or some boy's room. But when he lifted the curtain, he saw a girl with a panicked face sitting inside. The girl was about fifteen or sixteen years old, with amazingly white skin, as if it could be blown away, and some fat on her cheeks. When she stared at him with her round, dark eyes, he felt as if a kitten was looking at and scratching him.

Cui Xiuxin was flustered and embarrassed. Her face was like a swollen steamed bun, hot and swollen. She was stunned for a while before saying, "You...you...how did you get into the inner room?"

Li Yuzhi took several steps back and lowered her head, saying, "I didn't know the young lady was here, and I barged in without thinking. I deserve to die for offending the young lady."

Although Cui Xiuxin was so panicked that she didn't know what to do, she didn't lose her composure. She stamped her feet and said angrily, "Why don't you leave quickly!"

Li Yuzhi suddenly realized what was going on and bowed repeatedly while retreating in a panic.

Li Yuzhi had just left for a while, and Xiuxin was still in a state of confusion when she saw Jiang Shi coming in after lifting the curtain. Seeing her daughter's blushing face, she couldn't help but smile shyly and said, "Xiuxin, what's wrong? Who did you see just now?"

Xiuxin's face turned redder when she heard this, and she just lowered her head and said nothing. Jiang took Xiuxin to the inner room and said, "Xiuxin, the young man who just came in is named Li Yuzhi. He is the runner-up of this year's imperial examination. He has first-class character and literary talent. My daughter, you also met him today. What do you think?"

Even though Xiuxin was slow, she finally came to her senses. She half opened her mouth and asked in surprise, "Mother, did you deliberately bring that person in?" Xiuxin never expected that her mother would dare to do such a shocking thing.

Jiang sighed, "I had no choice but to do this, otherwise the old lady and your father would definitely marry you off to the Sun family, the Xie family, or other big families. I thought about it over and over again, and I came up with this plan. Although this is risky, with the power of our Cui family, even if Li Yuzhi doesn't rush to ask for marriage, or even if our Cui family forces him to marry, he will have no choice."

Cui Xiuxin pursed her lips and said nothing, lowering her head and said, "If I force someone to marry me, I'm afraid there's no point in that."

Jiang touched her daughter's face and said, "My daughter is so good. He will definitely like you when he sees you. If you marry well, I can rest assured."

In the evening, Cui Xiuxin was so worried that she only ate a few bites of dinner. Lanxiang helped her take a bath and saw that she was still depressed. She asked, "What's wrong with you? You have been absent-minded all day?"

Cui Xiuxin: "Lanxiang, you say..." She paused and didn't know where to start. She sighed first, her heart filled with the light sorrow that only belongs to a young girl. "Forget it, let it go."

Although Xiuxin had never experienced the taste of family fighting, she knew that the eldest lady, the two concubines, and the legitimate sons and daughters and illegitimate sons and daughters of the eldest master's family were fighting fiercely. She thought of the handsome man in the daytime and her mother's words, and she felt a little relieved, "I just hope that things can really go as smoothly as expected."

In fact, things did not go as smoothly as Jiang thought. For the first time in so many years, Cui Zhengkai was furious with his wife. He slammed the teacup in his hand to the ground, his face livid, "You are making a fuss!"

Jiang was startled, her eyes were red, "Master..."

"You are too reckless." Cui Zhengkai was so angry that his hands were shaking. "Let's not talk about whether Li Yuzhi is willing to marry our Xiuxin. Even if she is willing, how can a girl with a bad reputation before marriage gain a foothold in her husband's family? Moreover, I am having a hard time in the court now, and the direct descendants of the Cui family don't give me any help. Marriage is inevitable. I have only one direct daughter, Xiuxin, and I absolutely cannot marry her into a poor family!"

Jiang Shi burst into tears when she heard this, and cried, "Master, I didn't think so much. I only wanted Xiu Xin's best interests. With her personality, how could she understand the complexity of the inner house? If she married into a mansion, she wouldn't be as good as her."

Cui Zhengkai suppressed his anger after hearing this, but he didn't say anything. However, his face was pale and it was obvious that he was still angry. "Ruohan, you are confused."

Ruohan was Jiang's maiden name. When they were young, the couple were very close. Cui Zhengkai always called Jiang Ruohan, and later gradually changed to calling her Madam. Now Jiang was stunned when she heard him call her like that again.

"Whether life is good or bad is not only determined by where the third girl marries, but more importantly, it depends on the husband's heart. If the husband is willing to protect her, even if the third girl has no ulterior motives, who can hurt her in the slightest? If the husband is not

interested, even if he is full of schemes, he can do nothing. Don't you understand after marrying me for so many years?" Cui Zhengkai paused and said, "Ruohan, after Aunt Zhang gave birth to Minxin, she was not well and died in less than two years. I know the ins and outs of this very well, but I didn't pursue it because I have you in my heart, and I respect and love you."
Jiang's face turned pale when he heard this. Cui Zhengkai held Jiang's shoulders and said gently, "The third girl is also the apple of my eye. I will not let her suffer any injustice."
Jiang asked, "Does the master have a plan?"
Cui Zhengkai said, "Indeed."
"who is it?"
Cui Zhengkai said, "The second son of Sun Yangchun from the Jiangbei Sun family."

☆, Chapter 5: Breaking off an Engagement

Chapter 5: Breaking off an Engagement
The man took Xiuxin through the garden, walked along the corridor, and finally arrived at a palace. The eunuch at the door saw him and greeted him with a smile, "Greetings, King..." The man waved his hand at him, "Call a capable maid to find a pink dress for this girl."
"Yes, we will do it right away."
Seeing him walking freely in the palace, Xiuxin secretly guessed his identity. Then she changed her mind and felt that she was

reckless. Why did she follow a strange man like this? If he had no bad intentions, it would be fine. If he had any bad intentions, what should she do? When she thought of it, Xiuxin felt a chill down her spine.

"Let's go?"

Xiu Xin came back to her senses and exclaimed, "Where are we going?"

Seeing her dazed look, the man smiled and said, "Of course, go to the inner room. Do you want to change your skirt at the gate?"

This made Xiuxin lower her head, feeling her face burning. She heard the man chuckle in her ear, and she had no choice but to follow him to the inner room. The layout of the palace was indeed more luxurious than that of the Cui family. As soon as Xiuxin stepped into the inner room, she saw gold and jade everywhere, and she lowered her head and dared not look around.

After a while, a person who looked like a palace maid came in dragging a tray. She bowed to the man and said to Xiu Xin, "Miss, here are three pink skirts. Take a look and see which one you like."

Xiu Xin took the tray and thanked her. The maid bowed and said, "I'll take my leave."

Seeing that only Xiuxin and the man were left in the room, Xiuxin faced him face to face, but the man just sat on the chair with no intention of leaving. Xiuxin gritted her teeth and said with a red face, "Why don't you go out?"

The man laughed and stood up, his eyes full

of romance, "I'm just going out, what's the hurry." After that, he strode out and carefully closed the door for her. Xiuxin breathed a sigh of relief, chose a dress that was most similar to the one she was wearing, put it on, and then opened the door. As expected, the man hadn't left yet. He stood tall and tall at the door. When he saw her coming out, he praised her, "Not bad." Xiuxin glared at him. The man saw that Xiu Xin was still holding the dirty skirt in her hand, so he reached out and took it, "I'll hold it for you."
Xiu Xin may have been confused by the series of things, but she actually nodded, "Thank you, I'll be back soon."
Unexpectedly, as soon as I walked out of the door, I found that the sky had darkened, and it was actually snowing. Xiuxin stood on the eaves for a while, but the snow still didn't stop. She was secretly worried, thinking that if her mother couldn't see her again after being out for so long. It's time to worry.
"girl."
Xiuxin looked back and saw that it was the senior palace maid. "Young lady, please hold the umbrella. The road outside is slippery. Be careful when walking."
Xiu Xin was even more grateful, "Thank you, sister."
The palace maid smiled and said, "How can I be worthy of being your elder sister?"
Xiuxin hurried to the western banquet, but

the banquet had already ended. Twos and threes of ladies and girls were holding the hands of maids and getting on the carriage. Xiuxin was getting anxious when she heard her mother's voice, "Xiuxin."
"Mother."
"Oh, my sweetheart, you've worried me to death. Where have you been? I haven't seen you for such a long time." Jiang patted Xiuxin's hand, "You never make me feel at ease for a moment."
"Nothing." Xiu Xin said, "I had a few glasses of wine and went to the garden to get some fresh air."
Jiang said, "This is an important place in the palace. Do you think you are in the mansion and can walk around randomly? It's fine if nothing happens, but if something happens, who can protect you?"
Cui Yixin looked at Cui Xiuxin for a long while and exclaimed, "Xiuxin, why did you change your skirt?"
"I got my skirt dirty when I was going to the garden, and I happened to meet a maid, so I asked her to get me a skirt."
Jiang always treated Cui Yixin harshly. She held Xiuxin's hand and walked towards the carriage. "Stop talking so much. The snow is getting heavier. Let's hurry out of the palace."
After resting at night, Cui Xiuxin sat on the bed in a daze, holding the warm hot water bottle, thinking of the description of the man in the daytime, and secretly

spit in her heart. He didn't look like a playboy in his teens. Although he was younger than her father, he was after all a man over thirty. She never thought he would be like this... Xiuxin touched her hot cheeks, lay down anxiously, and prayed secretly before going to bed, never meeting him again.

It is said that because of Cui Xiuxin's performance at the Qionglin Banquet, everyone in the capital knew that the third lady of the Cui Mansion was a dull person, and she was not good at poetry and literature. Fortunately, in this era, women are virtuous without talent, so no one said anything. In fact, Cui Xiuxin just couldn't write poetry. She had read the Four Books and Five Classics, but she was a little less talented and could not understand it as quickly as others. Jiang was worried these days, fearing that because of the incident at the Qionglin Banquet, Xiuxin's reputation would be ruined and she would have a rift with her future in-laws. It was not until she received the visiting card from the eldest lady of the Sun family that Jiang felt relieved.

Although the marriage between the Cui and Sun families was not announced, both families had already expressed their intention. Mrs. Sun sent a visiting card specifically to talk to Jiang, meet Cui Xiuxin, and go back to choose a date to set the marriage.

The father of Madam Sun was a Jinshi, a great scholar, and once served as the prince's tutor, and was quite respected. But after all, her family background was weak, not as good as that of the daughters of aristocratic families. After she married into the Sun family, she gave birth to two legitimate sons. The eldest son had already married, and the second son was Sun Peifang. Madam Sun brought her second son Sun Peifang into the mansion, and there were maids and servants waiting at the door to greet them early in the morning. Madam Sun followed the maids and servants into the mansion, and after a quarter of an hour, she saw the second wife of the Cui family, Jiang, waiting at the door of the main room. Seeing her coming, Jiang greeted her with a smile on her face, "Madam, I have been waiting for you for so long, and I am finally here."

"Don't say that, I'm looking forward to seeing you." Madam Sun said as she took Jiang's hand and walked into the house. After the two sat down, Mingxiang and other maids presented various snacks and fragrant tea. Madam Sun had been nodding in her heart when she saw that everyone in the Cui Mansion was in a serious state. Now she was even more satisfied to see Jiang's noble and graceful manner. She couldn't help but ask, "Why don't you see the third lady?"

Jiang said, "Xiu Xin is still in school now. She will be back after school."

"Oh?" Madam Sun raised her eyebrows. "The third young lady is still studying now?"
Jiang said, "She just learned some female rules and regulations from the teacher, which is not worth much. She is just a little knowledgeable about documents and account books, so that she won't marry into a family and not be able to manage the household, which would be a joke."
Madam Sun said, "That's right. A woman without talent is virtuous. It's not good to have a reputation as a talented woman. It's great if she can read a few words and understand some documents."
Mrs. Sun's words were directed at Xie Yulan of the Xie family. Xie Yulan was her niece and Sun Peifang's cousin. However, Mrs. Sun had always disliked her, thinking that it was unbecoming for a girl to spend her days writing and trying to be outstanding.
The two chatted for a while, and then they heard Mingxiang lift the curtain and say, "The third lady is here."
Madam Sun looked up and saw a girl about fifteen years old walking in. She was wearing a light green vest on the upper body, a light yellow skirt on the lower body, and a white cloak on the outside. Her eyebrows and eyes were very beautiful, but her cheeks were still a little chubby, making her look childish.
Jiang waved at her, "Xiu Xin, come over and meet the eldest lady of the Sun family."
Xiuxin greeted Madam Sun, then lowered her

head and sat down beside Jiang. A little while later, a little maid brought over a small stove to warm her hands. Mingxiang brought her a cup of hot tea. Xiuxin took a sip of tea and felt that her whole body was finally warmed up. She felt comfortable all over and fixed her eyes on the food on the table. However, since there were guests, Xiuxin did not dare to act recklessly. She just lowered her head and listened to Jiang and Madam Sun talking.

Madam Sun saw Xiuxin lowering her head, her hands neatly placed on her legs, with the demeanor of a daughter of a noble family, and nodded secretly in her heart, and then asked Jiang Xiuxin's birth date and other things, Jiang answered them all. Madam Sun then turned the topic to her own son, "The girls in your family are really extraordinary, unlike my boy, who is a complete devil. As a mother, I have never been relieved."

"Madam, you are too modest." Jiang smiled and said, "There are four great young masters in the capital, and your second son is one of them. His character and talent are beyond reproach. How could he be a devil? Even the emperor has praised your son highly."

Madam Sun was naturally happy to hear this, "That's a compliment from His Majesty."

After hearing this, Xiu Xin understood it no matter how dumb she was. It was clearly the Sun family coming to look for their future daughter-in-law! Xiu Xin glanced at Jiang and thought to herself, didn't my mother tell me that she would marry me to the second-place winner, Li Yuzhi? What's going on now? Has something changed? She thought of the pair of mandarin ducks she met in the rockery at the Qionglin Banquet. Wasn't the woman called Sun Lang? Could it be Sun Peifang? If so, wouldn't she be marrying into a hell?

"Third Miss, what do you like to do on weekdays?" Mrs. Sun asked with a smile.

Cui Xiuxin came back to her senses and said respectfully, "I usually stay in my room to do some embroidery, or I play with my sisters." In fact, when she was free, she was either eating or on the way to find food. Fortunately, Jiang Shi reminded her to answer like this if someone did something for her, otherwise it would be impossible to tell the truth.

Madam Sun said again, "Let's talk together. It will be boring for Miss San to be confined here. Why don't we let Miss San go out to play? It will be cheaper for us."

Jiang knew what was going on and knew that Madam Sun wanted to discuss the marriage between the two families with her. She waved her hand and said, "Why don't you go outside and find your sister Minxin."

"Yes, mother." Xiuxin responded and left. Lanxiang followed Xiuxin and said with a smile, "It seems that the young lady will be very happy soon."

Xiuxin was preoccupied with her own thoughts and pretended not to hear anything. After a while, she said, "Lanxiang, how about we sneak to the front yard and take a look today?"

Lanxiang joked, "Even if the girl wants to meet her future son-in-law, there's no need to be so anxious, right?"

Xiu Xin was not anxious at all. She was like an ant on a hot pot. "No, I have to go and take a look now."

After walking for a quarter of an hour, they finally arrived at the front yard. Lanxiang pulled the servant who served the second master and asked him about the master who was meeting the second young master of the Sun family, Sun Peifang, in the front hall. Xiuxin asked, "Is there any way to see the person inside?" The servant was a lively person, "There is an annex behind the main hall, Miss San, just follow me."

Xiuxin followed the boy in and through the crack in the door, she could see clearly what was going on inside. Cui Zhengkai was sitting upright inside, and a young man in a blue robe was standing next to him. Xiuxin's heart was pounding, and she held her breath and moved closer to take a look. The young man in the blue robe happened to turn around, and Xiuxin saw his face, and she turned pale with fright.

That person was indeed the man I saw in the rockery that day!

The second young master of the Sun family actually had an affair with the girl of the Xie family!

If I marry him, how can anything good happen?

Cui Xiuxin was in a state of anxiety, while there was news that Cui Yixin, the second daughter of the Cui family, had been divorced by Xie Sanlang. Rumors were rife, saying all sorts of things. Lanxiang and Qinxiang were always upset by Cui Yixin's arrogance and said, "Evil will be punished." Cui Xiuxin felt sad, and she burst into tears.

Lanxiang misunderstood and wiped Xiuxin's tears, "My dear girl, how can you cry for that kind of person? How can she know the good of you?"

"Oh no, that's bad." Lianxiang ran in in a panic, her face full of panic, "Oh no, the second girl hanged herself!"

☆, Chapter 6: Burning Incense

Chapter 6: Burning Incense

Xiuxin was shocked when she heard this. She quickly put on her shoes and took Lanxiang and Qinxiang to the small courtyard where Cui Yixin lived. They hurried all the way. Before they reached the gate of the courtyard, they saw the courtyard was brightly lit. Little girls and servants gathered in groups of three or four with sad faces. Xiuxin walked into the courtyard and saw her uncle Cui Zhengyu, her aunt Feng, Cui Zhengkai, and Jiang. Yixin was still sleeping on the bed, with obvious marks on her neck. Feng hugged Cui Yixin and cried bitterly. Cui Zhengyu's concubines also cried beside her.

After Xiuxin arrived, several girls including Minxin, Yuxin and Cui Zhengyu's concubines also hurried over. In the room, some were gloating, some were talking, and some were crying with all their hearts, with different expressions. Xiuxin was surprised and pulled Ruixiang from Yixin's room to a quiet place and asked, "Why did the Xie family cancel the engagement?" For an unmarried girl, canceling the engagement was a big deal. If the husband's family canceled the engagement, it would mean that the girl was not virtuous. If the parents' family canceled the engagement, it would mean that the girl was greedy and ungrateful. It would be bad for the girl's reputation anyway, and it would be even more difficult for her to find a good marriage.

Ruixiang said, "Third Miss, I don't know either. This morning, I served Second Miss a meal and heard Xie's family handing in a letter of cancellation of engagement. The reason was not stated, I only heard that it said something official like "not a good match"."

"This Xie family is really going too far!" Cui Zhengyu's face turned pale and he stamped his feet, "Although my Cui family is not a branch of Qinghe, it is still a wealthy family in the capital. How dare they be so disrespectful! Tomorrow I will go and ask for an explanation!"

Cui Zhengkai said, "Brother, don't be impulsive. The Xie family can't cancel the engagement without a reason. Let's wait a few days. If the Xie family still doesn't have an explanation, it won't be too late for us to go later."

Cui Zhengyu could only nod when he heard Cui Zhengkai say this, "Let's do this for now."

The next day, Xie Zhenqing, the father of the current Concubine Xie, came to the door. He apologized to Cui Zhengyu as soon as he arrived. "This matter is really the fault of my Xie family, but we are helpless. Ten years ago, I was the governor of Jinzhou. My son was engaged to my good friend, the second daughter of Jinzhou Governor Qian Bosen. I cut a piece of concentric jade into half for my son and Miss Qian. Originally, these two were childhood sweethearts and were a perfect match. Who knew that the second Miss Qian was kidnapped by human traffickers when she was seven years old. Qian "Berson sent people to look for her outside for a year but there was no news. He was very sad. We naturally thought that it was difficult to find the young lady. Who knew that just a month ago, my son rescued an orphan girl on the street and brought her back home. She was originally just a maid, but who knew that the girl had the jade pendant that Miss Qian Er wore. I hurriedly sent a letter to inform Chamberson to come to the capital, but who knew that the woman was indeed Miss Qian Er. However, my son and Miss Qian Er were engaged first, so I can only write a letter to cancel the engagement. I hope Brother Zhengyu will forgive me."

Xie Zhenqing added, "This matter is entirely my Xie family's fault. We will not take a single cent of the betrothal gift. In addition, my Xie family will also announce the reason for the cancellation of the engagement to the world, so that the reputation of the daughter will never be damaged."

This was a reasonable statement, and Cui Zhengyu could not refute it. He could only sigh and blame his daughter for her bad luck. However, no matter what, no matter what the reason for the divorce, it would be very difficult for her to find another marriage. Thinking of his daughter's domineering and arrogant personality, Cui Zhengyu felt the veins in his temples throbbing uncontrollably.

In addition to Cui Zhengyu's headache, Jiang Shi also had a headache. The order of marriage in the Hua Dynasty was very particular. The elder brother went first, and the eldest daughter went first. If there was an older sister who was not engaged, the younger sister could not get engaged first. There were many cases of young girls getting married first in the folk. But in a wealthy family, it would be a laughing stock if they did so. Seeing that the marriage of her youngest daughter and the Sun family had been discussed almost, this happened suddenly, which really caught Jiang Shi off guard. She had to send someone to tactfully signal the Sun family to postpone the engagement schedule.

Xiu Xin took this opportunity to tell Jiang what she saw and heard in the Imperial Garden that day. Jiang was silent for a while and said, "My daughter, those young masters are all cheating. Let alone other things, there are always concubines in this house. After marrying a wife, those concubines will also come in one after another. Do you think everyone is like your father and mother? Even your father had two concubines and one concubine. If you marry, it still depends on whether you can please your husband and in-laws. Even if you don't marry Sun Peifang, and marry someone else, how can you know if he has someone else in his heart? Even if he doesn't have anyone now, how can you know if he will have someone in the future?"

Xiuxin fell silent after hearing these words. Her mother was right, but she was unwilling to accept it. She felt depressed when she thought that she might have to marry a man who didn't have her in his heart. Even in her mother's eyes, this little affair was not a big deal. It seemed that she was the only one who took it seriously. She thought of Li Yuzhi whom she had met at home. She wondered if someone like Li Yuzhi, who came from a poor family, was as romantic and passionate as other men. Yixin was hit hard this time. She didn't go out, but vented her anger by beating and scolding the maids in the yard all day. Xiuxin happened to meet Ruixiang in Yixin's room. Seeing that her face was covered with pinch marks, she couldn't help but feel distressed for her. Ruixiang knew that the third lady had the best temper. It goes without saying that the older maids like Lanxiang and Qinxiang, even the little maids who did the cleaning in the third lady's room had never been beaten or scolded. This time, seeing Xiuxin like this, Yue knelt down and cried, "Third lady, I really can't stay in the second lady's room anymore. No matter if I did anything wrong or not, they pinched and beat me." After that, Ruixiang lifted up her sleeves, revealing purple marks, "Third lady, please be kind and ask the lady to take me away!" Just as Xiuxin was about to speak, she heard a cold snort in her ear. It turned out that Yixin and Ruixiang were walking over. Ruixiang was immediately frightened and turned pale.

"Hey, third sister, your sister is not dead

yet, and you are going to snatch the maid from my room?" Yi Xin said sarcastically.

Xiu Xin said, "Second sister, you misunderstood. That's not what I meant. Rui Xiang just came to me to cry and I comforted her."

"No need!" Yi Xin snorted, "The people in my room don't need your comfort. Just take care of yourself." After that, she laughed and said, "I heard you are going to get married? But don't forget, as long as I, your sister, am not married, you have to accompany me. As long as I am not married, you have to accompany me for a year!"

Lanxiang couldn't hold back any longer after hearing that, and said first, "You are an old maid in the mansion, and you want to drag our daughter down with you. If there really is an old maid in our family who can't get married, will our master and mistress really let our daughter accompany you?"

Yi Xin was immediately furious, "How can a servant like you interrupt our master when he is talking! Rui Xiang, slap him ten times!"

Originally, Xiuxin understood that Yixin had suffered a blow today, so her words were a bit harsh. In addition, she was a gentle person, so she was not prepared to argue with her. Who knew that she would be so aggressive? If she didn't say anything, she was afraid that Lanxiang would be upset. So she stepped forward and said, "Lanxiang is my maid, there is no need for my second sister to teach her a lesson. If she makes a mistake, I will punish her. At worst, there are still the master and the mistress." What she meant was, it's not your turn to do it.

"Cui Xiuxin, there will be a day when you will regret it! Just wait and see!" Yixin's face turned pale and blue, and hatred flashed in her eyes. She kicked Ruixiang, who was kneeling on the ground, hard, and left with Ruixiang in hatred.

After this incident, Ruixiang might find it even harder to stay with Yixin, but it was not appropriate for her to stay with him. After thinking it over, Xiu went to ask Jiangshi for help and took her into Jiangshi's room.

Ten days later, it was the beginning of the month again. The Cui family, led by the first wife Feng and the second wife Jiang, took the female family members to the Zhengjue Temple outside the city to burn incense and worship Buddha as usual. The group of female family members, maids, servants, and other servants had at least ten carriages and went to Zhengjue Temple in a mighty manner. Xiuxin and Minxin rode in the same carriage. Xiuxin took out the fried five-spice dried fish from her bosom and ate it with relish. Occasionally, she took a fish and handed it to Minxin, "Do you want some?"

Minxin looked down at the greasy dried fish

in Xiuxin's hand and frowned barely noticeably, "No need."

"Okay." Xiuxin felt bored and started to eat with a crunch. When she arrived at Zhengjue Temple, there was still half of the dried fish wrapped in a ballet that she had not finished eating. Xiuxin rewrapped the rest and put it in her arms.

Thinking of the times when she always ran into that person every time she went out of the house, Xiu Xin followed Jiang closely, always having a bad feeling in her heart. It would be a coincidence that she would meet him again this time, right? So when she worshipped the Bodhisattva, Xiu Xin kowtowed to the Bodhisattva three times, chanting, "Buddha bless me, Bodhisattva bless me, please don't let me meet him again."

After worshipping the Buddha, Feng and Jiang followed the abbot to the Zen room to drink tea. Seven-year-old Yuxin pulled Xiuxin's clothes and whispered, "Third sister, how about we go to the back mountain to play?" Xiuxin tapped Yuxin's nose, "I dare not take you, you love to run around the most. At most, I can take you to the back garden of the temple."

"Good sister, just go with me." Yu Xin started to act coquettishly.

Xiu Xin raised her eyebrows and said, "Why don't we go to the back hall to see if there are any snacks or vegetarian meals?" After a while, it was time for dinner. The vegetarian food in Zhengjue Temple was very good. Although the ingredients were all vegetarian, the cooking methods were exquisite.

"I'd rather not." Yu Xin wrinkled her nose and turned her gaze to Cui Min Xin who was standing beside her. "Fourth sister, how about you accompany me?"

Minxin has always been cautious in her words and actions, so how could she possibly agree? In the end, Cui Yixin said, "Forget it, I'll take you there." That was the end of it.

At this moment, the fragrance of tea filled the room in the backyard. Li Yuzhi poured the brewed tea for the person opposite her, and said respectfully, "Teacher, do you mean to arrange this student to the Ministry of Personnel? But the runner-up and third place winners in the past would first be arranged to be editors in the Hanlin Academy."

Wang Fusheng took a sip of tea and said, "Rules are always dead."

Li Yuzhi was overjoyed when she heard this, and raised her hand to bow, saying, "Thank you, teacher, for the promotion." Being able to enter the Ministry of Personnel is indeed a better prospect than entering the Hanlin Academy. After a pause, Li Yuzhi said, "I just don't know how Chaozong is doing?" Wang Fusheng said, "I am his father and I should avoid suspicion. It is not easy for me to interfere in his work. I am afraid it depends on the opinion of the left prime minister Cui Jinyi." Li Yuzhi hesitated, "This..." Wang Fusheng smiled meaningfully, "He is not like you, who grew up in luxury and has a straightforward personality. He should also be allowed to go down and gain some experience."

Li Yuzhi said, "The teacher is right."

After chatting for a while, Li Yuzhi heard the bell ring three times and knew that the temple had served food, so she said, "Teacher, please wait a moment. I will go to the back hall to get some food."

☆、Chapter 7

Chapter VII

The Chinese dynasty attached great importance to the separation of men and women, and even in places like temples, the boundaries between men and women were extremely clear. Even the back hall where they had meals was like this, with men in the east courtyard and women in the west courtyard.

Before Xiuxin entered the west courtyard, she smelled a sweet fragrance that made her appetite grow. However, there were too many pilgrims today, and the west courtyard was crowded with people. The place where food was distributed was crowded. Xiuxin saw the snow-white steamed buns, yellow corn, tender white tofu, and various exquisite snacks being taken away bit by bit, and she became anxious. But she was still small and delicate, so there was no way she could squeeze in. She stood outside for a while and then walked to the small garden behind in disappointment.

In the center of the garden was a wishing tree, which was covered with red ribbons that fluttered in the wind, looking very beautiful. Xiuxin saw a large white stone under the wishing tree, with a smooth and clean surface, so she climbed up and sat on it, with her legs dangling in the air. The soft-soled embroidered shoes on her feet were also exposed, delicate and petite.

She was bored, so she casually flipped through the words on the wishing ribbons. One of them read, "I wish to find a person who loves me and we will be together till old age." The handwriting was beautiful and elegant, and Xiuxin guessed that it was written by a daughter of a famous family. It turns out that there are many girls who hope for a pure love, but which one can really be like that in reality? Which aristocratic family does not have three wives and four concubines? Even if the wife is given some respect, it is still hard to accept.

"Miss Cui."

Xiuxin was daydreaming when she suddenly heard a man's voice. Her heart skipped a beat and she thought, this man's voice is like the sound of a clear spring, so moist and elegant.

Because she was sitting high up and her vision was blocked by the hanging red ribbon, she leaned forward to push aside the embroidered ribbon in front of her eyes before she could see the face of the person in front of her. She was wearing a green robe, her black hair was simply tied up with a jade hairpin, she had an elegant appearance and a pretty face, it was undoubtedly Li Yuzhi.

Xiu Xin was startled, her cheeks blushing uncontrollably. She hesitated for a moment before climbing down from the big rock, bowed and said, "Master Li."

Li Yuzhi recently heard that the Cui family and the Sun family were planning to form a marriage alliance. She felt pained and helpless, and could only lament her miserable life. Now, she happened to meet Xiuxin in the small garden of Zhengjue Temple, and she felt even more sad. She had thought of letting go of Xiuxin and forgetting her. But she couldn't bear to let her go, so she called her out loud, saying that it would be good to see her more.

"Since we parted that day, how have you been lately, young lady?"

"Fine."

Because Xiuxin had met strange men several times recently, she didn't blush as much as before. Although she still lowered her head slightly this time, she secretly glanced at Li Yuzhi several times with her peripheral vision. Seeing that he was gentle and refined, and looking at her with affectionate eyes, she thought to herself that Sun Peifang liked talented women like Xie Yulan. Xiuxin silently rubbed her slightly bulging belly. The Xie family girl was full of knowledge, and I was full of fat. How could we compare? Li Yuzhi was chosen by her mother, and Sun Peifang was chosen by her father. The Li Yuzhi in front of her was obviously interested in her. Compared with Sun Peifang, she was much better.

Li Yuzhi looked at the girl in front of her, lowering her eyebrows and nodding her head. Although she couldn't see her full face, she could still see the round curve of her chin and the slightly red tips of her ears. She was moved for a moment and said without thinking too much, "I heard that the young lady got married recently? I have seen the second master of the Sun family. He has a very good face and is a son of an aristocratic family. His future is naturally limitless."

Hearing this, Xiuxin raised her head and shook her head repeatedly, causing the crystal pendant on her ear to draw a beautiful arc. "These things are still not happening. I don't know if you know that my second sister broke off the engagement with the Xie family and is still undecided. My second sister is not engaged, so how can it be my turn? Besides..." Xiuxin lowered her head, wanting to say something but stopping herself. She believed that Li Yuzhi would be able to guess what she was not saying with her insightful mind.

Xiuxin has been raised in a honeypot since she was a child, and has never been exposed to such messy things as house fighting, but because of this, she is born braver than others and does not have those concerns.

Li Yuzhi was a person of high character. She immediately understood Xiuxin's intention and was overjoyed. The gloomy feeling that had accumulated over the past few days disappeared completely. Suddenly, the sky became clear and the dawn began to shine. She bowed deeply to Xiuxin and said, "I understand what you mean, young lady. Don't worry, I will do my best to fight for you and will never let you down."

Li Yuzhi's meaning was so clear that Xiuxin blushed for a moment, lowered her head and said, "That's good," then she walked away quickly with her skirt lifted. Li Yuzhi stood there and looked at the beauty's back for a long time without coming back to her senses. Even when she returned to the Zen room, the joy on her face had not faded.

Wang Fusheng saw that Li Yuzhi's eyes and eyebrows were relaxed, no longer gloomy and melancholy, and couldn't help asking, "Did Yuzhi encounter any good things just now?"

Li Yuzhi shook her head, "It's unspeakable, it's unspeakable."

Wang Fusheng laughed and said, "Yuzhi, you

have won the second place, which is a great success. If you can be so happy, it can only be a small success. I guess you must have met the daughter of a noble family just now, right?"

Li Yuzhi was embarrassed when she heard this, "Teacher, please stop making fun of your students."

Wang Fusheng said, "I don't know which daughter you are interested in, but I can propose marriage for you."

Li Yuzhi bowed and said, "I would like to thank you in advance, but the matter has not been decided yet. I will trouble you again in the future. I hope you will help me with this."

"As the ancients said, a teacher is a father for life. You lost your father when you were young, so it is only right for me to propose marriage for you."

Li Yuzhi bowed again, "Thank you, teacher."

In other words, Xiuxin felt relieved after meeting Li Yuzhi. She felt that the Bodhisattva she had just prayed to was effective. She did not meet that pervert, but met the elegant Li Yuzhi. After being overjoyed, she thought that even if Li Yuzhi went to the mansion to propose marriage, she was afraid that her father would not agree. He wanted her to marry into the Sun family. She could only hope that her mother could give her some advice. Look at how well Sister Jinxin is doing now. Aren't Zhao Zichen and Sister Jinxin the envy of everyone? In other words, even if the couple is at odds, Zhao Zichen still has to rely on the power of the Cui family. How can he not treat his sister well?

Marrying down has its advantages. A woman of high birth can naturally control her husband more easily.

After lunch, Jiang took Xiuxin to worship Yue Lao. Xiuxin put her hands together and prayed to Yue Lao to give her a good marriage. After a moment of silent contemplation, she shook out a stick. Xiuxin picked up the stick and saw a poem written on it:

The Queqiao Bridge is built high to wait for good times, and the clouds will clear to see the bright moon.

Jiang also took the lot and said with a smile, "Oh, it's a very good lot."

Xiu Xin was not very knowledgeable in poetry and prose, but she roughly understood the meaning of the poem, so she said, "Should we ask Master Hui Yuan to interpret the divination for us and see what it means?"

Jiang said, "Okay."

Jiang asked a young monk, "Little Master, where is Master Huiyuan now?"

The young monk put his hands together, bent down and said, "Female donor, the master is meeting guests in the meditation room. If you want to see the master, why don't you follow me to the tea room next to the meditation room and wait for a while?"

"That's fine." Jiang was about to go with Xiuxin, but Mingxiang pulled Jiang's sleeve and whispered something in her ear. Jiang's face changed immediately. Because there were outsiders present, she couldn't speak out. She suppressed her shock and anger and reluctantly said to Xiuxin, "Xiuxin, go to the tea room with the young master to rest for a while, I'll come later."

Cui Xiuxin said hello and followed the little monk to the tea room.

The teahouse of Zhengjue Temple was elegantly and simply decorated. When Xiuxin entered the teahouse, she saw a small table filled with all kinds of utensils, including teapots, teacups, and a small tea stove. On the bookshelf not far away were several hand-copied sutras. Xiuxin picked one up and took a quick look. One was the Diamond Sutra, one was the Mahaparinirvana Sutra, and the other was the Lotus Sutra. When the old lady was alive, she loved these books the most. Every time Xiuxin went to see her, she saw her copying sutras. The incense in the bedroom was all sandalwood. To this day, there are more than a dozen sutras hand-copied by the old lady in the house.

Xiuxin was bored, so she picked up the Diamond Sutra and flipped through it briefly, "Thus I have heard, once the Buddha was in the country of Savatthi..." Well, she didn't understand a single word, and before she had finished reading for a while, her eyelids felt heavy, she yawned loudly, and couldn't help falling asleep on the small table.

I don't know how long I slept. I opened my eyes hazily and saw a man in front of me. He was wearing a moon-white robe, with black hair hanging softly on his shoulders without a hairband. He had a face as beautiful as jade and a complexion as beautiful as spring flowers, just like a banished immortal. For a moment, Xiu Xin didn't know whether she was dreaming or awake. She looked at him in a daze and said, "Where did you come from, immortal?"

The man smiled gently, like a blooming flower, "Little confused bug, how many days have passed, and you don't recognize me?"

Xiu Xin was startled and rubbed her eyes hard, then she saw the true face of the man in front of her. It was a narrow road for enemies to meet again, why was it this scoundrel again!

"why is it you again?"

Wang Fusheng looked at the little girl in front of him, who was staring at him with her round eyes. Maybe because she had just woken up, her hair was a little messy and her face was a little red. She really looked like... a little rabbit. Yes, that's right, a little white rabbit. Wang Fusheng's heart felt like it was scratched by a cat, and he couldn't help but want to tease her, "Why can't it be me?"

Why is it that praying to the Buddha

doesn't work? I can actually meet him everywhere!

I was the first one to enter the teahouse. Even if he came in by mistake, he should have left. I never thought that he would walk in openly and even pick up the tea set to make tea! It was like putting the host and the guest in the wrong place. I don't know what he was talking about!

"You! You..." Xiu Xin racked her brains and finally thought of a word, then blurted out, "You scoundrel!"

Since he was born, Wang Fusheng has been called a boy, but has also been praised as a great scholar of the time and a model of civil officials. However, he has never been called a scoundrel by any woman. This is quite new.

"How am I a scoundrel?" Wang Fusheng said, "I reserved this teahouse, and not only did you barge in without permission, you even fell asleep on my table. I took you in out of kindness and didn't chase you away. I was afraid you'd catch a cold, so I put a coat on you. But you're not grateful to me, and instead you call me a scoundrel?"

Xiu Xin saw that she was wearing a dark robe. She felt embarrassed and annoyed. "How can you prove that you reserved this teahouse?"

Wang Fusheng pointed to several scriptures on the bookshelf next to him and said, "These scriptures were copied by my mother. I brought them to the Buddhist temple for worship."

☆, Chapter 8: Marriage Robbery

Chapter 8: Marriage Robbery
When Xiuxin heard this, her cheeks felt hot. It turned out that she had entered the wrong room. However, she refused to admit it and argued, "Then you should have woken me up." How could a man and a woman be in the same room together?
"I called you." Wang Fusheng took a sip of tea elegantly, "but you didn't wake up. I was helpless too."
You act like you've been wronged... Do you want me to compensate you for your losses? Xiu Xin took off her black robe and handed it to him, saying shyly, "Here, it's for you."
Wang Fusheng took the clothes and put them on in front of her, his eyes full of romance, "Girl, including this time, you and I have met by chance three times before, right? Come to think of it, we are really destined to meet."
Xiuxin secretly complained, who would want to be destined to be with you... You look quite old, but still so unserious.
"It's so naughty..." Xiu Xin originally slandered secretly in her heart. Who would have thought that she actually whispered the last sentence. Wang Fusheng, who has sharp ears, heard it immediately, and the expression on his face He changed

immediately. It's enough to say that he is not serious. Why add the word "老"? He is the youngest?

Wang Fusheng stood up, sat next to Xiu Xin, and leaned toward her. Xiu Xin fell back in panic, feeling his warm breath hitting her face, causing waves of itching.

"You think I'm very old?" A dangerous atmosphere filled the air.

Xiu Xin blushed and remained silent.

"How old do you think I am? Huh?" Wang Fusheng came closer and closer, and the tips of their noses were almost touching.

Wang Fusheng's gaze moved from Xiu Xin's round eyes to her red and fat face, and finally settled on her small, pink lips. A slight itching crawled into his heart. , making him particularly...especially want...

"Well……"

Before Wang Fusheng realized what he had done, his lips had already sealed Xiuxin's lips. Hmm, very sweet, very soft, very wet, and with a faint fragrance.

But at this moment, Xiu Xin was so frightened that even her pores opened up. She could hear her heart pounding in her chest. All the blood in her body rushed to her brain. Her mind was filled with thoughts like, I was actually molested by a man!

Wang Fusheng was enjoying the kiss more and more, he really felt like he had found a treasure and couldn't bear to let go, he lightly teased her with the tip of his tongue, trying to break through the barrier, but the beauty clenched her teeth tightly, so he couldn't get in. He became more and more itchy, and wanted to swallow the beauty whole in one go.

It was not until he felt Xiuxin's whole body trembling and whimpering like a kitten that he suddenly let go of her hand. At this moment, Xiuxin's face was covered with tears, her face was pale, and her whole body was trembling. She was as pitiful as a hibiscus flower hit by rain, which was really lovable.

Knock knock.

Wang Fusheng was about to say a few words of comfort when there were several soft knocks on the door. Li Yuzhi's voice sounded respectfully, "Teacher, I just got some top-grade Rain-previous Longjing tea from Master Huiyuan. Why don't you taste it with me?"

Wang Fusheng gently covered Xiuxin's mouth and said in a low voice, "I am not feeling well today. Please rest here for a while. We will have tea and talk about Taoism another day."

Li Yuzhi said, "Teacher, you are not feeling well. Do you need me to ask a doctor to come and take a look for you?"

"No need." Li Yuzhi said, "It's nothing serious, just rest for a while, you can go."

"Yes." Li Yuzhi seemed to bow outside the door before leaving.

Wang Fusheng breathed a sigh of relief and secretly sighed that he was really bewitched by the devil and actually did such a thing. Even though he prided himself on being a romantic and unrestrained man, he had never forced himself on a woman, let alone a daughter of a noble family. Now that something like this had happened, he really didn't know how it would end.

On this side, Xiuxin cried so hard that her eyes were red, and her little body was shaking and hiccuping, looking so pitiful. Wang Fusheng took a jade pendant from his waist and put it into Xiuxin's hand, "Take it as a token of love, I will definitely marry you."

Xiuxin got so angry that she didn't care who the other person was. She threw the exquisite jade pendant to the ground and cursed, "Who wants your pickled things? I would never marry you even if I die!" After that, Xiuxin quickly got up, opened the door and ran away.

Seeing her precious daughter sobbing, Jiang was surprised and distressed. "Xiu Xin, could it be that you knew about it?" She hugged her daughter and comforted her softly while asking coldly, "Which blind servant told the young lady about it?"

All the maids and servants knelt down and cried, "Second Madam, we would never dare to do that."

Xiu Xin raised her head and looked at Jiang with her eyes swollen like walnuts. "Mother, what happened? What do I know?"

"Nothing." Seeing that Xiuxin's tone didn't seem to indicate that she knew about the incident, Jiang Shi felt relieved, but then she felt more anxious again. "Why are you crying like this? What happened? I haven't seen you the whole afternoon."

How could she bring up such a thing as being flirted with? Not to mention in front of the maids and wives, even in private, Xiuxin couldn't mention it to her mother, so she just lied, "I fell asleep alone in the tea room, and when I woke up I saw a mouse and got so scared."

Jiang smiled when she heard this and tapped Xiuxin's forehead lovingly, "When will you grow up? You were scared like this by a mouse. Well, it's getting late, let's go back."

Xiuxin got on the carriage and found that her great aunt Feng and Yixin were all gone, so she asked, "Where are my great aunt and the others?"

Jiang's expression froze for a moment, and she forced a smile, "Yixin caught a cold, so they went back first."

"Is it serious? How did you catch a cold?"

"It's nothing serious. You'll be fine after a few days of rest." Jiang said, "Stop talking so much. Look at how swollen your eyes are. You need to apply ice cubes when you get back."

"Yeah." Xiuxin nodded.

In the evening, Lan Xiang served Xiu Xin

and applied ice cubes to her eyes to reduce some swelling. Lan Xiang asked, "Girl, do you want to take a bath now?".

"Let them prepare," Xiu Xin said.

"Yes." Lan Xiang opened the door and went out.

After a while, Cuixiang Lianxiang and others carried the bathtub in, and some rough girls carried several large buckets of water in and poured them all into the bathtub. For Qin Xiang, sprinkle chrysanthemum, Imperata cognac root, mint and other cooling substances into the water, and then add whitening substances such as Angelica dahuricae, Atractylodes macrocephala, Bletilla striata, Bletilla, white Poria, white peony root, White bamboo silkworm, pearl powder, etc., mix and stir Then he said, "Girl, the bath water is ready."

"Okay, you guys go down first."

"Yes." Everyone retreated and closed the door.

Xiu Xin took off her clothes and immersed herself in the water. She felt a mixture of emotions. She thought of Li Yuzhi, her marriage with the Sun family, and... that person today...

Feeling upset from thinking about it, Xiuxin splashed some water on her face and sighed, "I'll leave it to fate." She only hoped that it would be like what was written on the fortune slip today, that the Que Bridge would be built high to wait for good times, and that the clouds would clear to reveal a bright moon.

Cui Yixin seemed to have caught a cold. She had not left her house in recent days. Even the maids in Yixin's room were rarely seen walking around. Cui Yixin's small courtyard was quiet all day, which was really suspicious. Xiuxin asked Lanxiang several times, but Lanxiang avoided the question. Xiuxin didn't think much about it. She just read a storybook, was in a daze, and chatted with Lanxiang. One day passed by.

However, Lan Xiang saw that Xiuxin was listless today and even ate less of her favorite sweet-scented osmanthus cake, so she took advantage of the fact that no one was around and asked, "What's happened to the girl recently? But what troubles have you encountered?"

Xiuxin sighed, "It's nothing, I just feel upset."

Lan Xiang pursed her lips and smiled, pushing Xiu Xin's shoulder, "Girl, are you afraid of spring?"

Xiu Xin gave Lan Xiang a light slap and said with a smile, "Lan Xiang, you have become more and more bold recently. You dare to make fun of me, just to see if I don't tear your mouth apart."

Lan Xiang hurriedly ran away and begged for mercy, "Girl, I don't dare to do it anymore, please spare me this time."

Having said that, although Jiang's information was tightly sealed and she didn't dare to let Xiuxin know even a little bit, she still couldn't prevent someone from letting it slip. The first one is Xiuxin's wet nurse, Mrs. Zhao.

Although Mrs. Zhao was Xiuxin's wet nurse and had nursed Xiuxin for several years, Xiuxin never liked to get close to her. Mrs. Zhao relied on her age and the fact that she had nursed Xiuxin before, and looked down on everyone except Lanxiang. One day, Zhao lost some money in a bet, and when she returned home, the little maid Danxiang had already locked the door. Mrs. Zhao was immediately furious and cursed at the door, "You little idiot, you locked the door before I came back, you have no eyes."

Danxiang held back her anger and opened the door. She couldn't help but mutter, "You haven't come back yet after all this. Who left the door open for you? You really think you are the master."

Mrs. Zhao had originally not intended to pursue the matter further when she saw Danxiang opening the door, but after hearing Danxiang's words, she burst out with anger over losing money, "You lowly thing, I'm not the master, and you, a third-class maid, are even less the master. What's the matter? Even our master has been wronged outside and has nowhere to complain, and you, a little maid, really want to make a fuss!"

Mrs. Zhao had a loud voice to begin with, and it was night, so her voice could be heard even further. Even Xiu Xin, who was having a drink in the bamboo forest, heard it. She put down the snacks in her hand, walked up to Mrs. Zhao and asked, "What grievances have I suffered that I don't have anyone to tell?"

When Mrs. Zhao saw Xiuxin, she was so frightened that her face turned pale. She knelt on the ground and slapped her mouth twice, "Miss, I was just talking nonsense, don't take it seriously."

Xiu Xin thought about all the strange things that had happened in the past few days and knew that something big had happened. She asked in a stern voice, "What is it? Tell me now!"

Mrs. Zhao cried, "Miss, I really can't tell you."

Although Xiu Xin had no scheming in her heart, she still had the authority to rule her subordinates, so she said, "Don't think I don't know that you usually cheat, play tricks, gamble, and spend money. I understand that you raised me and you are old, so I don't care about you. But since you told me about it this time, I will forgive your previous mistakes. If you don't tell me, I will report it to my mother and kick you out!"

Mrs. Zhao was frightened and her face turned pale. She kept saying, "Miss, I will tell you, I will tell you, but please don't tell Madam that I said this. If Madam knows, I will suffer the consequences."

Xiu Xin said, "Just tell me."

☆, Chapter 9 Misunderstanding

Chapter 9 Misunderstanding
"That day when the masters went to Zhengjue Temple to burn incense, the second young lady accidentally fell down the hillside at the back of the mountain. Somehow, she ran into the second master of the Sun family. The second young lady was injured, and the second master of the Sun family..."
"What?" Xiuxin asked.
"He carried the second young lady up on his back. This happened in front of everyone, and many people saw it. Now the news has spread even more widely, and everyone knows that the second master of the Sun family saved our second young lady."
So that's how it is. No wonder everyone has been acting strange these days. It turns out that something like this happened. It's strange to think about it. How could Yi Xin, who has always been cautious, fall down the back mountain? It would be fine if she fell into the back mountain, but she happened to meet the second master of the Sun family. This matter is strange no matter how you think about it. That day, Yu Xin said she wanted to go to the back mountain to play. Yi Xin has never been close to this sister, let alone spoil her. Why did she agree so easily that time? This is also a strange thing.

"Okay, you all know it, but you're just hiding it from me?"

Lan Xiang said, "We are afraid that the girl will be sad, so..." Seeing the change in Xiuxin's expression, Lan Xiang thought she was overly sad and comforted, "Girl, please don't be sad. It is the second girl's dignity that will be damaged if something like this happens. How can Mr. Sun be willing to marry her?"

Xiuxin shook her head, "I'm not sad."

When Lan Xiang saw this, she thought it was Xiu Xin who said something sarcastic. She was even more worried and ordered the little girl to report to the second lady. After a while, Mrs. Jiang hurried over. Seeing Xiuxin holding her chin in front of the mirror in a daze, she called out several times, "My son."

Xiu Xin said, "Mother, why are you crying? First of all, I have not yet been engaged to the second master of the Sun family. Now that the marriage is ruined, we have nothing to lose. Furthermore, Yixin and the second master of the Sun family are not engaged. It may not be a good thing for her to be in such a bad situation, and even if she gets married, she may not be very dignified."

Jiang saw that Xiuxin was not sad at all, and she was relieved immediately. "You made me worry for nothing. You are right. Although the Sun family is good, it is not necessarily a blessing to marry into it.

However, I can't swallow this breath. Cui Yixin is very calculating. She is jealous of our marriage and tried every means to take it away. Does she think we are easy to bully? Let's just wait and see."

"What is mother going to do?"

Jiang smiled proudly, "Don't forget, I have a sister who married into the Sun family. She is the legitimate second wife of the Sun family, the aunt of the second master Sun. Needless to say, I only let my sister whisper a few words in the ears of the old lady of the Sun family, and Cui Yixin will never be able to enter the Sun family!"

"Mother, we are sisters after all. Is it right to do this..." Xiu Xin was a little hesitant.

Jiang poked Xiuxin's forehead in dismay, "She's riding on your head, and you're still concerned about her. You're so gentle and indecisive, and you still have me and your father to protect you at home. If you become someone else's daughter-in-law in the future, she won't be as good as you."

Xiu Xin said, "There's nothing we can do about it. He has already developed this kind of temper. It's too late to learn now."

Jiang said, "Then I can only pick a few loyal and clever maids to go with you as a dowry. I think Lanxiang is very good. She is steady, clever and good at reading people's faces. I can feel more at ease with her around. But don't let her have any grudges against you. Once the master and servant fall out, she may plot against you behind your back. You can't guard against that."

"No, mother. Lanxiang is not that kind of person."

"You can only know a person's face but not his heart. Anyway, you pay attention to everything, and you have to take care of the servants under you and the elders above you. If you marry a husband who understands your feelings and loves you from the bottom of his heart, it would be fine. But if you marry a man who doesn't care about you and you can't control him, you will only be bullied."

When Jiang saw Xiuxin's silent look, she knew that she was uncomfortable in her heart, but there was nothing she could do. As a mother, she had to teach her first. If she didn't teach her well, it would be too late to teach her after she got married and became someone else's wife.

"Besides, there is no man in this world who doesn't like to cheat. Even your father..." Jiang paused and changed the subject. "You can't avoid such things. Sometimes you can only turn a blind eye. If the woman outside can't infringe on your power, just pretend you didn't see it. In addition, if you have to, you can give him the maid next to you. On the contrary, he can calm down and love you more. Among the maids in your room, Qinxiang is the best in terms of appearance and personality. She is the most suitable. But you have to be careful. You can only let her get close to you when you are with her. If she wants to climb into bed behind your back at other times, you just drive her out. Got it?"

After hearing these words, Xiuxin frowned, and her fantasy about love was almost shattered. She couldn't help but say, "Mother, are you worrying too much? I think father treats you very well."

Jiang's expression changed for a while before she said, "That's just superficial, just a little respect for me. Do you think I can really control your father?"

"Mother, has something happened?" Xiuxin sensitively felt that Jiang's tone was wrong when she talked about her father. It was not as affectionate as usual, but instead contained some hatred.

"Nothing." Jiang forced a smile, "Don't worry, it's getting late, you should go to bed early."

"Yeah." Xiu Xin replied.

Jiang helped Xiuxin fall asleep before letting Lanxiang turn off the lights and return to the main courtyard.

A few days later, Madam Feng came to Xiuxin's courtyard with her maid Guixiang. Xiuxin quickly put down her book, stood up and went to greet her, saying, "My aunt is here. I am so rude for not coming to greet her."

Feng said, "My dear girl, I am really rude

to you that your aunt has not come to see you for such a long time. Recently, the mansion has received a batch of brocade and daily jewelry for girls. I will bring them to you to choose from. In addition, there are also strawberries and cherries shipped by express horses from Lingzhou. I know you like to eat them, so I brought them here specially for you first."

"You're too polite, aunt." Xiuxin was secretly surprised. She and Feng were just casual friends at ordinary times, and they were just showing off. Why was she suddenly so polite now?

Feng held Xiuxin's hand with great care, asking about her health and well-being. She chatted for a long time before getting to the point. "Well, to be honest, my second daughter is really unfortunate. She was engaged to the Xie family before, but who knew that a Miss Qian would suddenly appear. My Yixin was so desperate that she chose a dead end. Fortunately, she escaped death and survived. She was going to the temple to pray for a good fortune and ask the Bodhisattva to bless her with a good marriage, but who knew that this incident would happen again. How would my Yixin cope if she didn't marry into the Sun family? But there has been no movement from the Sun family for half a month, and my master and I have been so anxious that our hair has turned half white."

Feng wiped the tears from her eyes and

continued, "Xiu Xin, you are a kind-hearted girl. Yi Xin and you are sisters. Seeing that she has encountered such a thing, can you bear not to help her?"

Xiu Xin completely understood what Feng meant. The smile on her face softened and she asked, "What does my aunt mean?"

Mrs. Feng smiled and said, "Doesn't your mother have a younger sister who married the second master of the Sun family? I heard that she is the housekeeper of the Sun family and is highly regarded by Old Madam Sun. If you can talk to your mother..." Mrs. Feng paused and smiled flatteringly, "If you ask her sister to mention it to Old Madam Sun..."

Xiuxin thought to herself, this Feng probably went to ask my mother first, and my mother rejected her, so she set her sights on me? The people in the first house are really interesting. They first planned to snatch my future husband away, but ended up making things worse and not being able to marry him. After such a thing happened, they should have just borne the consequences themselves, but they actually asked me to mediate? Does this Feng think I am really someone who can be manipulated? I was tolerant in everything because I didn't want to argue with them, but now they are really going too far!

Xiu Xin thought so in her heart, but said, "Don't worry, auntie, I will go talk to mother myself. But although mother usually favors me more, she doesn't listen to my opinions on important matters. I can only do my best."

Feng said happily, "Thank you so much. If it works, my aunt will definitely thank you profusely."

After sending Feng away, Xiuxin actually mentioned Yixin's matter to Jiang casually, "Now everyone knows that our Cui family has some connection with the second master of the Sun family. If the Sun family really doesn't marry Yixin, Yixin will either be an old maid in her natal family for the rest of her life, or shave her head and become a nun. What exactly is the Sun family planning?"

Jiang said, "It's not just my sister who is causing trouble. I heard from my sister that the eldest master and the first lady of the Sun family are also unwilling. Even the second master of the Sun family, Sun Peifang, is also unwilling. A few days ago, our eldest master went to discuss with the Sun family, but the Sun family didn't give a result and just dragged it out. This matter is not so easy to resolve."

Xiu Xin sighed, "Yixin is too clever for her own good."

Jiang snorted coldly, "She deserves it."

After another half month, the Sun family finally made some progress and sent a matchmaker to propose marriage. The people in the main house were overjoyed and went out to welcome the bride. But who knew that when the engagement letter was taken out, it was not a letter to marry a wife, but clearly stated "taking a concubine".

Cui Zhengyu's face immediately changed, and he was so angry that his face turned pale. He threw the engagement letter on the ground and said angrily, "This Sun family is really too much! How can I, a legitimate daughter, become someone's concubine?" Feng also cried and fainted on the spot. Her personal maid Guixiang was shocked, "Madam! Madam!"

After this incident, Feng was sick in bed for more than a month. Cui Zhengyu had no choice but to accept the Sun family's proposal. Because Yi Xin was not only rejected by someone else, but also had such a bad reputation. If she didn't marry into the Sun family, she would have nowhere to go.

These things made the whole Cui Mansion in turmoil, and there was no peace. Xiuxin's small courtyard was not affected. She was worried every day, because for some reason, Li Yuzhi had not come to propose marriage for a whole month. Normally, Sun Peifang married the daughter of the cabinet minister as his wife, and married Cui Yixin as his concubine. Li Yuzhi should have no worries, so why did she not make any move? Could it be that something happened?

Xiuxin was worried day and night, and Li Yuzhi was also very depressed.

Li Yuzhi became Wang Fusheng's favorite

student, so he often went in and out of the palace, and was very close to Wang Fusheng and Wang Chaozong. That day, he entered the palace as usual, and Wang Fusheng went to the palace to meet the emperor, so Wang Chaozong hosted a banquet for him. Wang Chaozong was not as temperamental as his father, and he was still a teenager, and he and Li Yuzhi got along well, so there was no red tape, and he directly called Li Yuzhi a brother, toasting and chatting happily.

Both of them were very drunk, so Wang Chaozong and Li Yuzhi laughed and supported each other as they went to the bedroom.

Wang Fusheng had only one son, who lost his mother when he was young, so Wang Fusheng brought him up personally. Li Yuzhi's bedroom was connected to Wang Fusheng's bedroom, separated by a small door. Wang Chaozong took Li Yuzhi to his bedroom and fell asleep on his bed. Li Yuzhi was not drunk yet. She barely stood up and looked around. She saw a small door on the west side, so she pushed the door open and went in. It looked like a man's bedroom. The furnishings in the room were simple, with a few books on the desk and a few calligraphy and paintings on the wall. Li Yuzhi didn't think too much about it, and thought that this room was also Li Yuzhi's, so she lay on the bed and fell asleep. He was also drunk, and fell asleep soon.

After an hour or so, Li Yuzhi woke up,

rubbed his temple, sat up, and saw a piece of pink fabric under the quilt. He was surprised and lifted the quilt, picked up the fabric and unfolded it. It turned out to be a pink pleated skirt with a lotus pattern. Li Yuzhi thought to himself, could this be the girl that Brother Chaozong was in love with? As he thought about it, he saw a beautiful "Cui" character embroidered on the waist of the skirt.

Cui?

Li Yuzhi was shocked. Could this be Cui family's thing?

As she put down her skirt, she saw a handkerchief inside. Li Yuzhi picked it up and saw a very beautiful word "Xiu" embroidered on the lower right corner of the white handkerchief. This must be a woman's personal belonging, and this word must be her name...

Wait, Cui, Xiu...

Li Yuzhi was stunned, as if struck by lightning, and the pain made his brain almost pop out! Cui Xiuxin! It was Cui Xiuxin! Xiuxin actually had an affair with Wang Chaozong! She even had such a personal item as a woman's!

☆, Chapter 10 Birthday Banquet

Chapter 10 Birthday Banquet

After discovering Xiuxin's personal belongings in Wang Chaozong's room, Li Yuzhi felt as if a huge stone was pressing down on his heart, making him breathless. He wanted to ask Wang Chaozong again and again, but it was really hard to ask such a private matter, so he could only ask indirectly, "Chaozong, I wonder if you are familiar with the Cui family?" Wang Chaozong was stunned, "Brother Li, why do you ask this?" Li Yuzhi forced a smile, "Well... I'm about to take up a post in the Ministry of Personnel. The Cui family is deeply rooted, so it's always good to get familiar with it in advance."

Wang Chaozong said, "You mean the Qinghe Cui family? The Cui family is huge, with dozens of collateral branches alone. The direct branch is headed by the current left prime minister Cui Jinyi." Wang Chaozong winked at Li Yuzhi mischievously, "He is my father's mortal enemy. Among the Cui family's collateral branches, the strongest one is Cui Yushi's branch. In addition to Cui Zhengyu and Cui Zhengkai, the younger generations of the Cui family are also outstanding. You know Cui Qihong, who was a Jinshi in the same class as us. Now he has been assigned to the Dali Temple and has a bright future."

Li Yuzhi asked tentatively, "I wonder how your relationship with the Cui family's children is?"

Wang Chaozong said, "Not bad. Cui Qihong, Cui Jinghong, and Cui Qinghong are all familiar to me. When we serve in the same court in the future, we must get along well with them."

"Then..." Li Yuzhi rolled her eyes and spoke with difficulty, "Then have you ever seen...the women of the Cui family?"

Wang Chaozong looked at him suspiciously, "Why are you asking about the women of the Cui family?" Wang Chaozong let out a long "oh", changed his tone, and said jokingly, "Could it be that Brother Li has taken a fancy to a young lady of the Cui family and came to me to inquire about her?"

At this point, Li Yuzhi could only force a smile, "Chao Zong, what are you talking about? When can I see a daughter of a rich family? How can I fall in love with anyone?"

Without getting any result from Wang Chaozong, the matter just hung on Li Yuzhi's chest, lingering and weighing on his heart. The ironclad evidence was there, and there was really nothing to refute. Even if the whole story was figured out, it would probably only add to the bitterness. Chaozong was a god-like figure, and the eldest son of the Wang family. How could he compare to him? He suddenly remembered the beautiful woman's bright smile under the wishing tree in Zhengjue Temple, and it really hurt his heart.

Gradually, because of this suspicion, Li Yuzhi even became estranged from Wang Chaozong and was not as close to him as before.

Meanwhile, the Cui Mansion finally calmed

down after the chaos caused by Cui Yixin's marriage. Cui Yixin was surprisingly quiet this time. She did not commit suicide or beat or scold the servants to vent her anger. Instead, she stayed quietly in the yard. This really surprised Xiuxin. Not long after, the wedding date was set, the eighth day of the fifth lunar month. Sun Peifang's wedding date with the daughter of the cabinet minister was set on the eighth day of the fourth lunar month, a full month later.

Being a concubine is inherently inferior to others. Even if you please your husband, you still have to kowtow to your mistress. The Hua Dynasty attaches great importance to the distinction between legitimate and illegitimate children, and the sons and daughters born to concubines are also inferior to others. How can you not feel aggrieved when you are controlled by others for your entire life? Cui Yixin really lost more than she gained.

After more than a month, Xiuxin became more and more anxious day by day, just like an ant on the hot pot. She was in seclusion in her boudoir and could not send any messages to others. She had no choice but to mention her marriage to Jiang in a tactful way.

Jiang said, "I have always wanted to marry you to a Jinshi from a poor family, but your father has been reluctant to agree. You are fifteen now, and Yixin has become someone's concubine. Your marriage should be settled, and it is not right to delay it any longer. However, your father seems to be still hesitating. I don't know what he is thinking."

"What exactly does father want to do?" Xiu Xin was anxious. She wanted to speak frankly but swallowed her words back. In the Hua Dynasty, men and women were most forbidden to have any private feelings before marriage. Even if Xiu Xin was anxious, she could not say something like she wanted to marry someone.

"You have to wait a little longer. I will talk to your father on your behalf. Don't worry, I will do my best to choose a good husband for you." Jiang paused and said, "My son, why have you lost so much weight recently? Do you want to ask Doctor Chen to check you out? Are you sick?"

Xiuxin has been having trouble eating and sleeping in the past few months, and has been worried all day long. The soft fat on her face has disappeared a lot, her chin has become pointed, and her eyes look even rounder and bigger.

Xiu Xin knew that she was worrying too much, so she smiled and said, "Mother, it's okay. Maybe the weather is getting warmer. I just need to take more supplements these few days."

Jiang ordered the kitchen staff to stew bird's nest and other nourishing foods for Xiuxin every day. Xiuxin snuggled up to her mother with a smile, "Mom, I like to eat roasted chicken. Can I have one roasted chicken every day?"

Jiang nodded at Xiuxin's nose lovingly, "You glutton, you should eat less of those greasy foods, they are not good for your stomach."

Xiu Xin said, "I'll just eat less. If I can't eat what I like, I won't have an appetite for anything."

Jiang said, "Look at how spoiled you are. Can you still be so willful after you marry into your husband's family?"

On the other hand, because Princess Duanyi's 70th birthday was coming up, the entire palace began to prepare for it two or three months in advance. Wang Fusheng was also very concerned about this matter and took time to discuss the birthday banquet with Princess Duanyi.

Wang Fusheng stood by the side, looking respectful, "Grandmother, your 70th birthday is coming soon. The emperor has specially rewarded you for this, including a pair of jade ruyi, a gold jade pillow, a double-sided embroidery of fortune and luck with gold thread, ten pieces of ice silk brocade, and a pair of Tianshan snow lotus and a pair of thousand-year-old ganoderma lucidum tributed from the Western Regions..."

Princess Duanyi sipped her tea gracefully and said, "Okay, I know everything. It's hard for His Majesty to still care about an old woman like me. I don't want to hold a big party this year. It's better to keep it simple. My old bones can't do it anymore. But the people in the palace, the princes' families, and many people from the aristocratic families must come. I think the birthday banquet doesn't have to follow the example of previous years. It can be just two days. On the first day, of course, we will entertain the people in the palace and the princes' families. On the second day, we will entertain the aristocratic families. The direct descendants of the Xie, Sun, Cui, and Jiang families, as well as the important side branches, must be invited. Those who have contacts in the officialdom and those who are close friends must be considered."

"Grandson knows, grandma don't worry." Wang Fusheng said in a deep voice.

Princess Duanyi looked at Wang Fusheng and smiled. "I am naturally confident in your work. How much money have you prepared for the birthday banquet this year?"

Wang Fusheng said, "This year, we have prepared 80,000 taels of silver, of which 30,000 taels are allocated by the Ministry of Revenue, and the remaining 20,000 taels are granted by the palace."

Princess Duanyi frowned and asked, "How come there are 20,000 taels more than last year?"

Wang Fusheng said, "This year is different from previous years. Grandmother is 70 years old this year, and she has reached the age of 70. The palace and the outside of the palace are all important. In addition, our house needs to be renovated inside and out. All the necessary equipment should be added and replaced. All these will cost money. In addition, I personally think that we might as well distribute 10,000 dan of grain to beggars and refugees around the capital during the birthday celebration. On the one hand, it will accumulate virtue for grandma, and on the other hand, our Wang family's dignity and reputation will be preserved. Isn't it the best of both worlds?"

Princess Duanyi nodded when she heard this, "You are very considerate, so I will do as you say." She paused and looked at Wang Fusheng meaningfully and said, "You have already passed your thirties, Chaozong His mother has been gone for many years. The person in charge of your house has been missing for more than ten years. You can't let Aunt Wang take care of the family affairs for you for a long time. You don't have to be laughed at by outsiders. You have to marry a step-brother to look good. I wonder what you think about this？"

Wang Fusheng bowed his hands, and inexplicably thought of someone's tearful eyes, tender lips, and cute nose. His heart skipped a beat, but the expression on his face did not change, and he still answered in a calm tone, "What grandma said is that my grandson has been busy with political affairs recently and really has no time to think about his marriage. It is better to discuss this matter after some time."

Princess Duanyi's face suddenly changed when she heard that, and her tone became anxious, "Busy? Are you so busy that you don't even have time to marry a wife? Or are those girls in your room making trouble? You are the backbone of our Wang family. You have reached a high position at a young age. How can you not understand this? Those girls in your room are all from small families. Could it be that they want to covet the power of household management? Especially that one!" Princess Duanyi seemed very reluctant to mention that person, "When you did that stupid thing, the whole world knew about it and it brought shame to the Wang family. It's okay if this matter is over, but if she wants to make any more trouble, be careful or I will kick her out!"

Seeing Princess Duanyi coughing in anger, Wang Fusheng lowered his head and admitted his fault, "I know I was wrong. I did those reckless things because I was young and ignorant. I must not be so foolish now. I'd better let grandma look after my marriage for me."

Princess Duanyi then suppressed the anger on her face and said slowly, "That's good. Your family is small, and if I can have a few grandchildren after marrying this wife, I will be blessed as an old lady."

Wang Fusheng bowed his head and said, "Grandma, you are right. I will do as you say."

A month later, Princess Duanyi's birthday banquet became the most lively and grand event in the capital. Even the queen in the palace brought the crown prince and several princesses to the Wang family to celebrate the birthday. More than a hundred other princes, emperors, and county kings were all present. It was very lively for a while, and the power of the Wang family was at its peak. On the second day, all the noble families and officials in the capital came with their families to celebrate. In the past two days, the gifts alone filled three rooms, and the banquet was like a stream, with endless laughter and joy.

Only the wife of the first wife and her daughter could attend such an event, so Minxin could not come. Yixin was ill recently and Yuxin was too young, so the only female members of the Cui family who attended were Feng, Jiang, and Xiuxin. The three of them rode in a carriage, and the maids and servants followed the carriage to serve.

According to the rules of the Hua Dynasty, male guests should enter from the east and female guests from the west. As soon as the carriage that Xiuxin was sitting in stopped, a maid with a very elegant appearance came to greet her. Feng handed over the bright red visiting card, and the maid bowed and said, "Madam Cui, Madam Cui, and Miss Cui, please follow me. The birthday banquet has not started yet. I will take you to the inner room to rest first."

Feng, Jiang, and Xiuxin said, "Thank you, Madam."

The three followed the maid and walked along the long corridor. Feng and Jiang were silent and held their breath. Xiu Xin was a child at heart. She looked around secretly and saw that the furnishings and architecture of the Wang family were incomparable to those of ordinary families. They even surpassed the residence of the Cui family in Qinghe. She was slightly surprised in her heart. The Wang family was really like a palace. While thinking, she walked for about two quarters of an hour before reaching an inner courtyard. The maid who led the way said, "Everyone, please rest here, drink tea, and eat some snacks. If you need anything, just let me know. The maids outside are waiting outside."

Jiang thanked them again, and the three of them entered the courtyard.

☆、Chapter 11 Reunion

Chapter 11 Reunion
When the three of them entered the courtyard, they saw rows of small pearwood tables in the courtyard, with snacks, fruits and other snacks on them. The ladies

gathered in groups of three or four to chat and laugh, making the place very lively. When Feng and Jiang came in with Xiuxin, a lady in a gorgeous dress came up to them immediately, smiling, "Sister, it's been so long, and I finally get to see you. Although we are sisters, we rarely get together. Today we must have a good chat."

Jiang said, "You are busy managing the household, unlike me who has nothing to do. I won't bother you too much."

Xiu Xin bowed and said, "Aunt, I wish you good health."

Madam Sun Er smiled and said "OK", then looked at Feng who was standing beside her and smiled slightly, "Madam Cui, your daughter Yi Xin will marry into our Sun family, so we will be considered relatives, and we should interact more often in the future."

Feng was a little embarrassed. "Madam Sun is right. We should indeed have more contact." In fact, how could marrying someone as a concubine be considered a relative? Her daughter was probably ruined.

The four of them talked for a while, and then Feng went to talk to other ladies. When Mrs. Sun Er saw Feng walking away, she snorted coldly, "I don't know how you raise your daughter. You raise such a shameless daughter."

Although Madam Sun Er usually managed the household well, she was always gentle and polite to both superiors and subordinates, and rarely spoke harshly. Jiang couldn't help but say, "Second Miss did something a little out of line, but from what you said, I wonder if there is any other reason behind it?"

"Sister." Madam Sun Er lowered her voice and said, "You don't know, that day in Zhengjue Temple, my second master was in the pavilion on the back hill. He heard the woman's cry for help and went outside with a servant. He saw your second daughter. Seeing that her injuries were not serious and that men and women should not touch each other, the second master thought of going back to call a maid to help her. Unexpectedly, she grabbed my second master and refused to let go. The second master had no choice but to carry her on his back. He originally wanted to leave her in a deserted place where no one could see her. Firstly, it would be bad for the girl's reputation, and secondly, it would be difficult for him to get away. But after carrying her for a few steps, he saw Feng's people coming over. It was really impossible to deny it. It was really shameless. She was still the daughter of a noble family, but she did such a thing as to seize someone else's marriage."

"So that's how it is." Jiang sighed, "I was originally wondering how Mr. Sun could do such a shameless thing, being so intimate with an unmarried young lady and letting others see it. According to what you said, this was probably planned by Feng and others from the beginning to the end."

"That's right." Madam Sun Er said, "The girl has no shame, and the mother has no brains, so they are only fit to be concubines." Madam Sun Er took Xiu Xin's hand and said, "My Xiu Xin has grown better and better in recent years. Her skin is so tender that it looks like water can be squeezed out. My second master is unlucky. I don't know which young man will be lucky enough to marry my Xiu Xin."

Xiu Xin said in a tender voice, "Aunt..."

Madam Sun Er laughed and said, "Oh, you're still shy."

"It's still a long way to go for my Xiuxin's marriage, and we have no idea about it yet. Let's wait and see." Jiang paused and changed the subject, "I haven't congratulated you yet, but your master has won the first place in the imperial examination this time, and will surely be highly valued by the emperor. But I don't know where your master will be assigned this time?"

Madam Sun Er said, "He is currently assigned to the Ministry of Justice. He originally had no ambition to make progress. Although he has some knowledge, he only writes and paints poems. Now that he has suddenly made progress, it is naturally my blessing."

Jiang said, "That's right."

The three of them were chatting casually

when Xiuxin looked up and saw a young lady coming in from the door. She was no more than twenty years old, with her hair done in a heart-shaped bun, and she was wearing a jacket embroidered with a school flower pattern, and a silk top embroidered with a lotus pattern. She was very beautiful, with curved eyebrows and beautiful eyes.

"Big sister!" Xiu Xin stood up and waved with a smile.

Cui Jinxin was also very surprised. She walked over quickly, bowed and called out, "Mother, Aunt."

Jiang sighed, and lovingly helped Jin Xin sit down by her hand. "It's been more than half a year since I last saw you. I really missed you. Let me see you. You've lost weight, lost weight."

Jin Xin burst out laughing and said, "Mother, every time you look at me you say I've lost weight. In fact, I'm not thinner at all. It's just that you're worried and you wish I could gain weight."

Madam Sun Er said, "That makes sense. As a mother, you can't help but worry about your children no matter how old they are. When my son Heng'er was sick, I couldn't sleep or eat well, and I lost a lot of weight. I was afraid that..." Heng'er was Madam Sun Er's only son, and she treated him more seriously than her own life.

Xiu Xin comforted him, "My cousin is fine now, so please don't worry."

Madam Sun Er smiled and said, "Everyone

says that this girl is a sweet and caring little cotton-padded jacket for her mother, and it really is true. Sister, I really envy you, your sons are all very promising, and your daughters are all very beautiful."

Jiang said, "That's true, but there are still many things to worry about. The first one is the marriage of our children. Qihong is still young, and Jinghong and my daughter Xiuxin are both at the age of engagement..." Jiang glanced at Jinxin as she spoke, "Although Jinxin and her husband are in harmony and love, they have been childless for three years. What will happen in the long run?"

Jin Xin's expression darkened, "If there is no news this year, I will give my beloved An Xiang to him. If she gives birth to a child, I will take her as a concubine."

Jiang frowned, "There is nothing we can do about it. If the concubine gave birth to a child, you would raise him by your side, and it would be the same." In fact, Jiang was just saying this to comfort Jin Xin. Raising someone else's child is different from raising your own. First, it is difficult to handle things. If you are too strict, people will say that you are treating him harshly. If you are too lenient, people will say that you have not fulfilled your responsibilities. Second, after all, he is not your own child, so there is a layer of separation. Besides, his biological mother is there, so it is inevitable that she will cause trouble.

Jin Xin said bitterly, "We'll talk about it when the time comes. There's still half a year left this year, I just hope there will be good news within this half year."

Madam Sun Er asked, "Did you see any doctor? What medicines have you taken?"

Jin Xin said, "I had previously hired Doctor Wei from Rong'an Hall to treat my illness. After taking the medicine for more than a year without seeing any effect, I asked someone to invite Doctor Wan, who usually treats Princess Duanyi, to see me. He prescribed some medicine, and I've only been taking it for less than half a year. I've been taking medicine all the time in the past two years. Doctors usually only said that I had a yin deficiency in my constitution and only prescribed some tonic medicine. Now, after taking my pulse, they said that I had almost recovered, and just told me to relax and wait for good news. But after more than half a year, there is still no news." Jin Xin shed tears as she spoke.

Xiu Xin felt very sad after hearing this, "Sister, please relax. I remember you drew a lot before you got married. The lot said that you just need to wait patiently, and happiness will come after suffering."

Jinxin held Xiuxin's hand, choking with sobs, "Sister..."

Jiang and Madam Sun also comforted her, and Jinxin stopped talking. At one point, another maid came to invite all the ladies and girls to the front yard for a banquet. Everyone stood up and followed the maids to the front. A large stage had been set up in the courtyard, and hundreds of tables were placed around the stage. On each table was a pot of wine and a pot with a large lamb leg cooking in it, with several dishes of stuffing placed around it. Feng, Jiang, Xiuxin, and Jinxin sat at a table, while Madam Sun sat with the women of the Sun family.

Among the sisters, Xiuxin has been close to Jinxin since childhood. Since she got married, Xiuxin only saw her a few times a year, and each time was in a hurry. This time, it was rare for everyone to get together, and Xiuxin was very excited. She pulled Xiuxin to ask questions, and Jinxin couldn't help but poke Xiuxin's forehead with her fingertips, "If you love to make trouble like this, I don't know who can control you in the future after you get married."

Xiu Xin said, "There is no such thing as being able to control a relationship between husband and wife. They should naturally treat each other with respect, just like our fathers and mothers."

Jiang said, "There is no such thing as perfection in this world. It's just a matter of forbearance."

Xiuxin didn't hear the hidden meaning, and took a large piece of lamb leg from the pot, dipped it in the stuffing, and put it into her mouth. Lamb is very tender, and the stuffing makes it even more delicious. Xiuxin took several big bites and soon finished all the lamb leg on the plate.

Jin Xin was puzzled, so she turned her head and asked Jiang quietly, "Mother, has something happened to you and father?"

Jiang sighed softly, pulled Jinxin's sleeve and said, "Come with me."

The two of them left the table and walked to a quiet place. Jiang said, "I'm just telling you this. Previously, although your father didn't have a concubine, he never came to the master bedroom every day. I thought he was busy with official duties, so he rested in the study. . But a few days ago, I sent a bowl of ginseng soup to the study for your father, but I heard..." Jiang paused, her face turned red, "It turned out that there was that kind of sound coming from inside. , He actually had a relationship with Mingxiang in my room. Normally, Mingxiang doesn't have any special color, but I didn't expect that little bitch to climb into the master's bed."

Jin Xin said, "Mom, just send this girl away. It's not worth being sad about."

Jiang shook her head, "Of course I want to send him away, and the master dare not stop me. But if there is one, there will be another. In the past, I could still keep him by relying on my beauty, but now I am old and don't like to deal with him. But men are always greedy for new things, how can I resist. These years I have been watching him like a thief, he is tired and so am I. I thought it would be better to buy a girl with a clean background to be his concubine, so that he won't be obsessed with cheating outside."

Jin Xin sighed, "So even my father and mother are like this. Is there no couple in this world who stays faithful to each other and stays together until the end of their lives?"

Jiang said, "That's just a thought before you get married. Men are like this. If you can control him, he will respect you for a day. If you can't control him, he will slap you in the face. I have seen through this a long time ago."

Speaking of which, after Jiang and Jin Xin left the table, Princess Duanyi arrived. All the maids bowed and praised her, "May Your Highness live a long and healthy life."

Princess Duanyi sat down at the main seat and said, "You all don't have to be so formal. Today is my birthday banquet. It is a blessing for me that you all have come. You just sit down and watch the show, drink wine, and eat food. Let's just have fun together."

Everyone should agree.

At that moment, a play started on the stage, and it was the play "Heaven Official's

Blessing". Xiuxin liked to watch plays very much, but she liked the lively fighting plays like "Havoc in Heaven". She didn't find such literary plays interesting, so she just lowered her head to eat. At that moment, another maid brought up a pile of crab roe and tofu. Xiuxin's eyes lit up, and she quickly scooped a big mouthful with a small silver spoon and put it into her mouth. She felt that the fresh taste of the crab roe mixed with the softness of the tofu was so delicious that it made her swallow her tongue in one gulp.

"Xiu Xin, Xiu Xin." Feng pushed Xiu Xin, who was holding a large mouthful of crab roe tofu, and said, "Princess Duan Yi is calling you."

☆, Chapter 12: Embarrassment

Chapter 12: Embarrassment
Xiu Xin was startled and quickly swallowed the crab roe tofu in her mouth. She walked out and stood behind the young ladies and bowed to Princess Duan Yi. "Greetings, Princess."

Princess Duanyi's eyes were full of smiles. "I am old, but I still find it interesting to see young people like you. You are the third daughter of the Cui family, right?"

"Yes." Xiu Xin answered with a frown.

Princess Duanyi laughed loudly. "I remember very clearly the boxing you performed in Qionglin Garden last time. It is rare for young girls to be both literary and martial. Come closer so I can take a closer look."

Xiu Xin had no choice but to walk a few steps forward past the crowd and stop in front of the steps, still with her head slightly lowered.

Princess Duanyi waved at her, "Come closer, come up, come to my side."

Xiu Xin was surprised. This princess was really strange. There were so many noble ladies standing below. Why did she only call me up? But the princess had given the order, so she had to bite the bullet and go up. When she arrived in front of Princess Duan Yi, she bowed and said, "Greetings, Princess."

Duan Yi shook her hand with a smile on his face, "Oh, let's not worry about those empty formalities. Look at me, you are so pretty, you look blessed."

Xiu thought to herself that because she was a little bit chubby, it was a bit of a stretch to praise her for being beautiful, so she could only praise her for being pretty. You know, Huachao considered thinness beautiful. For example, Xie Yulan, who was standing at the bottom of the stairs, was a typical thin beauty, as if she could be blown away by a gust of wind.

Duan Yi asked Xiu Xin what books she had read and what embroidery she had done as usual, and then let her go. At the end, she added, "Take this scallion-fried sea cucumber and this plate of charcoal-roasted pigeon on my table to Miss Cui San. I am old and have no teeth, and young people like to eat these."

Xiuxin was very happy, her eyebrows were about to fly up. Her favorite was charcoal-grilled pigeon, but the family's meals were all decided by the kitchen, and the menu was written every month and given to Jiang Shi for review. Xiuxin could not decide what to eat, and Jiang Shi was afraid that Xiuxin would have food stagnation, so she even ordered snacks in fixed quantities. After a while, the delicious and fragrant charcoal-grilled pigeon was served. Xiuxin tore off a pigeon leg and bit into it with a wow. The tender pigeon meat was crispy on the outside and tender on the inside, and it also had a spiced flavor. Xiuxin's eyes lit up as she ate.

Princess Duanyi looked at Xiuxin from a distance and smiled to her long-time confidant Yu Niang, "It's rare to see someone as straightforward as the third young lady of the Cui family these days. Even the fifth young lady of the Cui family is not as good as her."

Yu Niang glanced at Xiu Xin who was gnawing on the wings, then at Cui Wu who was sitting upright, and said with a smile, "Princess is right, this Third Miss Cui is indeed rare." Yu Niang glanced at Duan Yi, and continued, "It's just that her personality is too outspoken, like a child, and I'm afraid it will be difficult for her to take charge of a big family."

Duanyi said, "You can learn those mundane things later. What I hate most are those girls who put on airs. They are obviously only in their teens, but they act like they are mature for whom. They are full of ideas at such a young age. It's not expected that they will be successful after they marry into a husband's family. Wouldn't that just cause unrest in the family?" Duanyi was the daughter of the queen. Before she got married, she was the most favored girl in the palace, so she developed an open-minded character.

Yu Niang laughed and said, "Princess, you are right."

The noble ladies discussed privately, wondering what kind of drug Cui Xiuxin had given Princess Duanyi to make her think so highly of her. Cui Wu was even more so. With so many noble ladies standing in a row, although she didn't really want Princess Duanyi's attention, she was naturally uncomfortable when Princess Duanyi only praised Cui Xiuxin in front of so many people, which made her lose face. Moreover, judging from Duanyi's intention, could it be that she wanted to replace Wang Chaozong... Thinking of this, Cui Wu felt even more uncomfortable. The sons of the Wang family were like gods, and how could Cui Xiuxin be worthy of them?

Xiu Xin didn't realize that she had become a sitting duck for the noble ladies, so when Cui Wu came over with a wine glass in his hand, she didn't react. Cui Wu had always been arrogant, and apart from being close to the daughters of the Xie, Wang, and Sun families, he never paid attention to anyone else. Why was he taking the initiative to get close to her now?

Cui Wu raised the wine glass and said to Xiuxin, "We are a family and should be as close as sisters. Unfortunately, we have not had much friendship over the years. Sister, you are wrong for not getting close to your sister. Shouldn't you be punished with a glass of wine?" Cui Wu's words were so artistic. It was Xiuxin's fault that the two sisters were not close. Although Xiuxin knew it in her heart, she didn't like to argue with others. She simply raised the wine glass and toasted Cui Wu with a glass of wine, "Since my sister said so, I'll just drink this glass of wine." After that, she tilted her head back and drank it.

However, Cui Wu had no intention of letting her go. "One glass of wine is not enough. Today is Princess Duanyi's birthday banquet. Sister, you have brought honor to our Cui family. You should drink another glass for this." Cui Wu was known for his sharp tongue. After he said these two sentences, Xiu Xin had to pick up the wine glass and said, "Then I'll finish this glass." While drinking, she thought, when will Cui Wu ever stop? Does he want to get me drunk on purpose?

After two glasses of wine, Cui Wu saw that Xiu Xin's cheeks were flushed and her big eyes were wet. It was obvious that she was getting drunk. He raised the corners of his mouth and filled a glass for Xiu Xin, saying, "Sister, you are really straightforward. I will drink a glass with you, just for the sake of our friendship."

Xiu Xin knew that if she drank another glass, something might happen, so she quickly refused, "I can't drink much, I really can't drink any more."

Cui Wu thought, I just want to know that you can't handle the alcohol, how can I let you go, so he pretended to be aggrieved, "Sister, don't you want to acknowledge me as your sister? I guess I have offended you in some way, and you refused to drink even the glass of wine you offered me."

After she said that, Xiuxin had no choice but to drink all the wine in the glass. Now, her head was dizzy and her whole body seemed to be as soft as mud. She half leaned on Feng's body, looked at Cui Wu in a daze, tipped the glass down, and laughed, "Look, I drank...drank it all."

"You are really my good sister." Cui Wu said proudly, "Why don't we go and toast to Princess Duan Yi together again?" I just want to see you make a fool of yourself. Look at you like this, and see if Princess Duan Yi can still value you?

Feng also wanted to see Xiuxin doing well, so she pushed Xiuxin and said, "Xiuxin, why don't you go with Cui Wu? What are you dawdling for?" Xiuxin was already feeling dizzy, and after being pushed and pulled by them, she stood up unsteadily. She really took the empty wine glass and followed Cui Wu to go to Princess Duanyi.

Originally, the ladies of various families were toasting to the eldest princess, and there was nothing wrong with Cui Wu bringing Xiu Xin along. But Xiu Xin staggered along the way, and after a few steps she bumped into the table of Madam Wang, Wang Fusheng's mother, and knocked over a pot of wine on the table.

Madam Wang was talking to her relative, Princess Changping, when she was startled and felt unhappy. She thought that some girl was so careless and needed to be disciplined. When she turned around, she saw Xiuxin's drunken face. "I'm sorry." Cui Wu hurriedly supported Cui Xiuxin and smiled, "Madam, my sister drank a few more sips of wine and got a little drunk. Please don't blame me."

Old Lady Wang frowned immediately and thought to herself, how could the third daughter of the Cui family be so unstable and rash in her behavior? She didn't have the demeanor of a lady from a noble family at all. On the other hand, Cui Wu next to her was the one who knew how to act gracefully.

Cui Wu supported Xiu Xin and walked forward. When they were about to reach Princess Duan

Yi, he deliberately let go. Xiu Xin staggered up the stairs alone, holding a wine glass, and came to Duan Yi's side. She raised the empty wine glass high and smiled foolishly, "Congratulations to the Princess... Princess, may you live a long life and may you be blessed... as vast as the East Sea." After saying this, she twisted her body and fell forward, falling directly into Duan Yi's arms.

Duan Yi hugged Xiu Xin and cried out, "This kid must have drunk too much. Yuniang, please send two maids to take her to the side room in the backyard to rest for a while."

Yu Niang quickly agreed, called two maids over, and helped Xiu Xin away.

Yu Niang looked at Xiu Xin's back and said worriedly, "Princess, the third young lady of the Cui family is really not steady enough. It's really inappropriate for her to drink like this in public. The second master is now the backbone of the court. If the third young lady Cui is not presentable, it will be harmful to the second master."

Duan Yi pondered for a while and said, "Didn't you see Cui Wu trying to drink Xiuxin wine just now? That girl is indeed not very scheming, but she is cute and adorable, and can't be said to be unpresentable. The Second Master is already very busy in the court, and if he has to face a calculating wife after leaving the court, it would be too much."

Yu Niang wanted to say more, but seeing her master's expression, she had to hold back and said reluctantly, "Master, you are right."

On the other hand, Feng was secretly happy to see Xiuxin had made a fool of herself today. Then she saw two maids from the palace helping Xiuxin out, and a plan came to her mind. She also secretly left the table, found a big maid in green, gave her ten taels of silver, and whispered something to her.

Since Yi Xin was promised to the Sun family as a concubine, Feng hated Jiang's mother and daughter, thinking that Jiang was the one who interfered and instigated the old lady of the Sun family to make Yi Xin a concubine. Therefore, Feng held a grudge and thought that since you killed my daughter, I would kill your daughter to be fair and just.

Then, the eldest maid put the ten taels of silver in her sleeve, walked a few steps quickly and said to the two maids who were supporting Xiuxin, "Chengbi, Xinbi, the old lady asked you to go to the front to help, I will take this young lady to see her off."

Upon hearing this, Chengbi and Xinbi handed the embroidery heart to the maid. The maid's name was Yubi. She was the top maid in Wang Chaozong's room and the concubine appointed by the old lady to Wang Chaozong. However, Wang Chaozong had not touched her for half a year. Everyone in the mansion laughed at her, and she felt ashamed. She looked down at the lady beside her and hated her. Aren't you a rich lady? Look, I'll throw you into a man's room and ruin your reputation. Can you still marry in?

So, Yubi dragged Xiuxin all the way through the garden, into the front hall, and threw her onto the big bed in Wang Chao's chamber.

☆, Chapter 13: Erotic

Chapter 13: Erotic

As the head of the civil officials, Wang Fusheng was best at flattery and flattery. During the banquet, many officials tried their best to force him to drink, but he cleverly avoided them. However, today he ran into a tough problem, and that problem was the Protector of the Country, Liu Baozi. Liu Baozi is also a legendary figure in the Hua Dynasty. He was the chief escort of the escort agency, escorting escorts on the road all day long. Later, when the Hu people invaded the border of the Central Plains, he volunteered to join the army. In eight years, he went from an unknown soldier to the famous Zhenyuan General. Intimidated by his reputation, the Hu people handed in a letter of surrender and vowed not to invade the Central Plains for 30 years, which brought 30 years of peace and stability to the Hua Dynasty. The emperor appreciated his contribution and named him the Duke of Protecting the Country.

Liu Bao was born in the military, and he looked down on civil officials like Wang Fusheng the most. He always felt that they were full of benevolence and morality, but in fact they did nothing serious, so he always made trouble for Wang Fusheng. At the birthday banquet of Princess Duan Yi, Liu Bao came to Wang Fusheng with a large bowl to toast him. When Wang Fusheng saw him coming, he felt a pang in his heart, thinking that it was not good, and this troublemaker might come to cause trouble again.

Wang Fusheng evaded the question, "Lord Protector of the Country, I have already drunk a lot of wine today. I really can't drink any more. I hope you will forgive me."

Liu Baozi glared with his tiger eyes and blew his beard, "Fuck you, you are not giving face to me, are you?" After that, he put the large bowl on the table with a bang, picked up the wine pot and filled it with wine, "Boy, drink quickly, drink quickly, you are so dawdling like a woman. If you don't drink, you are looking down on me."

Liu Baozi, who is fifty-one years old this year, is not wrong to call Wang Fusheng, who is just over thirty, "boy". It's just that he is the only one in the whole court who dares to call Wang Fusheng "boy".

Wang Fusheng said, "Lord Protector of the

Country, I can't drink much. I really can't drink any more. I'm afraid my stomach can't handle this bowl. How about a smaller cup?"

Liu Baozi sneered, "Why should a man learn to drink from a woman's small cup? If I were you, you should drink from this big bowl! Boy, you don't dare to drink, do you?"

Forced into this situation, Wang Fusheng had no choice but to drink a large bowl of wine. Liu Baozi was also not polite, and gulped it down. Without changing his expression, he stretched out his big calloused hand and patted Wang Fusheng on the shoulder, causing Wang Fusheng to stagger. "Boy, you have a good alcohol tolerance."

Wang Fusheng thought he had a good alcohol tolerance, but after drinking such a large bowl, although the wine did not get on his face, he began to feel dizzy. Wang Chaozong saw that Wang Fusheng's eyes were a little dazed, so he came to Wang Fusheng and said, "Father, you should go to the bedroom and rest for a while. I will take care of it here, so don't worry."

Wang Fusheng was also feeling dizzy. He pulled himself together and bowed to the guests, saying, "Dear colleagues, I am not feeling well and will take my leave first. I hope you will forgive me."

Everyone should agree.

Wang Fusheng was supported by a servant and went to the bedroom in the front yard. The servant helped him wash his face and hands, drank a bowl of hangover soup, and lit a calming incense before leaving and closing the door. Wang Fusheng had just gone to bed when he heard a noise next door, as if something was knocking against something. He was startled. Could it be that there was someone in Wang Chaozong's room?

He stood up, pushed open the small door, and saw a person sitting on Wang Chaozong's bed, a woman. She was wearing a light green coat on her upper body and a lotus-colored pleated skirt on her lower body. At this moment, she was rubbing her forehead with her hands, mumbling, "It hurts, it hurts..."

Wang Fusheng wondered why the voice sounded so familiar.

Just as Wang Fusheng was about to get closer to take a look, the woman took off her outer coat, revealing a light pink double-breasted jacket, "It's so hot..."

Wang Fusheng had drunk some wine, and when he suddenly saw the woman taking off her clothes in front of him, he felt that the heat suddenly filled his brain and exploded. In the dim light, he saw the woman's back. Her waist was not very slender, but the skin on her neck was as white as top-grade porcelain, which made people imagine how smooth it would be to touch. He thought so and did so, and his big hand had already touched the woman's neck.

Men have higher body temperatures than

women. Wang Fusheng suddenly stretched out his hand and pressed it against Xiuxin's skin, scaring her sober. She turned around abruptly and met Wang Fusheng's burning eyes. "Hey? Deng, Tu, Zi?"

When Wang Fusheng saw that it was Cui Xiuxin, he couldn't help but feel more and more happy. Since that day when he left Zhengjue Temple, the figure of this little girl has been lingering around him day by day, making him look like a young boy who just started eating meat. It's true to say that It was embarrassing. At this moment, Xiuxin was disheveled and her beautiful eyes were full of tears. It was really sinful and aroused his most primitive desires. He couldn't control it for a moment. He rubbed her hard into his arms and sprayed hot air. On her face, "My little darling, I miss you so much." This is a standard line for a romantic young man to tease a decent woman.

Xiu Xin never expected that she would meet this deceitful disciple in the palace, and in such an embarrassing situation. She couldn't help but struggle, waving her little hands wildly, "You, let me go! Let me go!"

When Wang Fusheng saw Xiuxin waving her fists around with her big watery eyes, she was so adorable, his heart was burning with desire. He didn't care about her soft fists and hugged her tighter. "Be good, don't make trouble, don't make trouble, let me treat you well." After that, he kissed her red lips that he had longed for.

"Hmm…Hmm…"

It was indeed fragrant and smooth, like the finest tender tofu. Wang Fusheng traced a circle along her lips, nibbled them gently, and then he wanted to use the tip of his tongue to pry open Xiuxin's teeth. However, the beauty's teeth were clenched tightly, and he couldn't shake them even a little bit even if he tried his best. After he sucked the beauty's lips hard, he pressed Xiuxin on the bed and kissed her again. This time, his hand deftly got into Xiuxin's shirt and directly covered her full roundness. Xiuxin opened her eyes wide, exclaimed, and opened her teeth. Someone's tongue took advantage of this gap to deftly get in and play with the beauty's soft tongue.

Xiuxin had never encountered anything like this before. She thought that what he did to her last time in Zhengjue Temple was the limit. She didn't expect that he could put his hand... like this... in such a shameful place. But he was still not satisfied. His hand covering her roundness even began to move skillfully, causing Xiuxin to exclaim again.

Wang Fusheng was so amused that he couldn't let her go. Just as he was thinking about unbuttoning her outer jacket, Xiuxin's fist finally hit the right spot and hit him straight on the nose. Wang Fusheng felt a sore nose and groaned in pain. He covered his nose and frowned.

Xiuxin was about to open the door and run out in panic, but Wang Fusheng stopped her, "Do you want to run out in such a disheveled state? What will others think?"

Xiu Xin stopped walking when she heard that. When she turned around, she suddenly pulled out the red hairpin on her head and pointed the tip at her neck, her face full of determination, "If you dare to touch me again, I will die here." How important a woman's chastity is, her mother has said it many times. She must not let her future husband down.

Seeing Xiu Xin like this, Wang Fusheng was sobered up by the shock. He realized that the woman in front of him was not a prostitute in a brothel. He patted his head and thought to himself, what happened to me? He lost his usual level when he saw her. Even though he usually prided himself on being a romantic, he had never been so strong. This was really wrong, this was really wrong!

"Put down the red hairpin first, and I promise not to touch you again." Wang Fusheng lowered his voice and said, "Really."

Xiuxin couldn't believe him. If others knew what happened today, she would not survive. She felt a strong hatred for the man in front of her, so she might as well end it all. So she ran a few steps desperately and stabbed Wang Fusheng in the face with the red hairpin. Wang Fusheng saw her eyes full of hatred and raised the red hairpin to stab him. He instinctively dodged, but was still stabbed in the shoulder. Fortunately, Xiuxin's strength was not strong, and the stab was only half an inch deep, and blood immediately flowed out.

Xiu Xin was also startled when she saw the blood. She loosened her grip in panic and the red hairpin in her hand fell to the ground with a crisp sound. Wang Fusheng covered his shoulder, endured the severe pain, took out a bottle of hemostatic medicine from the cabinet and sprinkled it on the wound, which slightly stopped the bleeding. Xiu Xin was so scared that her face turned pale and trembled, "You...you...are you going to die?"

Seeing her like this, Wang Fusheng felt pity for her and said, "I won't die."

Thinking of what had just happened, Xiuxin couldn't help curling up into a ball and began to cry. Wang Fusheng saw the beauty's tears flowing like a river, and was about to say something to comfort her when he heard the voices of several women outside the house.

"Madam Cui, this is our brother's room." Yubi said.

Feng said, "Are you sure my third daughter is in your brother's room?"

Yubi said, "I saw your third daughter enter our brother's room with my own eyes.

Whether it is true or not, you can go in and take a look, Madam."
The door creaked open, and Yubi looked inside. As expected, she saw a bulge in the quilt. She was quite proud, "Look, isn't there someone here, Madam?"
Feng also thought she had succeeded and was about to walk over to lift the quilt, but the person sleeping in the quilt lifted a corner of it and half-raised his body. A majestic male voice came into Feng's ears, "Madam Cui, what do you want to do by breaking into a man's bedroom without permission?"
Feng was startled and cried out, then she saw Wang Fusheng looking at her gloomily, and her face turned pale immediately, "I didn't know that you were resting here, otherwise I would not dare to offend you. I'm sorry to bother you, so I'm leaving now."
Yubi was so scared that she knelt down and kowtowed to admit her fault, "Second Master, I didn't mean to do that. Please forgive me."
"Get out of here!" Wang Fusheng said.
"Yes, yes." Yubi crawled out and closed the door.
After the two walked away, Wang Fusheng's hand still stayed on Xiuxin's waist. There was a little bit of fat on her waist, but the flesh on her waist was really soft and felt so comfortable to touch...
"Hey, can you let me go now?" Cui Xiuxin

got out of the quilt and shook off Wang Fusheng's hand. Because she had been in the quilt for a few minutes, Xiuxin's face looked red, like a ripe apple, which made people want to take a bite. Wang Fusheng thought so and did so. He really leaned over and took a bite on her cheek. "My dear, you are so lovely."

Xiuxin was grateful for his saving her, but she also hated his frivolity, so she hit him hard with her fist. Wang Fusheng grimaced in pain and called her, "Little Lajiao, I saved you just now, why aren't you grateful?"

Xiu Xin glared at him hatefully, "It's obviously you who harmed me."

Wang Fusheng felt innocent and said, "I didn't make you sleep in this bed."

"You!" Xiu Xin was choked and clenched her fists in anger.

Wang Fusheng saw that the beauty was angry again, so he tried to please her, "Okay, get yourself ready. I'll go out and get rid of everyone outside. You can leave now while no one is around, so that no one can see you and make it difficult to explain."

☆, Chapter 14: Peace

Chapter 14: Seeking Peace
Jiang and Jinxin returned to the banquet together, but Xiuxin was missing, and even Feng was nowhere to be seen. Jiang's heart immediately rose to her chest. Jinxin

comforted Jiang and said, "Sister is that old now, she should be fine. Why don't we ask the Wang family first?"

After a lot of inquiries, a maid replied and told Jiang that Xiuxin was drunk and was sent back to the backyard by two maids. Jiang was still worried and begged the maid to go find her. Jiang was anxious, but Xiuxin suddenly appeared at the banquet. Jiang was relieved, "My child, where have you been? You made me worry to death."

Xiuxin forced a smile, "I, I slept in the backyard for a while, and I came back after I sobered up. Don't worry, mother."

Jiang looked Xiuxin up and down and saw that her lips were slightly swollen and her eyes were still full of spring. What was even more terrible was that there was a tender red mark on her neck, which was obviously... obviously a mark left by lovemaking... Jiang was so frightened that her whole body trembled. She managed to calm down, took out the brocade handkerchief from her sleeve, and gently wrapped it around Xiuxin's neck, "Don't catch a cold."

After sitting for a while, Jiang said goodbye to Princess Duanyi, saying that she was not feeling well and wanted to take her daughter with her. Duanyi naturally agreed. Along the way, Jiang's face was as gloomy as water, and she held Xiuxin's hand tightly, her nails almost pinched into Xiuxin's palm. Xiuxin cried out in pain,

"Mother, it hurts." Jiang's grip loosened slightly, but her face was still heavy.

As soon as they returned to Cui's house and entered the small courtyard where Xiuxin lived, Jiang reached out and pulled off the silk scarf around Xiuxin's neck, pointed at the tender red mark on Xiuxin's snow-white neck and asked, "Xiuxin, I ask you, what is this? What is this!"

Xiu Xin looked at herself in the bronze mirror and felt so ashamed that tears welled up in her eyes. She knelt down and said, "Mother, I... I..."

Jiang knew Xiuxin's personality, so she slowed down her tone and asked, "Xiuxin, let me ask you, what's going on? Who is that man? Who bullied you?"

Xiu Xin shook her head, "I, I don't know."

"I don't know?" Jiang was shocked. "How could you not know? How could you not know? What are you going to hide from me now?"

Xiu Xin cried, "Mother, I really don't know. I was forced to drink and sent to Wang Chaozong's room. That person, that person suddenly appeared. I really don't know..."

Jiang asked, "How old is that person?"

"He looks about thirty years old."

"If it's someone from the palace, it would be easy to find, but today is a birthday party, so it might be someone from outside." Jiang was anxious and in pain, and asked in a low voice, "Xiu Xin, tell me honestly, did he...did he reach the last step?"

Xiu Xin was puzzled, "What's the last step?"

Such an unspeakable fact was really hard to describe, so Jiang had to change the way he put it, "That is...did he take off your clothes?"

Xiu Xin thought about it and realized that her clothes were still on her body, so she shook her head and said, "No."

Jiang finally breathed a sigh of relief. At least it wasn't irreparable. "Xiu Xin, forget about what happened today. Forget it completely. Just pretend it never happened. Do you understand?

"Xiu Xin understands."

The matter was finally suppressed, and Jiang severely blamed Feng's mother and daughter for this mess. She really didn't expect them to do such a vicious thing. If no one offends me, I won't offend them. If someone offends me, I will offend them. After Cui Yixin promised to be a concubine of the Sun family, she originally didn't intend to pursue the previous matter, but now that they dared to harm her precious daughter, don't blame her for being rude.

On the other hand, despite all the attempts to conceal it, Princess Duanyi finally found out about Wang Fusheng's injury, which made her furious. "Don't lie to me. I'm afraid you were injured by one of the prostitutes in the brothel. If it weren't for them, who else would have the guts to hurt you? You're not young anymore, how could you do such a stupid thing? If people outside knew about it, where would you put your face? Where would the Wang family put its face?"

Wang Fusheng lowered his head and complained in his heart, "My grandmother, the truth is more serious than you can imagine. I, your grandson, have molested the daughter of the Cui family..." I don't know how this matter will end. Wang Fusheng couldn't help but be moved when he thought of Cui Xiuxin's lovely appearance. Otherwise, I should mention this matter tactfully to my grandmother. It would be best to marry her into the family.

"Second Master? Second Master! Did you hear me?" Duan Yi became even more angry when he saw Wang Fusheng's absent-minded look. "I was just talking to you. Did you hear me?"

Wang Fusheng hurriedly said, "My grandson heard it."

Duan Yi asked again, "Then tell me, what do you think of the third daughter of the Cui family?"

Wang Fusheng was puzzled. "The third daughter of the Cui family? What does grandma mean?"

"Although she is only a branch of the Cui family, Cui Zhengkai has been promoted rapidly in recent years and has assumed the important post of Censor. If you marry Cui Xiuxin, you will naturally gain the support of Cui Zhengkai. Besides, your relationship with Cui Jinyi has been too stiff in recent years. Marrying a girl from the Cui family will always help ease the relationship. In addition, this Cui Xiuxin is very much to my liking. Although her appearance is not very outstanding, she is cute and lovely, straightforward and simple. It would be great for you to have her as your wife and have Nanny Wang to guide you in household affairs." Duan Yi said.

Wang Fusheng was surprised and delighted when he heard this. He never expected that it was his grandmother who brought up this matter first. He could not help but curl his fists and cough a few times to suppress the smile that was about to rise to the corner of his mouth. He bowed respectfully and said, "Grandma, you have considered it very carefully. The third daughter of the Cui family is indeed very suitable. But I think this matter may need further consideration. And we don't know what Cui Zhengkai means. I'm afraid he has already made up his mind, so it's hard for us to say. It's better to test the waters first."

Duan Yi nodded, "You are right. Isn't the Hundred Flowers Festival coming up soon? I'll ask your mother to bring this up with Jiang, and you can secretly find out what Cui Zhengkai thinks."

"Yes, grandma." Wang Fusheng bowed.

Wang Fusheng and Duanyi were eager to know Cui Zhengkai's intention, but in fact Cui Zhengkai and Jiang were also trying to figure out what the Wang family meant.

After that incident, Cui Zhengkai had not set foot in the main room for a whole month, and had been sleeping in the study. Cui Zhengkai knew that Jiang was not able to calm down for a while, and he also felt regretful. After all, he and his first wife really had feelings for each other, so he frequently showed his goodwill and smiled apologetically. Jiang naturally ignored him. One day, the maids had just gone to bed after serving Jiang, when the door creaked open. The maids saw Cui Zhengkai and bowed, "Master."

"You guys go down." Cui Zhengkai said.

When Jiang saw Cui Zhengkai come in, she ignored him and turned her back.

"Madam." Cui Zhengkai smiled apologetically.

Jiang still ignored him.

Cui Zhengkai said, "It's been so long, why don't you forgive me? I promised you that I would never do it again. I drank a few more sips of wine that day and lost control. You've been the only one for me all these years, and you should know how I feel about you."

Jiang sat up suddenly after hearing this, threw the pillow at Cui Zhengkai's face, and cried, "You said you were drunk and denied everything, but you messed around with the maid in my room, and you are just throwing my face on the ground. You don't know how many people laugh at me behind my back. If you are tired of me, just tell me yourself. I am not the kind of person who can't tolerate others. I will naturally find you a beautiful concubine, so that people outside won't say that I am jealous."

Cui Zhengkai knew that Jiang was just speaking in anger, so he sat on the edge of the bed and wiped Jiang's tears. "When I was young, I had a lot of people around me. When did you ever see me put my heart on them? After I married you, wasn't I completely satisfied with you? It was my fault that something like that happened, but it's been a whole month, and I've been swearing, swearing, and begging for mercy. You should at least forgive me once, right, Madam?"

Seeing Cui Zhengkai's sincere words, Jiang couldn't help but feel a little soft-hearted when she thought of their 20-year-old love, so she said, "I have been married to you for more than 20 years, and we are an old married couple. I know how you have treated me over the years. Ordinary people have three wives and four concubines, and we are a noble family. According to common sense, what the master did is nothing at all. But master, you don't know that since the first day I married you, I have been completely satisfied with you. You should know that every time you get close to other women, it's like taking a knife to my heart."

Cui Zhengkai was quite moved. Is there any man in the world who doesn't like his woman to love him from the bottom of her heart? At this moment, he regretted it even more. "Madam, I was wrong. I failed you. Madam, please believe me this time. I will never do it again."

Jiang smiled softly, leaning into Cui Zhengkai's arms, with a faint smile on her lips. This is the way to control a husband, the means must be tough, but soft to a man, so that you can catch a man and control him for a lifetime. After this incident, Cui Zhengkai will only feel that he owes her, so why should he listen to her in everything?

Cui Zhengkai was delighted to see Jiang like this. He reached out and hugged Jiang. He thought to himself, I don't know what was wrong with me. My wife is so good, but he actually fell in love with Mingxiang, that little girl. In fact, she is not even as good as his wife's little finger.

After a warm and affectionate conversation, Jiang nestled in Cui Zhengkai's arms and chatted, "What do you think Princess Duanyi meant at the birthday banquet? There were so many noble ladies from aristocratic families, why did she make an exception for Xiuxin?" Thinking of a possibility, Jiang sat up suddenly and asked nervously, "Do you think the Wang family is thinking of marrying our Xiuxin to Wang Chaozong?"

Cui Zhengkai nodded. "You have a point. Do you remember when I mentioned to you that the Wang family was interested in forming a marriage alliance with the Xie family?"

"I remember, why, but what happened in between?"

Cui Zhengkai said, "I don't know the specific changes. From what Wang Fusheng said, it seems that the Wang family has no intention of marrying into the Xie family."

"Does that mean you like our Xiu Xin?"

Cui Zhengkai said, "That may not be the case. There is no news leaking out from the Wang family right now. Besides, our family is only a branch of the Cui family. There is also Cui Wu in the direct line of the Cui family. It is not our Xiu Xin's turn anyway."

Jiang snorted coldly, "That Cui Wu is comparable to our Xiu Xin. She is always proud of her status and thinks she is great. Everyone knows that Cui Wu is a stubborn and intolerant person. How can the Wang family be interested in her?"

Cui Zhengkai said, "No matter what she is, she is still the legitimate daughter of the Cui family and has a noble status. Not to mention marrying the legitimate son of the Wang family, I'm afraid the Cui family is intending to marry her to a prince."

Jiang said, "Promise her to the prince? Wait and see, it will be a wonder if she can hold on to the position of princess."

Cui Zhengkai sighed, "You, as a mother, always think that your daughter is the best, and naturally other people's daughters are inferior to your own."

Jiang said coquettishly, "That's right. Our Xiuxin is the best."

☆, Chapter 15: Testing

Chapter 15: Temptation

Since Cui Yixin broke off her engagement with the Xie family and was promised to the Sun family as a concubine, her status in the mansion has declined greatly. The maids and servants in the Cui mansion are used to changing their attitudes according to the situation, and even the housekeeper Li secretly gave the share that should have been given to Yixin to Xiuxin, and even went to Xiuxin to curry favor with her.

Now it is spring, the flowers in the mansion are in bloom, Xiuxin, Lanxiang and Qinxiang are busy tinkering with pollen. Seeing the old woman coming, Xiuxin didn't even raise her head, but Lanxiang raised her hand and said, "Mom, there are rules for how much silver and cloth our girl should get every month. Our girl is loved by the master and the mistress, so it is our own business if the mistress gives more. It would be our girl's fault if she took advantage of the rules of the mansion. We appreciate your kindness, mom, but those things should be given to whoever they are, and it is not easy for us to accept them."

The old woman couldn't help but feel a little embarrassed when she heard this. She groaned and said with a smile, "I was wrong.

You deserve to be beaten. I will just take these things away."
The old woman was holding the things, feeling indignant. She kept muttering as she walked, "Hey, I, an old woman, gave her things but she refused them. Do you really think you are the emperor's daughter and you don't have to worry about anything?"
"Madame Li."
When Mrs. Li looked up and saw that it was the fourth young lady, Minxin, she stopped and said with a fake smile, "Where is the fourth young lady going?" The fourth young lady has always been a little bit of a loser in the mansion, neither loved by her father nor her mother. The servants could not be said to be very dedicated to her, they were just perfunctory.
"I was just strolling around a few places. Madam Li came to see my sister?" Min Xin's eyes swept over the things in Madam Li's hand and she immediately understood, "Madam, these things are probably for my sister, right?"
When Li Ma Ma mentioned this, she felt a little embarrassed and said, "They are just small things. The Third Miss doesn't want them. I might as well give them to someone else and avoid being embarrassed in front of the Third Miss."
Min Xin smiled and said, "Madam, don't be angry. My sister is very straightforward and doesn't know how good you are. Madam, why don't you give the things to me and I

will tell my sister that she will definitely accept them. Then I will mention Madam to my sister, and then everything will be fine, right?"

Upon hearing this, Nanny Li smiled and said, "Young lady, you are right. Thank you for your concern."

Nanny Li then gave all the things to Minxin, who took them with a smile. But when Nanny Li turned around, her smiling face turned into a sinister one, with resentment emanating from her eyes.

Cui Yixin stayed indoors these days. Ruixiang was anxious when she saw her daughter becoming increasingly depressed.

"Girl, it's only two or three months before you get married. You have to cheer up. There are still many days to come. I heard that the daughter of the university scholar only knows how to recite poems and compose couplets all day long. She has an empty reputation as a talented woman. She is also dull and honest. She is definitely no match for you in terms of behavior and conduct. Even if she entered the house a month earlier than you, you can still surpass her. You have won the favor of the son-in-law and the old lady. With your status as a legitimate daughter, it is not impossible for her to be a concubine instead of a wife."

Cui Yixin shook her head dejectedly, "You don't know, although I haven't entered the house yet, I have already lost the hearts of my husband and mother-in-law. Even if I enter the house, I'm afraid I will just sit on the bench. It's not as easy as you think. To put it another way, even if I win the hearts of him and my mother-in-law, it is really difficult to replace a wife with a concubine. A wife is a wife, she should be respected, and a concubine is a concubine, just a plaything. Don't you see that my father has so many women inside and outside, but my mother's status is still transcendent. Didn't he say last time that he would send Aunt Zhen away, so he sent her away?" After saying that, she burst into tears again.

Ruixiang said anxiously, "Miss, don't be so discouraged. There is always a way out. The most hateful thing is Cui Xiuxin. She won the victory, but she was too arrogant. She even secretly took our room's share. Although we don't lack those things, how can we swallow this?"

Yi Xin angrily said, "Isn't it because of her that I am in this situation today? She looks innocent, but in fact, she is more vicious than anyone else. Just wait and see. If I am ruined, she won't have an easy life either! At worst, we will all go to hell together!"

As they were talking, the little maid in the room came to tell them that the fourth girl, Minxin, had come. Yixin frowned, "Why is she here? I don't usually interact with her." As she spoke, she asked someone to invite her in.

When Minxin saw Yixin, she started to cry, "How is Second Sister these days? As her younger sister, I was not able to accompany her in time. It's my fault."

Yixin saw that Minxin was dressed very simply, in stark contrast to Xiuxin, who was dressed in silk and satin. She was also quiet on weekdays, and it was obvious that she had been severely bullied. Therefore, she felt a little pity for her, "Sister, please don't cry. Although I'm unlucky, I can still get through it. Don't worry, sister."

Min Xin stopped crying and choked up, "It was my third sister who was too selfish and overbearing. She refused to help my second sister to speak to the Sun family. Second sister, you know that although my third sister and I have the same father, there is a world of difference between a legitimate and an illegitimate child. No one pays attention to me on weekdays, let alone serves me wholeheartedly. Even...even the monthly allowance is deducted..."

Yi Xin was puzzled, "Why, she even took your share?"

Minxin nodded softly, "Yeah."

"That's too much!" Yixin held Minxin's hand, and suddenly felt that the enemy of her enemy was her friend. "If you need anything, tell me. I can't do without yours. Sister Minxin, we are the same. We can discuss everything together in the future. What do you think?"

Min Xin nodded quickly, "Yes, thank you, sister."

Recently, Wang Fusheng and Cui Zhengkai have been getting quite close. Wang Fusheng frequently showed his goodwill to Cui Zhengkai, and his intention to win him over was very obvious. Wang Fusheng even asked Cui Zhengkai to go boating on the lake and enjoy the scenery together.

Originally, it was quite common for officials to hold banquets, but Wang Fusheng's attempt to win her over after Princess Duanyi had just expressed her opinion seemed to have a lot of meaning. Cui Zhengkai thought that his little daughter's marriage to Wang Chaozong of the Wang family was almost certain, and he could not help but feel very happy, so he naturally agreed.

Those who came to the lake to enjoy the night view were all officials of the Hua Dynasty, and they were naturally chatting and laughing, quite contented. And at the gathering between men, singing girls were naturally indispensable. For a while, there were people pouring wine, singing songs, playing the pipa, and the flowers were in full bloom.

Li Yuzhi had been in a bad mood recently, and she heard that the Wang family and the Cui family were planning to form a marriage alliance. Now she saw that her mentor Wang Fusheng and Cui Zhengkai were chatting very happily, and it was obvious that they both had the same intention. She couldn't help but feel even more depressed, and drank one glass of wine after another.

There was a singing girl named Yingge'er on the boat. Seeing Li Yuzhi's outstanding beauty, she couldn't help but admire her. She came over to pour wine for him and said tenderly, "Sir, why are you drinking alone? How about letting me accompany you?"

Li Yuzhi was already drunk. She looked to the side and saw a beautiful woman with heavy makeup looking at her with a smile. She suddenly thought of her pretty and lovely face without makeup. She felt so sad that she cursed softly, "Get out of here."

The singer was originally full of love, but after being scolded by him, her eyes turned red and she left in hatred.

Wang Fusheng, who was sitting opposite Li Yuzhi, smiled and said, "Yuzhi, don't be so rude to a beautiful woman. How can we miss a beautiful woman with wine on such a beautiful night?"

Li Yuzhi smiled bitterly and shook her head, "There are three thousand rivers, and I only drink from one. Apart from that one, I don't care about the others."

Wang Fusheng was stunned, then smiled and said, "I never thought Yuzhi was such a passionate person. Who is the young lady you told me about last time? I will propose marriage for you, so that I can fulfill your wish."

Li Yuzhi glanced at Cui Zhengkai standing beside her, and was slightly startled before shaking her head, "Thank you, teacher, but I'm afraid I'm not destined to be with that lady."

Wang Fusheng was used to being in the entertainment world, and the women on the boat were all top singers and actresses. Among them, there was an actress named Yuqin who played the qin, and he was quite familiar with her. Yuqin played a song, then stood up and leaned gently against Wang Fusheng, saying softly, "Master Wang, you haven't come to see me for a long time."

As soon as these words came out, Wang Fusheng was shocked. Ahem, it seemed inappropriate to flirt with another woman in front of his future father-in-law, so he pretended to be surprised and asked, "Who is the girl? Have I seen her before?"

Yuqin was also a perceptive person, and she immediately said, "Oh, I recognized the wrong person. I hope you will forgive me."

Wang Fusheng coughed dryly, "Nothing."

Seeing Wang Fusheng's behavior, Cui Zhengkai had to understand. He could not help but think of the mess he had with Chu Lanyuan, the top singer on the Qinhuai River when he was young. This matter was known to the world at that time. Cui Zhengkai thought to himself that Wang Fusheng usually acted pretentiously and looked like he was concerned about the country and the people, but in fact, he was a thief and a prostitute in secret. However, he had a good family background and was good at managing personal connections. He was highly valued by His Majesty. Looking at the whole court, except for Cui Jinyi's power, he was probably a person who could command the world with a single word.

After Wang Fusheng sent the singing girl away, he poured wine for Cui Zhengkai. Cui Zhengkai hurriedly said, "I dare not, I dare not." Wang Fusheng smiled and said, "Brother Cui's children are all very ambitious. Cui Jinghong is now working in the Ministry of Industry, and your Cui Qihong has just passed the imperial examination and is working in the Dali Temple. He has a bright future. But after the big success, we have to consider the small success. I wonder how Brother Cui thinks about the marriage of his children?" He deliberately emphasized the pronunciation of the word "female".

How could Cui Zhengkai not understand? He immediately smiled and said, "I am also worried about this. Qihong is still young, but Jinghong has already passed the age of twenty. I have also mentioned marriage to him, but he always said that he has not yet established a career, so how can he start a family? So this matter has been delayed. However..." Cui Zhengkai paused, "I have a little daughter who is still unmarried. She has reached the age of engagement, but now

she has not found a husband."
Wang Fusheng laughed when he heard this, "One family has a daughter and hundreds of families are looking for her. Brother Cui, just wait. The matchmaker will come to your door soon."
Cui Zhengkai felt relieved when he heard Wang Fusheng say this, and said with a smile, "Thank you for your good words, Lord Wang."

☆, Chapter 16: Hundred Flower Festival

Chapter 16 Hundred Flowers Festival
A few days later, it was the Hundred Flowers Festival, which was said to be the birthday of the goddess of flowers in heaven, Nuyi. This day was also a day for spring outings and flower viewing. Because of this story, the women in the capital formed a routine, and every day on this day, they would go to the Hundred Flowers Garden outside the capital to enjoy the spring flowers.
The Hundred Flowers Garden is planted by a dedicated person and covers a large area. There are also special gardeners who carefully cultivate it. On the day of the Hundred Flowers Festival, all kinds of flowers bloom in competition, which is beautiful. There are also pavilions, teahouses, wine shops, inns, and food shops inside for female guests who come to enjoy the flowers to rest and have fun.

Later, the Hundred Flowers Festival gradually changed its nature, becoming a place for noble ladies to show off and a place for noble ladies to compete with each other. If you perform well at the Hundred Flowers Festival, your reputation will spread, and finding a good marriage will be a piece of cake. Therefore, the Hundred Flowers Festival has become one of the festivals that noble ladies carefully prepare for.

Jiang also attached great importance to this Hundred Flowers Festival. Although her daughter's marriage to the Wang family was almost certain, there were still variables before things were finalized. Therefore, Jiang began to choose the clothes her daughter would wear at the Hundred Flowers Festival several days in advance, and it was bound to be eye-catching.

Xiuxin usually dressed plainly. When Jiang saw that her daughter only picked a butterfly-fronted blouse and a pomegranate skirt, she couldn't help but blame her, "Xiuxin, these two clothes are what you usually wear. They're fine for everyday wear, but won't you be outdone if you wear them to the Hundred Flowers Festival?" So she turned around and took out a light purple embroidered gold-thread blouse, a matching jacket, and a light green pleated brocade embroidered long gauze skirt, "Here, you've never worn this set before. Wear it the day after tomorrow, and I guarantee you'll be stunning."

Xiu Xin frowned, "Mother, isn't this too bright?"

Jiang said, "It's not bright at all. Little girls should wear bright clothes. Go try them on for your mother to see, and I'll go pick out some jewelry for you."

Xiu Xin had no choice but to change out. Jiang clapped her hands and said, "Oh, my daughter looks so beautiful in this outfit."

Xiuxin was helpless. Sigh, I really don't know what my mother is thinking. My appearance is obviously only above average among the noble ladies, but my mother always thinks that I am the most beautiful among all the ladies...

"Second Madam, Third Miss, and Fourth Miss are here." Cuixiang came in as she lifted the curtain.

"Why is she here?" Jiang was puzzled.

"My sister must have come here for something, Cuixiang, go and ask her to come in." Xiuxin said.

Min Xin walked in with her head lowered and bowed first, "Mother, Third Sister."

Jiang hummed and sat upright on the chair, "Minxin, why are you here today?"

Min Xin thought, "Mom, the day after tomorrow is the Hundred Flowers Festival. I wonder if Mom and Third Sister can take me with them?"

When Jiang heard this, he emphasized his tone with some contempt, "You want to go too?"

Normally, those who attend the Hundred Flowers Festival are the principal wives and legitimate daughters. Of course, there are also some concubines' daughters with outstanding performance from famous families. However, Min Xin is not outstanding in terms of appearance or talent, so it is really a bit difficult for her to attend the Hundred Flowers Festival, so Jiang frowned immediately.

Min Xin was so frightened when she saw Jiang's change of color that she immediately knelt on the ground, tears streaming down her not-so-big eyes, "Mother, it's not that I want to overstep my authority, but I'm already fifteen years old, and I want to go out with my sister to see the flowers and enjoy the scenery. If you think it's not good, you can just say that I'm your sister's maid."

Xiuxin thought that Minxin was not like herself. She had never been allowed to attend social events outside. She had never been out even once in her life. She felt sorry for her. So she said to Jiang, "Mother, I am also in need of a companion. Let Minxin go with me."

Jiang poked her forehead lightly with her fingertips, "You!"

"Mother..." Xiuxin grabbed Jiang's hand and said coquettishly.

"Okay, I'm scared of you." Jiang nodded helplessly, turned to Min Xin who was

kneeling on the ground and said sternly, "Behave yourself outside, okay?"
"I know, I know. Thank you, mother." Min Xin kowtowed to Jiang happily.
The day of the Hundred Flowers Festival soon arrived. Jiang took Xiuxin and Minxin in a carriage, Feng took Yixin and Yuxin in another carriage, and they took another carriage with four or five personal maids, and they drove to the Hundred Flowers Garden in the suburbs.
Minxin saw that Xiuxin was dressed very differently today, so she praised, "Sister, you look really beautiful today. You must be the most eye-catching one among all the flowers."
These words made Jiang feel comfortable all over, "Minxin, you are really good at talking."
Minxin smiled and said, "This is the truth. My sister is just beautiful."
Chatting and laughing along the way, the group soon arrived at the gate of the Hundred Flowers Garden. Xiuxin lifted the curtain and saw that many carriages of various colors had already been parked at the gate of the Hundred Flowers Garden. The ladies and young ladies got off the carriages and walked into the garden, chatting and laughing. It was very lively.
"Oh, this year's Hundred Flowers Festival is more lively than previous years." Xiu Xin said.
"Indeed, there are many more carriages this

year than last year," said Jiang.

As they were talking, they heard the sound of hurried horse hooves. Xiuxin turned around and saw a woman in red riding a tall horse with shiny black fur. The black horse, the red dress, and the woman's flying black hair formed an indescribably beautiful picture.

Xiuxin had seen this kind of horse in a book before. It had a black body with only four white hooves. It was called Wuyun Taxue and was a very valuable horse.

"Liu Manzi's daughter has also come to the Hundred Flowers Festival." Ma Yunyun, the daughter of the Minister of Revenue, said in a low voice.

Liu Manzi? Which Liu Manzi? Xiu Xin was wondering when the woman whipped Ma Yunyun's feet with a horsewhip, shocking her so much that she turned pale, "Ah, murder."

The woman pointed with her whip, her pretty eyebrows raised, "Ma Yunyun, if you dare to talk nonsense again, next time my whip won't be under your feet!"

Xiu Xin's eyes widened in shock. This... this woman was so special, different from any woman she had ever seen.

Jiang whispered in Xiuxin's ear, "She is the daughter of the Protector of the Country, Liu Baozi. Her name is Zhan Xue. When she was a child, she stayed at the border with the Protector of the Country for more than ten years and only returned in recent years."

"What? Zhanxue?" Xiuxin's voice was a little louder, causing Liu Zhanxue, who had just dismounted, to focus her gaze on Xiuxin like a knife. Xiuxin was frightened by this gaze and took three steps back, fearing that she would whip her.

Liu Zhanxue took a few steps closer and looked closely at Xiuxin's face, then looked at the carriage with the word "Cui" written on it parked next to her. Suddenly, he laughed loudly, patted Xiuxin's shoulder heavily, and said with a smile, "Hey, you are Cui Xiuxin, right?"

"I, I am..." Xiu Xin responded in a low voice.

"You know Kung Fu?"

"Ah?" Xiu Xin was confused.

"Didn't you show off your boxing skills at the Qionglin Banquet? Cui Xiuxin, I've heard of your reputation a long time ago. Come on, today we have a chance to meet, let's have a good competition to see who's better, your kung fu or mine!"

Seeing that Liu Zhanxue was about to make a killing move, Xiu Xin waved her hands and said, "Miss Liu, you misunderstood. The boxing I learned was given to me by my mother to strengthen my body. It's just fancy moves and cannot be used in a competition."

Liu Zhanxue sighed in disappointment, "Okay... forget it."

Xiu Xin suddenly felt that although Miss

Liu in front of her had a scary posture, her emotions were all visible on her face. She was much easier to get along with than people like Cui Wu who said nice things but were actually scheming. Therefore, she wanted to get close to her and hurriedly grabbed Liu Zhanxue's sleeve and said, "Miss Liu, although we can't compete together, we can appreciate the flowers together. How about that?"

Liu Zhanxue looked at the girl in front of her who was smiling at her with curved eyebrows and eyes, and she also wanted to make friends with her, so she agreed immediately, "Okay, let's go together."

Seeing the two of them being intimate and secretive, Jiang finally felt relieved, "Girls of your age should really get close to each other. If you don't have a companion to enjoy the flowers and scenery, the scenery will lose a lot of its charm."

Ma Yunyun, who was standing by, saw that Liu Zhanxue, who had just embarrassed her, was now as nice to Cui Xiuxin. She was so angry that she almost stamped her feet, and she turned her anger towards Liu Zhanxue towards Cui Xiuxin. Minxin looked at Ma Yunyun not far away, and curled her lips in a good mood. She trotted a few steps to catch up with Xiuxin, "Third sister, wait for me."

In the Hundred Flowers Garden, hundreds of flowers are in full bloom.

Soon after the group entered the garden,

Madam Sun Er and others came over. Madam Sun Er said, "Sister, Madam Cui, let these girls go play together. Why don't we get involved? Why don't we go to the teahouse to drink tea and chat. I heard that the teahouse has a lot of expensive flower teas."

Feng agreed immediately, but Jiang was a little worried about Xiuxin and hesitated. Xiuxin said, "Mother, I can take care of myself, don't worry." Jiang whispered in Xiuxin's ear, "It's not like home outside, be careful about what you eat, don't eat carelessly, understand?" Xiuxin agreed.

Jiang also instructed Liu Zhanxue, "Miss Liu, please take good care of our Xiuxin."

Liu Zhanxue patted his chest generously and said, "Don't worry, Madam Cui, I will take care of Xiu Xin."

Jiang was relieved and followed Feng, Madam Sun and others. Yixin had already fallen out with Xiuxin, so she pulled Yuxin to the other side. Yuxin still refused to leave and pulled Xiuxin's clothes, "Why don't you go with Third Sister?"

Yi Xin slapped Yu Xin's palm hard, "You are so tactless. Even if you want to be with someone, they may not pay attention to you."

After Yi Xin left, Xiu Xin was no longer embarrassed. Fortunately, she had Zhan Xue and Min Xin by her side, otherwise she would have been really alone.

Among all the flowers, Xiuxin's favorite is

peach blossom. Peach blossom is gorgeous and sweet. Only when you are in the peach forest can you really feel the breath of spring. The ancients said that the peach blossom is young and bright, which is really appropriate. Liu Zhanxue was not interested in those flowers and plants. He picked a peach blossom at random and pulled the petals in his hand out of boredom. After a while, the peach blossom was completely bald.

"Hmph, this is just like a cow chewing a peony, a waste of God's resources." Ma Yunyun said angrily not far away.

Cui Wu who was beside Ma Yunyun glared at her and said, "Be careful what you say. Haven't you suffered enough just now?" Cui Wu had always stood out among the noble ladies because of her distinguished family background and her scheming. Therefore, Ma Yunyun and her ilk listened to her very much.

Seeing Zhan Xue looking at her from afar, Ma Yunyun felt guilty for some reason and quickly hid behind Cui Wu, "Oh, she won't hear it, will she?"

Cui Wu snorted coldly, "Are you scared now? What did you show off just now?" He said while walking towards Xiuxin and the others with a smile, "Sister Xiuxin, what a coincidence, we meet again. The peach blossoms are blooming so beautifully this year. Why don't we spread a mat in the peach forest and ask someone to bring us all kinds of cakes, so we can enjoy the flowers while eating, isn't it nice?"

☆、Chapter 17: Conspiracy

Chapter 17: Conspiracy
Cui Wu snorted coldly, "Are you scared now? What did you show off just now?" As he spoke, he walked towards Xiuxin and the others with a smile, "Sister Xiuxin, what a coincidence! The peach blossoms are blooming so beautifully this year. I was thinking, why don't we spread a mat in the peach blossom forest and ask someone to bring us all kinds of cakes and tea? Wouldn't it be nice to enjoy the flowers while eating?"
Zhan Xue was not interested in these things to begin with, so she asked Xiu Xin for her opinion, "What do you think?"
Min Xin responded before Xiu Xin could, "Okay, okay, that's great, we can still eat, drink and have fun, it's a great idea."
Cui Wu originally disdained to speak to a concubine's daughter, but she disliked Xiuxin, so she inevitably used Minxin as an example to ridicule Xiuxin, "I'm asking Sister Xiuxin, who are you and how dare you answer me? Xiuxin, although you are from a branch family, you are also a member of the Cui family. Why don't you teach your concubine sister a lesson and teach her some rules? Don't let her out to embarrass herself."

Minxin's eyes immediately turned red with tears hanging in her eyes, and she felt that Cui Wu was being too much. Xiuxin said, "Cui Wu, Minxin is my sister. I can bring her out if I want. This is my family's business. Besides, Cui Wu, you have many illegitimate sisters. I remember your illegitimate sister Cui San came here last year, didn't you stop her? Right?"

When Cui San's concubine sister Cui Wu was mentioned, her face immediately turned ugly. Although Cui San was a concubine's daughter, she was particularly valued by Cui Jinyi. Not to mention the Hundred Flowers Festival, she even appeared in some places where only legitimate daughters could attend, stealing a lot of her limelight. After getting married last year, Cui Wu finally got rid of the big worry in her heart, and she was considered unique in the mansion.

Cui Wu was seething with anger, but she had a sweet smile on her face. "Sister Xiuxin, let's stop saying those spoiling words and quickly get someone to spread the mats. We are all of similar age, so it's great for us to get together and talk. If you don't agree, I won't agree."

Xiuxin had not forgotten that Cui Wu had deliberately made her drunk, so she tried to avoid her this time, and said, "Thank you for your kindness, sister. I also want to go to the Pear Garden and the Azalea Garden, and I won't stay in the Peach Garden."

Cui Wu said, "I remember that my sister likes peach blossoms the most, right?"

Min Xin said innocently, "Yes, my sister likes peach blossoms the most. There are a few peach blossoms in front of her window. My sister enjoys them every day and never gets tired of them."

"That's it." Cui Wu smiled even more proudly, "Since sister likes peach blossoms, why do you refuse such a good thing? Could it be..." Cui Wu paused and made a lonely expression, "Could it be that sister doesn't want to associate with me?"

Min Xin quietly pulled Xiu Xin's clothes and pleaded in a low voice, "Third sister, let's stay here. I think it's fun. Besides, it's a good thing for us to get closer to the direct descendants of the Cui family."

Xiu Xin had no choice but to agree.

Cui Wu then had the mats spread out, and the five of them sat around, with all kinds of cakes and tea placed on the stools. The aroma of tea and cakes filled the air. Xiu Xin remembered her mother's instructions not to mess with things, and she was a little wary of Cui Wu, so she resisted the temptation of cakes and didn't eat them, and even just took a sip of the tea.

Cui Wu said, "Sister Xiuxin, do you think the food in my Cui Mansion is not good? Why don't you want to eat a single bite?"

Xiu Xin said, "I have had stomach discomfort recently, and Doctor Chen at home told me not to eat anything other than the three meals, and even the three meals have to be reduced in size."

Cui Wu said, "Sister, please take care of yourself."

Ma Yunyun was originally a person who was not very calculating. She immediately said sarcastically, "So you are so weak, Xiuxin. I'm afraid you really need to take good care of yourself. I remember that there was a sickly young lady in the Sun family. She was over 20 years old, but she hadn't been engaged yet."

"My parents will decide my marriage, so there's no need to worry about it, Miss Ma." Xiu Xin said.

Ma Yunyun was frustrated, but she didn't stop talking. After a while, she turned her attention to Zhan Xue again, "Oh, now I remember, Miss Liu, you are seventeen now, right? You are four years older than me. I wonder what the Duke of the Protectorate has planned for your life?"

Zhan Xue snorted and said, "What a joke! I have the final say on my marriage. Why should I let others decide my lifelong affairs? If I want to get married, I will get married. If I don't want to, no one can force me."

Ma Yunyun smiled, thinking she had the upper hand, so she asked with a smile, "So, which family has Miss Liu decided to marry herself to? Tell us so we can hear it."

Zhan Xue glared at Ma Yunyun fiercely and slammed the cup on the table, splashing tea everywhere. "Why should I tell you what I want to do? Do you really think you are a big shot? My father has never disciplined me, but you are acting so arrogant in front of me!"

Ma Yunyun was so frightened that her whole body trembled, she shrank back and stopped talking.

Cui Wu hurriedly laughed and said, "Hey, Zhan Xue, don't be angry. Yunyun is still young and outspoken. If you get angry with her, it will seem that you are fussy, right?"

Zhan Xue was as straightforward as her father. She stood up and kicked over the small stove that was boiling tea. The tea immediately overflowed onto the table. "What kind of tea is this? It's really annoying. Cui Xiuxin, are you going to leave? You don't have to stay here with them."

Xiu Xin stood up quickly, smiled and nodded, "Okay." She bowed to Cui Wu and the others, "I'll go first."

Minxin followed Xiuxin and said, "Third sister, wait for me."

The three of them left the peach forest, chatting and laughing all the way. Zhan Xue told Xiu Xin and Min Xin about her experiences at the border. Xiu Xin was envious and yearning, "I once dressed up as a soldier and went to the battlefield to kill several Hu people with my own hands."

Min Xin widened her eyes in surprise,

"Aren't you afraid?"

"What's there to be afraid of? It's a pity that my father later sent someone to look after me, otherwise I would have to go to the battlefield as a female general."

"You are the only daughter of the Duke of the Protectorate. How can he allow you to take risks on the battlefield?" Xiu Xin said, "Now that your father has returned to the capital, you may never have the chance to become a female general. However, you can gather the maids in the mansion to practice martial arts and form a female guard team."

Zhan Xue clapped her hands and said, "Xiu Xin, you are so smart. Why didn't I think of it?"

"Ah!" Xiuxin and Zhanxue were talking happily, but suddenly they heard Minxin scream. Xiuxin turned around and saw that Minxin had fallen down at some point, her clothes were all dirty, her forehead was red and swollen from hitting something, and her palms were also scratched.

"Oh, how did you fall?" Xiuxin helped Minxin up, "Come on, I'll go with you to the garden to find a doctor."

Min Xin held Xiu Xin's hand and said, "No need, Third Sister. It was all my own carelessness, and the fall was not serious. I can go by myself."

Xiu Xin asked, "Can you do it alone?"

Min Xin said, "It's alright, you and Sister Zhan Xue go somewhere else to play, I'll go to the teahouse to find a doctor."

Xiuxin and Zhanxue walked out of the peach forest and into the pear garden. The pear blossoms were as white as snow and exuded a sweet fragrance. Seeing that the sun was getting late, Xiuxin said, "Let's sit here for a while and then go to the teahouse to look for my mother. Fortunately, this place is not far from the teahouse." Zhanxue replied, "Okay."

The two found a shady place and sat down. After sitting for a while, Xiuxin felt a wave of heat rushing to her face, making her dizzy and hot. She couldn't help but reach out and unbutton the first two buttons of her clothes. Zhan Xue saw that she looked different, her cheeks were red, and her eyes were blurry. She couldn't help but be surprised, "What's wrong with you?"

Xiu Xin shook her head, "I... I don't know, I... I feel so uncomfortable." She was about to unbutton her clothes. Although Zhan Xue was bold and unrestrained, she knew that she couldn't do such a thing in public, so she quickly reached out to stop Xiu Xin, "No, bear with it for now, I'll take you to the teahouse, there should be a doctor waiting."

Zhan Xue was just about to help Xiu Xin get up when she saw Cui Wu, the old lady of the Wang family, Princess Pingyang and others coming over. Cui Wu curled his lips when he saw Xiu Xin in such a state, and called out in surprise, "Oh, isn't that Sister Xiu

Xin?"
Xiu Xin secretly said "bad luck" and wanted to leave quickly to avoid those people, but after the effect of the drug took effect, her body became limp and she leaned in Zhan Xue's arms. Zhan Xue was wearing a red dress, but she only tied her waist tightly with a belt. Because of her martial arts training, her bones were larger than those of ordinary women. From the back, she looked like a man.
Previously, the old lady of the Wang family, following the order of Princess Duanyi, had mentioned the marriage of Wang Fusheng and Cui Xiuxin to Madam Cui Er. Jiang's words were vague, and it seemed that she was not very fond of this marriage, so the old lady Wang was a little angry. If it weren't for Princess Duanyi's order, she would still think that Cui Xiuxin's family background, appearance, and talent were not worthy of her son, and Madam Cui Er was even dissatisfied. Now, the old lady Wang ran into Cui Xiuxin hugging and kissing a man in the pear garden, and her anger suddenly increased to seven points, and she shouted in a stern voice, "Miss Cui, please stay."
Xiu Xin was cornered and had to stop and reluctantly turned around. When the old lady of the Wang family saw that the girl next to Xiu Xin was the only daughter of the Duke of Huguo, she secretly said that she had misunderstood. But Xiu Xin's whole body was limply leaning in Zhan Xue's arms,

and two buttons on her outer collar were unbuttoned. In addition, her eyes were slightly red, and she looked shy and weak, which immediately made the old lady of the Wang family suspicious. She shouted, "How can you girls be so rude in public!"

Xiu Xin was startled and tried to push Zhan Xue away to stand up straight, but she fell forward when she lost her balance. Zhan Xue had no choice but to hold her waist and hold her tightly in his arms. The old lady of the Wang family looked at the scene and her face changed immediately. She had also heard about the pickled stories of unmarried girls or widowed women comforting each other to relieve their loneliness. Now seeing Xiu Xin and Zhan Xue being so intimate, her suspicion became even stronger and her words became more serious. "What are you doing in broad daylight? Do you still have any shame? You are all noble ladies from aristocratic families and you don't know the slightest shame."

Zhan Xue was also angry when she saw the old woman cursing without knowing the truth. "Madam Wang, Xiuxin is sick and I am taking care of her. How can I be shameless? I am afraid it is inappropriate for the old lady to say such things without knowing the truth."

Mrs. Wang was choked by Zhan Xue and was speechless. Zhan Xue ignored her and picked up Xiu Xin and quickly went to the teahouse in the garden to find Jiang.

☆、Chapter 18

Chapter 18 Marriage
Jiang was chatting with Madam Sun Er in the teahouse. Thinking of Madam Wang's arrogant tone and condescending attitude, she frowned. "I never thought that the Wang family was talking about him." Madam Sun Er said, "I also think it's not appropriate. The Wang family is big and powerful. If she marries... Xiuxin, how can she manage the family? Besides, if Xiuxin is bullied in the future, your Cui family will not be able to help her."
Jiang nodded and remained silent.
"Madam Cui Er." Zhan Xue strode into the teahouse holding Xiu Xin in her arms. "Xiu Xin seems to be ill. Please take a look at her."
Seeing Xiuxin's red cheeks, slightly parted red lips, and blurred eyes, Jiang's heart skipped a beat and she quickly took her daughter from Zhanxue's hands, "Thank you very much, Miss Liu, for today. Let me ask you, what did Xiuxin eat outside today?"
Zhan Xue said, "She didn't eat anything. She didn't touch the cakes and pastries at the banquet set by Cui Wu, and she only touched her lips with the tea."
Jiang immediately understood that the problem was that the tainted liquid got on her lips, and it was probably on the edge of the cup. Jiang carried Xiuxin to the

upstairs room and asked Lanxiang to invite Doctor Chen, who usually treated Xiuxin. Doctor Chen felt Xiuxin's pulse and said in a deep voice, "Miss, someone has done something to you..."

"What happened?" Jiang asked anxiously, "Just tell me."

"Aphrodisiac."

"What?!" Jiang almost fell down, barely holding onto a chair to stand, "I never thought that a daughter of a famous family like Cui Wu would do such a shameless thing!"

Doctor Chen wrote a prescription and said, "Take this medicine in half an hour and you will be well again."

Jiang said, "Doctor Chen, there are some things that should be said and some things that should not be said. I'm sure you know that, right?"

Doctor Chen bowed his head and said, "Madam, I will keep my mouth shut."

As Doctor Chen said, Xiuxin woke up in half an hour. Jiang was extremely anxious. When she saw Xiuxin waking up, she asked, "Xiuxin, tell me, who did you meet along the way?"

"After I left the banquet hosted by Cui Wu, I stayed with Zhan Xue the whole time. Later... later I met the old lady of the Wang family and Princess Pingyang and others."

"Didn't you meet a man?"

"Man?" Xiu Xin shook her head. "No, Zhan

Xue has always been with me."
After hearing Xiuxin's words, Jiang was relieved, but she started crying again. "My daughter, when I'm not with you, something always happens to you. How can I marry you off with peace of mind? I've raised you in my hands since you were little. How could you know the ins and outs of a deep house? I'm so worried."
"Mother, don't worry. There will always be a way out when you reach the mountain. There will always be a way out when you reach the bridge. It's useless for you to worry. Maybe my daughter will marry a poor boy like Sister Jinxin, and then you won't have to worry about anything." As Xiuxin said this, she thought of the elegant Li Yuzhi. It was a pity that two months had passed and he still hadn't come to propose marriage. I really don't know if he has changed his mind and has found another lady from a famous family? But, is he such a person?
"Xiuxin, actually...actually..." Jiang hesitated to speak, looking embarrassed.
"Actually what?"
Jiang thought about it and decided not to tell her for the time being, so she smiled and said, "It's nothing, you take a good rest, and we will go back to the mansion later."
Embroidered heart should be.
The next day, the old lady of the Wang family reported what she saw at the Hundred

Flowers Festival to Princess Duanyi. Duanyi did not doubt it, "It is normal for girls to be close to each other. You are making a fuss."

Old Lady Wang said, "Mother, although that is what I said, I feel that Cui Xiuxin's behavior is not worthy of a daughter of a rich family. In terms of family background, she is only a branch of the Cui family, not as good as Cui Wu. In terms of talent, she is only slightly proficient in writing, not as good as Xie Yulan. In terms of appearance, the most outstanding daughter of this rich family is Princess Duanyang. No matter which aspect, Cui Xiuxin is far inferior to other noble ladies. How can she be worthy of my son?"

Duan Yi couldn't help but get angry when she heard her say that, "You are too demanding. There is no perfect person in the world. Cui Wu may have a good family background, but he is picky and stubborn and can't tolerate others. Xie Yulan may be talented, but she is in poor health and suffers from constant illness. Princess Duan Yang is indeed outstanding in appearance, but she only has a widowed mother and a poor family background. Wife, our Fu Sheng is indeed a dragon among men, but don't forget that he is now marrying a concubine. How many of those wealthy families are willing to marry their daughters to others as concubines?"

"This..." Old Lady Wang hesitated, "But I

also heard that Cui Xiuxin was immoral and abused her concubine's sister."

"Where did you hear that?" Princess Duanyi sat up straight. How could a woman who abused her step-sister be good to her stepson? Wasn't she just trying to get ahead? If that was the case, there would be no peace in the family.

"Yesterday at the Hundred Flowers Festival, the fourth daughter of the Cui family, Minxin, was injured all over. Her forehead was bleeding. I heard that it was Cui Xiuxin who pushed her."

"Oh?" Duan Yi groaned, "You should ask someone to investigate this matter. If it is true, this marriage should be considered carefully."

"Yes." Old Madam Wang replied respectfully.

Everyone in the Wang family knew about this, so it was natural that Jiang Shi could not have not heard of it. She was so angry that her face changed, and she rushed into Cui Minxin's courtyard with a few maids and servants.

"You little bitch, I thought you were an honest person, but I never thought you were harboring evil intentions and were willing to do such a thing as framing your own sister! I felt sorry for you for losing your mother when you were young, and I never treated you harshly. Yet you did such a thing. I must discipline you today!"

When Cui Minxin saw her stepmother and her men approaching in a threatening manner, she immediately knelt down, grabbed Jiang's skirt, and burst into tears. "Mother, mother, please listen to me. I really didn't know that such outrageous rumors would spread. I didn't say a word to anyone. When others asked me, I just said that I fell. I really don't know how such rumors spread..." As she spoke, tears fell like beads with a broken string.

Jiang Shi would not listen to her explanation, so she kicked her and ordered the maid, "Give her ten slaps, and see if she dares to do it again!"

"Yes." The maids rolled up their sleeves and slapped Minxin fiercely. After a few slaps, Minxin's cheeks were swollen and blood flowed from the corners of her mouth. Minxin cried and begged for mercy, "Mother, I am innocent, I am really innocent, I did not frame my third sister, I really did not..."

The fight was going on, but Minxin had already asked the little girl to invite Cui Zhengkai to come. Cui Zhengkai rushed to Minxin's yard and saw that Minxin's face was swollen from being beaten. He thought of her mother who died in vain, and he couldn't help but feel sympathy for her, so he shouted, "Stop, stop."

Jiang said angrily, "Master, are you still protecting her?"

Minxin cried even more sadly when she saw Cui Zhengkai coming, "Father, I am innocent. I really don't know how the rumor spread. I really didn't frame my third sister..."

Cui Zhengkai said, "Madam, those rumors may not have been spread by Minxin. Maybe it was spread by some maidservant downstairs. Isn't it too much for you to hit someone without knowing the truth?"

Jiang became even more furious when she heard this. "I went too far? If it wasn't her, then who did it? Which good maid would think of spreading such a rumor?"

"Well, now that you've been beaten, you should calm down, right? Minxin has been without a mother since she was a child. She's been miserable enough in the mansion, and no one has taken care of her over the years. Let's just let this matter go."

Jiang snorted, stared at Min Xin fiercely and said, "I'll let you go this time, but if you dare to do it again, I will never let you off easily."

Jiang was not happy with Cui Zhengkai's pleading for Minxin and was upset for a while. Cui Zhengkai coaxed her for a long time before Jiang calmed down. After calming down, Jiang told Cui Zhengkai what Wang Fusheng had said to her that day. Cui Zhengkai was also quite surprised, "Wang Fusheng mentioned it to me last time, and I thought he was talking about his son Wang Chaozong, but he was talking about himself."

Jiang also nodded, "Yes, I never thought that the Wang family would want to marry our Xiuxin to Wang Fusheng as a concubine.

Wang Fusheng is powerful and has a son that old. He has countless concubines and singing girls in his house. His affair with a singing girl was known to everyone. It is known that he is a playboy. If our Xiuxin marries him, won't she cry every day? You also know Xiuxin's personality, she is as innocent as a child, how can you deal with her?"

Cui Zhengkai frowned and said, "I also think it's not appropriate. But since the Wang family has proposed it, I'm afraid there is no room for us to refuse. You know how powerful the Wang family is. Even the direct descendants of the Cui family may not be able to resist them, not to mention that we are only a branch of the Cui family, and I am only a third-rank imperial envoy."

Jiang asked anxiously, "Could it be that if we don't agree, the Wang family can still force us to marry?"

Cui Zhengkai shook his head. "How can a woman like you understand what's going on in the court? The Wang family won't force us to marry. They will force us to agree."

Jiang sighed, "I really don't know why the Wang family fell in love with our Xiu Xin. It's really... unfair!"

Cui Zhengkai also sighed, "Madam, don't worry. You should always think positively. Just talking about Wang Fusheng, he is a unique figure in the Hua Dynasty. He is so young and yet he is valued by the emperor. He is talented and powerful. He is more than enough for our daughter."

Jiang snorted, "No matter how good he is, I don't want him."

"That's a woman's opinion!" Cui Zhengkai said, waving his sleeves.

On the other hand, Madam Wang reported the matter of Xiuxin to Princess Duanyi. Duanyi smiled and said, "I know Xiuxin is not that kind of person. She has such a simple personality and is not on guard against others. How could she abuse her concubine's sister?"

Old Lady Wang said, "Mother is right. I think it was the fourth young lady of the Cui family who fell that day and the news got out by mistake."

"Well." Duan Yi said, "There are many tricks here, so we don't need to delve into it."

"Yes." Madam Wang thought for a moment and said, "But... Mother, I mentioned this to Madam Cui at the Hundred Flowers Festival. She was vague about it and seemed not very happy about it. If the Cui family disagrees..."

Princess Duanyi curled her lips and smiled, and said confidently, "Wife, the Cui family will definitely agree, just wait and see."

Madam Wang nodded, "That's right. How can we not get the person our Wang family wants to marry?"

A few days later, Jiang was as anxious as an ant on a hot pot, fearing that the Wang family would send someone to propose marriage one day. That would be too late. She thought it would be better to cut off the fire from under the cauldron and immediately arrange Xiuxin's marriage. In this way, no matter how powerful the Wang family was, they would not be able to do anything about it. But she was worried about who she could marry Xiuxin to in such a short time.

Jiang finally told Xiuxin about this matter, and Xiuxin's face turned pale immediately, "Becoming Wang Fusheng's concubine?"

Jiang cried, "My daughter, I want to arrange your marriage right away, so that even if the Wang family is unhappy, they can do nothing about it. What do you think?"

"But...but..." Xiu Xin thought of someone as she spoke. She had already made up her mind. Now she could not care about those red tapes. She could only give it a try.

☆, Chapter 19: Affair

Chapter 19: Affair

Xiu Xin wrote a letter to Li Yuzhi that night, and after thinking about it, she used red thread to tie the jade ring into a knot and put it in the letter, and gave it to Lanxiang, "Lanxiang, tomorrow you go find a servant you trust to deliver this letter to Li Yuzhi, the official in the Ministry of Personnel. Remember to find someone who is reliable and keeps his mouth

shut, and don't let anyone else know."
Lan Xiang was immediately shocked, "Girl! How...how can this be possible?"
Xiu Xin was determined to fight to the death, and could not care less about that. She handed the letter to Lan Xiang, "I can't care about that now. I have to give it a try. Otherwise, how can I be content?"
Lan Xiang nodded and said solemnly, "Don't worry, young lady."
The next evening, Xiuxin had finished her dinner and was lying on the table, squinting her eyes and pretending to be asleep. Lanxiang was drawing an embroidery pattern beside her. "Look, girl. Does it look good?"
Lanxiang drew a bellyband embroidery pattern of twin flowers in bloom. Xiuxin said with a smile, "Little girl, are you thinking about love? You are not afraid of being laughed at for drawing this picture."
Lan Xiang smiled and said, "Miss, you are wronging me. I didn't paint this for myself. I painted this for you, my lady."
Xiuxin blushed, stood up and nagged Lanxiang, "Lanxiang, I don't have anything as your master, why are you worrying about me? What if someone sees me drawing this kind of picture?"
Lan Xiang smiled and lowered her voice, "Miss, tomorrow Master Li will come to propose marriage. Isn't it time for you to have a good time?"
Xiu Xin blushed slightly, "You just know

how to make fun of me."

The two were talking in private when Cuixiang suddenly came in hurriedly, lifting the curtain and calling out repeatedly, "Miss, Miss, something bad has happened, the Second Master is here."

"Father?" Xiuxin was about to ask what was going on when she saw Cui Zhengkai stride in, his face as gloomy as water and angry. Xiuxin knew something was wrong.

"All of you get out!" Cui Zhengkai shouted.

"Yes." Everyone left, only Lanxiang knelt down and cried, "Master, if the young lady is wrong, it is us servants who instigated it. Master, just punish us, don't punish the young lady."

Cui Zhengkai was furious, and immediately kicked Lanxiang in the chest, knocking her to the ground. "I will settle the faults that you servants have instigated later. Do you think you can hide away? Now I will settle the account with your master first, and you still don't want to get out of here!"

Lanxiang was kicked in the ribs and turned pale with pain. She walked out holding her chest. Seeing Cuixiang standing at the door blankly, she was at a loss and scolded, "What are you still doing here? Go to the front and call the lady!"

Cuixiang suddenly came to her senses and left in a hurry.

Cui Zhengkai saw that everyone had left and the door was closed, so he took out a letter from his sleeve and threw it on the table. Because he threw it too hard, the knot inside flew out and fell heavily on the table. When Xiuxin saw it, she knew she couldn't escape, but she didn't beg for mercy, just lowered her head and said nothing.

Cui Zhengkai originally thought that his daughter shouldn't do such a shameful thing, so he took out the token and wanted to hear her explanation. However, Xiuxin was silent, and he became even more angry. He slammed the table and said angrily, "Why are you lowering your head? Is this thing yours?"

Xiuxin had been raised in a pampered way since she was a child, and Cui Zhengkai loved her and had never said anything harsh to her. Now that Cui Zhengkai spoke harshly to her, she also became a little angry, and raised her head and said, "It's mine."

"It's yours!" Cui Zhengkai became even angrier when he saw Xiuxin's expression, but he laughed instead, "You deserve it. You still don't know you're wrong even now? Fortunately, you reported this thing to me. If it really got out, you would not only ruin your reputation, but also the reputation of the Cui family. How many people would point at me, Cui Zhengkai, and say that I didn't teach my daughter well!"

Xiu Xin was forced to cry, her eyes were red, "Father, I...I have no choice. I don't want to marry Wang Fusheng."

"Your parents' orders and the matchmaker's

words have no say over whether you will marry or not. You are so bold that you dare to pass on such things privately. Those women's precepts and rules have all been read in vain! If I don't discipline you well today, I'm afraid you will cause greater trouble in the future. Kneel down!"

Cui Zhengkai pushed open the door and shouted, "Bring me a cane! Bring me a cane quickly!"

Lanxiang was extremely worried when she saw Cui Zhengkai was getting angrier and angrier. Then she was even more frightened when she heard him repeatedly asking for a cane. She only secretly hoped that his wife would come sooner.

A servant brought a finger-thick cane to Cui Zhengkai. Cui Zhengkai closed the door and swung it at Xiuxin's back. The cane had barbs on it, and the swipe immediately tore her skin and flesh apart. Xiuxin's face turned pale in pain, but she just bit her lips tightly and refused to make a sound.

Cui Zhengkai said angrily, "Do you admit your mistake?"

Xiu Xin gritted her teeth and said, "I don't admit my mistake!"

"Good! Good! Good!" Cui Zhengkai said three good words in a row, and then whipped him three times. "You refuse to admit your mistakes, so I will beat you until you admit your mistakes. If a girl doesn't learn to be a good person and secretly gets married, I'm afraid she will be a disaster if she marries someone in the future!"

After saying that, he raised his hand again and was about to wave it down.

"Master!" A shrill cry sounded, and Jiang had already rushed into the room, with disheveled hair and no shoes on. She hugged Xiu Xin, who was about to faint, and cried, "Master, if you want to kill my precious daughter today, you can kill me first."

Cui Zhengkai was helpless. Seeing the four bloody scars on Xiuxin's back, he regretted that he had hit her too hard. But he still said, "You are still protecting her. It is because you protect her that she is so lawless!"

When Jiang saw Xiuxin's back covered in blood and her face pale with cold sweat, she felt so heartbroken that she stood up and said, "Master, Xiuxin is just a girl. Are you going to kill her by hitting her so hard? I know you think I'm an eyesore. Why don't you kill her first and then kill me, so that we two can be together in the underworld! No one will control you even if you marry dozens or hundreds of women!" She cried and pulled Cui Zhengkai with a pair of scissors, asking him to kill her as well.

Cui Zhengkai was at his wit's end after being harassed by Jiang, and when he saw Xiuxin lying on the ground, unconscious, he regretted it so much, "I was just too angry at the time, I won't hit her again in the future."

Hearing this, Jiang became even more angry,

"There will be a next time, are you going to beat my Xiu Xin again next time!" She started crying again, and kept calling out, "Why don't you call Doctor Chen!"

A servant responded quickly and ran away.

Cui Zhengkai saw Jiang carefully hugging Xiuxin to the bed and wiping her sweat. He did not dare to leave and just stood there alone. Seeing that he was still standing there, Jiang scolded again, "What are you still standing here for? Do you want to beat her a few more times because you didn't beat her to death?"

Cui Zhengkai hurriedly retreated after hearing this.

Doctor Chen came trotting over soon after. He took one look at the wound and said, "The girl is seriously injured this time. I will prescribe some external medicine first, and then some internal medicine."

Jiang asked, "When will this injury heal?"

Doctor Chen said, "It will probably take more than half a month. Then I will come and prescribe some scar removal medicine. I guarantee that there will not be a single scar left."

Jiang said, "Then I'll trouble you, Doctor Chen."

The next morning, Xiuxin finally woke up. She leaned forward slightly and felt the pain of the thorns on her back. She couldn't help but groan. Jiang woke up immediately after hearing this sound, "Xiuxin, are you awake? Are you feeling okay? Does it hurt?"

Xiu Xin shook her head, "It doesn't hurt, mother, don't worry."

Jiang took out the letter and the knot from her sleeve, with a determined look in her eyes, "Daughter, you must not take this fight in vain. I will do whatever you want even if it costs me my life. Don't worry, I will keep this letter and the knot with me. I will send someone to communicate with Li Yuzhi. I will also talk to your father. We have been married for so many years, and I don't believe he would not care about the relationship between husband and wife at all."

Xiu Xin's eyes welled up with tears and she choked up, "Mother..."

Jiang asked again, "Tell me, who did you ask to pass this letter on your behalf? How did it end up in your father's hands?"

Xiu Xin said, "I asked Lan Xiang to pass it on for me. I don't know how it ended up in my father's hands."

Jiang murmured and said, "You take a rest. I'll be back soon." At the same time, she called Qinxiang and Lianxiang to come in to take care of Xiuxin, and went out to find Lanxiang.

When Lanxiang entered the room and saw that Jiang was unhappy, she guessed about 70% of the situation in her heart, and bowed and said, "Second Madam."

Jiang slammed the table and said, "Lanxiang, let me ask you, Xiuxin gave you the letter

and Tongxin, who did you give it to?"
Lan Xiang knelt down immediately, "Second Madam, I gave the letter to Xiao Yongzi at the front door. In the past, whenever the young lady wanted to buy some small toys or rouge and powder outside, she would ask him to do it. I saw that he was cautious and tight-lipped, so I gave it to him this time. I didn't tell him what it was. I put the letter in a brocade bag and asked him to give it to Lord Li."
Jiang had always trusted Lanxiang, and after hearing her sincere words, her doubts were alleviated by about 70%, so she said, "Go and call Xiao Yongzi to me."
That little Yongzi was only fifteen or sixteen years old, born quite clever, smiling whenever he saw anyone, so he got along well with many maids. Now when the little Yongzi saw Jiang coming to find him, he knelt down and slapped himself twice as soon as he entered the door and cried, "Second Madam, it's all my fault. I didn't do a good job and caused trouble for the master."

☆, Chapter 20

Chapter 20 Secret Encounter
Jiang said sternly, "Can you tell me what's going on?"
Xiao Yongzi cried, "Yesterday morning, Miss Lanxiang gave me a brocade bag and asked me to give it to Lord Li Yuzhi. I often buy

little things for the third lady. This time, I thought that this thing must belong to the third lady, so I didn't dare to open it. I put the thing in my sleeve and went out the door as usual. Unexpectedly, when I was walking, I accidentally bumped into Sixi who was beside the second master, and the brocade bag flew out. Originally, this was nothing, but I don't know how, the second master came over and took the brocade bag from my hand, which caused trouble for the third lady. I deserve to die, I deserve to die." As he spoke, he slapped himself twice. Jiang said, "If what you said is true, you can just give your subordinate ten strokes of the cane. But if what you said is false, and you betrayed your master and deceived your superiors and subordinates, don't blame me for being cruel. You go down first, and I will investigate this matter thoroughly."

Jiang thought, judging from Xiao Yongzi's appearance, what he said was probably true. But why did Cui Zhengkai appear so coincidentally, and why did he notice the brocade bag and take it away? Maybe someone had tipped him off. If this was true, it would be very difficult to catch the person behind it.

The two older maids around Xiuxin grew up with her and have a deep relationship with her, but it is not ruled out that they would do something bad. Of the two second-class maids, Cuixiang is always flustered and shows her emotions on her face. She doesn't look like someone who would do such a thing. Lianxiang is dull and doesn't like to talk on weekdays. I don't know what she is like. In addition, it is hard to guarantee that someone else may have heard about this and reported it. It is really difficult to verify.

Thinking of this, Jiang couldn't help but rub her temples with a headache. As the saying goes, it is easy to dodge an open attack but hard to guard against an arrow from the dark. Xiuxin still has her protection now, but she has encountered accidents one after another. I really don't know how she will deal with it when she marries into someone else's family in the future... When she thought of this, Jiang's head ached.

On this side, Jiang Shi tried every means to send his confidant to deliver Xiu Xin's letter and the knot of love to Li Yuzhi. On the other side, Li Yuzhi had packed her luggage and was ready to leave. Several classmates and old friends came to say goodbye, and Li Yuzhi said goodbye to them reluctantly, "Everyone, Yuzhi will be gone for half a year, please take care of yourself, and we will meet again." Everyone bowed and said, "Yuzhi, you have just taken office in the Ministry of Personnel and you are already very important. Go to Chenzhou for inspection. Next time you return to Beijing, you will be promoted to a higher level in no time."

Li Yuzhi said, "Thanks for your good wishes, I will say goodbye now."

Li Yuzhi got on the carriage, and the servant in front whipped the horse whip, and the carriage galloped away.

"Brother Li, Brother Li!" Wang Chaozong rode over and stopped Li Yuzhi's carriage.

"Brother Li, you are so disloyal. You didn't tell me that you were going to Chenzhou. If my father hadn't told me, I wouldn't have been able to send you off."

Li Yuzhi couldn't help but feel bitter when she saw him. She just bowed and said, "I didn't want to disturb anyone when I went to Chenzhou on official business. Besides, you are now working in the Ministry of Industry, so you must be busy with official duties, so I didn't tell you."

Wang Chaozong felt that he and Li Yuzhi were not as close as before, but he didn't know the reason. He thought that he was immature and offended him with his words, so he showed a reluctant expression, "Brother Li, you will be gone for half a year, remember to write to me. If you encounter any trouble, you can also write to let me know, I will go to find my father, and he will definitely help you solve it."

Li Yuzhi looked at Wang Chaozong's sincere eyes and sighed secretly in her heart. Wang Chaozong was frank and open-minded. She deliberately alienated him, but he never remembered it and treated her as before.

She only sighed that she was born in a humble family and did not dare to fight. Thinking of this, Li Yuzhi forced a smile and said, "Chaozong, you should go back. We will say goodbye now."

Wang Chaozong also bowed and said, "See you later."

Li Yuzhi's carriage galloped out, and Wang Chaozong was still standing there watching Li Yuzhi's carriage go. The servant sent by Jiang Shi just arrived and saw Li Yuzhi's carriage going farther and farther away. He couldn't help but jump up and call out, "Master Li! Master Li! Master Li!"

But Li Yuzhi had already gone far away, how could he hear it?

Wang Chaozong saw that the boy was dressed like someone from a wealthy family, so he asked curiously, "Which family are you from? What are you doing here to see Master Li?"

How could the servant tell such a confidential matter to an outsider? He just side-glanced at him and said, "You are not Lord Li, how can I tell you?"

It is said that the servant went back to Cui's house and reported to Jiang. Upon hearing this, Jiang could only sigh sadly that they were not destined to be together. The servant was also smart, so he asked, "Second Madam, do you want to send this letter to Lord Li?"

Jiang shook her head. "First, it is not safe to send such private items to Li Yuzhi. If they are intercepted by someone with ulterior motives, Xiuxin's reputation will be completely ruined. Second, Li Yuzhi was appointed by the court. How could she leave her post without permission? Third, even if Li Yuzhi rushed back thousands of miles for my daughter, it would take a lot of time to go back and forth. How would you know when the Wang family would come to propose marriage?"

The servant fell silent after hearing this. Jiang looked at the letter in his hand, sighed again, and put it into the incense burner beside him. The yellow flames licked up and immediately turned it into ashes.

Xiuxin spent more than half a month in bed before her wounds completely healed. The scars on her back were scabbed and hard to the touch. During this period, Cui Zhengkai also came to see her several times. Xiuxin naturally could not be angry with her father, but comforted Cui Zhengkai. Seeing Xiuxin like this, Cui Zhengkai felt more and more ashamed, and his heart softened. "Xiuxin, if you really don't want to marry Wang Fusheng, I will do my best to deal with it for you, but... as a father, I am limited in my ability and I am afraid I can't do it." In any case, Xiuxin is his youngest legitimate daughter. She has been born cute and lovable since she was a child, and he doesn't want to see her sad about her marriage.

Xiu Xin heard Cui Zhengkai say this and choked up, "Father...it's all because of my daughter's willfulness..."

Cui Zhengkai patted Xiuxin's hand and said, "Don't worry." Before leaving, Cui Zhengkai instructed the maids to take good care of her, and also asked someone to bring a lot of nourishing things such as bird's nest, ginseng, snow lotus, etc. to Xiuxin's yard.

Cui Zhengkai was looking for an opportunity to explain his intentions to Wang Fusheng. It happened that Wang Fusheng's 40th birthday was coming up in a few days, so he specially wrote an invitation and sent it to the palace. Wang Fusheng was about to marry into the Cui family, so how could he not go to his future father-in-law's birthday? Not only did he have to go, but he also had to prepare as many birthday gifts as possible. So he took out the priceless jade coral and a pair of white jade ruyi from his warehouse and went to Cui's house to celebrate his birthday.

The Cui family has been very busy these days. The servants in front and the maids in the back are all busy. Xiuxin's injury has not healed completely, and she did not go to the banquet in front. She stayed in the small courtyard, reading a few books and eating a few snacks to pass the time. So many things happened during this period. Minxin and Yuxin both don't get along with her when they meet. Minxin came a few times, but she sent her away on the grounds of being unwell. Since the last incident, Xiuxin felt that Minxin was secretly planning something. There was a layer of separation between her and her, so she also avoided her.

Xiuxin was chewing on a newly harvested spring peach when she saw Qinxiang approaching with a smile, "Girl, look who's here to see you." Xiuxin was just wondering when she saw a woman in red striding in with great spirit, "Xiuxin, it's really hard to see you. Today is your father's birthday, why don't you go to the front instead of staying in this small courtyard?"

Xiu Xin was surprised and happy. She jumped up and held Zhan Xue's hand, saying, "You are finally here. I have been bored these days. No one came to accompany me." While pulling her hand, she brought the fruit plate and candied fruit to Zhan Xue, "Here, have some fruit. These are sweet spring peaches."

Zhan Xue shook her head. "I don't like eating these. I'm used to eating large pieces of mutton and goat milk at the border. I'm not used to eating these delicate things."

"Oh." Xiu Xin spat out the peach kernel in disappointment, turned around and pinched another candied fruit and stuffed it into her mouth, stuffing her cheeks so full that she looked like a little rabbit. Zhan Xue couldn't help but stretched out her finger and poked Xiu Xin's cheek and said, "Hey, I see you eat a lot, why are you thinner than before?"

It's because of worry. When she thought about her marriage, Xiuxin sighed, "Oh, don't mention it. I think you have heard about it. The Wang family might be interested in having me as the concubine of Wang Fusheng, the second master of the Wang family. You said that Wang Fusheng's son Wang Chaozong and I are the same age, so he must be the same age as my father? It makes me feel uncomfortable just thinking about it." Xiuxin opened her heart completely in front of Zhan Xue, "And what I want is to be with someone for the rest of my life. Wang Fusheng's first wife is a mark that can never be erased. How can I be happy if I marry him?" The husband in Xiuxin's mind is like Li Yuzhi, elegant and affectionate. It's a pity...she is not destined to be with him.

Zhan Xue also felt the same way. She was now seventeen years old, the oldest among the unmarried noble ladies, but she still had no idea about marriage. The Duke of the State Guard was so anxious that his hair turned a few gray. But no matter what, Zhan Xue had one thing to say: she would rather die than marry someone she didn't like, and the Duke of the State Guard could do nothing about it.

So Zhan Xue said, "Xiu Xin, I think what you said is very true, but you haven't met that Wang Fusheng yet, so how can you conclude that you will look down on him? I heard from my father that he..." Zhan Xue paused and swallowed the word "oily-haired and powdered face", "He is very good-looking and elegant. Maybe you will fall in love with him as soon as you see him?"

Xiu Xin nodded, "You're right. Why don't we go to the front and take a look?"

When Zhan Xue heard Xiu Xin say this, she had no choice but to agree, so the two of them changed into maids' clothes and secretly went to the front yard.

☆, Chapter 21 Rejection

Chapter 21 Rejection

Although Cui Zhengkai's birthday banquet was not as grand as the one held by Princess Duan Yichang, it was still quite grand. Most of the officials in the capital came to congratulate him. In addition, after the news of Wang Fusheng's marriage to the third daughter of the Cui family spread, the officials in the court guessed that Cui Zhengkai would soon become Wang Fusheng's father-in-law, so they naturally gave him some face and gave him more generous birthday gifts.

Cui Zhengkai was busy dealing with officials in the court, while Jiang was busy entertaining female guests who came to the mansion. The entire Cui Mansion was very lively.

Xiuxin and Zhanxue changed into maids' clothes and walked to the front yard with their heads down. Zhanxue was not afraid, because no one recognized her anyway. Perhaps because the mansion was busy today, no one noticed Xiuxin. A maid in purple even put a wine pot in their hands and ordered them to pour wine for the guests.

Xiu Xin and Zhan Xue looked at each other in bewilderment, "This..."

Zhan Xue blinked at Xiu Xin and said, "This is a good opportunity."

Xiu Xin still had some concerns, "This is not a good idea. First, if we go out rashly and are recognized, it will cause trouble. Second, if my father sees me, I'm afraid I won't be able to escape a scolding."

"It's nothing. Even if someone saw it, they would just say a few words. What can they really do to you?"

Xiu Xin thought for a moment and said, "Or maybe we can just hide in the back room and have a look?" The wound on her back still hurts a little, and it's unacceptable to forget the pain after the wound has healed.

Zhan Xue nodded, and the two of them went to the back room. It happened that there was no one guarding the room today, so the two of them sneaked in, locked the door, and looked out through the crack.

Cui Zhengkai was the host and sat at the top seat. The first person sitting on the left was undoubtedly Wang Fusheng, and the first person sitting on the right was Liu Baozi, the Duke of the State. During the banquet, everyone was toasting each other.

Soon, someone came to toast Cui Zhengkai, and Cui Zhengyu also chatted and laughed with everyone at the banquet.

Because the view through the crack in the door was narrow, Xiuxin could only see the people on the right, and could not see anyone on the left. The two hid inside and watched for a while, and Xiuxin became a little anxious, "Oh, how can I tell which one is Wang Fusheng if they are like this?"

Zhan Xue said, "Don't be anxious, take another look." Zhan Xue was staring at a person with pleasure. The person was sitting in the seventh seat on the right. He looked young, about sixteen or seventeen years old, wearing a white suit. He had handsome eyebrows and eyes, and there were little dimples on the corners of his mouth when he smiled, which made her heart beat fast.

Zhan Xue was fascinated, but Xiu Xin became more and more anxious. She pushed Zhan Xue and asked, "Which one do you think is Wang Fusheng?"

Zhan Xue said, "I don't think he looks like any of them. I heard from my father that he has just turned thirty, but... the guests on the right are either very old or very young. I don't think he looks like any of them."

Xiu Xin was getting anxious when she saw a man in black holding a wine glass walking towards the upper seat from the left. He held the wine glass in his hand with an elegant posture and a voice like pearls falling on a jade plate. "Today is the 40th birthday of Censor Cui. The ancients said that a man is free from doubts at the age of 40. This is the prime of his life. Why don't we toast Censor Cui together and wish him a long life and eternal youth."

"Well said." All the officials stood up and praised.

Cui Zhengkai stood up quickly, raised his glass and said, "Thank you all for coming to my humble home to celebrate my birthday. I am grateful." After saying that, he raised his head and drank the wine in the glass. Everyone else also drank it before sitting down again.

Zhan Xue pushed the dazed Xiu Xin and said, "Hey, what's wrong with you? What are you looking at?"

Xiu Xin came back to her senses, her eyes still fixed on Wang Fusheng, and she murmured, "Why is it him again?"

"Who are you talking about?"

Xiu Xin shook her head, "No, I didn't say who."

As soon as Xiu Xin finished speaking, Cui Zhengkai raised his glass and said, "Sir Wang, I offer you a toast. Your presence in my humble abode today brings honor to me."

"I don't dare." Xiu Xin was just wondering, but suddenly she heard the scoundrel continue to laugh, "I don't deserve it. I will have to rely on you in the future."

Son-in-law?!

It was like a thunderclap. Cui Xiuxin was so shocked that she couldn't recover for a long time. Her long nails almost pinched into the tender flesh of her palm. How could it be him?! Thinking of the few times she met him outside, he flirted with her every time. That man... that man is obviously a playboy, a very romantic person. It's infuriating that he doesn't know how to restrain himself at his age. It's obvious that he has no shame! Now, the person she is going to marry is him? When she thought of this, Xiuxin wanted to die.

Zhan Xue saw Xiu Xin's face changing from gloomy to bright and dark. Sometimes she looked shy, sometimes furious, and sometimes sad and desperate. She couldn't help but ask curiously, "Xiu Xin, what's wrong with you? Is it because of that Wang Fusheng?" She blinked her eyes and said mischievously, "I think that Wang Fusheng is a little older, but he is handsome and good-looking. What do you think? Do you like him?"

Xiu Xin stood up angrily and turned back, "Only a fool would like him!"

"Hey? Where are you going?" Zhan Xue said.

"Go back and change your clothes." Xiu Xin pulled Zhan Xue's hand, "Let's go back quickly. If I'm caught by my father again, I'll be in big trouble."

Zhan Xue looked back at the handsome young man reluctantly, "Xiu Xin, is your family so strict with you?"

"I'm not from a general family like you." Xiu Xin pulled Zhan Xue along the way, "Our four major families have the strictest family education. If someone finds out that I sneaked into the front yard, there will be another disturbance."

Zhan Xue returned to Xiu Xin's courtyard and changed her clothes. Before leaving, Zhan Xue gave Xiu Xin a small knife made of gold, "It's rare that we get along so well. Take this small gift. I'll come to see you next time I have a chance." Xiu Xin pulled out the knife. She saw that the knife was only as big as her index finger, but the workmanship was very delicate. The scabbard was engraved with intricate patterns. The blade was pulled out, shining, and it was quite pleasing to look at.

"How can I accept such a precious gift from you?" Xiu Xin said.

"Why can't I accept it? Just take it. Next time you get something good, you can give it back to me as a gift." Zhan Xue said as she walked out. "It's getting late. I'll go home first."

"Yeah." Xiu Xin nodded, and sent Zhan Xue out of the courtyard and to the small garden.

After the banquet, Cui Zhengkai kept Wang Fusheng and invited him to the main room for tea. Wang Fusheng knew that he had something important to discuss, so he agreed. Cui Zhengkai asked someone to bring the top-grade Biluochun and personally made tea for Wang Fusheng, showing great hospitality. Wang Fusheng naturally declined again. In this way, the two chatted for a long time before Cui Zhengkai got to the point. "Sir Wang," Wang Fusheng hurriedly said, "Brother Cui, why are you being so polite? Just call me Fusheng directly."

Cui Zhengkai coughed dryly before saying, "Fusheng, at the Hundred Flowers Festival, your mother has discussed with my wife about the marriage between my daughter and you... I have discussed this matter with my wife, and I feel that my daughter has a stubborn temperament and little talent, so I am afraid it is difficult for her to be a good match. I hope that Lord Wang will find another good match."

Although the words sound nice, they clearly mean rejection. Upon hearing this, Wang Fusheng snorted coldly and put the teacup in his hand on the table, "Master Cui, do you think I am not worthy of your daughter?"

"I dare not, I dare not." Cui Zhengkai was several levels lower than Wang Fusheng in rank after all. Seeing Wang Fusheng's change of color, he hurriedly bowed and said, "Sir Wang, you are the backbone of the Wang family and a key official of our dynasty. Not to mention that my daughter is worthy of you, even if you are a princess, it's just... as the saying goes, a great man is not a good match. My daughter has been weak since she was a child. I have spoiled her and never brought her up well. It is really a stretch for her to be with someone as talented and beautiful as you, Sir Wang. I hope Sir Wang will reconsider."

When Wang Fusheng was young, he liked women with charm and talent, like Chu Lanyuan. Later, as he grew older, he found dignified and elegant women very attractive, like his first wife Bai Ruozhi. Now, after meeting Cui Xiuxin several times, he found that cute and lovely women also have some charm. Originally, Wang Fusheng didn't think he had to marry Cui Xiuxin. He had seen countless men in the past ten years, and women were nothing in his eyes. Now, the reason why he was eager to marry Xiuxin was, firstly, he felt that Cui Xiuxin had some attractive qualities, and secondly, Princess Duanyi happened to ask him to remarry her, so he agreed. However, he never thought that Cui Zhengkai was so ungrateful, which made him determined to marry Cui Xiuxin. He immediately changed his color and said, "I understand what Lord Cui meant. It's just that I, Wang Fusheng, think your daughter is worthy, so your daughter is worthy."

Cui Zhengkai wanted to say more, but Wang Fusheng waved his hand and said, "Forget it, let's leave it at that for today. I hope Master Cui will consider my daughter's marriage carefully. Don't let this little thing ruin Master Cui's bright future!"

These words were clearly threatening. Cui Zhengkai's face turned pale, but he could do nothing but sigh.

Wang Fusheng's trusted servant named Mo Yan saw Wang Fusheng leaving Cui Zhengkai and looked unhappy, so he asked, "What's wrong with you, sir?"

Wang Fusheng cursed, "You are such an ungrateful person."

Mo Yan was also a man of insight, so he smiled and said, "My master is not in a good mood today, why don't we go boating on the lake and drink to relax?" Boating on the lake and drinking naturally requires the company of singing girls and actresses. Seeing that Wang Fusheng remained silent, Mo Yan thought that Wang Fusheng had got the point, so he added, "Miss Yuqin must be thinking about me, she sent people to ask about me several times."

☆、Chapter 22 Confrontation

Chapter 22 Confrontation
Wang Fusheng was silent for a while and glanced at Mo Yan. "You are good at giving advice." Mo Yan didn't hear the sarcasm in his tone and smiled happily. "It's all because of my good training." Wang Fusheng looked at him and kicked him in the buttocks. "I didn't keep you under control when you were by my side, but you rebelled and secretly exchanged things with people outside. Tell me, how much benefit have you

taken?"

Mo Yan was startled and quickly knelt on the ground and kowtowed, "Master, I am innocent. Apart from Miss Yuqin who sent people to look for me a few times, how could anyone else have anything to do with me?"

Wang Fusheng knew that this could not be stopped, so he just had to avoid going too far. So he fanned the folding fan in his hand and kicked him lightly, "Come on, get up. I'll only forgive you this time. If you do it again, I won't let you off easily."

Mo Yan was overjoyed, he kowtowed on the ground and followed Wang Fusheng happily, "Hey, Master, where are you going?"

Wang Fusheng recalled the last time he met Xiuxin in the back garden. He turned around and said, "Let's go to the back garden of Cui's mansion for a stroll."

After Xiuxin sent Zhanxue to the back garden, she stopped and saw the pavilion was covered with wisteria flowers, which were in full bloom. She walked into the pavilion and sat down. It was getting dark, the sun was setting, and the clouds in the sky were dyed with purple and red, which was beautiful. Xiuxin half leaned against the pillar, holding her cheek. When she thought about her marriage, she was so worried that she wanted to cry, and she sighed deeply.

"My beauty, what are you worried about?"

Xiu Xin was startled. When she turned

around, she saw the man holding a folding fan and walking into the pavilion. He was smiling, his eyes were charming, and his dark clothes made him look even more handsome and elegant. After cursing him in her heart, she stood up reluctantly and bowed to him, "Lord Wang."

Wang Fusheng was surprised, "Hey, do you know who I am?"

Xiu Xin walked up to him and snorted coldly, "Of course I know who you are. I also know that you will come to my house to propose marriage soon."

Wang Fusheng saw that Xiuxin was unhappy, her face was tense, and even her palms were clenched tightly. He knew what was going on, "I'm coming to your house to propose marriage. Are you happy?"

Yue, you big-headed ghost!

"Wang Fusheng, listen to me, I am not willing to marry you!" Xiu Xin said word by word with a firm expression. Her already big eyes opened even wider, showing a kind of determination.

Wang Fusheng smiled when he saw her like this. He approached Xiuxin step by step until he pushed her into a corner. "Cui Xiuxin, no one in the whole court has ever called me by my full name. You are the first one. It shows that we are destined to be together and to be husband and wife."

Xiuxin was angry and ashamed, she spat at him and said, "Shameless! I would rather become a nun than marry you, I would rather die than marry you, not to mention that I already..." Xiuxin stopped talking halfway, she almost wanted to bite off her tongue, why am I so quick to speak!

Wang Fusheng knew that she was not being coy, but really looked down on him. He had all the women he wanted, but now he was ignored by this little girl! He laughed in anger, pinched Xiuxin's chin, forced her to raise her head, and approached her dangerously, "You already what? Huh?"

Xiu Xin turned her head away, "Nothing! Let me go."

It was not so easy for Wang Fusheng to let her go. He put his left hand around her waist and got closer to her. "I tell you, it doesn't matter what you are like. I am determined to marry you. What's more..." He paused, his expression changed, and he leaned close to Xiuxin's ear and whispered, "We have already had physical contact, haven't we? If you marry someone else, it may not be appropriate, right? The pink pleated skirt you took off last time is still with me, huh?"

"You!" Xiu Xin was simply overwhelmed by the shamelessness of the person in front of her. She wanted to struggle but failed. Her face turned red with anger. She said bitterly, "You are so old and still do such despicable things. There are actually people who praise you as a model of civil officials. It shows that you are just an empty reputation. The morals of the world

are going downhill!"
"So old?" Wang Fusheng is only in his early thirties. He considers himself a suave and handsome person. Now someone actually calls him "very old"? He thought that last time in Zhengjue Temple, this little guy seemed to have scolded him for being old and unruly?

For the first time, he felt that his self-confidence was greatly affected, "Am I really that old?" There were obviously no wrinkles.

Xiu Xin turned around and avoided his embrace, "What does your age have to do with me? I will never marry you anyway!" After saying that, she ran away.

Mo Yan felt that his grandfather had become very strange since he went to Cui Mansion to attend the birthday banquet. When he was free, he would ask him to bring a bronze mirror and ask him while looking at him, "Mo Yan, do you think I am old?" "?"

Mo Yan was asked strangely, "How come I am old? I am in the prime of life. Aren't people always praising me for being as beautiful as Pan An, with a dragon and a phoenix?"

Wang Fusheng nodded towards the bronze mirror, then touched his chin, "You are right. But..." He received these compliments when he was just a young man. Now no one has ever complimented his appearance. Could it be... When Wang Fusheng thought of a certain possibility, his heart turned cold. Could it be that he is really old?

"Mo Yan, can you please search for me some recipe for maintaining youth?" Wang Fusheng asked.

"Okay, I'll do it right away." Mo Yan trotted out, thinking as he ran, the master is really weird today, forget it, don't think about it, the important thing is to do the things the master asked me to do.

A few days later, Yuqin snuggled up to Wang Fusheng charmingly, twisting Wang Fusheng's hair with her white jade fingers, "Master, I heard Mo Yan say that you want a recipe for youthful appearance? Speaking of youthful appearance, I have quite a few. Do you want to try it?"

Wang Fusheng raised his head and drank a glass of wine, then pinched the beauty's face, "Do you have any? Bring it here so I can see it?"

Yuqin twisted her waist and handed the written prescription to Wang Fusheng. Wang Fusheng looked up in confusion, "It's for application?"

Yuqin gave him a seductive look and said, "Of course it is applied with compresses. I have tried all these recipes. After using them, my skin becomes as smooth as a peeled egg."

Wang Fusheng put the prescription into his sleeve, stretched out his hand and pinched the beauty's slender waist, "My beauty, if it is really useful, I will reward you greatly."

Yuqin called out coquettishly and fell into Wang Fusheng's arms, her fingertips like water lilies pointed at Wang Fusheng's heart and said, "I don't want your reward, Master. As long as you think about me more and think about me in your heart, I will be satisfied."

Speaking of which, Xiuxin has been suffering from spring sleepiness recently. She has been feeling listless all day long, and even her appetite has decreased. She has lost a lot of weight, and all the soft flesh around her waist has receded completely. Lan Lan is so anxious. Xiang Xin tried her best to get Xiu Xin's favorite food to be brought from the kitchen, but Xiu Xin still had a poor appetite.

In fact, Xiuxin knew that she was depressed and couldn't find anything to eat. The Wang family had sent people to propose marriage a few days ago. Although Cui Zhengkai had not yet responded, he had no choice but to agree. Either I simply become a sister-in-law, I'm afraid I have no choice.

Hey, my mother still wants to arrange a marriage for me before the Wang family proposes marriage, but who knows in the whole capital that the third girl of the Cui family is about to be the child of Wang Fu of the Wang family? Who dares to wade into this muddy water at this time?

At this point, we can only accept our fate.

"Girl, look what this is?" Lanxiang lifted the curtain and walked in, pushing Xiuxin, who was lying on the table and looking sleepy.

Xiuxin opened her eyes and saw the iron fork and wire mesh in Lanxiang's hands. Her eyes immediately lit up, "Barbecue? Lanxiang, are we having barbecue today? Mother has always forbidden us to do so. Why did she agree today?" Lanxiang smiled and said, "Madam saw that you had no appetite, so she told me to bring out all the utensils from the warehouse because you like it."

Xiuxin said, "Since we are having barbecue, it will be more fun if we have more people..." Yixin and Yuxin could not be called. "Why don't we go to the front yard to see if my two brothers have come back and call them over? We can set up the stove in the garden, wouldn't that be better?"

Lanxiang nodded and sent a little girl to the front yard to call Cui Jinghong and Cui Qihong. It was also a coincidence that Cui Jinghong and Cui Qihong had both returned from their jobs, and Jinxin happened to be back to her parents' home to play and was chatting with Jiang in the room, so the four brothers and sisters gathered together, set up their utensils in the garden, and started to grill meat.

"Xiu Xin likes to eat venison the most, roast more venison." Jin Xin said with a smile, "Oh, second brother, you watch the fire and burn the clothes carefully."

Cui Qihong is only eighteen this year, and is still young, so she smiled and said, "Big sister, you are exactly like mother."

Jin Xin laughed and scolded, "You are such a sharp-tongued person. You are almost 20 years old. Will you still be like this when you get married?"

Cui Qihong got behind Cui Jinghong and said, "Brother, you haven't married yet. It's too early for me. Let's have some fun for a few more years. Women are so troublesome. If you pamper her, she will rebel. If you treat her coldly, she will cry again."

Xiu Xin put her hands on her hips and said, "Second brother, be careful with your words. Be careful not to slip your tongue. My elder sister and I are both women. When have you ever seen us crying?"

Cui Qihong made a face and said, "Third sister, when did you become a woman? You are clearly just a yellow-haired girl!"

Cui Jinghong calmed down and tapped him on the head, "You just love to talk nonsense!"

Jin Xin said, "Our third sister is about to get engaged. She was still a little girl a few years ago, but now she is getting married."

When this was mentioned, Xiuxin's smile disappeared. She sat down sullenly, turning the venison with tongs. "I would rather be a nun than marry that man."

☆, Chapter 23: Incompatible Horoscopes

Chapter 23: Incompatibility

Jinxin knew Xiuxin's thoughts best, so she advised, "Xiuxin, 10% of things in the world are not satisfactory. How can there be such a perfect thing that is satisfactory to everyone? For example, although I married a man of my dreams, but..." As she spoke, her eyes became red, "Xiuxin, I have heard of Wang Fusheng. Although you and him seem inappropriate on the surface, you will spend your whole life together. If you really become a nun, not to mention the pressure on the Cui family, can you endure the lonely life?"

Xiu Xin thought for a long time and shook her head silently. If she became a nun, all the flesh in front of her would be gone.

Jin Xin said, "That's it. You still have to fight for your good life by yourself. Maybe after you get married, things won't be as bad as you think."

How could it not be bad? After she got married, she had to deal with a philandering, two-faced husband, a cunning mother-in-law, complicated household affairs, and a stepson who was as old as herself. Thirdly, Wang Fusheng had several concubines, one of whom was the world-famous Chu Lanyuan. With such a dazzling concubine, how could she still have a good life?

Cui Jinghong said, "Well, it's rare for the four of us to get together today, so let's talk about something happy. Second brother, give me some chili powder. The meat is almost burnt and you don't even know how to turn it over."

Xiu Xin opened her mouth and took a bite of a large piece of venison. The venison was fat and tender, and the freshness and fragrance overflowed after taking a bite, which really made her mouth water. She couldn't help but smile at Cui Jinghong and said, "Brother's barbecue is really the most delicious."

Cui Jinghong pinched Xiuxin's nose lovingly, "If it tastes good, eat more. You've lost weight recently, and it makes me sad to see you."

"Yeah." Xiu Xin nodded, cut the venison into small pieces with a knife and stuffed them into her mouth. She had already made a decision in her heart that since some things are powerless to change, it is better to accept them calmly. It is useless to be sad.

A few days later, Cui Zhengkai responded to the Wang family and agreed to the marriage proposal. The Wang family then sent someone to take Xiuxin's horoscope and send it to the Imperial Observatory for comparison. After the Imperial Observatory's Director Zhao compared Xiuxin and Wang Fusheng's horoscopes, he personally went to the palace to report to Princess Duanyi and Old Lady Wang: "From the horoscope, the third daughter of the Cui family is a person of great wealth and honor, with a phoenix in the sky, but..."

Duan Yi asked hurriedly, "Just what?"

"It's just that Miss Cui San and Lord Wang's horoscopes conflict with each other. If they are forced to be together, at best it will harm Lord Wang's fate, and at worst it may affect the fortune of the entire Wang family." The director of the Imperial Observatory bowed.

Duan Yi was shocked, "How could this happen?"

When Old Lady Wang heard this, she was secretly happy. She had never liked Cui Xiuxin, but now that their horoscopes were incompatible, it gave her a good reason to postpone the marriage. "Mother, in this case, should we reconsider the marriage between my Fusheng and Cui Xiuxin?"

Duan Yi was also disappointed. He waved his hand tiredly and said, "Let's discuss this later. I'm also tired. Let's leave it at that for today."

Incompatible horoscopes and bad luck are taboos for couples. If it is found during the marriage negotiation that the horoscopes of the two are incompatible, the marriage will most likely be cancelled. Therefore, the old lady of the Wang family became more active and thought about finding another noble lady to be Wang Fusheng's concubine.

At the same time, Cui Mansion.

Jiang whispered something in Xiuxin's ear,

and Xiuxin's eyes widened in shock, "What? You actually changed my horoscope?"

Jiang said proudly, "Our four major families place the greatest importance on the horoscope when it comes to marriage matching. I specially asked someone to calculate it. The horoscope presented here is incompatible with Wang Fusheng's. This marriage will definitely not be possible."

Xiu Xin was delighted, "Is that really the case?"

Jiang nodded, "Of course. If the Wang family cancels this marriage, our Cui family can be saved, and you don't have to marry them. Isn't that the best of both worlds?"

Xiu Xin was so excited that she jumped a few steps in the room. She felt that the depression that she had suppressed in her chest for the past few days suddenly disappeared, and her eyes and eyebrows were shining again. "Mother, you still have a way."

"Of course." Jiang hugged Xiuxin and said, "After the matter with the Wang family is over, I will find a clean family for you to marry into, and everything will be fine then." Jiang had a good plan, but the devil is always one step ahead of the good, and Wang Fusheng was not that easy to fool.

Princess Duanyi thought about it and decided to ask Wang Fusheng for his opinion. So she asked someone to call him to the main hall. "Fusheng, some things are better to believe than not. This is a major matter for the Wang family, so it's better to be cautious. What do you think?"

Wang Fusheng thought for a while, his mind was as clear as a mirror, and he curled his lips and said, "Grandmother, I think this incompatibility is not a big deal. There are many people in the folks who marry people with incompatible horoscopes, and I have never heard of any disaster caused by the conflict of horoscopes. Let's take a step back. Although Cui Xiuxin and I have incompatible horoscopes, we can ask the people from the Imperial Observatory to see if there is a way to resolve it."

Duan Yi nodded, "You are still thoughtful. Tomorrow, invite the director of the Imperial Observatory and Cui Xiuxin to come as well. Let them see if there is any way to resolve the problem."

"Yes." Wang Fusheng bowed.

The next morning, the Wang family's carriage was waiting at the entrance of Cui's house. Jiang took Cui Xiuxin on the carriage. Xiuxin felt uneasy along the way and whispered, "Mother, do you think the situation will change?" Jiang was also unsure, "Let's wait and see, I don't know what the Wang family wants..."

After arriving at the palace, there was already a maid waiting at the door to greet them. As soon as the carriage stopped, someone came up to them and said, "Mrs. Cui, Miss Cui, please follow me."

Jiang and Xiuxin followed the maid and walked for a quarter of an hour before entering the main hall. Sitting at the main table was the elegant and graceful Princess Duanyi, who had silver hair all over her head. The first person sitting on the side was Old Lady Wang. Wang Fusheng, who was standing by the side, saw Xiuxin come in, and his lips curled slightly, showing her a determined smile. His smile made Xiuxin's heart skip a beat.

Damn it, what is this scoundrel planning?

Xiu Xin changed her mind and realized that since she had determined her birth date and horoscope, he couldn't do anything about it, so this marriage would definitely not take place!

"Greetings to Princess Duanyi." Xiu Xin bowed along with Jiang, and then bowed slightly to Madam Wang, "Madam Wang."

Duan Yi smiled and said, "Second Madam Cui, Third Miss Cui, I am sorry to bother you with this trip today. This is Lord Zhao, the director of the Imperial Observatory. Lord Zhao, please take a look at the faces of Third Miss Cui and my grandson. Is there any way to resolve the conflict between the two?"

The director of the Imperial Observatory first looked up at Wang Fusheng who was sitting at the top, and then began to read Xiuxin's face. After looking at her for a while, Lord Zhao gradually showed a look of joy.

Duan Yi asked hurriedly, "How?"

Lord Zhao said happily, "Princess, although Cui Xiuxin's horoscope conflicts with Lord Wang's, and water and fire cannot coexist, the solution is very easy. The two of them only need to wear bracelets made of sandalwood to add wood energy and reconcile water and fire. Not only will the couple not conflict with each other, but they will complement each other, even more powerful."

Duan Yi's brows immediately lit up when he heard that. He said three good words in a row, called Xiu Xin over, held her hand and said, "Look, you are destined to be my granddaughter-in-law. It just so happens that I have two strings of Buddhist beads made of sandalwood on my wrist. You and Fu Sheng can each have one string, which is just right." As he spoke, he took off the Buddhist beads on his hand and put them on Xiu Xin's wrist without saying anything.

Xiu Xin looked down at the string of Buddhist beads on her wrist, then glanced at Wang Fusheng's smug face. She felt dark inside, her body was shaky, and she almost fainted. Wang Fusheng shamelessly stretched out his hand to Duan Yi, "Grandma, where is your grandson's?"

Duan Yi took the other string off and placed it in Wang Fusheng's hand. "I have carried these two strings of Buddhist beads with me for decades. You two must take good care of them, understand?"

"Grandson knows." Wang Fusheng solemnly put

the beads on his wrist.

Duan Yi said to Jiang, "In this case, the matter is settled. Madam Cui, we will be relatives in the future, so we should have more exchanges. Don't rush back today, why not stay and have dinner together."

Jiang forced a smile and said, "Since the princess has said so, I will respectfully obey your order."

Xiuxin knew in her heart that this was probably a good show arranged by Wang Fusheng. The matter of fate is mysterious and changes from time to time. As long as it makes sense, he is really using his own method to treat others. It is extremely insidious. Xiuxin thought sadly that the marriage certificate of the Wang family would be presented in a few days. When the marriage certificate is signed, it will be ironclad and there will be no change.

Wang Fusheng was a gentleman in front of others, a role model for civil officials, and was polite in every move. In front of Jiang, he regarded himself as a junior and was extremely respectful. If he hadn't deliberately rubbed Xiuxin's thigh when no one was paying attention, Xiuxin would have almost been deceived by his serious appearance.

When Xiu Xin's leg was touched by his hand, her whole body froze. She stared at him in disbelief, her cheeks quietly reddened, "You!"

Wang Fusheng smiled softly, looking like a

street scoundrel. "Me? What about me?"

Xiu Xin was now in the Wang family, with people coming and going. Xiu Xin swallowed the words "you touched my thigh" because of the crowd, and cursed in a low voice, "Shameless guy."

Wang Fusheng had no idea that he was a scoundrel, and asked, "Shameless, how am I shameless?"

Xiuxin was so angry that her face turned red and she left angrily.

Wang Fusheng looked at her from behind, and felt a little itchy in his heart. Recently, she seemed to have lost some weight, the soft flesh on her cheeks had disappeared, her face became sharper, and her big eyes looked more lively. When she got angry, her rosy face really made him want to reach out and pinch it. Wang Fusheng thought about it and laughed first, "Little thing, I'm suddenly looking forward to the day when I marry you."

☆, Chapter 24

Chapter 24 Engagement

A few days later, the Wang family's official marriage certificate was delivered to the Cui family, with a complete list of betrothal gifts written on it. The number and value of the betrothal gifts written on the Wang family's list quickly spread throughout the capital. In addition to Jiang and Cui Xiuxin, the entire Cui family was beaming with joy, and congratulations were endless. Even Cui Zhengkai couldn't help but be full of joy. After all, marrying Xiuxin into the Wang family was a great thing for him and the entire Cui family.

In contrast, Yixin's wedding date was getting closer and closer, but no one in the mansion was interested in her. After all, marrying someone as a concubine was not a great honor for the family. Moreover, because Yixin was a concubine, the dowry that should have been allocated to her was much less. Only Feng secretly gave her a portion of her dowry. At this point, Feng could only secretly wipe away tears and lament that her daughter had a miserable life.

"Miss, you are so happy." Xiuxin's wet nurse, Mrs. Zhao, stepped into Xiuxin's boudoir with a smile on her face, "I heard that the marriage certificate of the Wang family has been sent. I, an old woman, would like to congratulate you first!" Mrs. Zhao was not a person who could read people's expressions. She didn't see that Xiuxin looked bad, so she thought she could get some reward by coming in at this time. Seeing that Xiuxin lowered her head and kept silent, she didn't know to stop talking. She still smiled and said, "The Wang family is big and powerful. If you marry into it, you will be the wife of the head of the family, and your husband is the right prime minister of the dynasty. It's really the best. Our third girl is so lucky."

Xiu Xin threw the purse in her hand on the table in annoyance, "Madam Zhao, if you have nothing to do, go talk somewhere else. Why are you talking about this in front of me?"

Lanxiang quickly winked at Mrs. Zhao, "Mrs. Zhao, our young lady is busy making purses and has no time to chat with you. There is still work to do in the backyard, why don't you go out and get busy."

Mrs. Zhao finally came to her senses, said a few words in embarrassment, and left. She had thought she could get something good out of this, but she was criticized again, so she kept mumbling to herself all the way to the corridor outside. Min Xin happened to come over, and she quickly bowed and said, "Fourth Miss."

Min Xin smiled and asked, "Where is Aunt Zhao going?"

Mrs. Zhao sneered, "Where else can she go? The girl has married into a wealthy family, how can she still look down on me, a wet nurse? I am just being sentimental, and I am still thinking that the girl will consider the kindness of an old woman like me who nursed her."

Min Xin said, "Mammy is also an elder in this mansion. Third sister is very happy recently, but she didn't give Mammy a reward?"

Mrs. Zhao said, "Oh, my aunt, where is the reward? She looks so unhappy over there. She is not satisfied with marrying the prime minister. Could it be that she wants to marry the emperor?"

Min Xin rolled her eyes and smiled, "Don't be angry, Madam. You may have encountered her when she was in a bad mood. Maybe it will be better if you go tomorrow."

Mrs. Zhao spat, "I'm not going to get into trouble."

Minxin walked along the corridor and entered Xiuxin's courtyard. Through the window screen, she saw Xiuxin, Lanxiang, and Qinxiang gathered together to make purses. She walked up and knocked on the door gently, "Third sister, I'm Minxin."

"Minxin, come in." Xiuxin said.

"Third sister, is this the purse embroidered for second sister?" Minxin pushed the door open, picked up Xiuxin's purse and took a closer look. "The pattern is really beautiful. Third sister, why don't you let me see the embroidery pattern? I'll embroider an identical one for her according to it." In Huachao, it has always been a custom that when the eldest sister gets married, the other unmarried sisters will embroider a purse for their elder sister as a dowry. Therefore, although Xiuxin and Yixin are not good friends, she must embroider this purse.

After Xiuxin was plotted against, she became more cautious. After thinking for a while, she turned around and took out the embroidery pattern and gave it to Minxin. "Here, this is it. It's all thanks to Lanxiang's skillful hands."

Lan Xiang smiled and said, "Young lady, please don't make fun of me. When it comes to painting, I am just a layman. Our eldest girl is the best among them."

Min Xin thought, "That's right. Big sister is proficient in everything from music, chess, calligraphy and painting. She is a rare talent. But third sister, you are also very good. You married the chief civil official of the dynasty. Many girls envy you, third sister."

Xiu Xin curled her lips slightly, "Min Xin is envious too? It would be great if you could marry her for me."

Min Xin was horrified, "Third sister, are you kidding me? I am just a concubine's daughter, how can I be worthy of the legitimate son of the Wang family?"

"Fourth sister, I was just joking, but you took it seriously. We should quickly embroider this purse, because third sister is getting married on May eighth." Xiuxin held Minxin's hand and said with a smile.

On the evening of the sixth day of May, Ruixiang from Yixin's room rushed into Feng's room in a panic, "Madam, the second young lady... the second young lady has a rash on her body and a high fever. Madam, please go and take a look."

Feng quickly stood up and asked a doctor to

examine Yi Xin. After the doctor felt her pulse, he said that she was poisoned. Everyone was horrified and showed the doctor everything Yi Xin wore. The doctor took out a purse and sniffed it gently. Finally, he said, "This is it. There is poison powder in this purse. Once the skin touches it, you will get rashes all over your body."

Ruixiang looked at the purse and exclaimed, "Isn't that embroidered by the third lady for our second lady?"

As a result, Feng's face changed immediately, "Xiuxin actually dared to murder her own sister. This is an unforgivable crime. I must go and ask for an explanation today!" So she took a few maids and servants and rushed to Xiuxin's courtyard in a hurry.

Xiuxin's courtyard was also brightly lit and noisy. Feng led people in and saw Jiang sitting beside Xiuxin's bed, crying. Feng looked closely and saw that Xiuxin's body was covered with the same rash as Cui Yixin's, which looked very scary.

"This..." After hesitating for a while, Feng took out the purse and threw it on the table. "Second Madam, your daughter poisoned my daughter, and the evidence is conclusive. Now you have to give an explanation! Don't think about getting away with it!" As she spoke, she sat down on the chair.

Jiang wiped away her tears and said, "My

Xiuxin was also poisoned and had rashes all over her body. How could she harm your Yixin and herself?"

Feng said, "Who knows if she is harming others or herself? Do you dare to say that this is not the purse that Xiuxin gave to Yixin?"

"This..." Jiang hesitated.

Seeing Jiang's behavior, Feng thought she had won. She snorted and became more aggressive. "Jiang, your good daughter actually poisoned her own sister. If this gets out, will your Xiuxin still want to marry into the Wang family?"

Jiang looked weak, "How could this be? How could my Xiuxin do such a thing?"

"You still don't admit it?" Feng became more and more angry.

At this time, Lanxiang came over, took the purse on the table, looked through it carefully for a while and said, "Madam, this purse was not made by my daughter."

Feng was stunned, "What did you say?"

Lanxiang turned around and took out an identical purse and said, "The purses made by my daughter always have the word 'embroidery' embroidered on them. Although my daughter has indeed embroidered purses with this kind of pattern, this one is definitely not given by our daughter to the second daughter."

Feng's face immediately turned ugly, like an eggplant hit by frost. "This..."

Lanxiang tilted her head and thought for a

while, then let out a long "oh" as if she had just remembered something, "Oh, I remember now, I remember that the fourth girl took the embroidery pattern away. Since this purse is not our girl's, then it must be the fourth girl's. I remember that after the fourth girl finished making the purse, she showed it to my girl."

Jiang immediately said, "The matter is clear now. Now my daughter Xiuxin has also been poisoned. It is most likely that she was harmed by that little bitch. My son!" She cried and said in hatred, "What are you standing there for? Why don't you go and tie up that little bitch?"

Feng also responded dryly, "She really should be taught a lesson! A concubine's daughter is so arrogant that she wants to cause trouble!"

Minxin was dragged to the courtyard by Jiang, who ordered her to be severely whipped ten times, returning the whippings Cui Zhengkai had given her last time with interest. This time, the little girl next to Minxin also went to the front yard to report to Cui Zhengkai, but this time Cui Zhengkai turned a deaf ear and only said, "She did it herself, she has to bear the consequences herself, let her go."

After the ten lashes, Jiang was still not satisfied. She slapped Minxin hard and said angrily, "I felt sorry for you because you lost your mother at such a young age. I treated you well and gave you everything you deserved. I even took extra care of you. But you were not only ungrateful, but also tried to harm Xiuxin. I really raised an ungrateful person! You are living a good life, but you insist on going down a dead end. Don't blame me, your legal mother, for being cruel!"

Min Xin glared at Jiang and snorted, "You have never treated me badly? Who in the entire Cui Mansion treats me as a legitimate master? But what about your own daughter? You are afraid of dropping her if you hold her in your hands, and afraid of melting her if you hold her in your mouth! We have the same father, why is her life so good!"

Jiang sneered, "You are the one who was born into a good family. It would be fine if you just accepted your bad fate, but you still made trouble. You are in this situation now, and it is your own fault!"

Jiang paused and looked up at everyone, "All of you keep a close eye on the fourth girl and don't let her leave the courtyard. Do you hear me?"

"Yes," everyone responded, knowing in their hearts that the fourth girl was completely ruined.

Yixin and Xiuxin were both poisoned and had rashes, but the difference was that Yixin's fever subsided after a few days, and the rash gradually disappeared. However, Xiuxin's rash did not subside at all, but grew more and more, and the high fever did not subside. Jiang was so anxious that she cried every day and lost a lot of weight.

In the evening, Jiang invited Doctor Chen to see the patient. Doctor Chen felt Xiuxin's pulse through the curtain and said, "Second Madam, logically speaking, after the Third Miss took the medicine I prescribed, the rash should have disappeared long ago. Moreover, the Third Miss's pulse is steady and strong, and she doesn't sound like a sick person. I think..."

Jiang said slowly, "Doctor Chen, you have to look carefully. My daughter Xiuxin has rashes all over her body and has a high fever. Is she suffering from smallpox?"

"Ah?" Doctor Chen took a few steps back and said in embarrassment, "This..."

Jiang put a gold ingot into Doctor Chen's hand and said, "Just say that the poison powder caused the smallpox symptoms and send Xiuxin to the countryside to be isolated and recuperate. Do you understand?"

Doctor Chen suddenly understood and said repeatedly, "I understand, I understand."

☆, Chapter 25: Pretending to be sick

Chapter 25 Pretending to be sick
The next day, the news that Cui Xiuxin, the third daughter of the Cui family, had fallen ill and was sent to the countryside to recuperate spread throughout the capital.

People in the capital were discussing the matter and were looking at the Wang family's statement. Unexpectedly, Princess Duanyi said that she would never cancel the engagement and that the Wang family would definitely wait for Cui's third daughter to recover before getting married. Everyone praised the Wang family for being a model of aristocratic families and being affectionate and righteous.

Xiuxin was nominally sent to the countryside for quarantine, but Jiang secretly sent her to Jiang's mansion in Chenzhou, Jiang's natal home. Along with Xiuxin were Lanxiang, Qinxiang, Cuixiang, and Lianxiang, as well as the grooms and servants, in a total of three carriages.

On the day of her departure, Xiuxin wore a light green top, a lotus-colored gauze skirt, and a veil on her face. The curtains of the carriage were so tightly drawn that the entire carriage was covered completely, and outsiders could not see a single clue of what was inside.

Jiang held Xiuxin's hand and cried, "My son, I can't go with you. You must be careful at your uncle's house. I see that the Wang family will never cancel this marriage unless you... otherwise. The only way now is for you to live at your uncle's house first. After a month, I will let my brother spread the word that you died suddenly of illness. In this way, your marriage with the Wang family will naturally be invalid."

Xiu Xin was also very sad, "But mother, even if I can successfully marry off as my uncle's daughter, I... I am not your daughter after all... I am afraid that even if I see you in the future, I will have to call you aunt."

Jiang said, "What can I do? For your lifelong happiness, this sacrifice is worth it. As a mother, I can't just watch you marry into a dangerous place, right?"

Xiu Xin sighed, "The Wang family is really too bullying, forcing us to resort to this desperate measure. But mother, you must control the servants' mouths and never let the news spread. If the Wang family gets to know, I'm afraid there will be another storm."

Jiang said, "I have already arranged this. My daughter, remember that before your death is announced, you must not take off your veil and let others see your appearance. Do you understand?"

Xiu Xin nodded. The two of them said goodbye to each other for a long time before Jiang got off the carriage and watched the three carriages gallop away. She returned home sadly when she could no longer see their shadows.

The direct line of the Jiang family is in Chenzhou, and Jiang's eldest brother Jiang Yunhai is the current head of the Jiang family. Before this, Jiang had already sent a letter to explain the whole story, so Jiang Yunhai had already prepared Xiuxin's room and all the necessary items, and sent someone to the ferry to pick up Xiuxin.

After traveling all the way by water, Xiuxin was exhausted. Lanxiang helped Xiuxin get off the boat and saw two servants in green jackets standing at the ferry to greet people. "Is it the third daughter of the Cui family?"

Xiu Xin nodded, "That's right."

The servant smiled and said, "Our master sent us to pick up Miss Cousin. Please get in the car quickly, Miss Cousin."

Xiu Xin took a carriage to Jiang's house. A maid came to the door to greet her. She helped Xiu Xin get out of the carriage and said, "Cousin, you are finally here. The master has been missing you for several days."

Xiuxin thanked her and followed the nanny slowly. Chenzhou is a wealthy place in the south of the Yangtze River. Although the Jiang family is not as powerful as the four major families in the capital, it is also the largest aristocratic family in the south of the Yangtze River. Therefore, the furnishings in the mansion are also quite exquisite. The pavilions, towers, bridges, flowing water, and gardens are very different from those in the capital, showing a different kind of exquisiteness, which Xiuxin secretly marveled at.

When she walked to the main hall, she knew that she had reached her uncle and aunt's residence, so she moved more carefully. She saw two people sitting upstairs, one was a middle-aged man in his forties wearing a blue gown, and the other was a middle-aged beautiful woman in gorgeous clothes. She knew that they were her uncle and aunt, so she took off her veil, stepped forward and bowed, "Greetings, uncle and aunt."

Jiang Yunhai loved his sister Jiang the most in his early years. Now he saw that Xiuxin's eyebrows and eyes were quite similar to Jiang's. In addition, she behaved well. She was really a crystal clear little beauty. Therefore, he immediately felt pity for her. "Ah, niece, you really look like your mother. From now on, just treat this as your home. Now that you are here, my unruly daughter will have a companion." Jiang Yunhai paused and moved his eyes to the fifteen or sixteen-year-old girl on the side, "Zixuan, why don't you come and meet your sister!"

The girl was as noisy as Cui Yuxin. She immediately jumped up to Xiuxin and pulled her hand, saying in a sweet voice, "Sister, it's great that you're here. I'm the only girl in my family, and I don't even have anyone to cheer me up on weekdays."

Xiu Xin smiled and said, "Then we can just stay together."

Jiang Yunhai's legitimate wife, Wu, also smiled and said, "Xiu Xin, just tell me what you lack."

Xiu Xin bowed and said, "Thank you, aunt."

In this way, Xiuxin finally settled down in

the Jiang family in Chenzhou. Everything was fine in the Jiang family, except that she occasionally missed Jiang and Jiang Zixuan was too annoying, Xiuxin was very happy in the Jiang mansion.

Half a month later, it happened to be the Dragon Boat Festival on the fifth day of the fifth lunar month. Lanxiang had already made a sachet to ward off evil spirits. The sachet contained cinnabar, realgar wine, and fragrant herbs, and was wrapped in embroidered silk cloth. It was fragrant and then tied into a rope with five-color silk threads. It was very beautiful when worn around the waist. However, what Xiuxin was most interested in was not the sachet, nor the realgar wine, but the fragrant rice dumplings.

Qinxiang peeled off the leaves and served it to Xiuxin on a plate, and she scooped out the food with a spoon to avoid getting her hands dirty. Among all kinds of zongzi, Xiuxin's favorite was the candied fruit zongzi, which tasted sweet and refreshing. Before she knew it, Xiuxin had already eaten two. Lanxiang saw that Xiuxin had a big appetite and couldn't help but say, "Miss, you should use less of this sticky stuff. Don't you remember that you used too much cakes last time and caused a stomachache at night?"

Jiang Shi had always told her since she was a child that eating too much was not good for her, so Xiu Xin didn't eat much either.

She cleaned her mouth with tea and said, "Let's save it for tomorrow." Qin Xiang smiled and said, "If you were at home, would the Second Madam still indulge you to eat as much as you want?" Xiu Xin said, "But we are at home, aren't we?"

As the master and his servants were talking, a girl in bright yellow clothes came in through the curtain and said with a smile, "Sister Xiuxin, Sister Xiuxin!"

Jiang Zixuan ran in. Xiu Xin helped her up and asked with a smile, "What are you so happy about?"

Zixuan said excitedly, "I heard that there is a dragon boat race in Qianjiang today. My dear sister, come with me to take a look."

Xiu Xin shook her head, "No way, I can't go with you." Now is a sensitive period, how can she go out and show her face in public? What if someone spreads the news that the third daughter of the Cui family has recovered from her illness to the capital, wouldn't everything be lost?

Zi Xuan said coquettishly, "Sister, please come with me. The dragon boat race is very lively. It only happens once a year. Besides, we can sit in the boat and watch. Sister doesn't have to show up in public, so there's no need to worry."

Xiu Xin was originally a lively person, and she was slightly moved by what she said, so she said, "Okay, we can go, but we have to inform my uncle and aunt first."

Zi Xuan said, "Don't worry about these sisters. I have already informed my father and mother."

The bow of the dragon boat is carved into the shape of a dragon head and dyed with colorful colors. The boatmen are all wearing yellow short shirts and red headscarves. With the shouting of rowing horns, dozens of dragon boats are speeding away like arrows from a string. The scene is very spectacular. On both sides of the Qianjiang River, there are dozens of boats floating in twos and threes. These are used by the wealthy families in Chenzhou to watch the dragon boat race. Other people are crowded on both sides of the river or on the bridge.

Zixuan was lively and ran to the bow to watch the fun. She jumped and shouted when she saw something exciting. She turned around and pulled Xiuxin from the cabin, "Sister, what can you see in there? Come out." Xiuxin shook her head quickly, "No, I can't go." Zixuan said, "Sister, aren't you wearing a veil? This place is so far from the capital, who can recognize you as the third daughter of the Cui family? Relax your mind."

Xiuxin was also eager to go, so she got up and followed Zixuan to the bow. The bow had a wide view, and the breeze on the river blew Xiuxin's light green gauze skirt like a butterfly flapping its wings. Zixuan was beside Xiuxin and talked to her with a beaming smile. Xiuxin was influenced by her and forgot the unhappiness of recent days, and smiled.

At this time, another ship was approaching Xiuxin's ship from behind. On the bow, a man in white stood facing the wind, like a jade tree, but his brows were furrowed, as if he was worried. The boatman on the bow said, "Mr. Li, today is such a lively day, why are you still frowning?"

Li Yuzhi shook her head and smiled, "Nothing, I just thought of the old things in Beijing, and I feel a little melancholy." It has been a month since he came to Chenzhou. The governor of Chenzhou intends to marry his daughter to him. He has no intention, but now he has reached the age of twenty, and his mother is urging him to get married. It is time for him to find a girl who matches him and get married. But when he thinks of her, he is still upset. The bitter feeling in his heart cannot be shaken off no matter what. Li Yuzhi sighed in his heart. Maybe she has already been engaged to Wang Chaozong?

Zixuan was originally fascinated by the dragon boat, but she accidentally saw a young man in white standing on the bow of the boat next to her. He had black hair and elegant demeanor, and her eyes were fixed on the young man for some reason. Can't move it. Xiu Xin followed Zixuan's gaze and looked to the side. Her whole body seemed to be frozen and motionless, and her heart began to beat loudly. Li Yuzhi, he is actually here?

It turned out that he was sent here for official duties, and he also fled to Chenzhou. It seemed that something was destined for the two to meet again. The more he thought about it, the more excited he became. She wanted to call him Mr. Li, but she couldn't. In public, Xiu Xin was determined not to do such a thing, so she could only look at him silently, hoping that he would turn his gaze.

As if being induced, Li Yuzhi turned around. His eyes first crossed Zixuan's face, and then settled on Xiuxin's face. Although the girl was covered, those eyes were unusually familiar, because those eyes had appeared in his eyes countless times. In a dream.

"Master Li..." Xiu Xin called silently in her heart, her eyes anxious. Did he recognize me? She had so many things to say to him. She wanted to ask him, why hasn't he come to Cui's house to propose marriage for so long?

☆, Chapter 26 A strange combination of circumstances

Chapter 26 A strange combination of circumstances

Li Yuzhi felt as if a thunderbolt flashed through his heart. This girl's eyes were so similar to Xiuxin's, and her figure was somewhat similar. However, he was not sure that Xiuxin should be in Cui Mansion in the capital. How could she come to Chenzhou?

Seeing Li Yuzhi's complicated expression, Xiuxin knew that he was not sure. She was so anxious that she almost wanted to take off the veil she was wearing. She held back for a long time before turning around and wanted to go back to the cabin to write a note and quietly throw it to him. Zixuan saw Xiuxin return to the cabin and asked, "Sister Xiuxin, don't you want to take a look? Why did you come back?"

Zixuan's voice was not loud, but it was loud enough for Li Yuzhi to hear clearly.

Xiuxin, Cui Xiuxin, it was actually Xiuxin, she actually came to Chenzhou! Li Yuzhi was so excited that he wanted to ask the boatman to stop the boat and rush aboard to see her! After changing his mind, he thought again, no, this can't be done, this boat belongs to the Jiang family, so she must be living in the Jiang family now, as long as there is a chance to go to the Jiang family, there will be a chance to see her.

Thinking of this, I couldn't help but smile again.

Something must have happened, otherwise how could she come to Chenzhou when she was about to get engaged? Could it be that she was not engaged to Wang Chaozong at all? When she thought of this possibility, Li Yuzhi's heart was so excited that it seemed to jump out of her chest.

"Yuzhi, why are you so happy?" A slightly hoarse male voice sounded, bringing Li Yuzhi back from her thoughts.

Li Yuzhi bowed and said, "Teacher, I just remembered some funny things in the past, so I laughed."

Wang Fusheng curled his fist and coughed softly, "You have been in Chenzhou for a month. What have you gained?"

Li Yuzhi said, "Chenzhou is a place of wealth in Jiangnan, but several big families are very powerful. Many of them not only monopolize the tea, salt, cloth and other businesses, but also interfere in government affairs. They even privately raise thousands of slaves, which are like an army. Therefore, all the governors of Chenzhou have been unable to do anything. They really can't control it, and they can't control it."

Wang Fusheng nodded, "It's indeed a difficult problem. I came to Chenzhou this time to supervise the construction of flood control dikes. Since the governor of Chenzhou has no money to spend, we have to use our brains to get help from a few noble families."

Li Yuzhi lowered her head and said, "Teacher is right. I am thinking of a way to solve the problem of the money needed to build the flood embankment." After a pause, Li Yuzhi said, "Teacher has caught a cold recently. It is better not to stand at the bow and sit in the cabin to drink a cup of hot tea."

Wang Fusheng coughed and shook his head, "Nothing, just some fresh air. Today is the Dragon Boat Festival, so if I don't watch the dragon boat race, wouldn't it be a waste of time?"

Xiu Xin returned to the cabin, took out a piece of paper, and wrote a line of words with a pen: Master Li, have you been doing well since we parted at Zhengjue Temple? I have something important to ask you, Master Li, can you find a chance to meet me? Cui Xiu Xin stayed.

Xiuxin rolled up the note and was about to go out of the cabin to find an opportunity to throw it to Li Yuzhi when she suddenly heard a familiar male voice and her whole body froze. She heard the man talking intermittently and was suspicious. She lifted a corner of the curtain and looked out. There was clearly a tall man standing next to Mr. Li in white. The man was dressed in green, tall and graceful.

Surprisingly, surprisingly, it was Wang Fusheng, why did he come to Chenzhou? Xiuxin was so frightened that her hands trembled, and she quickly let down the curtain.

The sharp-eyed Wang Fusheng noticed the curtain of the boat next door move, and saw the word "Jiang" written on the boat. He couldn't help but feel suspicious, "Yuzhi, is the boat next to us owned by the Jiang family of Chenzhou?" He remembered that the

Jiang family of Chenzhou was the home of Cui Xiuxin's uncle.
"

Wang Fusheng got on the carriage early in the morning, and the group headed to Shangxin Garden in the suburbs of the city. Wang Fusheng was thinking all the way, what would her reaction be when she saw him later? He thought about it, and his heart became more and more uneasy. He wished he could grow wings and fly to Xiuxin to see what her expression was when she saw him.

No matter what, even if Xiuxin was pretending, he always hoped that she would be happy when she saw him.

Thinking of this, Wang Fusheng became a little nervous again. Alas, he sighed in his heart. He was also a man who had seen big scenes. He really didn't know why he had become so worried.

However, Wang Fusheng had never expected that this would be the scene when he saw Xiuxin. Xiuxin was riding on a horse, and a man in red stood beside her. Xiuxin nervously held the reins. Suddenly, the horse suddenly ran, and Xiuxin screamed and fell off the horse. Wang Fusheng was still far away from Xiuxin at this time, and he ran forward a few steps, his heart hanging in his throat. Falling from such a high place is not a joke, at the least, the hand will be injured, and at the worst, it will be...

Wang Fusheng closed his eyes briefly, and

when he opened them again, Xiuxin was lying in the arms of the man in red. Wang Fusheng breathed a sigh of relief, and a green fire burned from his chest to his head. Who was this man? He actually appeared in Shangxin Garden? He was still holding Xiuxin! He actually held her for such a long time without letting go?

Green clouds cover the sky...

Wang Fusheng felt his face turning green.

Wang Fusheng was about to rush over to catch the adulterer, but the man actually flirted with Xiuxin in front of him, touching her face, pinching her arms, and... It is simply unbearable to look at, it is so immoral, so immoral!

In anger, Wang Fusheng didn't care about anything else and wanted to rush over and catch him in the act. Mo Yan finally stopped him, "My Lord, if you expose this kind of thing, it's the Wang family that's in trouble."

Wang Fusheng clenched his hands tightly, his eyes almost spitting fire, "Cui Xiuxin! No wonder you were so reluctant at first, it turned out that..."

After Xiu Xin and Zhan Xue returned to Shang Xin Garden, Lan Xiang came up to them and said, "Miss, the Second Master is here."

Why is he here? Xiu Xin's heart was beating fast, and she said to Zhan Xue, "You should go back to your room first, he has come to Shang Xin Garden."

Zhan Xue blinked her eyes, "It feels like a long time since we last met. I think Wang Fusheng still cares about you." Xiu Xin spit at her and said, "You are still an unmarried girl. It's easy for you to say such things. You have no shame."

Zhan Xue smiled and pushed her, "Okay, go and take care of my aunt, or your husband will be waiting anxiously."

Xiuxin walked into the room with a smile on her face. Wang Fusheng had been waiting for her and was drinking a glass of wine. Xiuxin saw that he looked unfriendly, and her heart skipped a beat. The smile on her face also disappeared, and she called out softly, "Husband..."

Wang Fusheng put the wine glass heavily on the table, raised his head and looked at Xiu Xin coldly, "You still remember to come back?"

Xiu Xin thought his question was inexplicable, "Of course I know I'm back."

Wang Fusheng saw Xiuxin's calmness, and the fire in his chest grew stronger and stronger, almost burning away his rationality. He finally stopped the urge to kill and asked, "Where did you go just now?"

Xiu thought that the Wang family valued appearance and moral character the most. If she said she went out to ride a horse, she might just cause trouble. So she just said, "I just had dinner and went out for a walk. Why did you come here suddenly, my husband?

You didn't even send me a message before you came?"

Wang Fusheng snorted coldly, "If I had sent you a letter in advance, would you still be able to see the show?"

Xiu Xin asked in confusion, "What's going on?" Xiu Xin was full of confusion. Why was Wang Fusheng so weird today? His face was so ugly, and he kept saying weird things...

"You..." He wanted to say it directly, but he held back. He thought, Xiuxin seemed so innocent, how could she suddenly have a lover? And she brought him to Shangxin Garden in broad daylight? Even if she was stupid, she wouldn't do such a thing, right? But who was that man? Could it be that his eyes could deceive him?

"Are there any guests in Shangxin Garden?" Wang Fusheng asked tentatively.

Xiu Xin's face changed. No way, he knew about Zhan Xue as soon as he arrived?

Wang Fusheng's heart broke when he saw Xiuxin's expression change. Did she really hide something from him? Did she really do something immoral?

"Husband, I was wrong. I shouldn't have kept it from you..."

Haha, you should have discussed it with me in advance before you started dating a strange man?

"I won't do this again next time." Xiu Xin said pitifully, "You're not angry, are you?"

It would be strange if I wasn't angry!

"Zhan Xue and I are good friends. After I married you, it became difficult for us to see each other, so I invited her to Shangxin Garden for a small gathering..." etc!

"Battle Snow?"

"It's the daughter of the Duke of Protectorate, Liu Zhanxue."

Wang Fusheng stared at Xiuxin with eyes wide open, "The one who was riding with you just now was the daughter of the Duke of Huguo?"

"Exactly."

Wang Fusheng was immediately happy, "So it's her. Tsk, I've heard that the daughter of the Duke of the Guard loves to dress like a man. She's unique in the capital. Why didn't I think of it?" Wang Fusheng said as he looked Xiuxin up and down carefully, as if he was examining his beloved treasure. "Are you feeling better? You seem to be in better shape."

"Much better." Xiuxin complained in her heart, how could it not be good if she left the Wang family?

Wang Fusheng had been missing her to begin with, and he had just experienced such a shock. Seeing Xiuxin looking at him with a smile, his heart was inevitably moved. He stretched out his hand and pinched Xiuxin's delicate nose, "I have finished my recent official duties. Except for attending the morning court every day, I will stay with you in Shangxin Garden."

Xiu Xin instinctively said, "No."

"Hmm?" Wang Fusheng's face changed slightly. Xiuxin quickly added, "Zhanxue is also in Shangxinyuan, and she is still an unmarried girl. Isn't this bad for her reputation?" Xiuxin meant that since Zhanxue is here, it would be inconvenient for you to stay there, so you might as well go back to the Wang family. Goodbye.

Wang Fusheng thought for a moment and said, "It's okay. Shangxin Garden is so big, I just need to stay away from her. Besides, although unmarried girls should not show their faces in public, they don't have to avoid men completely. Otherwise, where do those romantic stories of cousins come from?" What he meant was, I don't care, but for the sake of that Miss Liu, let her get as far away as possible and don't get in the way of my husband and me.

Xiuxin knew he was talking about Xie Yulan, the daughter of the Xie family. She had an ambiguous relationship with her cousin, but they were not destined to be together. Some time ago, when Xiuxin and Wang Fusheng were about to get married, Xie Yulan resolutely cut her hair and became a nun in order to reject the marriage proposal from the young Marquis of Hengyang. At that time, the sensation caused by this incident was no less than the incident 20 years ago when Concubine Xie was selected to serve the emperor in the palace.

Xiu Xin sighed, "Xie Yulan was a strong-willed woman. She could give up all her glory for the man she loved, but her beloved husband could easily marry someone else, and there would be more women in the future. It's pitiful and lamentable. How much room could Sun Peifang have in her heart for Xie Yulan, who had shaved her head and become a nun at that time?"

Wang Fusheng said, "The most important thing for a woman is self-respect and self-love. Xie Yulan, as the legitimate daughter of the Xie family, was involved with her cousin and ruined her reputation. It was her own fault."

Xiu Xin didn't comment. In fact, she admired Xie Yulan in her heart. It was rare for her to have such determination to do this. Although it was not worth it for her to make such a sacrifice.

Liu Zhanxue's eldest maid Qingxue was brought back from outside the Great Wall. In addition to having some martial arts skills, she is also calm and reliable, courageous and resourceful. She has given Zhanxue many suggestions on many things, "Miss, the second master of the Wang family is back. Shouldn't we go back? Otherwise, if there are rumors outside, it will be bad."

But Zhan Xue is not an ordinary person. "What are you afraid of? I am not even afraid of the Hu people, so why should I be afraid of those rumors?"

"But the girl is still unmarried. If we

meet in Shangxin Garden, wouldn't it be embarrassing?" Qingxue saw that Zhanxue seemed a little shaken, and continued, "Besides, doesn't the girl already have a man in her heart? I guess that man is also the son of an aristocratic family. These aristocratic families attach great importance to these red tapes."

Zhan Xue was finally persuaded, "Okay, let's go say goodbye to Xiu Xin after lunch."

Qingxue then smiled, "Okay, I'll go pack my luggage right away."

After Xiuxin and Wang Fusheng finished lunch, Qingxue knocked on the door and said, "Madam Wang, my daughter wants to say goodbye to you. Please come out for a moment."

Xiu Xin hurriedly got up and opened the door, "Why are you leaving?" She has only lived here for a few days. It's all Wang Fusheng's fault. He came to Shangxin Garden for no reason and it's a rare opportunity to spend a few days with Zhan Xue.

Qingxue smiled and said, "My daughter has been bothering Madam for a few days. It's time to say goodbye."

Xiu Xin could only say, "Well, well, ask her to wait for a while, and I'll pack up and see her off."

Xiu Xin only has Zhan Xue as her close friend, and Zhan Xue also rarely meets a close friend, so the two of them are reluctant to part. They held hands and talked for a long time beside the Shangxin Lake, reluctantly.

Wang Fusheng looked at him from a distance and felt a little jealous. Xiuxin rarely smiled at him and would always stay away from him. Even though her attitude towards him had softened a little now, Dan Ye had never seen her smile so happily at him. What's more... Wang Fusheng stared at Zhan Xue fiercely. This young lady of the Liu family didn't look like a girl at all. From such a distance, she looked no different from a man...

Wait...

A thought tickled his tense nerves. Zhan Xue looked so manly, and Xiu Xin was...

He was just daydreaming when he saw Zhan Xue hugging Xiu Xin on the other side. Xiu Xin neither struggled nor was surprised, but just let her hug her. It was a long time before they let go.

Wang Fusheng held his forehead with a headache, "No, I have a headache..."

Mo Yan asked worriedly, "Master, what's wrong with you? Do you want to see a doctor?"

The author has something to say: There will be updates tomorrow.

☆, Chapter 53 Kitchen

Chapter 53: Kitchen
Xiuxin has been in a trance since Zhanxue left, not for any other reason, but because

the man Zhanxue had set his eyes on was none other than her "son" Wang Chaozong. But it was obvious that the Wang family had no intention of marrying. Therefore, Xiuxin kept making excuses, saying that she had not found the person she was looking for, so as not to make her sad. Zhanxue mentioned that matter to her just now. According to her, if the husband she married was not him, she would rather not marry for the rest of her life. When she thought of this, Xiuxin sighed sadly in her heart.

"Embroidered Heart!"

"Ah?" Xiu Xin suddenly came to her senses after being called by Wang Fusheng. "What's the matter?"

"What are you thinking about? You've been absent-minded the whole afternoon." Wang Fusheng put down the book in his hand. "Look at you, your sleeves are stained with ink, didn't you see it?"

Xiu Xin stopped grinding ink and looked down. As expected, there was a large black stain on her pink cuff. She cried out, "How could this happen?"

Wang Fusheng felt a little sour. Xiuxin had been in such a state of despair since Liu Zhanxue left. Could it be that she was really...

In the boudoir, lonely women often comfort each other to relieve their loneliness. But those are dirty things between widows, and an unmarried girl like Xiuxin should not understand these things. Moreover, the Cui family has very strict family education. Xiuxin didn't even know about the relationship between men and women before, let alone such things?

But how do we explain their extraordinary intimacy?

When Wang Fusheng thought of this, he felt like there was a small thorn in his heart. He wanted to pinch it but it was too small to pick up. If he left it alone, he would feel uncomfortable and found himself in a dilemma.

"Husband, I'm going to change my clothes. Please wait for me for a moment." Xiu Xin said.

Wang Fusheng said, "Come on, I see you've been sitting with me for so long and you're getting bored. Let's go to the Shangxin Lake and pick some osmanthus flowers. Don't you love osmanthus cake the most?"

At this moment, Xiu Xin showed a sincere smile, "Okay, I'll go prepare a cloth bag now."

Wang Fusheng saw Xiuxin's smiling face and felt relieved. "I'll wait for you by the lake."

Although Shangxin Lake is not as big as Wangjiayang Lake, it is exquisite and small, and the scenery on both sides of the lake is superb, giving it a unique Jiangnan flavor.

"The layout and furnishings of this Shangxin Garden are very similar to the pavilions and towers in the south of the Yangtze River. Although these are very common in Yanzhou and other places, they are rarely seen in the capital." Wang Fusheng said.

"Of course. This was built by my father in imitation of the Su Garden where my mother lived before she got married."

Wang Fusheng smiled and said, "It's because your mother loves you so much that she is willing to give you such a nice villa as a dowry."

"Of course my mother loves me." Xiu Xin said, "Since I was a child, every time I was sick, my mother took care of me personally and never asked anyone else to do it."

Wang Fusheng couldn't help but sigh. His mother was very strict with him. He would be punished to kneel down if he made the slightest mistake. Now, he respected and appreciated her, but they were rarely intimate. He shook his head and laughed as he thought that his son was old enough to get married, but he was sighing about this. It was really boring.

Xiuxin picked a small bag of osmanthus flowers in a short while, "Let's go, I want to make this osmanthus cake myself this time."

Wang Fusheng was quite surprised, "Can you do it?"

Xiu Xin glared at him, "Of course I can. I'm not very good at music, chess, calligraphy, or painting. What do you think I spend my time on?" Wang Fusheng laughed and said, "You're honest."

Wash the osmanthus with well water, boil it in clean water for a while, pick it up and put it in honey. On the other hand, put the gelatin powder into the pot, boil and stir, then add osmanthus honey and brown sugar.

Lanxiang had already prepared a mold with a flower pattern on the side, and Xiuxin scooped up the boiling juice and poured it into the mold.

At this time, Qin Xiang's voice sounded outside the door, "Second Master, why are you here?"

Xiu Xin looked up and saw Wang Fusheng striding in. She was stunned and looked at him at a loss, holding a big spoon in her hand. "Husband?"

Wang Fusheng saw how adorable she looked when she was dumbfounded, and asked with a smile, "What's wrong? Are you frightened?"

Xiu Xin shook her head and said as she pulled Wang Fusheng out, "Didn't the ancient saying say that a gentleman should stay away from the kitchen? Even a scholar would not come here. Why are you here, my husband?"

"We should follow the ancient rituals, but we should not be blind. If we follow the old rules in everything, won't we be stuck?" Wang Fusheng said with a smile, "Take the example of a gentleman staying away from the kitchen. Does it mean that a gentleman is not a gentleman if he stays close to the kitchen? On the other hand, does it mean that a gentleman is a gentleman if he stays away from the kitchen? A gentleman and a kitchen are two different things."

Xiu Xin was still a little confused, "Does my husband mean that a gentleman should not stay away from the kitchen?"

Wang Fusheng shook his head and said, "This is just one of the meanings. Just like now, the court is always clinging to old rules. Many things have blinded their eyes, and they only stubbornly adhere to the ancestral etiquette and laws."

"Seeking innovation and change?"

Wang Fusheng looked at her in surprise, "You know?"

Xiu Xin shook her head, "Zhan Xue told me."

Although Xiu Xin didn't care about politics, she knew the basics, such as the fact that Wang Fusheng and his party were trying to reform and implement new policies, while Cui Jinyi and his party were strongly opposed and obstructed the implementation of new policies. The dispute between the Wang and Cui families had gradually intensified, and the confrontations in the court were increasing day by day.

Wang Fusheng nodded, "That's right. But although these four words are easy to say, it's probably extremely difficult to take a step forward..."

Xiuxin looked at Wang Fusheng and for the

first time felt that he was not just the eldest son of the Wang family who was seeking fame and reputation, nor a playboy. He actually had many deep thoughts and ambitions that she could not understand.

"My husband, will your new policy make everyone's life better and better?"

"That's natural," Wang Fusheng said, "otherwise there would be no point in implementing the new policy."

Xiu Xin stopped and said, "Although I don't understand, I believe in you. Your new policy must be better than that of Cui Jinyi."

Wang Fusheng was overwhelmed with emotions. It had been three years since the new policy was implemented, but he had encountered countless obstacles and it was difficult at every step. Many times, even he thought about giving up. Because after giving up, life was much easier. Many times, if he was not the legitimate son of the Wang family, the position of right prime minister would have been changed long ago. However, at this moment, Xiu Xin could trust him so completely, which made him feel extremely relieved and happy.

Wang Fusheng secretly grasped Xiuxin's hand hidden in her wide sleeves and squeezed it gently, "With what you said, I can't give up easily, otherwise wouldn't I be betraying your trust?"

In the evening, Lanxiang brought up the osmanthus cakes that Xiuxin had made during the day. Pieces of flower-shaped, crystal-clear lotus flower cakes were placed on a delicate blue-and-white patterned plate. If you look closely, you can see small osmanthus flowers. If you smell it closely, you can also smell the faint fragrance of osmanthus. It is really delicious.

Wang Fusheng was studying a rare Go book at the table, and he couldn't help but look up when he smelled the smell. Xiuxin couldn't help it, so she took a piece of slightly warm osmanthus cake and put it in her mouth, and took a bite with a whine. Wang Fusheng saw that Xiuxin was eating so sweetly, and he also had an appetite, so he came over and sat beside Xiuxin, watching her silently.

Xiu Xin swallowed the whole piece of osmanthus cake, then turned her gaze to Wang Fusheng, "What's wrong? Husband, you don't want to read anymore?"

Wang Fusheng felt a little suffocated. He couldn't just say that he wanted to eat too, could he? Xiu Xin was too slow. If it were any other girl, she would have come over to him and coquettishly fed him herself.

Fortunately, Xiu Xin was not too stupid and gave him a piece. "Husband, would you like to try it too?"

Xiuxin had beautiful hands. Her skin was naturally fair, and one of her bare hands was as white as fine porcelain. Her fingers were long and slender, and there was no bright red nail polish on her nails. At this moment, she was holding a crystal clear osmanthus cake in her hand. In just a moment, Wang Fusheng had the urge to swallow the cake together.

"Feed me."

Xiu Xin's eyes widened slightly and she stared at him with her mouth slightly open.

"Hmm? Don't want to feed your husband?"

Xiuxin didn't dare to refuse him openly, so she could only bite the bullet and hand the osmanthus cake to his mouth.

Wang Fusheng ate the osmanthus cake bite by bite while holding Xiuxin's hand. When he took the last bite, he lowered his head, smiled wickedly, and put the osmanthus cake and Xiuxin's finger into his mouth together. Xiuxin was completely stunned and her face turned red. However, Wang Fusheng did not intend to let her go easily. After swallowing the osmanthus cake, he lightly swept his tongue around Xiuxin's fingertips. Xiuxin hurriedly pulled out her fingers, but her two fingers were slightly wet, which made her feel indescribably embarrassed.

Wang Fusheng laughed softly, "Look at you, your face is so red." However, she lowered her head with a slightly red face, which was really lovable. Wang Fusheng couldn't bear it, so he stood up and picked up Xiuxin horizontally, put her gently on the bed, and pressed his whole body on her.

Xiu Xin's face turned pale in an instant. At this moment, how could Xiu Xin not understand what was about to happen? However, the pain she had felt last time made her tremble with fear when she thought about it.

How could Wang Fusheng not understand the person under him in such a state? He couldn't help but sigh in his heart and lowered his head to kiss Xiuxin's forehead.

Xiuxin closed her eyes tightly. She felt his delicate and long kiss spread from her forehead to her nose, then to her cheek, and finally he gently kissed her lips.

Xiuxin's hands tightly clasped the bed sheet, as if this could be her only support. However, Wang Fusheng's right hand slowly came down, held Xiuxin's hand, and interlocked their fingers.

There was a faint sweet scent of osmanthus between Xiuxin's lips and tongue, which made Wang Fusheng's movements become more rapid, no longer gentle at the beginning, and his tongue pressed in forcefully, rubbing back and forth between Xiuxin's lips and tongue. Wang Fusheng's breathing became more and more rapid, and Xiuxin's face became more and more red.

Finally, Xiuxin couldn't stand it anymore and pushed him softly. Wang Fusheng finally let go. Xiuxin took a break and gasped for air, "I... I'm almost suffocating..."

Wang Fusheng was so shocked by these words that he stretched out his hand and pinched Xiuxin's nose, "Don't you know how to breathe through your nose?"

Xiu Xin stared at him blankly for a long while before she said stupidly, "I forgot..."

Wang Fusheng laughed even more when he heard this. He hugged Xiuxin and kissed her on the lips, "You are such a living treasure."

The author has something to say: The relationship between a man and a woman originally started with the most primitive impulse. The male protagonist has a crush on the female protagonist, so he can't help it. This shows that the female protagonist has formed a fatal attraction to him. There is a saying that goes, you don't have to worry about a man being lustful, as long as he likes your lust.

☆, Chapter 54 Wontons

Chapter 54 Wontons

Wang Fusheng laughed for a while and then stopped, because Xiuxin pouted her mouth and had tears in her eyes. In colloquialisms, the meaning of "live treasure" is to describe a person who is stupid. She felt that she was despised. Compared with others, she was a little slow, but she didn't want to be like that.

"What's wrong with you?" Wang Fusheng said anxiously, "I was just joking."

Xiuxin wiped away her tears and looked at him pitifully.

The beauty was in tears, her eyes sparkling.

Wang Fusheng couldn't hold back any longer and lowered his head to kiss her again. This time he was extremely restrained, kissing her gently and lingeringly. Even Xiuxin's hands gradually loosened the bed sheet and she embraced Wang Fusheng's waist in a daze. Wang Fusheng naturally felt it, and a burst of joy flashed in his eyes. He kissed Xiuxin hard, and while reaching out to untie Xiuxin's belt, he lowered his head to kiss her snow-white neck.

When the two of them had taken off their clothes, Xiu Xin looked down and saw the huge creature. The horrifying scene from that night once again came into her mind. How could such a big thing fit in? No wonder it hurt so much.

"Husband..." Xiu Xin shrank back in fear, "It will hurt..."

Wang Fusheng coaxed, "Dear, it's natural that it hurts the first time. Not only will it not hurt this time, but it will be very comfortable."

Xiu Xin cried and shook her head, "I don't believe it."

"Don't believe it? You'll believe it after you try it." He was about to go in with his gun. However, Wang Fusheng was careless and didn't catch Xiuxin, so Xiuxin found a gap and rolled over to get out. She jumped down barefoot, crying and trembling as she huddled in the corner, "No, I'm scared."

Wang Fusheng looked down at his proud little brother, then at Xiuxin's pitiful

appearance, sighed, and waved to Xiuxin, "Come here, I promise not to touch you."
Xiu Xin looked at him suspiciously.
Wang Fusheng added, "If you don't come over again, I'll be angry."
Xiuxin walked over reluctantly, looked at him timidly, and curled up at the foot of the bed.
Wang Fusheng grabbed her wrist and pulled her, and she fell into his arms again. They lay down again, and he held her hand and covered his burning and terrifying place. Xiuxin had experience with this, and comforted herself in her heart, just like holding a stick, rubbing it up and down.
In this way, we finally got through this chaotic and difficult night.
The next morning, the two got up, Lanxiang and Qinxiang came in to help Xiuxin get up and wash. Qinxiang came over to help Wang Fusheng get dressed, Wang Fusheng glanced at Xiuxin next to him, and said lightly, "Forget it, I'll do it myself." The two dressed neatly, and then Qinxiang began to tie Xiuxin's hair. Wang Fusheng looked at Xiuxin's black and shiny hair, smiled slightly, and said to the two, "You go down first."
"yes."
After the two of them left, Xiu Xin turned around and said to Wang Fusheng, "I haven't finished tying my hair yet."
Wang Fusheng picked up the comb on the table and said, "Today, I will tie your

hair for you."

Xiu Xin was surprised, "You can braid your hair?"

Wang Fusheng did not answer, but his hands began to shuttle back and forth between Xiuxin's black hair. Finally, Xiuxin looked in the mirror and saw that her hair was in a flying cloud bun. Although it was not as beautiful and neat as Qinxiang's, it was still acceptable.

"When did you acquire such a good skill?" Xiu Xin thought so in her heart and said it out loud. Looking at his skilled appearance, she believed that he had tied hair for many women.

Wang Fusheng felt relieved when he heard this. It seemed that the little girl was jealous. "Don't worry, from now on, I will only braid your hair."

Xiu Xin snorted in her heart, who cares!

Wang Fusheng was very good at serving women, and then he picked up the ink to draw eyebrows for Xiuxin. Xiuxin's eyebrows were not thin, but a little thick, but they were very neat. Wang Fusheng was drawing eyebrows for Xiuxin, thinking that he originally liked a pair of willow-leaf thin eyebrows the most. If this pair of eyebrows was born on someone else, he would probably not even look at it. But this pair of eyebrows was born on Xiuxin, so no matter how he looked at it, it was pleasing to the eye and beautiful.

In fact, if Wang Fusheng had not come,

Xiuxin and Zhanxue had originally planned to go for a stroll in a small town not far from Shangxin Garden. Xiuxin had lived in seclusion for a long time and was not allowed to go out of the house easily. Although she knew the hustle and bustle outside, she mostly saw it through the gaps in the curtains of the sedan chair. Zhanxue did not have so many concerns. If she wanted to go out, she could just change into men's clothes. Anyway, she had a boldness that men did not have. Even if her skin was whiter and her figure was slimmer, others would not forget the idea of a woman. However, if Xiuxin dressed up as a man, she would not look like a man at all. Zhanxue simply said, "Why don't you wear women's clothes, cover your face with a veil, and follow me out. Naturally, others will think you are my wife."

Xiuxin thought that she probably wouldn't meet those dignitaries in this small town and no one would recognize her, so she happily agreed.

Alas, thinking of this, Xiuxin sighed in her heart. She finally had a chance to go out, but now it was gone. It was all because of Wang Fusheng...

After breakfast, Wang Fusheng took the Go book and sat under the bamboo forest to study. He was a domineering person, but he insisted that Xiuxin accompany him. Xiuxin was so bored that she was about to doze off, so she asked someone to bring a desk, a bench, a pen, ink, paper, and other tools, and sat next to Wang Fusheng to paint.

In theory, Xiuxin has some talent in painting. She is naturally lazy and is spoiled at home. She behaves according to her own preferences and is not forced to do anything. She learned painting from her master for a while and then gave up, which made her master feel sorry. Xiuxin is open-minded and says, "I don't seek fame. I just paint for fun. It's fine if I have this level."

Wang Fusheng turned his head to look, and saw that the snow-white painting paper had taken shape in a short while, with bamboo poles and bamboo leaves, sparse and orderly, very elegant. Wang Fusheng completely moved his eyes away from the book and fixed his eyes on Xiuxin. Although he knew that Xiuxin's paintings were good, he didn't expect it to be more than just good. Although this level is a certain distance from the current national masters, if he sells this painting, he can also exchange it for more than ten taels of silver.

An hour later, Xiu Xin finally finished the bamboo forest painting. The bamboos in Xiu Xin's painting were strong and thin, straight and unbending, and the bamboo leaves were sharp and sparse. Adding to the rocks beside, it was really interesting and meaningful. Wang Fusheng said, "Since you have finished the painting, why don't you let me write an inscription for you?"

I had only done the embroidery painting to relieve boredom, and had not really thought about writing an inscription on it. But when Wang Fusheng said so, I handed the pen over.

Although Wang Fusheng was not good at painting, his calligraphy was unique among the officials of the Hua Dynasty. Wang Fusheng picked up the pen and wrote a poem. Xiuxin leaned over to take a look and saw that his handwriting was vigorous and powerful, with a lot of style between the horizontal and vertical strokes.

Xiu Xin sighed, "It's really well written."

Wang Fusheng raised his eyebrows, "That's it?"

Xiu Xin nodded, "That's it."

Wang Fusheng: "…" Isn't this praise too concise and too common?

After the two of them had lunch together, Wang Fusheng suddenly said, "There seems to be a small town not far from Shangxin Garden, called Ning'an. I heard that the Biechuan Temple there is quite effective. Since we are free today, why don't we go there later?"

Xiu Xin looked up in surprise, "Of course that's good."

Although Ning'an Town is not far from the capital, it is very different from the capital. Xiuxin secretly lifted the curtain of the sedan chair a little and looked out. The rows of houses outside were all green tiles. The small tiled houses were not big, but each one was exquisite. There were a few stalls in the street, and someone shouted, "Wontons, hot wontons..." Xiuxin swallowed her saliva greedily.

Wang Fusheng looked at her sideways and chuckled, "Why don't we go downstairs and take a walk?"

Xiu Xin clapped her hands and nodded like a chicken pecking at rice, "Yeah yeah."

Wang Fusheng took Xiuxin's hand and got off the carriage. The wonton stand was not far away, and Xiuxin could smell the aroma of meat and the fragrance of chopped green onions. But Wang Fusheng took Xiuxin in the opposite direction of the wonton stand, and Xiuxin was so anxious that she almost stamped her feet. But Wang Fusheng walked slowly, neither hurried nor slow, and finally entered a silk and satin shop.

The shopkeeper was also a shrewd man. He saw at a glance that the two men were of extraordinary status, and hurriedly came up to them and said cheerfully, "My two guests, what kind of fabric would you like to buy?"

Wang Fusheng saw Xiuxin standing there absent-mindedly, obviously her mind had flown to the wontons. He sat down slowly and said, "Boss, take out all the good things in your store. I want to take a look at them slowly."

When Xiuxin heard that Wang Fusheng actually wanted to take his time to look, she said with a bitter face, "What don't we have at home?"

Wang Fusheng wanted to tease her, so he deliberately said, "We have everything at home, but it's not bad to occasionally see what new stuff is out there." At the same time, he said to the shopkeeper, "Go, go, bring out your best stuff."

The shopkeeper said, "Okay, you two wait a moment."

Xiu Xin sat for a while, and finally couldn't help it, "Husband..."

"Um?"

"I'm hungry……"

"oh?"

Wang Fusheng pretended to be stupid.

"Let's go have a bowl of wontons, shall we?" Xiu Xin blinked her big watery eyes. "How about it?"

Wang Fusheng couldn't help it anymore, and stretched out his hand to pinch Xiuxin's face, "You, if you have anything in the future, just tell me directly. I am your husband, if you hide it from me, what kind of husband and wife are we?"

…… …

dividing line.

☆, Chapter 55 Sweetness

Chapter 55 Sweetness

It turned out that this guy was teasing her. He knew what she was thinking but pretended not to know. This was really too much! If it was her previous temper, Xiuxin would have turned her face away from him. But now it was different. Xiuxin had to endure it and said, "Husband... I know." Then she grabbed his sleeve and shook it, "Let's go?"

Wang Fusheng tapped her nose lovingly and said with a smile, "Greedy cat."

Just at this moment, the shopkeeper and several assistants took out the best silk in the store and said, "Sir, please take a look. Do you like any of them?"

Wang Fusheng glanced over and saw a few with nice patterns, so he randomly pointed to a few and said, "I want all of these."

After saying that, Wang Fusheng walked out. A servant had already come in from behind to take out the silver and carry the cloth into the large carriage.

After a while, they arrived at the wonton stall. The stall owner was an old couple, wearing coarse cloth clothes, with gray hair. One was rolling the wonton skin, and the other was wrapping the stuffing, cooperating very well.

"Two bowls of wontons, please."

"Okay." The old man responded cheerfully, "Please wait a moment, sir. It will be ready soon."

Maybe it was not the right time yet, there were not many customers eating wontons, only a few people sitting in twos and threes. The tables and chairs were clean, but Wang Fusheng just felt a little uncomfortable, standing straight beside Xiuxin, unwilling to sit down. Xiuxin also knew that he had probably never stopped at such a street stall, so she spread out her wide skirt and looked up at him, "Do you want to sit down?"

Wang Fusheng lowered his head and saw that Xiuxin's light green skirt was spread out on the stool, with enough space for two people to sit.

Seeing that Wang Fusheng was silent and looked strange, Xiuxin was afraid that he would not let her stay to eat wontons, so she flattered him, "Sit down."

Wang Fusheng hummed in a dignified manner and sat down. He tried hard to suppress the corners of his mouth from rising and put on a very conciliatory look, "Ahem, I'll just sit down for a while."

The old man who was cooking wontons saw this scene and smiled softly to the old woman beside him, "Look, that couple is really interesting."

The old woman smiled and said, "Hey, that's right. The young man looked at the young lady with eyes full of honey, but the young lady didn't see him at all. They are also a pair of little enemies."

The old man chuckled and said, "It will always be perfect. Weren't you unwilling to marry me at the beginning?"

The old woman spitted, "How dare you bring that up."

"The wontons are ready." The old man brought two bowls of hot wontons and said with a smile, "My two guests, please enjoy your meal."

The wonton soup was clear, with thin scallions floating on top. The plump wontons were bright in color, making people salivate at the sight. Xiuxin scooped one up with a spoon, put it in her mouth and took a bite. The wonton skin was smooth, and the meat filling was fresh and elastic. It was really delicious, even better than what she had eaten in the mansion.

Seeing Xiuxin's expression, Wang Fusheng also tried taking a small bite. It tasted good, so he slowly ate the whole bowl of wontons.

Mo Yan on the other side was stunned. He nudged the Yun guard next to him with his elbow and said, "Hey, look, is that still our master?"

Guard Yun was Wang Fusheng's personal bodyguard. He usually had a cold face, and this time was no exception. He replied concisely, "Yes."

Mo Yan looked at him in confusion, "What a blockhead."

Although Biechuan Temple is located in a small town, it is close to the capital and surrounded by beautiful scenery, so it is very popular. Many dignitaries and even royal relatives would make special trips to Biechuan Temple to burn incense.

Biechuan Temple is located on the top of Zhongling Mountain, and it takes an hour to climb up. When they were at the foot of the mountain, Wang Fusheng asked Xiuxin, "Do you want to take a sedan chair?" Xiuxin saw that the surrounding scenery was very beautiful, and it would be meaningless to take a sedan chair, so she shook her head and said, "No."

Wang Fusheng waved the fan in his hand, said nothing, and said, "Then let's go."

There is only one mountain road from Zhongling Mountain to Biechuan Temple, paved with long and short bluestone slabs, with lush trees and birds singing overhead. Halfway through the road, you may even come across a small waterfall, hanging diagonally in the mountains, like a silver ribbon.

Xiu Xin exclaimed in excitement, shaking Wang Fusheng's sleeves, "Look, look, it's really beautiful, isn't it?"

"Beauty, of course it is beautiful." Wang Fusheng said this, but there was no scenery in his eyes. His eyes were looking at Xiuxin's profile. Her eyebrows, nose, and lips were all delicate and lovely, more beautiful than the scenery of Zhongling Mountain.

After walking for a while, Xiu Xin was already sweating from exhaustion. Not only did she feel backache, but she also felt sharp pains in her toes. "No, my feet hurt. I can't walk anymore..."

Although Wang Fusheng was a scholar, his physical strength was definitely stronger than Xiuxin's. "I asked you when I was at the foot of the mountain, but you said you

didn't want a sedan chair."
Xiu Xin simply sat down on a large rock nearby and panted, "I really can't leave..."
Wang Fusheng looked at her helplessly. After a while, he sighed and said, "Then let's rest for a while before we go." After resting for a while, the sky gradually darkened. Wang Fusheng asked, "How is it? Do you have the strength to walk?"
Xiu Xin shook her head, frowning tightly, "My feet still hurt."
Wang Fusheng then stood up nervously and said, "Maybe your feet are rubbed and bruised?" He winked at Mo Yan. Mo Yan understood what he meant and immediately ordered several guards to surround the two men with their backs to them.
Only then did Wang Fusheng squat down in front of Xixin and reached out to hold Xiuxin's leg.
Xiu Xin was shocked, "What?"
"What else can we do?" Wang Fusheng turned around and said with a smile, "Look at your foot. If it's seriously injured, it will be bad. Besides, it will be dark soon. Are you going to spend the night in this mountain?"
Xiuxin really didn't expect Wang Fusheng to do this. At first, she thought he was a hypocrite. He was the prime minister of the dynasty and talked about morality, but in fact he was a playboy and a young man. Later, she thought he might not be what she thought at the beginning. He played the

flute very well, wrote calligraphy very well, had a lot of literary talent, and seemed to be a little concerned about the country and the people.

However, she never expected that he would squat in front of her and even take off her shoes for her! This really made her a little flattered.

"Isn't this... inappropriate?" Xiu Xin hesitated and tried to retract her legs, "I... can... ah!"

As he was talking, Wang Fusheng took off Xiuxin's shoes with force, and saw a few bloodstains on the tips of Xiuxin's socks, which showed that she was injured. He continued to take off her socks, and sure enough, several toes were worn out, and there was a big blister.

"How could this happen?" Wang Fusheng became suspicious and reached into his shoes, and felt something hard, as if a piece of porcelain had been sewn into the shoes!

"Who on earth is it? How could they have such a vicious mind!"

Xiu Xin asked in confusion, "What's wrong?"

"You, don't you know that someone has sewn a piece of porcelain into your shoes? You may not feel it when you first wear the shoes, but after wearing them for a long time and walking more, the pieces will float up and cut your feet."

"No wonder..." Xiu Xin was extremely frightened, "Who wants to harm me?"

Wang Fusheng said, "I will check it carefully after we go back." He put the socks on Xiuxin and held her up sideways. "It's not far from the top of the mountain. I will carry you up. Mo Yan, bring me a cloak."

"Yes." Mo Yan hurriedly took out the cloak from the luggage. Lan Xiang took the cloak and covered Xiu Xin's entire body, covering most of her face, leaving only a pair of big black eyes.

Xiu Xin gently pulled Wang Fusheng's collar, her face burning, "That...husband."

"Um?"

Xiu Xin buried her face in her cloak and said sullenly, "Thank you."

Xiuxin had been acting in front of him these days, and only this sentence was sincere.

Although Xiuxin was not heavy, it was still a climb up the mountain, and soon Wang Fusheng was so tired that his clothes were soaked with sweat. Fortunately, the guards had already rushed to the top of the mountain to ask for a sedan chair, so Xiuxin sat in the sedan chair and was carried up the mountain.

After the few people settled down in Biechuan Temple, Xiuxin and Wang Fusheng rested in two adjacent guest rooms. While helping Wang Fusheng wash up, Mo Yan winked and said, "Master, you could have waited until the sedan chair arrived before setting off, but you carried the lady for a

while. I'm afraid you did it on purpose to please the lady?"
Wang Fusheng slapped him on the head and said, "You are smart, but you can say this to me behind my back, but don't gossip about me, understand?"
Mo Yan touched his head and said, "How can that be possible? I am the most tight-lipped servant."
On the other side, after Xiuxin finished bathing, she sat on the bed in her inner clothes. Lanxiang also took off her outer clothes and sat on the bed. The master and servant were talking intimately and secretly.
"Miss, I am really good to you. Let's not talk about other things. But as for the fact that I carried you up the mountain, there are not many masters in Beijing who can do it." Lan Xiang said with a smile, "Also, this morning, I saw that you looked depressed, so I came to ask me. I casually told you that you wanted to go to Ning'an Town with Miss Zhan Xue. Who would have thought that he would bring you here in the afternoon." Lan Xiang covered her mouth and chuckled a few times, "In my opinion, as long as you can soften in front of me, I will obey you in everything, right?"
Xiu Xin rolled her eyes at her and said, "Lan Xiang, you are still an unmarried girl, yet you have so many things to say about these things." She smiled as she spoke, "Okay, okay, let's not talk about him

anymore. He's so boring."

Lanxiang teased Xiuxin's armpits and said, "Not talking about him? If not talking about him, who should we talk about? Isn't he the only one who has something to say now?"

Xiu Xin shrank back and said in a serious tone, "Stop joking. Let's be serious. Who do you think could have harmed me?"

The author has something to say: Why do people just not have the patience to see what happens next? Is the male protagonist a scumbag? I don't think so. The female protagonist is not scheming, which is the setting of this article. That's why the title of the article is called What is the House Fight, which means that the female protagonist is confused. Let alone becoming the queen of the house fight, she even has to ask what the house fight is…

☆、Chapter 56 Sound Sleep

Chapter 56: Sound Sleep

Lanxiang pondered for a moment, her expression becoming serious. "The Wang family is a complicated place, and there are many people who have reasons to harm you. Let alone the concubines Zhou, Chu, Chengbi, and even Nanny Wang in the Second Master's room. Who knows which one of them would harm you?"

Xiu Xin curled up on the bed and nodded silently. After a moment, she said, "But

there are not many people who can touch my clothes."
Lan Xiang's eyes lit up, "Miss is right. We brought two embroiderers from the Cui family. Most of your clothes, shoes and socks are made by them. Could it be that they made them?"
Xiu Xin shook her head slowly, "Not necessarily. Those embroiderers have been with me for many years, they wouldn't betray me so quickly, what good would that do to them? Besides, you just said that most of my clothes, shoes and socks were made by them, but not all of them. I remember Princess Duanyi asked the people in the Wang family's embroidery room to make a lot of things for me, didn't she?"
"Girl, you should think about it more carefully."
Xiu Xin's eyes showed some determination, "We will investigate this matter after we return. I will not offend anyone unless they offend me. No matter who harms me, I will never let them have an easy time."
The two were talking when there were several soft knocks on the door. "Xiu Xin, are you ready to rest?"
Xiu Xin and Lan Xiang looked at each other. Lan Xiang smiled, stood up, opened the door, and bowed, "Second Master."
Wang Fusheng nodded dignifiedly, "Yes."
Lanxiang lowered her head, smiled, turned and walked out, closing the door behind her. Wang Fusheng sat down beside the bed and

put down the medicine bottle in his hand. "I brought you some medicine for your wound. Let me apply it on you." As he said this, he was about to grab Xiuxin's legs under the quilt.

Xiu Xin pulled her legs inwards, a little shy, "Husband, I can do it myself."

Wang Fusheng had already grasped her left ankle accurately, and with one force he pulled one of her feet out of the quilt. "I'm your husband, why are you shy?"

Xiuxin's two toes had been simply wrapped with gauze. Wang Fusheng held Xiuxin's feet and unwrapped the gauze layer by layer, and then carefully poured the powder on the wound. The powder irritated Xiuxin's wound, and the pain made Xiuxin gasp and frowned tightly.

Wang Fusheng stopped moving, his eyes full of concern, "Does it hurt?"

Xiuxin has been afraid of pain since she was a child. At this moment, the pain made her eyes slightly wet. She nodded and said, "Yes."

Wang Fusheng lowered his head and breathed softly into the wound, then raised his head and asked her, "Is this better?"

Xiuxin's heart was pounding, and she couldn't calm down for a long time. She pulled her foot back at a loss, stammering, "No, no, it doesn't hurt anymore."

Wang Fusheng felt soft in his heart when he saw Xiuxin like this. He stretched out his hand and pinched Xiuxin's chin, "So cute."

Xiuxin felt that the hand pinching her chin was terribly hot, and she wanted to shake it off immediately, the farther away the better. However, Wang Fusheng not only did not let go, but even got closer.

Their breaths intertwined, and Xiuxin saw her own reflection in Wang Fusheng's black eyes. For some reason, she felt uncomfortable all over.

This is a quiet Buddhist place. Wang Fusheng just touched Xiuxin's lips lightly and let her go.

Xiu Xin breathed a sigh of relief.

Wang Fusheng said, "The other foot."

Xiuxin had no choice but to stretch her other foot out of the quilt with a bitter face. This foot was not as seriously injured as the other one. After applying medicine on her, Wang Fusheng said, "Don't wrap your foot with gauze anymore. It will block your breathing and make it harder to heal."

"I see." Xiuxin looked at him and suddenly remembered that she and he had met by chance in Xiangguo Temple. She rashly broke into his room and slept in his room. Now, only more than half a year, she has become his wife. How things have changed.

Wang Fusheng saw a copy of the Diamond Sutra on Xiuxin's bedside and was very surprised. "You're actually reading Buddhist scriptures?"

Xiuxin had indeed asked someone to get this Buddhist scripture for her, but she didn't do it to study it in detail, but to hypnotize herself... But how could she say such a shameful reason? She only said vaguely, "I suddenly felt interested in it recently. I have nothing to do today, so I just flipped through it casually."

Wang Fusheng knew Xiuxin very well, so he deliberately said, "Since you are interested in Buddhist scriptures, that's good. My mother also has some insights into Buddhism. When we return home, you can keep my mother company."

"Ah?" Xiuxin knew that Madam Wang had to copy Buddhist scriptures every day. If she went with her, wouldn't she also be forced to copy Buddhist scriptures every day? This life would be unbearable...

Wang Fusheng saw Xiuxin's little face wrinkled like a chrysanthemum, and he was already happy in his heart, but he said seriously, "Well, it's settled. My mother will definitely be very happy." After saying that, he was about to stand up, as if he was going to leave.

"Hey." In a hurry, Xiu Xin grabbed his sleeve and shook it flatteringly, "I don't know much about Buddhism, so don't tell mother. If I don't know anything, it will make mother unhappy."

"Ahem." Wang Fusheng could hardly hold it in any longer. He coughed dryly a few times to force the corners of his mouth to lower their upward curves. He said in an awkward manner, "But... Mother has always wanted someone to accompany her. You are my wife and also her daughter-in-law. It would be most appropriate for you to accompany her to copy Buddhist scriptures and recite Buddhist teachings for an hour every day."

"Husband." Xiu was anxious and didn't care about being reserved. She put her arms around Wang Fusheng's waist and said, "Mother likes quietness the most. She doesn't like me being in front of her all day."

Wang Fusheng turned around and said in an ambiguous tone, "Madam, why are you so proactive today?"

Xiuxin suddenly realized and quickly let go of her hand, lowering her head, her face feeling as if it was on fire.

Wang Fusheng was pleased and kissed Xiuxin's red cheek. "Okay, I won't tell my mother."

That night, Xiuxin lay in bed for a long time, unable to fall asleep. When she closed her eyes, she could see the frivolous smile on Wang Fusheng's face, and the scene of her tightly hugging his waist. Xiuxin turned over in annoyance.

Lanxiang was resting on the small couch outside. After hearing Xiuxin couldn't fall asleep for a long time, she simply stood up and asked, "What's wrong, girl? Does your wound hurt?"

Xiu Xin responded in the darkness, "Nothing, I'm just feeling irritated today, I'll go to sleep in a while."

After tossing and turning for a long time, Xiuxin didn't know when she fell asleep. When she woke up, she saw Wang Fusheng's face. Xiuxin was dazed and thought she was dreaming. She said incoherently, "Well, why is it you again?"

Wang Fusheng secretly laughed when he heard Xiuxin say this, and picked her up with the quilt, "Xiuxin, it's time to get up."

Xiu Xin opened her eyes again with difficulty, and seeing Wang Fusheng's perfect handsome face, she reached out and pulled his skin, giggling, "You are so handsome."

It was the first time that Wang Fusheng heard Xiuxin praising him. He was immediately overjoyed. He pecked Xiuxin on the lips several times and laughed softly, "It's rare to hear you praise me." In the past, she always called him "old and indecent."

Xiu Xin finally woke up completely this time. Seeing that Wang Fusheng was holding her in his arms so early in the morning, she turned around awkwardly and said, "I want to wash up."

Wang Fusheng finally let her go and said, "I'll wait for you outside. Wu Le will host the morning class today. Let's go and listen."

Because they were in the temple, Lanxiang and Qinxiang dressed Xiuxin very simply. She wore a moon-white dress with cloud patterns embroidered on the collar and a blue silk ribbon tied around her waist, which hung quietly from her waist. She didn't wear any hair accessories on her hair, which was only tied slightly at the back with a blue silk ribbon, and a small bun was combed in the front.

When Xiuxin pushed the door open and walked out, Wang Fusheng was stunned. He had always known that Xiuxin was very pretty, but today, dressed like this, she looked like she had walked out of a painting, as quiet as water, simple and elegant.

"Husband?" Xiu Xin called him several times before Wang Fusheng came back to his senses. "Let's go to the Buddhist temple."

When Xiuxin and Wang Fusheng arrived, all the novices had also arrived. Master Wu Le was sitting cross-legged on a cushion with his eyes closed, holding a Buddhist rosary in his hand.

"Master Wu." Wang Fusheng bowed first, "I have long admired your name. Today, I am here with my wife to disturb you. I hope you will grant me permission to listen."

Wu Lu opened his eyes, stood up, smiled and returned the greeting, "How can I refuse a distinguished guest? Please take a seat."

"Thank you." Wang Fusheng then took Xiuxin to sit on the cushion on the right side of the front row.

A quarter of an hour later.

"Hoo...Hoo..." Xiuxin did not get a good rest yesterday and was woken up by Wang Fusheng early in the morning. She was already feeling sleepy, and then the old monk started to lecture on Buddhism. The sleepiness immediately surged in like the Yellow River, so much so that she made soft sounds of deep sleep in the Buddhist hall.

Wang Fusheng bowed and said, "Master Wu, I am sorry for being rude to my wife."

Wu Lu waved his hand and said, "Madam, you have a pure mind and a single-minded focus, which is really rare. This state of mind is also the transcendent state that we have always pursued."

Master Wu Le's words were really well-written. Even Wang Fusheng couldn't tell whether Wu Le was really praising Xiu Xin or mocking her. He could only apologize again, "I'm so sorry." He patted Xiu Xin's face and said in a low voice, "Wake up."

Xiu Xin didn't sleep deeply to begin with, so she woke up after being patted. Only then did she realize that she had fallen asleep, and she was so embarrassed that she wanted to find a crack in the ground to crawl into.

Master Wu Le smiled at Xiu Xin and said, "There is no Bodhi tree, nor is there a mirror. The Buddha nature is always pure, where is the dust? To understand the profound Buddhist teachings, it is most important to maintain an innocent heart. If you have those impure thoughts, you will not be able to practice well no matter what."

Xiuxin didn't quite understand what he said,

but she intuitively knew it wasn't a bad thing, so she felt relieved and breathed a long sigh of relief.

The author has something to say: There will be more tomorrow. Muah. Are you ready to spread some flowers today?

☆, Chapter 57: Farewell

Chapter 57: Farewell

An hour later, the morning class finally ended. Wang Fusheng and Master Wu Le went to the Zen room to drink tea and discuss the Dao. Xiu Xin simply walked around the temple alone.

This Biechuan Temple is located on the top of Zhongling Mountain, with high skies and vast clouds, and beautiful scenery. Standing in the courtyard at the back door and looking down, you can see lush trees, continuous peaks, and jagged rocks. Standing on the top of the mountain, you can vaguely see the prosperous town below the mountain, with busy traffic and numerous buildings and ships. A little monk bowed to Xiuxin, "Do you want to go to the dining hall for dinner, lady donor?"

Xiu Xin thought of the exquisite food at Xiangguo Temple, and her eyes lit up, "Is there anything?"

The little monk answered honestly, "Only steamed buns and white porridge."

"Oh." Xiu Xin said disappointedly, "I'll go later." After all, it can't be compared with the Xiangguo Temple, which is very popular.

Xiu was not hungry, and there were still some snacks in the bag she brought last night. She stretched out her right hand, feeling the soft touch of the cool breeze passing through her fingers.

Alas, Xiu Xin sighed inwardly after a while. With such a beautiful scenery, she could neither play the zither nor the flute to cheer it up. Could she bring a paintbrush from the study? If it was Zhan Xue, she would probably be able to take out her sword and dance with it.

As Xiuxin was thinking this, she heard the sound of a zither. She listened for a while, then went down the stairs to the right and came to a bamboo forest. Through the dense bamboo leaves, Xiuxin saw a man in green clothes playing the zither. There was incense burning on the zither table, emitting waves of elegant fragrance.

The ancients said: You must bathe and burn incense before playing the zither. But today, no one cares about that anymore. It seems that this young man is really elegant. After all, there are differences between men and women. Xiuxin listened to the music for a while, then tiptoed back. But when she turned around, the man saw through her tracks and said, "Miss, please stay."

Oops.

Xiu Xin frowned, but instead of stopping, she quickened her pace and ran outside.

"girl!"

As Xiuxin ran, she thought, what's the point of calling her a girl? I've already been married, so I should call her Madam.

"Ah!" Xiu Xin was not careful and tripped over a dead bamboo, falling heavily to the ground with a thud. Xiu Xin grimaced in pain and was struggling to speak, but a slender white hand stretched out in front of her, "Girl, let me help you up."

Xiu Xin couldn't really let him help her up, so she stood up on her own, patted her clothes and walked forward.

"Girl." The man called her again.

Xiu Xin stopped and slowly turned around, but did not look up, "What's the matter, sir?"

The man smiled slightly and said, "Miss, do you know what song I just played?" The man's voice was quite nice. Not as magnetic as Wang Fusheng's, but clear and pleasant.

"I don't know." It would be strange if she knew.

"The phoenix seeks the phoenix."

Xiu Xin didn't care what he was playing. She bowed to him and said, "I didn't mean to disturb you just now. Please forgive me." Then she left in a hurry.

The man watched Xiu Xin walk further and further away, his eyes full of longing. When Xiu Xin's figure disappeared, a guard in black came out from the depths of the bamboo forest, "Master, do you want me to investigate the origins of this woman?"

The man shook his head slowly and said firmly, "No need, we will meet again if we are destined to."

Xiuxin returned to the wing room and had some snacks with tea. Lanxiang came in and asked with a smile, "Miss, do you know where Qinxiang went?"

Xiu Xin stuffed the rose cake into her mouth and said vaguely, "I guess he went out to have fun somewhere?"

Lan Xiang said mysteriously, "She went to ask for a marriage." Then she joked, "That little girl must be missing a man. Master, you should quickly take her out and find a man."

Xiu Xin swallowed the rose cake and said, "Yes, you and Qin Xiang are both grown up. You are seventeen and she is sixteen. It is indeed time to consider your marriage."

Lanxiang cried out, "Miss, we were talking about Qinxiang, why are you bringing me up again? I have been blessed by the Madam and Miss since I was a child, and Miss has just married into the Wang family and still needs my help, how can I get married at this time?"

Xiu Xin was deeply impressed, "Lan Xiang... I really can't live without someone by my side right now. I will find you a good family after some time."

Lan Xiang said, "We'll talk about the future later. I might never marry in my life. Didn't Princess Duan Yi's Yu Niang never marry in her life?"

Xiu Xin said, "Yuniang came from the palace, how can she be the same?"

As the master and servant were talking, the door creaked open and Wang Fusheng pushed it open.

"Second Master." Lanxiang bowed and walked out.

Wang Fusheng saw Xiuxin eating the leftover snacks from yesterday, and felt very distressed. He stepped in and brought a plate of red bean paste buns to Xiuxin, "Eat this."

Xiu Xin took it with a smile, opened her mouth and took a bite, "Where did you get this?"

Wang Fusheng sat next to Xiuxin and said, "I know you don't like those steamed buns and porridge, so I asked the canteen to make them for you."

The sweet and soft bean paste melted between her teeth, and Xiuxin suddenly felt the sweetness spreading from her throat all the way to her heart. She felt her whole body was sweet.

Soon, all three red bean paste buns were eaten. After finishing, Xiuxin remembered something and said with a sad face, "Husband, have you had breakfast?"

Wang Fusheng reached out and wiped the bean paste off the corner of Xiuxin's mouth, "I've already used it."

Xiu Xin breathed a sigh of relief and drank a sip of tea, "That's good."

"Let's go." Wang Fusheng took Xiuxin's hand

and walked out.
"where to?"
"Just come with me." Xiuxin was lazy all the time. She didn't like to move around after dinner. She would either stay in her room or read a storybook. Wang Fusheng was worried that she would have food stagnation, so he led her to the main hall.
The two of them burned incense and worshipped Buddha, then walked around the temple and finally went to the back door. Xiu Xin stood in the middle of the room, looking sideways to the right. Could the young man still be there?
"What are you looking at?"
"Ah?" Xiu Xin turned her head sharply, "No, I didn't see anything."
Wang Fusheng did not think much of it and continued, "Although the scenery of Biechuan Temple is very beautiful and it is a good place to cultivate one's character, the food is too poor. Let's stay for a while and then go down the mountain and have lunch in Ning'an Town before returning home."
Xiuxin was happy but also a little reluctant. She looked at him with her big watery eyes and said, "Are we leaving now?" She was happy that there would be delicious food when she returned, but what she was reluctant about was of course the free and easy days.
Wan Fusheng pinched her nose and asked, "Why, you don't want to?"

"Not really." Xiu Xin sighed in her heart.

Wang Fusheng said, "There have been a lot of things going on in the court recently, and I can't relax, so I have to go back to Beijing."

"I know all this." Xiu Xin paused and said, "I am already very satisfied to be able to come out for these few days."

In the afternoon, the two returned to the palace. As soon as Wang Fusheng returned, a senior eunuch came to deliver an imperial decree, saying that he was urgently summoned to the palace. Wang Fusheng knew that something important must have happened, and his face became solemn. He bowed and said, "Please wait a moment, eunuch. I will change my clothes and come right away."

The eunuch urged, "Lord Wang, please hurry up. The Emperor is very anxious."

Wang Fusheng hurried into the palace to meet the emperor. When he arrived, important ministers such as Cui Jinyi were also present, as well as the emperor's two princes, the second prince and the fifth prince.

"These corrupt officials are so hateful! Even if I eat their flesh and sleep with their clothes, it is still hard to appease my anger!" The emperor gritted his teeth and threw a memorial to Wang Fusheng, "My dear Wang, take a look at this memorial from the Magistrate of Luzhou."

Wang Fusheng quickly read through it and was shocked. "How could this be? That's two hundred thousand taels of silver. Are those officials really too bold?"

The emperor coughed a few times and said, "Nowadays, there are starving people everywhere, and there are rebels everywhere. Not only in Zhouzhou, but even the adjacent Tongzhou and Taizhou are in turmoil. There is also a local emperor named Liu who got a jade seal from somewhere and said that he is the true emperor... cough cough! It really makes me angry to death."

Wang Fusheng knelt down and said, "I failed to notice this."

Cui Jinyi and other important officials also knelt down and said, "Your Majesty, please punish me."

The old emperor waved his hands and said, "Now is not the time to decide whether to punish or not. The situation in Luzhou, Tongzhou, and Taizhou must be stabilized as soon as possible. I have sent the Protector of the Country, Liu Baozi, to capture the thieves, but I still need someone to go to rectify the administration and comfort the victims. Who of you is willing to go?"

As soon as these words came out, everyone fell silent. Everyone knew that this job was not an easy one. Now that the three states were in turmoil, who knows what would happen if they went there at this time.

After a long silence, Wang Fusheng's voice rang out in the hall, "I am willing to go."

"Good!" The emperor slapped the table and

praised, "Lord Wang is indeed a pillar of the country and a key minister of our Hua Dynasty!"

"Father, I am willing to go with you. Lord Wang is my teacher, and I would like to learn a lot from you on this trip." said the Second Prince Hua Yun.

"Good!" The emperor said again, "Then you can go with Lord Wang. It's better to see more outside than to stay inside the palace walls."

"Yes." Hua Yun bowed.

The fifth prince Hua Ling, who was standing quietly on the side, curled his lips almost imperceptibly. This idiot, could it be that he thought that just clinging to the Wang family would be enough? He didn't even think about who Wang Fusheng was, and how could he easily let himself get involved in the struggle for the kingship?

The author has something to say: Dear friends, the young master who appears in this chapter is not a male supporting role. This novel basically has no male supporting role. Except for Li Yuzhi who made a cameo appearance...

☆, Chapter 58 Pregnancy

Chapter 58 Pregnancy
After washing up that day, Xiu Xin curled up in bed and read a side story. It was another story about a talented scholar and a beautiful lady. A scholar who was well-

versed in poetry and literature met a rich lady and fell in love with her at first sight. After a glance, the lady gave the scholar dozens of taels of silver. The scholar went to Beijing to take the imperial examination and won the first place. In the end, the lovers finally got married.

As Xiuxin read on, she said to Lanxiang outside the screen, "It's a good story, but it doesn't make sense. To be the top scholar, you have to pass the provincial and metropolitan examinations. But if you passed the metropolitan examinations, how can you not even take out a few dozen taels of silver?"

"Those are all written by those poor scholars to comfort themselves, who cares whether they are readable or not?" Wang Fusheng came in at some point and put his hand on Xiuxin's shoulder. Xiuxin was startled and turned her head to look, but Lanxiang in the outer room had already left.

"You're back." Xiu Xin closed the book, "Did the emperor summon you because something important happened?"

"There were riots in Luzhou, Tongzhou, and Taizhou. The emperor sent me to deal with the aftermath. I will leave tomorrow."

"You're leaving tomorrow?" Normally, Xiuxin should be happy to hear that he was leaving, but at this moment, she was more worried.

"I heard that the Duke of Protectorate sent troops to suppress the rebellion. Isn't there war there? Won't it be dangerous for you to go?"

"No. I have guards around me at all times. Besides, I don't have to lead troops to fight. I have the Protector of the Country for everything. Those mobs are nothing."

Xiu Xin felt a little relieved and said, "I'll go pack your luggage for you." Then she was about to get up.

Wang Fusheng put his arms around her waist and hugged her. "Okay, do you know what I use every day? What do I need to bring this time?"

Xiu Xin shook her head honestly.

"That's it." Wang Fusheng hugged her tightly in his arms, "You don't have to worry about these things, just stay in the mansion and gain a few pounds." He pinched Xiuxin's waist and said, "Look how thin you have become."

Xiuxin was not used to such intimacy and struggled twice in his arms.

Wang Fusheng pushed her down completely, looked her straight in the eye and said, "I will be gone for at least a month, at most three or four months, Qingyi won't be able to come back."

Xiu Xin turned her eyes away and hummed softly.

"I……"

Xiuxin is no longer the ignorant Xiuxin she used to be. How could she not understand Wang Fusheng's meaning at this moment? Her pretty face turned red.

Wang Fusheng pecked Xiuxin's lips twice, "Is that ok?"

Xiu Xin didn't know how to answer him, but she didn't mean to refuse either. She just slowly closed her eyes.

Wang Fusheng was overjoyed, excited and delighted. He hugged Xiuxin and kissed her several times. Finally, he kissed her until she was dizzy and dizzy. "You are such a troublesome little thing." Since the stormy night, the two had not had sex. That night, Wang Fusheng felt sorry for Xiuxin's tenderness, so he kept forbearing, making Xiuxin gasp and sweat a little, but he still didn't move. Until Xiuxin felt a tingling and empty feeling rising from her lower abdomen, her legs couldn't help but clamp together, panting, "Husband..."

Wang Fusheng hummed, "What's wrong?"

Xiu Xin felt a little embarrassed, but she thought that she had to endure this tonight anyway, so she simply closed her eyes and said, "Just come directly."

"Xiu Xin..." Wang Fusheng reached out to touch it. It felt slippery, so he could no longer endure it and went straight to the point.

There is no need to describe in detail the passionate lovemaking that night.

The next day, when Xiu Xin woke up, she reached out to touch someone, but found that there was no one beside her. She woke up with a start, "Lan Xiang! Lan Xiang!"

Lanxiang pushed the door open from outside

with her hair down, "What's wrong with the girl?"
Xiu said anxiously, "Quick! Help me get up."
Lanxiang looked at her in confusion, "Miss, why did you get up so early today? It's not even daybreak yet."
Xiu Xin then looked outside and saw that it was still dark. "But where is the Second Master? Is he gone?"
Lan Xiang chuckled, "It's not even daybreak yet, why would the Second Master leave? He just got up to go to the bathroom and will be back soon."
Xiuxin was embarrassed and lowered her head. Lanxiang heard light footsteps coming from the other side of the screen. After helping Xiuxin lie down, she went out and closed the door.
Wang Fusheng came back from the toilet and saw Xiuxin was awake. He thought Xiuxin had a nightmare and hugged her in his arms. "Why are you awake now? Did you have a nightmare?"
Xiu Xin shook her head. She didn't know why she woke up so early today.
Wang Fusheng kissed her on the forehead. "You were so tired yesterday, but you woke up so early today? Could it be that I didn't try hard enough yesterday?"
This made Xiuxin blush, she clenched her fist and punched Wang Fusheng's chest softly a few times, "You are talking nonsense." Yesterday, he had tasted the

sweetness and pulled her to do it three times in different positions. Xiuxin felt a little full but didn't feel any pain. Finally, she couldn't hold on any longer and fell asleep.

The beauty's fist made Wang Fusheng feel comfortable all over. He smiled softly, "I will be gone for a few months. You must take good care of yourself. If you feel bored, you can stay in Shangxin Garden for a few days. I will tell my mother. If you have been wronged, tell my grandmother. She will take care of it for you."

"Yeah." Xiu Xin nodded, buried her head in his chest, and made a muffled sound.

Wang Fusheng continued, "This time, I plan to take Chaozong with me. He grew up in this prosperous capital, and it's time for him to go out and see the sufferings of the world."

Xiuxin was surprised and looked up, "Chaozong is going too?" Wang Chaozong is his only legitimate son, isn't he afraid that something might happen to him?

"If you want to be successful, you can't stay in this gentle place forever."

Xiu Xin was not in a position to comment on the matter, so she said, "It's up to you to decide, but you have to be more vigilant about Chao'er's safety."

Wang Fusheng smiled and said, "Of course I have already taken care of this."

The two of them talked in private on the bed for a while, and then it was dawn. Wang

Fusheng got up and put on his clothes. Xiuxin also wanted to get up, but Wang Fusheng pushed her back, "You should sleep a little longer. You have dark circles under your eyes."

Xiu Xin asked, "Don't you need me to take you there?"

"No, just take a rest." Wang Fusheng buttoned the last button, opened the door with a creak, and walked out. Xiuxin half sat up, watching him slowly walk away, a strange emotion arose from the bottom of her heart, this emotion made Xiuxin's nose a little sour, and her eyes a little hot.

Xiu Xin reached out and wiped her eyes.

I don't know when he will come back...

After Wang Fusheng left, Xiuxin began to investigate the matter of broken porcelain slag sewn into the shoes last time. She started with the two embroiderers that Xiuxin brought with her, and then went on to investigate the people in the embroidery room. After several inquiries, she finally found out that the embroiderer who made Xiuxin's shoes was surnamed Liu, and was a servant of the Wang family.

Duan Yi was furious, but Liu was crying out that she was wronged. "Princess, it is true that I made the Second Madam's shoes, but I really didn't do anything to her! I am wronged!"

Nanny Wang, who was standing beside her, saw this and slapped Liu across the face, cursing, "How dare you, a servant, harm the

Second Madam! Such a servant who offends her master should be dragged out and beaten to death."

Seeing that Nanny Wang was not doing things in a proper manner, Xiu Xin said, "Nanny, Princess Duanyi and the old lady are here. When will it be your turn to decide how to deal with the servants?"

Nanny Wang looked a little embarrassed and took a few steps back, "I have overstepped my authority."

Madam Wang said, "The evidence is irrefutable. You made the shoes. Who else could have done it? Take her out and give her thirty lashes. Then throw her out of the house. Whether she lives or dies depends on her luck."

"Princess, Princess, please spare my life. I am innocent."

Xiuxin originally felt that there was something hidden here, and seeing Liu's head broken and bleeding all over the floor from knocking her head, she felt a little sorry for her. She bowed to Duanyi and said, "Grandma, although Liu is abominable, she has been in the Wang family for quite some time, and she is also old. It would be better to drive her out of the house."

Duan Yi thought for a moment and said, "Well, well, I'll do as you say."

After the matter was settled, Lanxiang said to Xiuxin in the room, "Miss, are you just going to let this go? There must be someone behind Liu."

Xiu Xin said, "Of course I know. Otherwise, why would Liu, an embroiderer, come to harm me? But this matter can only be put aside for now, and we will wait and see in the future."

After Wang Fusheng left, Xiuxin lived a comfortable and peaceful life. She strolled around the garden every day, made some snacks, read some storybooks, drank tea with Princess Anyang to relieve her boredom, and bickered with Aunt Chu. The days passed by like this. A month passed like this.

On this day, Xiuxin had just woken up from her afternoon nap. Lanxiang lifted the curtain and came in, saying, "Miss, today is the Mid-Autumn Festival on August 15th. Princess Duanyi sent someone to tell her that you should go to Yuehua Tower to attend the family dinner tonight."

Every year during the Mid-Autumn Festival, the Wang family would have a great time, and this year was no exception. The entire palace had started preparing early, buying a lot of things and replacing all the utensils in the palace. The family banquet at Yuehua Tower during the Mid-Autumn Festival was not only attended by the Wang family's direct descendants, but also by branches in Huai'an and Qingyuan. Descendants, old and young gathered together, and it was very lively.

Over there, people were singing operas in the stands, while here, Xiuxin was absent-mindedly eating mooncakes with five nuts.

Duanyi sighed when she saw how lively the place was today, "It's a pity that Fusheng and Chaoge'er are not here." Princess Anyang said, "Grandfather, the Second Master's affairs in Ouzhou are going very smoothly, and the emperor is very happy. He may come back in a few days." As Anyang spoke, she touched Xiuxin with her arm and joked, "When the Second Master comes back, you don't have to stay alone in the empty room anymore."

Xiu Xin's face immediately turned red, "Sister, what nonsense are you talking about?"

Duan Yi laughed and said, "Xiu Xin is thin-skinned, and you still tease her. Unlike you, your face can be used as a wall."

"Grandfather, you are wronging me. I am just being thick-skinned in front of you. I am just trying to make you smile."

Duan Yi said cheerfully, "You are the only one who can make me happy."

At this time, the maids brought trays and served abalone to everyone. Xiuxin didn't care, she took the soup bowl, picked up the spoon and scooped a mouthful of it into her mouth. In an instant, Xiuxin felt the fishy smell rushing to her head, her stomach cramped, and she vomited immediately.

☆, Chapter 58 False Alarm

Chapter 59: False Alarm
"Oh, what happened to my sister?" Anyang

exclaimed, covering his mouth.

Xiuxin frowned uncomfortably, wiped her lips with a handkerchief with a pale face, and Lanxiang brought tea to Xiuxin to rinse her mouth, "Miss, are you okay?"

Anyang asked with concern, "Do you want to ask a doctor to come and check on your sister?"

Duan Yi, who was standing next to him, was different from the others. His face was filled with joy. "Xiu Xin, are you feeling unwell somewhere else? For example, you are sleepy?"

Xiu Xin thought for a moment and said, "This is also possible."

Duan Yi's face was filled with joy, "Oh, hurry up, call in Imperial Physician Chen to have a look at Xiu Xin."

Seeing Duanyi also thinking of that, Anyang was also delighted, "Indeed, I would like to congratulate you first."

Duan Yi was overwhelmed with joy, and held Xiu Xin's hand with concern, "Xiu Xin, if you are not feeling well, why don't you go back and rest?" At the same time, he said, "Quick, someone bring a cloak to the second lady, so she won't catch a cold."

Xiu Xin was escorted back to the East Courtyard like a star. Lan Xiang was also very happy, "Miss, I'll bring you a cup of hot tea."

Xiu Xin sighed, "What's wrong with everyone today? Why is everyone acting weird?"

Lan Xiang smiled and said, "Miss, have you

had your period this month?"
Xiu Xin shook her head, "Not yet, a few days late."
Lan Xiang felt relieved, and her smile deepened, "Miss, I think you are pregnant."
Xiu Xin was startled, "Are you pregnant?"
Xiu Xin looked down at her flat abdomen and asked, "How is this possible?"
"How is that impossible?" Lanxiang asked, "Didn't the Second Master spend the night in the girl's room before he left?"
"But..." Xiu Xin was suddenly confused, her mind was in a mess, and her heart was in a mess. The whole East Courtyard was also in an uproar because of this seemingly true news.
An hour later, Imperial Physician Chen finally arrived. Duanyi, the old lady, Anyang and others gathered in a circle, staring at the hand of Imperial Physician Chen resting on Xiuxin's wrist, holding their breath. Even Xiuxin behind the curtain couldn't help but clench her quilt nervously. If she was really pregnant, what should she do? She was going to be a mother?
After a long while, Imperial Physician Chen stroked his goatee and said, "Madam is not pregnant. She is vomiting because of the cold air entering her body and the discomfort in her stomach. I will prescribe some medicine to regulate her stomach and dispel wind and cold. It's nothing serious."
Everyone was disappointed, especially Duan

Yi, who couldn't hide the disappointment on her face. An Yang secretly raised his lips, but in the next moment he put on a look of regret and said to Duan Yi, "Grandfather, my sister is still young and can give birth to a child."

Duan Yi nodded, holding Xiu Xin's hand and said, "Since you are ill, you should take good care of yourself. But you are born with few children, so you have to take good care of yourself so that our Wang family can have more children."

Xiuxin herself was still a child at heart, and had never thought of this. Seeing so many people surrounding her, she suddenly felt a little embarrassed. After a long while, she said, "Grandma, I know."

Duanyi also truly loved Xiuxin. He held Xiuxin's hand and said, "The weather is getting colder now. You must take care of yourself. I see that you have lost a lot of weight recently. If you need any supplements, just tell me and I'll ask the people in the kitchen to make them for you."

"Thank you, Grandma."

Madam Wang also said, "Since you are ill, you should take good care of yourself. However, the Women's Court Meeting will be held in a month, so you should also prepare for it. After all, you are now the daughter-in-law of my Wang family." The Women's Court Meeting is an annual event hosted by the Queen. All women above the third rank in the capital can participate. At that time, the women must show their unique skills, such as embroidery, calligraphy, poetry, painting, etc. Finally, the Queen will select the best one.

Xiu Xin was very familiar with this Women's Court Meeting, because every year her mother would dress herself up gorgeously to attend the meeting. In fact, it was more like a competition for these noble ladies to compete with each other for beauty than a Women's Court Meeting.

"I understand, mother." Xiu Xin replied.

Xiuxin's illness was mild this time, and she recovered after taking a few doses of medicine. Duanyi sent a lot of supplements, including ginseng, bird's nest, snow lotus, etc. Xiuxin's face became rounder after eating them. A few days later, Wang Fusheng sent a letter with a simple sentence: I miss you very much, are you well?

Xiuxin wrote back: Everything is fine, I miss you very much.

The last two words "甚念" were added by Lanxiang at her insistence after she saw it. However, after she recovered from her illness, Xiuxin was no longer so timid. The next day, the old lady summoned Xiuxin to the west courtyard and asked her about music, chess, calligraphy and painting, but she could not show any of them. Old lady Wang looked at Xiuxin's round face and felt a little disappointed.

This girl, her appearance is not

outstanding, her family background is not outstanding, her talent is not outstanding, I don't know what Duanyi and Fusheng like about her? Could it be that they like her stupidity? The old lady looked Xiuxin up and down, thinking that although she is not outstanding in everything, at least her behavior and etiquette are not wrong. However, she is the legitimate daughter of the Cui family after all. If she doesn't even have this little ability, the Cui family's way of raising daughters is questionable.

"This women's court meeting is just an excuse for the Queen to gather everyone together for fun. Although the ranking is not important, we cannot lose face for the Wang family." Old Madam Wang paused and said, "But you don't have anything to show for yourself. What will you do then?"

Xiu Xin hesitated for a while before saying, "Mother, maybe I can draw a picture."

The old lady said, "Really?"

Xiu Xin nodded reluctantly, picked up a brush and casually drew a landscape painting. After Mrs. Wang carefully looked at it, the expression on her face finally relaxed a little, "It's quite interesting, but the brushwork is a bit rough, and it needs to be improved." After a pause, she continued, "You need to study it diligently these days. I have a painting by Cui Hongzhen, a great master of our dynasty, in my room. I'll have someone bring it to you

later to show you."
Madam Wang paused and said, "Is Cui Hongzhen your uncle?"
Xiu Xin responded respectfully, "Mother, that's right."
Madam Wang nodded. "Just learn from it. I want to see one of your paintings every day. Do you understand?"
"Yes." Xiu Xin was respectful on the surface, but she was roaring in her heart. One painting a day? Her hands would be broken from painting.
That day, Xiu Xin went to the West Courtyard to hand in her homework. As soon as she entered the door, she heard Old Madam Wang exclaim, "What? Is there such a thing?"
Xiu Xin came in and asked, "What happened?"
Anyang was also there, and he told Xiuxin, "The riot in Luzhou has just been quelled, but the bandits and rebels who caused the riot have not been completely eliminated. One group of rioters somehow learned of Chao Ge'er's identity and captured him to threaten my uncle."
"What?" Xiuxin's heart was in suspense. "Chao Ge'er was kidnapped?"
Anyang continued, "Don't worry, Chao Ge'er is fine, it's just..."
Seeing Anyang hesitate to speak, Xiuxin asked anxiously, "What's wrong?"
Madam Wang added, "You are Chao'er's biological mother, so I should tell you that Chao'er was saved by the daughter of

the Duke of Huguo."

"Zhan Xue?" Xiu Xin widened her eyes.

"The bad thing is that they spent a night outside alone." Old Lady Wang held her forehead with a headache, "What should we do? Her daughter is involved with our Chao Ge'er, and the Duke of the Protectorate is not easy to deal with. Aren't we forced to swallow this bitter pill in silence?"

Xiu Xin advised, "Mother, maybe things are not as bad as you think. The daughter of the Duke of Huguo is of noble birth and beautiful. Maybe she can be a good match for Chao Ge'er."

Madam Wang frowned tightly and uttered a cry, "How could I not know Liu Baozi? He was born in a peasant family, how could he raise a good daughter? Besides, I heard that his daughter grew up outside the Great Wall and was good at wielding swords and knives. This time, when she rescued Brother Chao alone, she killed quite a few people."

Xiu Xin thought to herself, Zhan Xue's path was indeed different from that of ordinary people. Others were heroes saving beauties, but she was a beauty saving a hero.

"Mother...but things have come to this point. We can't afford to offend the Duke of Protectorate. What else can we do?" Xiu Xin said.

Old Madam Wang opened her eyes and looked at Xiuxin, thinking to herself that she was not satisfied with this daughter-in-law at first, but compared with Liu Zhanxue, she liked her better. At least Xiuxin was well-mannered, polite, and came from a noble family.

"Xiu Xin." Old Madam Wang held Xiu Xin's hand and said, "Please think of a solution for me. We must not marry a Hedong lion like Liu Zhanxue."

Xiu Xin was just looking forward to Zhan Xue marrying into the family, so she just comforted him with soft words, "Mother, things are not as bad as you think. We will slowly think of a solution, mother, don't get angry and hurt yourself."

Madam Wang wiped away her tears and said, "I really don't know what sin I committed to bring about such a disaster."

That night, Xiuxin wrote a letter to ask Wang Fusheng's opinion on the matter. She praised Zhan Xue with many words and finally concluded: The Liu family has a beautiful girl. If you want to marry her, you will find a good match.

Wang Fusheng, who was still in Luzhou, received Xiuxin's letter and read it. The little doubt in his heart grew wildly like spring rain. Why was Xiuxin so eager to ask me to agree to marry Liu Zhanxue? Could it be that she hoped that after Liu Zhanxue married, the two of them could hang out together every day in a legitimate way?

Wang Fusheng shook his head, shaking off the messy thoughts in his mind.

However, Wang Fusheng thought of the scene he saw in Shangxin Garden, where Liu

Zhanxue was dressed as a man, and his own Xiuxin was rolling around with her...
When the two of them were together, Xiuxin's unrestrained and completely relaxed smile never appeared in front of him.
Wang Fusheng clenched his fists in jealousy as he thought about it. No! We can't let Zhan Xue marry in!
The author has something to say: The last chapter was tragically locked... What did I write? Wasn't it clear enough? Oh, heaven and earth, I don't want to be a little fresh.

☆, Chapter 59 Return

Chapter 60 Return
Wang Fusheng had been feeling uneasy since he received Xiuxin's letter. On the one hand, he had been away from Beijing for three months, and now he was in the desolate Zhouzhou, with weeds and ruins everywhere, which made him miss his beloved. On the other hand, he became more suspicious and wished he could grow wings and fly to Xiuxin's side.
At the same time, Wang Chaozong was also sighing and frowning. The father and son looked at each other with sad expressions on their faces.
"Chaozong, don't worry, I will never let you marry Liu Baozi's daughter and push you into the fire pit." Wang Fusheng closed the

file and said heavily.

Wang Chaozong was standing nearby. Hearing this, he sighed, "Father, it's easier said than done. Now everyone in the world knows that I was saved by Liu Zhanxue, and I even spent a night outside. I can't wash myself clean even if I jump into the Yellow River. Liu Zhanxue is not like Cui Yixin, the second daughter of the Cui family. She single-handedly saved me from the bandits with her own strength. Now, her legend has spread all over the world. Doesn't even the emperor praise her?"

"Even so, we just need to deny it. Even though you and she spent the whole night outside, you just need to say that you were separated and were never together. No one can verify this. When the time comes, I will send some gifts to the Liu family in the name of the Wang family, and then I can stop the gossips in the world."

Wang Chaozong always listened to his father's words, but this time he raised some doubts, "But if this happens, will it damage Miss Liu's reputation? After all, she is my lifesaver..."

Wang Fusheng asked, "Are you really planning to marry her? If you are willing, I don't want to bother with it. Liu Baozi has hundreds of thousands of soldiers and horses under his command. There is nothing wrong with the marriage between our Wang family and the Liu family."

Wang Chaozong shook his head quickly, "No,

father, I just think it's a little unfair to Miss Liu." Wang Chaozong has been strict with himself since he was a child, and he is most unwilling to do immoral things, so how can he be a heartless person? This is very different from Wang Fusheng, who has been cunning since he was a child, saying one thing in public and another in private, otherwise he would not have been able to climb to the position of Prime Minister at such a young age.

Wang Fusheng frowned and said, "There is no such thing as fairness or unfairness in the world. People in the world are destined to be unfair from the moment they are born. Besides, you don't need to worry. Liu Zhanxue is the daughter of the Duke of Huguo. Is she worried about getting married?"

"Yes. Everything will be arranged by father." Wang Chaozong said.

Half a month later, the situation in Luzhou was almost settled. After the rebellion was almost purged, Wang Fusheng killed a large number of corrupt officials and fostered a large number of his own followers. After the situation in the three states stabilized, Wang Fusheng and Wang Chaozong prepared to return to Beijing.

More than ten days later, Wang Fusheng and his party finally arrived in the capital. When Wang Fusheng and his party arrived in the capital, it was already early winter, the weather was getting colder, and the leaves on the ground were all golden.

Wang Fusheng was riding on his horse and immediately spotted Xiuxin among the welcoming crowd.

She wore a light yellow moire jacket with a circle of fine white fox fur at the collar, which made her face look even more pink and translucent. Below was a Confucian skirt of the same color, and a pair of pointed embroidered shoes on her feet, which were dazzlingly beautiful.

Wang Fusheng stared at Xiuxin greedily, wishing he could jump off his horse and hug the lovely girl. Unfortunately, there were a lot of people around him, so Wang Fusheng could only endure it secretly.

"Greetings, Grandma, Mother."

Wang Chaozong also followed Wang Fusheng and bowed, "Greetings to great-grandmother, grandmother."

Princess Duanyi held Wang Fusheng's hand tremblingly and said, "You've lost some weight."

Wang Fusheng said with a smile, "I'm not thinner at all. It's just that you haven't seen me for a long time, so you always feel that your grandson has become thinner." As he said this, he glanced at Xiuxin who was standing next to Duanyi. Duanyi laughed at this and said, "Okay, you two young people should stop flirting in front of an old woman like me. It's more important to give me a great-grandson as soon as possible."

Xiu Xin's face flushed slightly, and she

said angrily, "Grandma, why are you bringing this up again?"

Wang Fusheng smiled shamelessly and said, "Don't worry, grandma. You will definitely have a great-grandson soon."

Princess Anyang smiled and said, "Well, we are standing in the wind now, it is important to go inside quickly."

Everyone should agree.

Because Wang Fusheng and Wang Chaozong returned home, the Wang family was very lively all night. It was already late at night when they finally settled down. As soon as Xiuxin entered the room, Wang Fusheng hugged her waist from behind, buried his head in the back of her neck, and took a deep breath, "Little girl."

Xiu Xin had long been accustomed to such intimacy, so she just struggled slightly and said, "Itchy."

Wang Fusheng turned her around and held her in his arms, "Did you miss me?"

Xiuxin really hadn't thought about him. These days, she was forced by Mrs. Wang to practice painting and had no free time every day, so she really had no time to think about him.

Wang Fusheng knew what was going on when he saw Xiuxin's expression. He felt a little sad and pinched Xiuxin's nose hard, saying, "You are such an ungrateful person. You really have never thought of me?"

In this situation, Xiu Xin neither admitted nor denied it, and her pretty face flushed red.

Wang Fusheng also knew that he couldn't push her too hard. After all, he had made so many mistakes before, so she naturally wouldn't forgive him so quickly. He only hoped that she would be satisfied if she could have one tenth of the love he had for her.

"Embroidered Heart..."

"Hmm?" Xiu Xin raised her head and looked at him with her big eyes.

Unexpectedly, Wang Fusheng suddenly kissed her lips, blocking her breath. She tasted as sweet as ever, and her lips were still as soft as ever, but Xiuxin's reaction was still immature. Fortunately, she did not push him away.

The two of them naturally indulged in a passionate love affair, with the red quilt fluttering in the wind.

Wang Fusheng had been away for more than three months, and was extremely hungry. He had tortured Xiuxin so much that she was exhausted. In the early winter night, she was sweating profusely. Wang Fusheng was not much better. He hugged Xiuxin and was sweating all over.

Xiuxin remembered what her mother had said: a man is most likely to agree to a woman's request after he is satisfied. So, she rolled her eyes, rubbed towards Wang Fusheng, and called him in a tender voice, "Husband."

It was rare for Xiuxin to take the

initiative to get close to him. Wang Fusheng hugged Xiuxin in his arms and asked, "What's wrong?"

"What do you think about the marriage between Zhan Xue and Chao Ge'er?"

Wang Fusheng didn't expect Xiu Xin to say such a thing at this time. She acted so servilely, actually for that Liu Zhanxue? Thinking of this, his heart sank, and he replied with a smile, "Why, do you have any ideas?"

Xiu Xin hugged Wang Fusheng's waist and said, "Everyone in the capital knows that Zhan Xue saved Chao Ge'er. If our Wang family does not say anything, it will be difficult to stop the world from talking about it. Besides, this Duke of the Protectorate commands the most powerful troops in the world. If we marry him, it will also be good for our Wang family. Isn't this a natural thing?"

Wang Fusheng sneered, "You think very far ahead."

Xiu Xin didn't realize that Wang Fusheng's face had changed, and continued, "Besides, Zhan Xue is a martial arts expert and a true heroine, and Chao Ge'er is also a talented man. Aren't they a perfect match?"

Wang Fusheng said, "I see that you are very happy to have Liu Zhanxue marry you. Could it be that you are planning to keep her company?"

Xiu Xin nodded and said, "It would be great if Zhan Xue could marry into our family.

She is my only close friend in the boudoir."

Wang Fusheng didn't show any expression on his face, but he was thinking secretly in his heart, you want her to marry in so much, but I can't fulfill your wish! Even if Liu Baozi brings his soldiers to cause trouble, I will never compromise!

When Xiuxin woke up the next day, it was already 3:45 in the morning. When she woke up, she was looking into Wang Fusheng's eyes. Xiuxin was startled, "Ah, husband, you didn't go to the morning court?" Wang Fusheng laughed and said, "Little lazy guy, don't you see what time it is now? I just came back from the morning court."

Xiu Xin sat up and said in annoyance, "Why didn't Lan Xiang wake me up?"

Wang Fusheng said, "Don't blame her. I told her not to wake you up. Come, let me take a look."

Xiu Xin hurriedly covered her quilt and asked in panic, "What are you looking at?"

Wang Fusheng reached in and said, "What else can I see? See if you are injured."

Last night, Wang Fusheng was too indulgent and used too much force. Xiuxin felt uncomfortable but didn't care. Now Wang Fusheng insisted on watching, so she blushed. "No, no, how can this be possible?"

Wang Fusheng loved to see Xiuxin blushing. "What's wrong with that? I'm your husband, and there's nothing I can't see. I brought

some ointment here. Apply it on you, and you'll feel better."
Xiu Xin took the ointment from his hand and pulled the quilt tightly, "I'll do it myself."
Wang Fusheng said, "Okay, do it yourself." Then he scratched her nose and turned to walk out, "Remember to wipe it."
Speaking of which, that day, just after the morning court session ended, Liu Baozi stopped Wang Fusheng at the palace gate, "Wang's boy! Stay!"
Wang Fusheng had already prepared for this, so he turned around gracefully and saluted, "What's the matter, Lord Protector?"
Liu Baozi was a man of the military, so he said whatever he wanted to say. He immediately widened his eyes and cursed, "Stop using these sour words on your grandfather. Just tell me what kind of nonsense you said in the court today. Are you going to deny it? My daughter saved your son in vain?"
Wang Fusheng smiled and said, "Your Majesty, you are wrong. How could my Wang family be like this? Your daughter saved my son's life, and I will never forget it. I will prepare generous gifts and go to your house to thank you in person the next day."
"Your grandma is a fucking jerk. If you don't want to admit it, then just don't admit it. What are you talking about?" Liu Baozi only has Zhan Xue as his precious daughter. Seeing her depressed today, he

felt so distressed that he immediately pulled out his sword and plunged it into the mud with a hiss. "My son, I, Liu Baozi, have made a statement today! You have to marry the Wang family whether you want to or not!"

"Oh... My Lords, my Lords, peace is the most precious thing, peace is the most precious thing." Rong Zhenghe, the chief eunuch beside the emperor, said in a shrill voice, "This is at the gate of the palace."

Wang Fusheng was calm in the face of the emergency. "Lord Protector of the Country, we must be reasonable in everything. Your daughter certainly saved my son's life, but my son and your daughter are innocent and have nothing to do with each other. Lord Protector of the Country can't force my son to marry your daughter, can you?"

Liu Baozi blew his beard and glared, "My son, I will definitely let your son marry my daughter! Just wait and see!"

The author has something to say: Sorry, everyone is going out for a trip during the Mid-Autumn Festival. I will update as usual from today.

☆, Chapter 60 Forced Marriage

Chapter 61: Forced Marriage
Looking at the Hua Dynasty, the only person who dared to openly antagonize Wang Fusheng besides Cui Jinyi was the Protector of the Country Liu Baozi. He commanded a large

number of troops and had countless generals under his command. He was a person who could shake the Hua Dynasty with just one stomp of his feet, and even the emperor had to give in to him. But Wang Fusheng was determined to look down on her daughter, so how could Liu Baozi not be furious?

After returning home, he was still furious and kicked over an incense burner. "This brat is too much! Wang Fusheng is such a talker. It's clearly a done deal, but he can just talk it back!"

Zhan Xue was not the kind of girl who would get sad about the passing of time. She was so angry that her eyebrows were raised and she crossed the flower spear on the shelf. "Dad, why don't we just charge into the palace and get the person out! No matter what, let's get married first."

Liu Baozi said, "Girl, do you think you are a bandit in the mountains? You want to rob people? Moreover, Wang Chaozong is the legitimate son of the Wang family after all. Can you rob him just because you want to?"

Zhan Xue said gloomily, "This won't work, and that won't work either. So what should we do?"

Liu Baozi pondered for a moment and said, "There must be a way. I will go ask the military advisor to see if he has any good ideas."

On the other hand, Xiuxin was really worried about Zhanxue. Wang Fusheng was very tough, and Mrs. Wang thought so too.

Xiuxin had no choice but to find Princess Duanyi to see what she thought. She thought that since the old lady loved her so much from the bottom of her heart, she must have a different mind than ordinary people.

So, Xiuxin didn't even take a nap. She had lunch and rested for a while before going to the West Courtyard where Princess Duanyi was. Yu Niang beside Duanyi bowed to Xiuxin and said, "Second Madam, the princess has gone to bed. Second Madam, please come back later."

Xiu Xin said, "No problem, I'll just sit and wait for a while."

After waiting for almost half an hour, Duanyi finally woke up and walked out with the help of Yu Niang. Xiuxin hurried forward to hold Duanyi's right hand and called her sweetly, "Grandma."

Duan Yi glared at Xiu Xin lovingly, "You naughty girl, you never come to my temple for no reason. Just tell me what you want today."

Xiu Xin smiled and said, "Grandma, I have been here for no other reason than to come here recently. I think you have also heard about how the daughter of the Duke of Huguo saved our Chao Ge'er, right? What do you think about this, Grandma?"

Duan Yi pondered for a while, "Xiu Xin, what do you think?"

Xiu Xin had already prepared a set of arguments in her mind, "Grandmother is known as the most talented woman in the Hua

Dynasty, and she has a very broad mind. Everyone in the world fears Zhan Xue like a tiger, but how can ordinary people compare to Zhan Xue? Not to mention that she has the ability to bravely break into the enemy camp alone, but this kind of heroism and courage is incomparable to the thousands of gold in the world. I believe that grandma will never look at Zhan Xue with worldly eyes, right?"

Duan Yi laughed, "You. You seem to be an honest person, but you have such a powerful mouth. According to you, if I look down on Zhan Xue, then I am narrow-minded?"

Xiu Xin lowered her head and said, "Granddaughter-in-law would never dare to do that."

Duan Yi smiled for a while, then stopped smiling and sighed softly, "I not only like Zhan Xue, but I also admire her. Nowadays, all the daughters of the Hua Dynasty are arrogant, competitive, and scheming. Compared with them, Zhan Xue is indeed a standout. But Xiu Xin is bad because of her identity."

Xiu Xin asked doubtfully, "Her identity?"

Duan Yi said, "Don't forget, she is the daughter of the Duke of Protector of the Country. Our Wang family is the leader of the four great families and is in the limelight. If we marry the Duke of Protector of the Country, most of the political and military power will be in our hands. I am afraid that the emperor will become suspicious. If that happens, the Wang family will probably suffer a devastating disaster."

Xiuxin gasped, "This..." Xiuxin thought, "Grandma, is this also the reason why you took a liking to me in the first place?" Because I am just the daughter of a third-rank censor?

Duan Yi said, "This is just one aspect."

Duan Yi held Xiu Xin's hand, "You are a lovely girl, don't worry about Chao Zong's affairs. I will choose a suitable marriage for Chao Ge'er and get him engaged early, so that the Protector of the Country can't make trouble even if he wants to." As he spoke, he sighed, "This Liu Baozi is brave enough on the battlefield, but he still lacks a brain in politics."

Xiuxin nodded, "Grandma, I understand." She was really stupid. She had to wait for Duanyi to point it out before she understood. Wang Fusheng must have thought of all this a long time ago, right? No wonder Wang Fusheng never considered Zhan Xue from the beginning.

But, are Zhan Xue and Wang Chaozong really going to let it go like this?

Xiu Xin thought of Zhan Xue's deep affection and couldn't help but sigh, "It's just not meant to be."

When the matter between Zhan Xue and Chao Zong came to a stalemate, on the other side, an imperial edict was issued from the palace, which said that the fifth daughter of the Cui family, Cui Wu, was dignified and virtuous, talented and virtuous, and a role model for women. She was named the fifth prince's principal wife and their marriage would be held on an appropriate date.

When this incident happened, the entire Hua Dynasty was in turmoil.

First, the fifth prince Hua Ling was born to the unpopular Concubine Duan, and originally had little hope of winning the throne, but now he has the Cui family as a strong backer, which is like adding wings to a tiger. Second, this shows that the Wang family and the Cui family are completely on opposite sides, because everyone knows that Wang Fusheng is the tutor of the second prince Hua Yun.

Wang Fusheng was also troubled by this matter. When he discussed it with Duan Yi, his face looked very ugly. "It seems that Cui Jinyi is willing to put all his wealth on the line to go against me."

Duan Yi said, "Let them make trouble, we must not get involved in the storm of succession. Fusheng, you are the helmsman of the Wang family. If you stand on the wrong side, the whole ship will capsize."

Wang Fusheng said, "Grandmother, I know the pros and cons of this. But the second prince Hua Yun is not a powerful character to begin with, and he has been spoiled by his mother, Concubine Hua, since he was a child. So, apart from the advantage of his mother being favored, what can he use to compete with the scheming Hua Ling? If Hua Ling really ascends the throne one day, will our Wang family still have a good life?"

"Our Wang family's century-old foundation is deeply rooted. How can it be shaken at will?"

Wang Fusheng sighed, "It is indeed difficult to shake it, but doing so will definitely cause great damage to its vitality."

"What do you mean?" Duan Yi asked in a low voice.

Wang Fusheng shook his head. "It's hard for my grandson to make a decision right now. Let's wait and see."

After Wang Fusheng bid farewell to Duanyi, he returned to the East Courtyard and happened to meet Xiuxin talking to Wang Chaozong in the East Courtyard. Xiuxin was now the legal mother of the family, so she naturally put on a good front and personally poured a cup of tea for Chao Ge'er, saying earnestly, "Chao Ge'er, do you have any idea about your own marriage?"

Wang Chaozong bowed and said, "It's up to my father and mother to decide."

Xiu Xin turned around awkwardly, "Did your father tell you that he would marry the daughter of the Marquis of Xinyang to you?"

Wang Chaozong lowered his head and said, "It has been mentioned. But it has not been decided yet."

Although the Marquis of Xinyang is a marquis, he has no real power and is a veritable idle marquis. The daughter of the Marquis of Xinyang is a well-known talented woman. At the moment, this marriage is really a perfect match.

Xiu Xin thought about how she had resisted in every possible way, and she felt a little sympathy for Chao Ge'er. "Chao Ge'er, do you have a girl you like?"

Chaozong's face turned red immediately when Xiuxin asked him this question, "Mother..."

Xiu Xin held her cheek with her hand, "Forget it, this is an unnecessary question. Whether you have a girl you like or not, you can only marry the one your parents choose for you. But if you meet her in the future, just take her home, understand?"

Chaozong was quite embarrassed. Although Xiuxin was nominally his biological mother, she was only sixteen years old, the same age as himself. He always felt it was a little strange to mention this matter to him.

"You are a competent stepmother. You haven't even married your daughter-in-law yet, but you're already talking about taking a concubine." Suddenly, Wang Fusheng's voice came from behind Xiuxin. She was so shocked that her back tightened and she turned her head sharply, "Husband?"

Wang Fusheng glanced at Wang Chaozong calmly, flicked his sleeves and said coldly, "Xiu Xin, come in with me."

The author has something to say: I will update every other day.

☆、Chapter 61 Intimacy

Chapter 62 Intimacy
Xiu Xin really didn't know what had angered Wang Fusheng, so she followed him into the house with her nerves tensed, and timidly called out, "Husband."
Wang Fusheng sat down and drank a bowl of cold tea to calm his anger. "Xiu Xin, you are my wife, Wang Fusheng. Instead of taking care of the household chores, you are worrying about Chaozong's marriage?"
Xiu Xin felt wronged and angry after hearing his harsh words. "I am Chao Ge'er's stepmother. Shouldn't I ask about his marriage? Besides, this is Chao Ge'er's marriage after all. Don't you ever ask about his opinion?"
Xiuxin's words brought up an old problem in his heart. He had forced Xiuxin to marry him in the first place. Even if he had used every possible means, how could he know that she wasn't just acting in front of him now?
"Since ancient times, parents have decided on their children's marriages. Can it be possible that Emperor Chaozong can marry whomever he wants?" Wang Fusheng paused and narrowed his eyes. "Xiu Xin, even if Chaoge'er doesn't like Liu Zhanxue, even if he loves her so much, he has to marry the

daughter of Marquis Xinyang!"

Xiu Xin was so angry that her chest rose and fell, and she looked at him with moist eyes, "You..." If it were her usual temper, her son would have quarreled with him by now, but now, Xiu Xin forced herself to suppress her surging anger and said, "I didn't intend to interfere in Chao Ge'er's marriage, but I just asked him a little question, why do you have to make such a fuss?"

Wang Fusheng was originally in such a state of emotional upheaval due to the doubts in his heart. Now, seeing Xiu Xiu lowering his head, biting his lips aggrievedly, with a tear slowly sliding down his cheek, he secretly regretted that he had said too much. He hurriedly hugged Xiu Xin and wiped her tears. "Why are you crying now? It's all my fault, all my fault." As he spoke, he felt so distressed.

Xiu Xin cried even more sadly, tears rolling down her cheeks, "You yelled at me..."

Wang Fusheng felt even more guilty when he saw Xiuxin like this. He coaxed Xiuxin again and again, and Xiuxin finally stopped crying and laughed. She reached out and poked Wang Fusheng on the forehead, "Okay, you can't do this to me again in the future."

How could Wang Fusheng not respond?

In fact, this trick was also taught to Xiuxin by Jiang. A man will calm down when he sees a woman crying. If the timing is right, he can even get some extra benefits.

A few days later, news of the emperor's marriage approval spread.

The reason was simple. Liu Baozi went to the emperor at night and was willing to hand over the military power of the Northwest Army in exchange for an imperial decree granting marriage. The emperor was unwilling to do so and immediately issued an imperial decree to announce to the world that Liu Zhanxue, the daughter of the Protector of the Country, would be betrothed to Wang Fusheng's son Wang Chaozong.

The strongest of the hundreds of thousands of soldiers in Liu Baozi's hands were the 150,000 troops in the northwest. Now that he had handed over the military power, Liu Baozi only had 50,000 remnants in the southwest. Even if Liu Baozi married into the Wang family, it would be difficult for him to succeed. The emperor was naturally happy to make it happen.

Once the emperor issued the decree, the Wang family had to acknowledge it even if they didn't want to, and they could only accept the decree and express their gratitude. Of course, this also included Wang Fusheng.

Old Madam Wang was so angry that she fell ill and lay in bed for several days. Xiuxin personally served by her bedside. Old Madam Wang held Xiuxin's hand and was quite moved.

She used to look down on Xiuxin, but now she is so pleasing to the eye. Alas, when she thought about having another female demon in the family in the future, Old Madam Wang couldn't help rubbing her forehead and exclaimed, "There will be no peaceful days for our Wang family in the future."

Xiu Xin comforted her, "Mother, please be at ease for now. Not to mention that Miss Liu may not be as bad as you think, even if she is really like that, she has already married into our Wang family and is our Wang family's daughter-in-law. Are you still worried that there is no way to control her?"

When Old Lady Wang heard this, she felt a little relieved, "That's what you said."

Compared to Madam Wang, Wang Fusheng seemed quite calm after the imperial edict was issued, and he didn't even say a word, which made Xiuxin a little nervous. Now that the weather was getting colder, Jiang sent someone to send two peacock feather felts to Xiuxin, one for Xiuxin and the other for Wang Fusheng. Xiuxin was naturally very happy, and after putting them on, she couldn't let go, "My mother still loves me."

After a pause, she asked, "Lanxiang, has the second master returned?" She also wanted to let him try out the other piece of felt embroidery.

Lan Xiang answered quickly, "Yes, now..."

She paused, "In the study."

Xiu Xin was not so easily fooled now. She took off the peacock feather felt and asked with a frown, "Where did he go?"

Lan Xiang hesitated for a while and finally told the truth, "Second Master... Second Master went to Aunt Chu's place."

Xiuxin felt something tighten in her heart, as if something was gripping her heart, making her feel suffocated and her vision blurred. Lanxiang saw that Xiuxin's face was pale, and she called out worriedly, "Miss, what's wrong with you? Are you feeling unwell?"

It took Xiuxin a long time to recover. "It's nothing. I've been married to him for almost half a year, and he hasn't been to the concubines yet. If it gets out, people will say I'm jealous. It's better this way."

Seeing Xiuxin like this, Lanxiang didn't know how much of what she said was true, but she could only comfort her, "If the girl can really think this way, it would be great."

After all, from Lanxiang's point of view, not to mention that there are already two concubines in this mansion, it is likely that there will be another one at any time. If the girl cannot see through this, won't she shed tears every day in the future?

Xiuxin ate her meal as usual, but for some reason, she felt that the meal was tasteless. Even her favorite grilled pigeon tasted bland.

Qinxiang, who was serving Xiuxin, asked, "Miss, are the meals not to your liking? Should I ask the kitchen to bring you another table?"

Xiu Xin shook her head, "No need."

After the meal, Lanxiang asked Xiuxin if she wanted to go out for a walk to help digest the food. Xiuxin just felt tired and said, "I'm a little tired. I want to rest." Lanxiang agreed and asked the little maids to bring in water for Xiuxin to wash.

Xiu Xin took off her hairpins and rings, wearing only a small jacket with a front opening, and curled up on the bed, flipping through a book of martial arts novels. She had recently bought this book from Wang Fusheng, and she had been reading it with great interest yesterday, but for some reason, she could not get into it at all today.

She put the book down and listened to the sounds outside. The wind was blowing, and there was a rustling sound of wind blowing through the leaves.

She felt a chill.

QQ.

There were two knocks on the door.

"Miss, are you ready to rest? It's a little cold tonight. Do you want a hot water bottle to keep you warm?" It was Cuixiang's voice.

Xiu Xin responded, "Okay, bring it in."

The hot water bottle covered her in the

quilt and gave her a warm feeling. She hugged the hot water bottle, but she couldn't stop thinking, maybe he is hugging Aunt Chu now? He hasn't been to Aunt Chu's room for half a year. Aunt Chu came to make trouble a few days ago. Now she should be satisfied.

Xiuxin thought about it and comforted herself, saying that if he went to someone else's place, she would be relieved. Anyway, the two concubines were not of high birth, so they could never surpass her.

But why did her nose still feel so sore?

Xiu Xin couldn't help but bury her whole face in the quilt.

Suddenly, her body fell into a warm embrace, and a familiar voice sounded from above her head, "Xiu Xin."

Xiu Xin's body and mind seemed to be filled with a warm current. She secretly wiped away her tears, sat up, pushed him, and said angrily, "You are full of cold air."

Wang Fusheng said, "It's raining heavily outside. The weather is getting colder." As he spoke, he took off his coat and put it on the small couch beside the bed. He got on the bed and hugged Xiuxin in his arms. His hand touched the hot water bottle and he couldn't help laughing, "Oh, I was just wondering whether I should ask someone to bring in a hot water bottle. You are so thoughtful."

Xiu Xin held the hot water bottle tightly in her arms and said, "This is mine. I won't give it to you."

Wang Fusheng only noticed at this moment that Xiuxin's eyes were red, "What's wrong with you? Did you cry?"

Xiu Xin said stubbornly, "No, maybe I caught a cold recently."

Wang Fusheng got an unexpected surprise today. "Do you think I stayed at Aunt Chu's place? That's why you're crying?"

Xiu Xin held the hot water bottle and turned sideways, "Aunt Chu and Aunt Zhou are all my people, it is only natural for me to go to their place. As the second wife of the Wang family, I still have this kind of broad mind."

Wang Fusheng's excitement was extinguished by Xiuxin's words, but he changed his mind and thought that there was still a long time to come, and Xiuxin would eventually understand his feelings. With this thought, he put the matter aside and fell asleep with Xiuxin in his arms.

The author has something to say: Dear friends, would you like to leave a message?

☆, Chapter 62: Meet Again

Chapter 63: Meet Again

When Xiuxin woke up the next day, she found herself being held tightly in Wang Fusheng's arms, with his big hand on her waist and her nose against his chest. Her long, shiny black hair was tangled with his, indistinguishable from each other.

Xiu Xin suddenly understood the meaning of married couple. The ancients said: "Married couple, love each other without doubt." It's a pity that the married couple refers to the original wife, and she is just his concubine.

Xiuxin stretched out her bare hands and ruffled the hair of the two people, her heart full of thoughts. She first met him last year. She caught a glimpse of him at Cui's house. How could she have imagined at that time that a year later she would be sharing a bed with this man and snuggling with him?

Perhaps Xiuxin accidentally pulled Wang Fusheng's hair, and he murmured something as if he was half awake. He moved his hand on Xiuxin's waist down and hugged Xiuxin with more strength so that Xiuxin was pressed tightly against Wang Fusheng's chest.

This posture made Xiuxin feel a little restrained, and she couldn't help but push him gently.

Wang Fusheng relaxed a little, and Xiuxin was able to catch her breath.

Xiu Xin raised her eyes to look at him. His eyebrows were like swords, but without any aura of killing. He looked handsome and upright, with a high nose bridge and wide and thin lips. In fact, in terms of appearance alone, he was really very good. Although Wang Chaozong looked about 50% like him, he was not as handsome and eye-catching as him. Of course, maybe it was because Wang Chaozong was still young.

"Why, do you think your husband is so handsome now?" Wang Fusheng suddenly opened his eyes, looking mischievous.

Xiu Xin refused to admit it. "I just noticed that your skin is a little rougher than before. Is it because the wind and sand in the northwest are very strong?"

Wang Fusheng was shocked. "Rough?"

Xiu Xin nodded, "Rough."

Wang Fusheng reached out and touched Xiuxin's cheek. It was smooth, white and elastic. Then he touched himself. Eh? It seemed... it seemed a little rough.

Being disliked...

But I am twice her age and will only get older. She has always been so cold to me. If I become an old man, wouldn't that be...

When Wang Fusheng thought about it, he broke out in a cold sweat. He quickly put on his clothes, got up and walked out.

Xiu Xin grabbed his sleeve and said, "Aren't you taking a day off today? Are you still going to the palace?"

Wang Fusheng put on his outer robe, buttoned it up and said, "I have something to do outside. You can sleep a little longer."

Xiu Xin nodded, "Okay."

When Wang Fusheng opened the door and came out, Mo Yan had just stood up. Seeing Wang Fusheng actually leaving the room, he came forward in surprise and said, "Isn't the

Second Master taking a day off today? Why are you up so early? The Second Madam hasn't gotten up yet, right?"
Wang Fusheng rubbed his face with his palms and asked, "Mo Yan, are you looking at me, the youngest?"
Mo Yan said, "Second Master, what are you talking about? Second Master is in the prime of life, handsome and in full bloom, how can he grow old?"
Wang Fusheng glared at him, "Come on, come on, I'm too lazy to listen to your nonsense. Find me the ointment I got from Yuqin last time."
Mo Yan saw Wang Fusheng and his wife getting closer day by day, why did the second master mention the jade piano now?
When Wang Fusheng saw Mo Yan standing still, he glared at him, "What are you still bothering about? Why don't you get it for me quickly?"
"Hey, okay." Mo Yan responded and left quickly.
Although Wang Fusheng was off today, there were still many people coming and going, and he was entertaining people non-stop. Xiuxin got up early and went to the West Courtyard to pay her respects to Duanyi and Old Lady Wang. It happened that Princess Anyang and Qian also came to pay their respects, so the four of them gathered together to chat.
"Has the Third Master's condition improved recently?" Duan Yi asked.

Qian sighed and said, "He is not the same as before, neither better nor worse, but it is winter now and his wheezing has become more severe, which is really worrying."

Madam Wang said, "The third child's illness relapses almost every winter. Last year, we invited Doctor Cui from the palace to see him, but there was no improvement. We must be more careful this year and make sure he doesn't catch a cold."

Qian bowed and expressed his gratitude.

Duan Yi took a sip of tea and fixed his eyes on Xiu Xin who was sitting at the end. "Xiu Xin, our family is about to marry the daughter of the Duke of Huguo. You are Chao Ge'er's biological mother, so I will let you take care of this matter. How do you think?"

Xiu Xin was shocked, "Grandma, my granddaughter-in-law is still young and may not be able to handle such an important task."

Duan Yi sighed, "You will have to take care of these things sooner or later. Although you are young, you should learn to manage the household. This time Chao Ge'er is getting married, because the emperor has granted the marriage, the court has allocated 20,000 taels of silver. Our mansion has also contributed 20,000 taels. He is grown up, and it would be ridiculous for him to live with you and your wife all the time. Isn't there a piece of land behind the East Courtyard that belongs to our Wang family? Why don't we just build a courtyard there for Chao Ge'er and his family?"

Madam Wang responded, "Mother has considered it carefully, but Chao'er's marriage is imminent, and I'm afraid it will be difficult to build the courtyard before the wedding."

Duan Yi said, "I know that too. We are going to marry the daughter of the Duke of Huguo on October 8th, so we won't have enough time to build this courtyard. But there is no rush, we can build it slowly. We can just vacate Shangxin Garden for their wedding room."

Princess Anyang smiled and said, "I'm afraid we'll have to set aside a room in Shangxin Garden to be used as a weapons room. Isn't it rumored that the daughter of the Duke of the Protectorate loves to wield swords and clubs?"

Xiu Xin said, "Among the noble ladies of our Hua Dynasty, there is really no one like Miss Liu, who is both talented in literature and martial arts, and has a kind heart. Even the emperor praises her highly."

Princess Anyang smiled half-sinisterly and half-sinisterly, "Oh, you are lucky to have such a good daughter-in-law."

Xiu Xin just smiled and said nothing.

Anyang took a few sips of tea slowly before speaking, "Grandmother, Chao Ge'er is engaged, and it's time for our Xiaozong's marriage to be settled. After much thought, I think the daughter of Minister Ma of the Ministry of Personnel is very suitable. Both her appearance and family background are a perfect match for our Xiaozong."

Duan Yi asked, "But your maiden name is Yunyun?"

Anyang said, "Exactly."

Xiuxin was worried, why was it her? Ma Yunyun and she had some grudges against each other. With Ma Yunyun's petty personality, what would happen if she married into the same family? However, Xiuxin changed her mind and felt relieved. Now she was on the same level as her mother-in-law. If she really dared to act rudely in front of her, it would be a violation of her superiors and would be considered unfilial! Xiuxin sighed inwardly, this was also a rare benefit of marrying Wang Fusheng.

Anyang continued, "I think Xiaozong and Chaoge'er are about the same age, so why not let them get married together? What do you think, grandmother?"

Duan Yi hesitated for a moment, "Is this inappropriate?"

Anyang said, "What's wrong with this? Xiao and Chao are brothers. Wouldn't it be more lively if they set the wedding date together?"

Duan Yi remained silent.

Finally, it was Old Lady Wang who spoke up, "If that's the case, then let's do it together. Following Chao'er's example, our mansion will also pay 20,000 taels of silver."

Anyang was overjoyed and bowed to express his gratitude.

In this way, Xiuxin bid farewell to Duanyi and Old Lady Wang, left the West Courtyard and returned to the East Courtyard. At this time, Wang Fusheng was meeting guests in the study room of the East Courtyard. Xiuxin didn't like to disturb him in the study room, not to mention that he had guests. She walked around the study door and went to the main room.

Who would have thought that at this moment, the door of the study creaked open, and a tall and graceful young man in a purple robe with sword-like eyebrows and heroic eyes walked out.

Xiu Xin took a casual glance and suddenly remembered that the man was the young man who played the zither that she met in Biechuan Temple. At that time, he told her that he played "The Phoenix Seeks the Phoenix"...

Xiuxin was confused and wanted to walk past quickly with her head down, but the man called her back, "Miss, please stay."

Although Xiu Xin didn't know who this person was, she knew from his clothes that he was either rich or noble, and must be a relative of the royal family. Xiu Xin stopped and asked, "What do you want, sir?"

The young man smiled and said gently, "Miss,

do you still remember me?"
The author has something to say: Update la la la la la la... Dear friends, did you spread flowers today?

☆、Chapter 63: Actors

Chapter 64: Actors
Although Xiu Xin knew little about zither music, she was familiar with a piece like "The Phoenix Seeks the Phoenix". The meaning of this piece is obvious: a glance from a beautiful woman, the zither music, and the two holding hands across the world.
Xiu Xin bowed and said, "I am Wang Fusheng's wife, Cui. It is really inappropriate for you to call me Miss."
Hua Ling was shocked when he heard this. When he first met her in Biechuan Temple, he thought she was the daughter of the Wang family. He never thought that she was actually Wang Fusheng's second wife. He had heard earlier that Wang Fusheng married the daughter of a branch of the Cui family. It seemed that this woman was the one in front of him. Hua Ling secretly hated her. If it was someone else, it would be fine. He could just take her away. Unfortunately, she was actually Wang Fusheng's woman... Hua Ling narrowed his eyes. No matter what happened in the future, he couldn't afford to offend the Wang family now.
Just then, Wang Fusheng pushed the door open and walked out. He looked suspiciously

between Xiuxin and Hualing, then bowed to Hualing and said, "Fifth Prince, this is my wife."

Hua Ling retracted the expression on his face and said with a smile, "So you are Lord Wang's wife. I am so sorry for your disrespect."

Xiu Xin bowed to Hua Ling and said, "Greetings to the Fifth Prince."

Hua Ling supported Xiu Xinxu and said, "Why do you have to do such a big ceremony?"

Xiu Xin calmly stepped back to stand behind Wang Fusheng and said, "I'll take my leave first."

Hua Ling's gaze involuntarily followed Xiu Xin. Her back was slender and weak, and her jet-black hair fell to her waist, like silk.

"Fifth Prince." Wang Fusheng could see Hua Ling's thoughts. He was already a little angry in his heart, but his smile was even more charming. "Fifth Prince, please come this way."

Hua Ling came back to his senses and bowed, "I am sorry to bother you, Lord Wang today."

"It is truly an honor for me that Your Highness has come to my humble home. Why should I bother you?" Wang Fusheng smiled as he led Hua Ling out of the house.

That evening, Xiuxin waited until three o'clock in the morning but Wang Fusheng still didn't come back. Xiuxin hugged the pillow, but couldn't hold on any longer and fell asleep in a sideways position.

That morning, Xiuxin had just woken up when Cuixiang came in with toiletries and other things, "Madam, I will help you wash up."

Xiu Xin yawned, "Why is Lan Xiang not here today?"

Cuixiang said, "Miss Lanxiang went outside to see those two vixens."

Xiu Xin exclaimed, "What vixen?"

Cuixiang was the type who could not hide her secrets, so she said immediately, "The Second Master came back drunk last night, and brought back two beautiful actors. I heard they were from the Fifth Prince's mansion, one is called Lu Yao and the other is called Hong Ying."

Xiu Xin suddenly felt a tightness in her chest, and asked calmly, "How is the Second Master going to place them?"

Cuixiang said, "I don't know, I only know that the Second Master has placed them in Wutong Garden in the East Courtyard."

"Wutong Garden?" This place is quite close to Aunt Chu's courtyard. Could it be that she is really planning to take in the house? Xiu Xin sat up straight and said, "Hurry, help me get dressed."

"yes."

Xiuxin deliberately dressed more formally today, with an exquisite gold hairpin in her hair, and her lipstick was darker than usual. Xiuxin looked at herself in the bronze mirror, with delicate makeup and gorgeous clothes, this is what a wife should look like.

Cuixiang followed Xiuxin and asked, "Where is Madam going?"

Xiuxin did not answer, but walked faster and faster, going straight to the side room where Wang Fusheng had stayed last night.

Wang Fusheng came home very late yesterday and slept until the beginning of the 9th hour today.

"Tea."

Wang Fusheng had just asked for tea when the door creaked open. Mo Yan came in with a teapot and poured Wang Fusheng a cup of tea, saying, "Second Master, you are finally awake. Second Madam has been waiting for you for an hour."

Wang Fusheng raised his eyebrows and asked, "What's wrong? Why is she waiting for me?"

Mo Yan secretly complained that it was you who did this, "Second Master, I guess it's because of the two actors you brought back yesterday."

"So it was for them." Wang Fusheng seemed to have just remembered, "They..." Wang Fusheng thought about it and thought that he could take this opportunity to see Xiuxin's reaction, so he said, "Let the second lady come in."

When Xiu Xin walked in, Wang Fusheng almost didn't recognize her. She was covered in jewels and glittering clothes. Wang Fusheng thought she was Princess Anyang. Didn't his little Guai always dress plainly and cutely? Why did her temperament change so much now?

"Second Master." Xiu Xin bowed first.

Wang Fusheng held Xiuxin's hand affectionately and asked, "What's the big deal today?"

Xiu Xin shook her head, "No."

"Then why are you dressed so formally?"

Xiu Xin said, "There is a new person coming into the mansion today, so it should be more grand."

With just this one sentence, Wang Fusheng knew that Xiuxin was jealous. She wore this battle robe to declare war on him. He couldn't help but pinch Xiuxin's nose and said, "Can you tell me where the newcomers are in the mansion? Why are you bothering to dress like this?"

Xiu Xin asked, "Isn't that the red and green in Wutong Garden?"

"So you're talking about them." Wang Fusheng pretended that he had just remembered that there were two such people in the palace. "They are the actors sent by the fifth prince. Green waist is good at dancing, and red cherries are good at singing. Oh, they are two wonderful people."

Xiu Xin almost wanted to stretch out her claws to scratch Wang Fusheng's smug face, but she managed to suppress it with great effort and said against her will, "I would like to congratulate the Second Master on getting two beauties."

Wang Fusheng looked at Xiuxin's tightly clenched palms, her long nails almost digging into the flesh, and stopped teasing her. He straightened Xiuxin's curled fingers and clasped their fingers with his own, "Xiuxin..."

Xiuxin was angry at the moment and struggled to pull her hand out, but Wang Fusheng held it tightly. With one force, he pulled her into his arms. "Xiuxin, don't you think that those two people came from the Fifth Prince's mansion? Do you really think that my room can accommodate them?"

Xiu Xin suddenly became quiet, "Then you..."

Wang Fusheng pinched Xiuxin's cheeks and said, "Of course I have to accept the person given by the Fifth Prince, but I just keep him in the mansion to keep him idle. Our Wang family can afford to support two idle people."

Xiu Xin blushed a little, "Husband."

Wang Fusheng was suddenly delighted. "You are so stupid and cute."

Since she was little, Xiuxin has been called stupid many times. Her brothers and sisters also say she is stupid. Is she really stupid? However, even if these two are not good enough, there will always be other concubines in the future, right?

"Okay." Wang Fusheng pinched Xiuxin's ear, "It's better for you to be a little dumb. Being too smart can easily backfire."

Xiu Xin raised her head, the tassel on her gold hairpin swaying gently, "My husband, aren't you afraid that those two people will cause trouble in the mansion? Or maybe they are spies sent by the fifth prince."

Wang Fusheng said, "It's nothing. I don't think they can cause any trouble."

Wang Fusheng was so sure that they would not cause any trouble, but he didn't know that just two days later, a big incident happened in the Wang family.

The author has something to say: Everyone, I really have no choice after work. Every day after overtime, I just want to fall asleep. I will never abandon this article, but I really can't guarantee regular updates. I'm really sorry. I can only say that everyone should check it every few days, and there should be updates. There is not much content left in this article.

☆, Chapter 64 Storm

Chapter 65: Storm

When Xiu Xin heard this, she was shocked. Chao Ge'er had always been tactful, gentle, and knew right from wrong. How could he do such a thing? No wonder Wang Fusheng was so angry that his face turned pale. He shouted angrily, "Come here, capture that rebellious son! I want to torture him!"

Xiuxin grabbed Wang Fusheng's sleeve and advised, "Brother Chao has never been like this. Ask him carefully, maybe there is something going on."

Wang Fusheng was already furious, and when he heard Xiuxin say this, his anger did not diminish at all, "No matter what the reason, that rebellious son did such a thing, he deserves to be beaten by the family law this time!"

The cause of this matter was Chao Ge'er's personal maid Yubi. Yubi was a maid given to Chao Ge'er by Old Lady Wang. Everyone in the palace knew about this, but Wang Chaozong had never touched her. This time, somehow, Wang Chaozong and Lu Yao's scandal was discovered this morning. Although Wang Fusheng had no intention of taking Lu Yao and Hong Ying into his room, they were both actors given to Wang Fusheng by the fifth prince. No matter what, Wang Chaozong should not touch them, as it would be suspected of incest.

Xiu Xin just thought that this matter might have spread throughout the capital, and Zhan Xue would be so sad if she knew about it.

At this moment, Wang Chaozong was already kneeling in the ancestral hall. Wang Fusheng pushed open the door of the ancestral hall and without thinking, kicked Wang Chaozong hard in the back, knocking him to the ground.

Wang Fusheng used a lot of force in this kick, but Wang Chaozong didn't say a word. He bit his lower lip tightly with his upper lip, and his face turned pale.

Wang Fusheng was still not satisfied, so he turned around and took out a bramble from behind the ancestral hall door and hit Wang Chaozong with it fiercely, "You evil creature, you actually did such a disgraceful thing on the eve of your wedding! I don't know what evil I did in my previous life to give birth to a creature like you!"

Wang Chaozong became even more silent when he saw that his father was extremely angry. Wang Fusheng was originally only about 60% angry, but when he saw Wang Chaozong like this, his anger increased to 100%. He became even more ruthless and hit Wang Chaozong hard again and again.

Mo Yan and the others saw Wang Chaozong's body quickly covered in blood and flesh, and they were all so frightened that they kept silent and shrank their heads. Only Mo Yan was willing to stand up and persuade him, "Second Master, please stop, look at what you have done to my brother?" Wang Fusheng pushed Mo Yan in hatred, "This evil creature should be beaten to death!"

Mo Yan saw that the situation was not good, and hurriedly winked at the servants below. The servants understood and ran out to find Old Lady Wang and Princess Duanyi. Mo Yan also ran out and knocked on Xiuxin's door, "Second Madam, Second Madam, go and persuade the Second Master, he wants to beat Chao Ge'er to death."

Although Xiuxin knew that Wang Fusheng was going to attack her, she had never thought it would be so serious, so she dropped what she was holding and ran out. Xiuxin pushed open the door of the ancestral hall, and saw Wang Fusheng raising his hand and hitting Wang Chaozong hard on the back. Chao Ge'er collapsed to the ground, his back covered in blood and flesh, his eyes closed, his face pale, and he didn't even make a sound.

Xiuxin's heart immediately rose to her throat, and she quickly reached out to grab the whip, "Stop hitting him, are you really going to beat him to death?"

Wang Fusheng didn't notice that Xiuxin came to grab the thorn, but he saw a long bloody mark on Xiuxin's snow-white palm. It looked horrible, and he felt guilty and regretful for a moment, "What are you doing here?"

Xiuxin said, "I know that as a father you are very disappointed with your son, but you should at least ask the whole story and the cause and effect before you judge him. How could you beat Chaoger like this without knowing the right or wrong?" Wang Fusheng felt regretful when he saw how Chaoger was beaten, and he felt even more guilty when he saw the long blood mark on Xiuxin's palm.

Wang Fusheng was about to send someone to call the doctor when he heard the servant outside shouting, "Princess Duanyi and the old lady are here."

Wang Fusheng had no choice but to walk a few steps forward to greet him. Duan Yi came over trembling and panting, and stepped into the door of the ancestral hall. "You only have this one son. What will you do if you beat him to death today?"

"Grandma…" Wang Fusheng reached out to help, but Duan Yi angrily dodged his hand.

"Originally, I shouldn't have been involved in Chao'er's affairs. It turns out that you are his father. But if you use such heavy hands, I will not be able to bear it. The Wang family ancestors in the ancestral hall are watching you!"

When Xiuxin saw Duanyi coming, she felt relieved and quickly called for Chen, the imperial physician who often treated Duanyi. Old Lady Wang squatted down to check the wounds on Chaozong's body. His back was bloody and there was not a single piece of healthy flesh. She couldn't help but feel sad and cried, "It's a pity that you don't have a mother to love you. You have suffered such a serious injury." At the same time, she scolded the maids and servants around her, "Are you all dead? Why don't you find a soft chair and carry Chao back?"

After all this hustle and bustle, it was already night.

Everyone's attention was on Ge'er, and no one noticed the injury on Xiuxin's hand. However, Lanxiang noticed it. She saw that Xiuxin's right hand was a little swollen, and there was a long bloodstain that looked very scary.

"Girl, do you want to ask a doctor to take a look?"

Xiu Xin shook her head and said, "It's

nothing, just a minor injury. Go to the pharmacy to get some medicine and bandage it up." After a pause, she said, "Go get a cloak, I'll go to Wutong Garden."

Wutong Garden was adjacent to Aunt Chu's courtyard, deep and remote. Xiuxin walked to the door, tightened her cloak, walked to the door of Luyao's room, and knocked.

Not long after, Green Waist's voice sounded from inside the door, "Who is it?"

Lan Xiang said, "The Second Madam is here."

Lu Yao hurriedly opened the door and bowed politely, "This servant greets the Second Madam."

Xiuxin looked at Lu Yao carefully and found that she was indeed slender, like a willow swaying in the wind, especially her slender waist that could be held in one hand. She was truly a beauty.

"Sit down." Xiu Xin sat down in the main seat. "I have no other reason to come here tonight, but to ask you about you and Chao Ge'er."

Lu Yao may have been prepared, and immediately knelt down and cried, "Second Madam, the young master and I are compatible, please help us."

Mutual affection?

Xiu Xin almost laughed out loud, "You've only been in the palace for a few days and you've already become close friends with Chao Ge'er?"

Lu Yao kowtowed to the ground several times, "A few days ago, I ran into you by chance in the East Courtyard Garden. I fell in love with you after seeing your graceful demeanor, and you also secretly fell in love with me. You and I are in love with each other."

Xiu Xin felt that Lu Yao was very good at avoiding the main point, and she said sternly, "You two are in love? Do you know who you belong to in this palace?"

"Your servant..." Lu Yao's eyes were a little flustered.

"Or do you think you have no chance in front of the Second Master, so you set your sights on Chao Ge'er?" Xiu Xin smiled slightly, "Lu Yao, although you are given by the Fifth Prince, you will have to let my Wang family deal with you once you enter the palace. It's not impossible for me to sell you out."

When Lu Yao heard this, his face turned pale as paper and a gleam of anger flashed in his eyes.

Xiu Xin said no more and turned and left.

In the end, the Wang family did not sell Lu Yao. First, Lu Yao was the Fifth Prince's. If they sold her, wouldn't it be a slap in the face of the Fifth Prince? Second, Wang Chaozong begged Wang Fusheng to keep Lu Yao. Finally, Mrs. Wang said, "This matter should not be publicized. She is just a woman. Just keep her as a maid for Brother Chao."

Although Xiuxin felt that Luyao was a nuisance, she couldn't say anything more.

On the other hand, the annual women's court meeting is approaching. Led by Duanyi, Old Lady Wang, Princess Anyang and Xiuxin are all carefully planning for this women's court meeting.

The author has something to say: Updated. Sorry for the long wait.

☆、Chapter 6511 Miscarriage

Chapter 66

After Chao Ge'er was injured, Lu Yao regarded herself as a member of Wang Chaozong's family, lived in Chaozong's courtyard, and took care of him all day long. In addition, she was good at winning people's hearts, and the maids in the East Courtyard all loved to play with her. Lu Yao began to act like a concubine, and even Old Lady Wang said that Lu Yao was very dedicated.

Xiuxin naturally disliked her, but she didn't do anything big wrong, and Xiuxin couldn't act like a "mother-in-law" to her, so she could only suppress it for the time being.

November 28th is the annual Women's Day Meeting.

Princess Duanyi, along with Madam Wang, Princess Anyang, and Xiuxin, entered the palace together. Four sedan chairs were approaching the palace gate, and dozens of sedan chairs of different sizes had already been parked in front of them. The chief guard at the palace gate was checking the number of people and invitations one by one. The waiting process was a bit long, and the ladies all got off the car and talked and laughed. Duanyi took Xiuxin to greet the wives of the Xie, Sun, and Cui families, as well as the wives of the princes. Xiuxin returned the greetings one by one. Everyone praised her.

Xiu Xin was clear-headed and knew that these noble ladies were not praising her at all. They were obviously doing so for the sake of the Wang family.

After half an hour, everyone entered the palace gate. A special maid came forward to lead the way and took everyone to the Queen's Phoenix Palace. After everyone sat down, they all waited for the Queen in silence. Not long after, they heard a palace maid shouting: The Queen has arrived.

Xiu Xin hurriedly followed the crowd, stepped out from the table, knelt down, and praised: "Your Majesty, the Queen, is here to see you."

After the Queen called out, she swept her eyes over everyone one by one, and finally fixed her eyes on Xiu Xin, and said, "Isn't this Xiu Xin from the Cui family?"

Xiu Xin had never thought that the Queen would mention her alone, so she quickly bowed with fear and trepidation, "Your Majesty the Queen."

The queen seemed to have thought of something interesting. She chuckled a few times and said, "The last time I saw you, you were fighting in the palace. This time, you are already the daughter-in-law of the Wang family. Do you want to fight again this time?"

Xiu Xin said hurriedly, "My humble servant is only good at showmanship and not worth seeing. Today, I want to present you with a painting."

The queen groaned, "That's great."

After some greetings, the Queen said, "Now that the winter plum blossoms are just beginning to bloom outside, why don't we take the winter plum blossoms as our theme today, whether it's writing poems, embroidery, playing music, or painting, it's all fine, what do you think?"

Everyone responded, "We will obey the Queen's words."

What a coincidence, among the entire room, only the Fifth Miss Cui, who is now the Fifth Prince's wife, chose to paint like Xiuxin.

Xiuxin mixed the paint and was about to start painting when she saw Cui Wu looking at her with provocative eyes. After all, Cui Wu was now the fifth imperial concubine, so Xiuxin couldn't confront her as before, so she just looked away. Xiuxin didn't have the mind to compete, and this women's court meeting was just the queen gathering everyone together for fun, so why bother to fight for those titles?

An hour later, Xiu Xin and Cui Wu both

handed their paintings to the Queen.

The Queen evaluated them one by one. When it was Xiu Xin's and Cui Wu's turn, the Queen said, "From the perspective of composition and brushwork, the Fifth Concubine's painting is slightly better, but Xiu Xin's painting of winter plum blossoms is more interesting. The white snow covers everything, but there is only one winter plum blossom standing alone, with bright red flowers blooming, which makes people feel the spring breeze blowing in their faces. It is really interesting."

The Queen held the two paintings and weighed them for a while and said, "Generally speaking, Xiu Xin's painting is slightly better. Come, enjoy it."

"Yes." A palace maid was already beside him, holding a tray and bringing over a gold hairpin with extremely exquisite workmanship.

Xiuxin kowtowed to express her gratitude.

Madam Wang was overjoyed, "Xiu Xin, these few months of hard work have really not been in vain."

Xiuxin pursed her lips and said nothing. This Cui Wu had always been petty, and she had stolen her limelight. Who knew how she would take revenge in the future? Xiuxin felt a throbbing pain in her head just thinking about it.

Sure enough, during the noon tour, the newly promoted Fifth Imperial Concubine came towards her with an aggressive and arrogant manner. Xiu Xin bowed to Cui Wu first, "Greetings to the Fifth Imperial Concubine."

Cui Wuxu responded, "How does this Imperial Garden compare to the Wang Family Garden?"

Xiu Xin said, "The Imperial Garden gathers all the beauty in the world and all kinds of rare treasures together. How can the Wang family compare to it?"

Cui Wu said, "Is that so?" Cui Wu smiled, "But marrying into the royal family also has its own worries. The first one is the issue of offspring. As the fifth prince's wife, I have to give birth to a grandson as soon as possible. I am not as lucky as you. Lord Wang already has a legitimate son, so you don't have to worry about it. Besides, even if your child is born, he can enjoy wealth and glory, and he won't have to worry about anything. After all, he is the eldest son."

Xiu Xin did not want to argue with her, so she just smiled and replied, "Of course, sister, you married into the royal family, and there are many things to worry about. You are not like me, who just wants to be free and happy."

"You..." Cui Wu's face changed with anger. Wasn't she saying that even if she, Cui Wu, was the Fifth Prince's consort now, the new women who entered the Prince's Mansion in the future would not give her a good life?

Old Madam Wang was in the front accompanying the wife of the Marquis of

Xinyang to appreciate the plum blossoms. When she turned around and saw that Xiuxin had not caught up, she called out, "Xiuxin, come quickly."

"Yes." Xiu Xin responded, bowed and said, "I will take my leave first."

Cui Wu looked at Xiu Xin and stomped his feet angrily, then walked back biting his lip, "Cui Xiu Xin, just wait and see!"

"Greetings, mother." Xiu Xin followed Madam Wang to enjoy the snow, but she didn't expect to hear a clear male voice. Xiu Xin raised her head and met the narrow and long phoenix eyes of the fifth prince Hua Ling. Xiu Xin's heart skipped a beat and she quickly looked away.

"My son." The queen smiled when she saw Hua Ling. "Why are you wearing so little?" She looked at the eunuch chief at the side in reproach. "How do you serve the master? Why don't you bring a cloak over?"

Hua Ling said, "It's okay, mother. Although it snowed a little today, it's not very cold yet, so I didn't feel cold."

For some reason, Xiuxin always felt that Hua Ling's gaze was directed at her intentionally or unintentionally, making her very uncomfortable, and she wished she could burrow three feet into the ground.

After everyone saluted, they all praised the Fifth Prince for his handsome appearance, extraordinary bearing, etc. Xiu Xin hid behind Old Lady Wang and kept silent.

Hua Ling said, "I know all the ladies, but I don't know..." Then he walked to Xiu Xin and asked, "Who is this?"

Xiu Xin was so embarrassed that she didn't know what to do and even forgot to respond.

It was Old Lady Wang who spoke first, "This is my wife's daughter-in-law."

Hua Ling smiled slightly, "Oh, so she is Lord Wang's wife."

Xiuxin clenched her hands tightly, feeling extremely nervous. She had clearly met him at Wang's house last time, so why was he pretending to be confused?

The Queen was a very capable person. She quickly noticed something was wrong and smiled while holding Hua Ling's hand, saying, "Hey, why isn't the Fifth Imperial Concubine here? I just saw her following behind us."

A palace servant replied, "Reporting to the Queen, the Fifth Imperial Concubine has returned to her bedroom."

The queen smiled and said, "Look, this is really unfortunate. You came all the way to look for her, but she returned to the palace."

Hua Ling's gaze still vaguely fell on Xiu Xin, and he twitched the corners of his mouth slightly, "It's quite unfortunate... Your son will take his leave now."

Only after Hua Ling left did Xiu Xin feel relieved.

In the evening, the carriage drove to the east courtyard. Xiuxin got off the carriage and saw Wang Fusheng.

It was snowing lightly at the moment, and Mo Yan was holding an umbrella behind him. He stood straight at the gate of the courtyard, his blue uniform swaying in the wind, the white sash around his waist dancing like a butterfly, his face as white as jade, his black hair like a waterfall.

Xiu Xin's heart softened in an instant. She walked over, held his hand, and whispered, "Are you waiting for me?"

Wang Fusheng's palms were warm. He gently stroked Xiuxin's cold hands. "Of course. Is everything okay?"

Xiu Xin sighed, "I'd better not go to this palace easily in the future."

A sinister look flashed across Wang Fusheng's eyes. "Some people are too arrogant. They dare to covet other people's things. They are too self-conscious."

Xiu Xin said, "Fusheng, although that is true, we cannot follow the royal family..."

Wang Fusheng stopped Xiuxin from talking, "I understand what you mean, I have my own plans."

Although Xiuxin didn't like the fifth prince, she didn't want Wang Fusheng and Hua Ling to become enemies from then on. After all, no matter how powerful the Wang family was, they were just an aristocratic family. Even if the imperial power declined, they were still the royal family after all.

On the other side, Cui Wu was also upset because of what happened during the day. As

Hua Ling went to Concubine Shi's place today, he pretended to be sick again. This time, although Hua Ling came after nearly an hour, he finally came. Cui Wu curled his lips proudly, grabbed Hua Ling's hand and pressed it on his chest, "My husband, my chest hurts so much."

Hua Ling suppressed his impatience and said softly, "Chest pain again? Do you want to call the imperial physician to take a look?"

Cui Wu leaned over sweetly, "As long as you come, my husband, my chest will not hurt anymore."

Hua Ling said, "You really should ask the imperial physician to take a good look at your illness and prescribe some medicine for you to take for a few months. It has to be cured completely."

Cui Wu hummed, "My husband still cares about me."

Hua Ling was feeling annoyed when he suddenly heard the eunuch outside say, "Fifth Prince, the Queen is calling you urgently."

Hua Ling was as if he had been pardoned. He quickly broke free from Cui Wu's hand and said, "My mother urgently summoned me. Perhaps there is something important to discuss. I will go first. You should have a good rest."

As soon as Hua Ling entered Fengqi Palace, the queen sitting at the head of the table shouted sternly, "Kneel down!"

Hua Ling knelt down hurriedly, "Mother..."
"Do you know how difficult your current situation is? The Emperor has always favored Concubine Xie, and the Second Prince's faction originally had the support of the Xie family. And what about you? You have no connection with any of the four families of Wang, Xie, Cui and Sun. It was not easy for the First Prince to marry the legitimate daughter of the Cui family, and we are evenly matched with the Second Prince. Do you want to offend the Wang family at this critical juncture? You are confused!" The late Empress Dowager disliked Concubine Xie, and forced the Emperor to make Li the Queen in the name of filial piety. Otherwise, Li had no favor in the palace and no background, and she would never be able to ascend the throne of Queen.
Hua Ling knelt down and bowed his head, saying, "I was wrong."
The queen sighed, "Nowadays, it's wrong for you to look at some people for even a second! If you are dissatisfied, take up that position first. If you want her then, it won't be a matter of a word."
Hua Ling smiled slightly, "I understand, that Cui Xiuxin will be mine sooner or later."
Another month passed, and the wedding day of the two brothers of the Wang family was getting closer. Old Madam Wang was determined to cultivate Xiuxin, so she assigned some things to Xiuxin to do, so

Xiuxin had no time to rest for this month. Old Madam Wang saw that Xiuxin handled things in an orderly manner, and had the demeanor of a lady from a noble family, and she became more and more satisfied with Xiuxin. However, Nanny Wang had some complaints, "Madam, the second wife is still young after all, and she is asked to arrange the marriage of Xiao'er and Chao'er. If something goes wrong..."

Old Madam Wang said, "I think Xiuxin is very good, just let her do it." After a pause, she continued, "Madam, you are old too, it's time to take a rest, enjoy yourself and stop worrying so much."

There was a sinister flash in Nanny Wang's eyes, and her wrinkled face smiled hypocritically, "The old lady is right, she is right..."

Although Old Madam Wang was becoming more and more satisfied with Xiuxin, there was still no news about Xiuxin's pregnancy. The old lady couldn't help but get a little anxious. She couldn't help but mention it to Xiuxin, "Xiuxin, I remember you used to be plump and slender, but now you have lost weight. Although you look a lot better, it is not good for your health. It seems that I still need to nourish your body more..."

After a pause, she continued, "Only when you are well can you give me a grandson soon."

Xiu Xin blushed, "Mother..."

In fact, she was also wondering, Wang

Fusheng had been irrigating the uterus diligently these days, why was there no news? Xiuxin's hand gently rested on her belly, should she go and pray to Guanyin for a child?

Compared to Madam Wang, Wang Fusheng was not in a hurry. "You are less than seventeen years old this year, there is no need to rush." He kissed Xiuxin and said, "It will be bad for your health to have a baby so early."

Xiu Xin giggled, "Maybe I'm pregnant now."

On the second day, Xiu Xin was checking the detailed purchase list for the past month when she suddenly felt a dull pain in her lower abdomen. She curled up, holding her stomach, and said, "Lan, Lan Xiang, I... my stomach hurts..."

Lanxiang saw Xiuxin's pale face and sweat on her forehead, so she hurriedly supported Xiuxin and shouted, "Quick, quick, someone come! Girl, girl, what's wrong with you?"

Xiuxin felt a dull pain in her lower abdomen, and intuitively felt something flowing out of her lower abdomen. She held her stomach tightly, vaguely aware of something, and tears began to flow. "No, no, no... Lanxiang, Lanxiang, hurry, hurry and get a doctor, hurry!"

"Okay, I'll go right away, I'll go right away!" Lanxiang had just let go of Xiuxin's hand when she saw a small pool of blood slowly flowing out from under Xiuxin's pink silk skirt. Lanxiang was so frightened that her face changed immediately, and she covered her lips and exclaimed, "Girl!"

The author has something to say: There will be more tomorrow

☆, Chapter 66 Crisis

Chapter 67 Crisis

Wang Fusheng came out of the meeting room. For some reason, his heartbeat suddenly accelerated, as if something was about to happen. He put his hands in his sleeves and looked up at the sky. It was gray and looked like it was going to snow. The wind was strong and cold, penetrating into his bones.

The chief eunuch came out from behind, bowed to his luggage, and said in a shrill voice, "Sir Wang, the north wind has suddenly risen, and the temperature has dropped sharply. This is the goose feather blanket that His Majesty gave you. Sir Wang, please put it on."

Wang Fusheng took the goose-feather blanket and bowed deeply to the emperor. "Thank you, Your Majesty."

After bidding farewell to the chief eunuch, Wang Fusheng walked out quickly. Unconsciously, his steps were getting faster and faster, and soon he saw his dark blue carriage.

Mo Yan came forward and said in an urgent tone, "Second Master, you finally came out. Something happened to the Second Madam!"

Wang Fusheng felt his heart hanging in his throat falling straight down, as if it was about to fall into the abyss, but his face remained calm, and even his tone of voice did not change, "What's wrong with her?"

A trace of pain flashed across Mo Yan's face, "Second Madam...she seems to have had a miscarriage!"

Miscarriage!

It was as if a thunderbolt had exploded overhead. Wang Fusheng almost couldn't stand. He took several steps back before he could stand. His mind was a little dazed. After a long while, he quickly lifted the curtain and got into the car, asking, "How is she?"

Mo Yan said, "I don't know yet. Imperial Physician Chen has already rushed over."

During the whole journey, Wang Fusheng looked very calm, and even looked at the unfinished documents. But Mo Yan kept urging him, "Hurry up, hurry up."

After finally reaching the east courtyard of the palace, Wang Fusheng handed all the documents to Mo Yan and said, "Put them in the study."

"yes."

Mo Yan responded, and when he looked up, he saw that Wang Fusheng's men had already slipped into the inner room.

"How is it?" the old lady asked in a low voice, with a hint of hoarseness and anxiety in her voice.

"The bleeding has stopped, but the second

lady's nearly one-month-old fetus cannot be saved." Imperial Physician Chen hesitated for a while and continued, "Also, the second lady has lost her health this time. It will be difficult for her to get pregnant again in the future."

The old lady sighed sadly upon hearing this and sat down on the armchair behind her, "This child is unlucky."

When Wang Fusheng stepped into the room, the first thing he heard was the old lady's words. His face became a little gloomy, "Why did she suddenly have a miscarriage?" This child, this child, was lost just like that before he had time to be happy about its existence.

Imperial Physician Chen was frightened by the pressure emanating from Wang Fusheng, and said stumblingly, "The Second Madam's constitution is extremely weak and cold, which should be caused by taking cold and yin substances for a long time."

Wang Fusheng clenched his fists instantly, "What do you mean by the cold and gloomy thing?"

"Safflower, musk, and the like."

The old lady glanced at Xiu Xin who had her eyes tightly closed on the bed and said, "Who on earth could have done such a shameful thing? I will never forgive her!"

Wang Fusheng closed his eyes and said in a voice as powerful as thunder, "Investigate thoroughly! Investigate thoroughly!"

After everyone left, Wang Fusheng was the

only one left in the room. He held Xiuxin's hand, and Xiuxin slowly opened her eyes.

"I..." Before he could finish his words, tears started to flow from his eyes, "I was too confused, I didn't know... I..."

Wang Fusheng held her hand tightly, "I understand, I understand."

Xiu Xin thought about who had done such a cruel thing, and her whole body was shaking with hatred, "Who is it? Who is it? Who wants to hurt me like this?"

Wang Fusheng said, "I will investigate thoroughly and not let any one go!"

Xiu Xin just shook her head with tears in her eyes and slowly loosened her hand, "So what? The child is gone... gone..."

Wang Fusheng really didn't know how to comfort her, so he went out and started to investigate the matter thoroughly. The whole palace was in a panic.

The next day, Jiang came to the palace. Xiuxin had to suppress her grief and said that she just had a cold.

Seeing that Jiang had lost a lot of weight and her eyes were swollen, Xiu Xin couldn't help but ask, "Mother, is there something wrong at home?"

Jiang said, "Xiu Xin, I have no other choice but to come to you. There is a literary inquisition going on in the court right now. Your father wrote a poem last month, but somehow, someone reported it and said that your father had treasonous intentions. Now... now he has been imprisoned in Marble!" As she spoke, she burst into tears.

Xiu Xin really felt like a thunderbolt had exploded in her ears from a clear sky. "Mother, what did you say?"

Jiang continued, "I don't know who is against your father. Although Cui Jinyi promised to mediate, there has been no news in the past few days. I think now there is only..."

Xiu Xin leaned forward, her waist still aching. She thought for a while and said, "There is a literary inquisition going on in the Hua Dynasty now, and this is the most unclear thing. I think someone is trying to harm my father. Mother, don't worry for now. My father is a third-rank imperial censor after all, and he is from the Cui family. Now that the charges have been determined, the people in the Dali Temple dare not do anything to my father. Don't worry for now. I will discuss with my husband and see how to deal with this matter."

Jiang nodded with tears in her eyes and got up and left.

However, as soon as Jiang left, Xiuxin covered her lower abdomen tightly and called out repeatedly, "Lanxiang...Lanxiang..."

Lanxiang pushed the door open and asked anxiously, "Miss, what's wrong with you?"

Cold sweat broke out on Xiu Xin's forehead, "Has the Second Master come back?"

Seeing Xiuxin like this, Lanxiang said worriedly, "Second Master just came back, Miss, do you want to call Imperial Physician Chen to come and take a look?"

"No need." Xiu Xin bit her lower lip tightly, "Help me up..."

"Girl, no."

"Help me up!" Xiu Xin struggled to stand up, put on only a cloak, pushed open the door and walked out in the cold wind. Before she took a few steps, she felt a sharp pain in her lower abdomen. Her feet went weak and her whole body fell forward.

"Ah..." Her waist was supported by a pair of big hands, and then her body was embraced in someone's arms.

Wang Fusheng opened the goose feather felt and wrapped Xiuxin in it. "Xiuxin, how can you run around outside in such a cold day?" There was a hint of tenderness and a hint of blame in his tone.

Xiuxin burst into tears immediately, "Husband, husband, I beg you, please save my father."

Wang Fusheng reached out and wiped the tears from Xiuxin's cheeks. "Master Cui is my father-in-law. Even if you didn't say it, how could I not save him?"

Suddenly, Xiu Xin felt a warm current emanating from her heart, "Husband..."

Although Wang Fusheng is the prime minister of the dynasty and the eldest son of the Wang family, he still has the greatest imperial power. The emperor is old and confused, and now is the most critical moment. How could it be so easy to save Cui Zhengkai?

Xiuxin was already weak after her miscarriage, and she caught a cold at some point, which made her even worse. She had a vague fever and talked nonsense day and night, shouting for help, sometimes for her father, sometimes for help, sometimes for her child.

Wang Fusheng was so worried about saving Cui Zhengkai that his hair turned white. In the end, Wang Fusheng almost used the power of the entire Wang family to put pressure on the emperor. The emperor reluctantly released Cui Zhengkai from the Dali Temple, but demoted him two levels to the fifth-rank deputy censor.

That day, Wang Fusheng had just returned to the palace when he was called to the west courtyard by Duan Yi.

"Grandson greets grandmother."

Duan Yi hummed, "Has my in-law been rescued?"

"yes."

"What do you think about this?"

Wang Fusheng only said, "Knock on the mountain to scare the tiger."

Duan Yi nodded, "It seems that the Royal Family is ready to make an effort."

For hundreds of years, the Hua Dynasty was dominated by clans of all sizes, especially the four families of Wang, Xie, Cui and Sun, which were powerful and deep-rooted.

Gradually, the imperial power declined.
"Now, it seems that the emperor is dissatisfied with this situation and wants to cut off the branches of our clan with a knife." Wang Fusheng said.
Duan Yi said, "I'm afraid this is not the worst. The worst thing is that the emperor wants to uproot us."
Wang Fusheng snorted, "That would require him to have the strength."
Duan Yi said solemnly, "Don't underestimate the current emperor. The royal family alone can't do anything, but what if he joins forces with the Cui and Xie families?"
"This..." Wang Fusheng pondered for a while and said, "What do you think, grandma?"
A ruthless light flashed in Duan Yi's eyes, "If it really comes to that, my nephew and I will become enemies!"
Wang Fusheng said, "I see that the emperor has not made any major moves yet. If he really wants to attack our Wang family, how can we just sit there and wait for death?"
After bidding farewell to Duanyi, Wang Fusheng returned to the East Courtyard. Seeing Qinxiang coming out of the door, he asked, "Is the Second Madam feeling better? Has the fever subsided?"
Qin Xiang bowed and said, "The Second Madam's fever has not completely subsided, but she doesn't feel as hot as she did this morning, but she is still not awake."
Wang Fusheng frowned tightly when he heard this, and his face was full of worry.

Mo Yan hurriedly said, "Second Madam is a blessed person, she will definitely be able to turn danger into safety."

Wang Fusheng nodded and asked as he walked away, "Have they confessed?"

Mo Yan said, "No idea."

Wang Fusheng's hand touched the curtain and he paused. "I don't want to wait any longer. Just use whatever method you have on them."

"Yes." Mo Yan took the order and left.

After opening the curtain and going in, Wang Fusheng reached out and touched Xiuxin's forehead. It was indeed still a little hot. He felt so distressed that he couldn't help but kiss her on the lips, "Only you have the ability to make me so confused."

"Water..." Xiu Xin stammered out these words.

Wang Fusheng hurriedly got up and poured a glass of water. He tested the temperature first and found it was warm before feeding it to Xiuxin with a silver spoon. However, Xiuxin couldn't open her mouth, so the water couldn't go in at all and flowed out along her lips.

Wang Fusheng had no choice but to take a sip of it himself and then feed it to Xiuxin.

After feeding her a small bowl of water, when Wang Fusheng took the last sip of water and leaned over to kiss Xiuxin's lips, Xiuxin's eyeballs moved and she opened her eyes.

Wang Fusheng pried open Xiuxin's teeth with his tongue and skillfully fed the water in his mouth into Xiuxin's mouth, "Are you still thirsty?"
Xiu Xin shook her head.
"Your father has been released from the Dali Temple, but he was demoted two levels and is now a fifth-rank deputy censor."
A glimmer flashed in Xiuxin's eyes, "Really?"
"of course it's true."
The author has something to say: Update tomorrow.

☆, Chapter 67 Falling Out of Favor

Chapter 68: Falling from Favor
"That's great..." Xiu Xin had just finished saying this when she closed her eyes and fell straight down.
"Xiu Xin!" Wang Fusheng whispered and then shouted outside, "Go and get the imperial physician!"
Cui Xiuxin was seriously ill this time. She had a high fever for seven or eight days and lay in bed in a daze. Wang Fusheng did not even attend court for Xiuxin's sake. He stayed by her bed all day without taking off his clothes. After a few days, his beard was untidy and his body was thin. How could he still look like a prime minister?
But in the end, even Imperial Physician Chen was helpless, and could only say that it all depended on Second Madam's own will,

and if she could get through it, then she would get through it, and if she couldn't, then...

Wang Fusheng's body swayed, as if he couldn't stand.

Seeing Wang Fusheng like this, Old Lady Wang sighed and said, "Come with me."

"Kneel down."

Wang Fusheng knelt on the cushion in the ancestral hall as he was told.

"Fusheng, let me ask you, what position does Cui Xiuxin hold in your heart?"

Wang Fusheng moved his lips a few times, and finally spoke hoarsely, "More important than my life..."

The old lady raised her whip and hit Wang Fusheng, "You unfilial son! Your body and hair are given by your parents, and you are willing to risk your life for a woman! For her father, you took the whole Wang family on the line, and for her, you made the whole Wang family panic. Now, you want to ruin yourself for her again?"

Wang Fusheng bowed his head and said, "Mother, I know I am wrong, but I have no choice."

The old lady sat down dejectedly. "I know you love her, but loving her too much is like falling into an abyss. You are the Prime Minister of the dynasty and the helmsman of my Wang family. Are you going to abandon my Wang family for a woman?"

"Mother……"

Madam Wang said, "Well, you should know

exactly what to do. I don't need to say more."

The news of Xiuxin's serious illness could not be concealed, and it reached Jiang's ears. Jiang was so grief-stricken that she came to the palace and cried several times, and no one could persuade her to stop.

"My son, my son..." Jiang cried out of breath, and asked, "Who is it, who hurt my son?"

Lan Xiang wiped her tears and said, "I don't know yet. The Second Master has arrested many of the maids and servants, but we still have no clue. The food that the young lady eats every day is brought in from outside, made in her own small kitchen, and also made in the Wang family's big kitchen. It is really difficult to find out where those red flowers and other things come from."

Jiang lowered her head and said, "Now that our Cui family has suffered such a great disaster, Xiuxin has had a miscarriage this time, and it will be difficult for her to have children in the future... Even if she survives this disaster, I'm afraid she will have no one to rely on. Wouldn't it be difficult for her to live in the Wang family?"

Lanxiang shed tears and said, "Who said it wasn't?"

Jiang couldn't hold back her tears again, and threw herself on Xiuxin and cried, "My poor child!"

"Mother..." Xiu Xin opened her eyes slightly.

Jiang screamed in shock and hurriedly held Xiuxin's slender hand, "Daughter, are you awake?" At the same time, she touched Xiuxin's forehead and felt the coolness. She felt relieved and chanted "Amitabha", "The fever has finally subsided."

"Mother, you are here?"

Jiang caressed Xiuxin's cheek lovingly, "How could I not come? The last time I came to see you, you lied to me and said you caught a cold... Who would have known..."

Xiu Xin shook her head. "After what happened in our family, how can I let my mother worry again?"

Jiang said, "My daughter, the Wang family is complicated. Now our Cui family has lost power, and you..." Jiang retracted the words "difficult to give birth again", "Wouldn't it be more difficult for you to gain a foothold in this Wang family? Why don't you go back with me to recuperate for a while?" Jiang meant that this time she would take her daughter back to recuperate for a period of time, at the shortest time being a year and a half, or at the longest three to five years, or even not send her back at all.

"Mother, I still need to discuss this matter with Second Master. Besides, the person who harmed me has not been identified yet. How can I just walk away like this?"

Jiang nodded, "Indeed."

Lan Xiang said, "Second Master is investigating this matter and has already locked up many maids and servants these days."

Xiu Xin asked, "Who are they?"

"They are all people from the dining hall and some maids in charge." Lanxiang said.

Xiu Xin pondered for a moment, "Imperial Physician Chen said that my illness was caused by long-term use of safflower, musk and other substances. I believe that person must have a lot of safflower and musk on hand. Why don't we search the mansion to see who has these things."

Jiang said, "Even if it existed before, it would have been lost now that something happened. How can it still be in your hands?"

Xiu Xin thought, "That's not necessarily true. The person who wants to harm me must be no small figure. Wang Fusheng has already locked up many people. He must have thought that the matter was over, and it's probably time to let his guard down. If we search now, we might really find something."

As soon as Xiuxin finished speaking, Cuixiang came in through the curtain and said, "Miss, the Second Master has sent many people to search the yard."

Jiang and Xiu Xin looked at each other and said, "You and he are thinking alike."

Soon, the truth came out.

When Nanny Wang knelt in front of her with tears in her eyes and begged Xiuxin to spare her life, Xiuxin felt only numbness and coldness in her heart.

Seeing Xiuxin was indifferent, Nanny Wang turned around and cried to Wang Fusheng, "Second Master, Second Master, I am the wet nurse of the late Madam. You should not give face to the monk but to the Buddha. For so many years, I have managed the big and small matters of the East Courtyard for my daughter. I have no merits but I have worked hard. The reason why I am against the Second Madam is that I can't stand her occupying my daughter's position... I..."

Wang Fusheng's expression did not change, and he sat upright like a mountain.

Nanny Wang thought there was hope, so she knelt down and kowtowed a few times, "Second Master, no matter what, you have to do this for my daughter's sake...ah!"

Who could have imagined that Wang Fusheng would kick Nanny Wang in the chest, sending him flying several meters away. Nanny Wang immediately covered her chest and spat out a mouthful of blood.

Wang Fusheng turned his face away, as if looking at her any longer would be a disgrace to his eyes, "Drag her out and let her die on her own. This is the last of my friendship with Qing Ruo."

Wang Fusheng and Xiuxin walked out together. Xiuxin coughed a few times with a handkerchief covering her throat. Wang

Fusheng hurriedly calmed her down and asked, "Are you feeling better?"

Xiu Xin nodded.

At some point, it started snowing outside. Goose-feather-like snowflakes were falling and swirling, and a thin layer of snow had accumulated on the roof and the ground. Xiuxin had a small hand warmer in her sleeves, but even so, she still felt very cold.

"Xiu Xin, I'm sorry."

Xiu Xin turned her head and looked at him, "Why do you say that?"

"It's my fault that our child..."

Xiu Xin shook her head and said, "No, it's just my bad luck."

"Embroidered Heart..."

Xiuxin turned around and smiled brightly at him, "I'm fine. Second Master is a man who does great things. You don't have to worry about me." Xiuxin paused and said, "I'm not feeling well now. Second Master doesn't have to come to my place every day. If Second Master doesn't like the two concubines, he can take in another concubine." These were what Old Lady Wang told her. Since she couldn't give birth to a child, what qualifications did she have to keep him?

Wang Fusheng felt like a tangled mess in his heart. Indeed, as the old lady said, he loved her too deeply, but her heart was not with him. It was just his wishful thinking from beginning to end. What could he do?

"The wedding of Xiao'er and Chao'er is getting closer, and we should start making arrangements. Unfortunately, I haven't recovered yet, and I really don't have the energy. I think we can only ask Princess Anyang to come and help with the arrangements. What do you think?" Xiu Xin continued.

Wang Fusheng responded in a confused manner, "It's up to you to decide. You go back first, I'll go to the study."

Wang Fusheng didn't even look at Xiuxin again, and walked to the right.

What Wang Fusheng didn't know was that the moment he turned around, Xiu Xin suddenly burst into tears.

Before she got married, she hoped to find a true lover and live together till old age. After she married him, she only hoped to live a peaceful life in the Wang family. Now, she wants to keep him, but he has lost the qualification to keep her. No, I didn't care in the first place, not at all... Although I think so, why does my heart hurt so much?

Xiu Xin has fallen out of favor after all.

For nearly half a month, Wang Fusheng had not set foot in the main courtyard.

Lanxiang was indignant about this. "Second Master is too heartless. It's not the girl's fault that she got into this situation. He doesn't even show any sympathy for her at this time. Aunt Chu has been so arrogant lately. Only Aunt Zhou is polite to the girl."

"Lanxiang, be careful what you say." Xiuxin warned.

Lan Xiang stopped talking. "I'm just speaking up for the young lady. Do you really want to let Aunt Chu bully you like this?"

Xiu Xin said calmly, "She wants to bully me? She doesn't have that ability. Even if my Cui family is about to collapse, I won't allow a concubine who came from a brothel to bully me. In fact, it's easy for someone like Aunt Chu. We just need to ignore her."

"But……"

Xiu Xin shook her head and rubbed her temples, "I'm tired..."

"Yes, I'll go make the girl's bed."

QQ.

There were several light knocks on the door outside.

Xiu Xin leaned forward and asked, "Who is it?"

"The Second Master is here." It was Cuixiang's voice.

Xiuxin's hand holding the teacup shook, and the hot tea spilled onto her hand, scalding her index finger red.

Then, the door creaked open and he walked in. The first thing Wang Fusheng saw was Xiuxin's scalded index finger. He frowned slightly. Why was she still so worried? He wanted to hold Xiuxin's hand and blow on it for her, but he pulled his hand back halfway through.

Xiuxin's heart was beating hard in her chest, and she looked at him, feeling confused.

"It's already been a month, why haven't you gained some weight?" He pinched Xiuxin's thin cheeks as if with ease, "The fat on your face has all disappeared."

Xiu Xin just asked, "Why is the Second Master here today?"

Wang Fusheng suppressed the smile on his face, "You finally don't want to act in front of me anymore? You've been acting for so long, are you finally tired? Huh?"

Xiu Xin remained silent.

Wang Fusheng was furious. He pinched Xiuxin's shoulders with both hands, as if he wanted to crush her bones. "Speak, speak, tell me what you really think. After going through so many things, don't you know what I'm thinking? You actually pushed me to another woman! Tell me, do you still have feelings? Hmm? Do you?"

Xiuxin burst into tears immediately, biting her lower lip tightly, and remained silent. At this point, she had lost the old lady's favor, had lost her natal family's support, and could not have children. What was she good for? What could she do? What could she do?

"Cui Xiuxin, do you have me in your heart? Even a little bit?" He asked her in a low voice, with a hint of despair, "Tell me, tell me."

Xiuxin looked into Wang Fusheng's eyes and

slowly, slowly shook her head.

Wang Fusheng laughed strangely, let go of Xiuxin's shoulders, turned around, "Cui Xiuxin, you are too hard-hearted." He walked to the door, one hand already on the door, suddenly, he felt a small whirlwind sweeping over, and then his waist was hugged, Xiuxin cried silently behind him, "I... I have no choice, it's... it's the old lady's intention..."

Although it was just a few words, Wang Fusheng understood everything immediately. He turned around and hugged Xiuxin, feeling both happy and resentful. "I am your husband. You should discuss everything with me. If I don't force you today, will you never talk to me again in your life?"

Xiu Xin cried and hiccuped, "She is your mother after all, how can I say anything?"

Wang Fusheng said, "She is my mother, and we really shouldn't go against her. But we can unite and put on a show for her. After a while, she will calm down and won't insist anymore."

Xiu Xin stared at him blankly, "Can it be like this?"

Wang Fusheng burst out laughing, "You are just stupid."

Xiu Xin thought, "Can the old lady believe it so easily?"

Wang Fusheng said, "She has believed it. For the past month, hasn't she thought that I favored Aunt Chu?"

Xiu Xin lowered her head sadly, "Aren't

you?"

"Of course not." Wang Fusheng liked to see her jealous look, so he lifted her chin and kissed her on the lips, "Could it be that she doesn't have a wing room?"

Xiuxin's knot in her heart that had been there for a month was finally untied. She felt as if she had seen a bright and beautiful moon. For the first time, she took the initiative to put her arms around his waist and smiled.

The author has something to say: There will be updates tomorrow.

☆, Chapter 68 Wedding

Chapter 69: Wedding

Xiuxin was busy with her two brothers' marriages and accompanied Old Lady Wang. As time went by, Old Lady Wang began to feel sorry for Xiuxin. "You are a kind girl, but you are not blessed enough." Xiuxin said, "Mother, being able to accompany you is my greatest blessing."

Old Madam Wang sighed, "Fusheng is the same. He hasn't even entered the main courtyard for such a long time. He spends the whole day in Aunt Chu's small courtyard. It's really outrageous!"

Xiu Xin's smile remained unchanged. "Second Master likes Aunt Chu, that's a good thing. It would also be good if Aunt Chu could give birth to a grandson for you."

"She...she can..." Old Madam Wang knew she

had said something wrong, so she quickly stopped what she was about to say and said, "Xiu Xin, how is your health?"

Xiu Xin said, "Imperial Physician Chen said he has not recovered yet."

The old lady sighed and said, "It would be a great thing if you could get your body back in shape."

Xiu Xin suppressed the upward curve of the corners of her mouth and was secretly happy in her heart that Wang Fusheng's method was indeed effective. Now the old lady no longer had to endure it.

December 18th was the wedding day of the two brothers Wang Xiaozong and Wang Chaozong. The palace was decorated with lights and colors, and everyone was in high spirits. The maids and servants were all dressed in new clothes, walking back and forth, chatting and laughing all the time.

Xiuxin and Princess Anyang were busy together and had a lot of fun. They finally worked until nightfall. Firecrackers rang out and two red sedan chairs carried by eight people were carried to the main gate. Xiuxin and Princess Anyang went out hand in hand to greet them. As they reached the main gate, they heard a commotion. Xiuxin looked up and saw Zhan Xue wearing a phoenix crown and a shawl. She lifted her veil and stepped out of the sedan chair. She whipped Ma Yunyun's sedan chair with a loud bang. She was so majestic that the people on the other end of the sedan chair didn't even dare to breathe.

"I won't argue with you, but you really think I'm a good person. Although Wang Xiaozong is from the eldest master's room, Wang Chaozong is two months older than him. How dare you put your sedan chair in front of mine? Is there still a hierarchy of seniority?"

No one dared to step forward to persuade her, and finally Xiu Xin took a few steps forward to stop Zhan Xue, "Today is your wedding day, it's important to put on the veil quickly, it's embarrassing for everyone if you make such a fuss now."

Zhan Xue put the whip back at her waist after hearing this, covered her head with the veil and sat back in the sedan chair. Xiu Xin winked at the best man, who immediately responded, "Please let the bride out of the sedan chair." The best man then helped Zhan Xue get out of the sedan chair. Ma Yunyun also got out of the sedan chair with the help of the best man.

The crowd gathered around the two newlyweds and walked through the archway, around several corridors, and arrived at the main hall of the palace. The two newlyweds stepped over the threshold, and Wang Xiaozong and Wang Chaozong walked towards the two brides.

"Ouch, wrong, wrong!" The best man yelled, and led Wang Chaozong towards the taller Zhan Xue, "Chao brother, this is your bride." He then led Wang Xiaozong towards

Ma Yunyun, "Xiao brother, this is your bride."

After the ceremony, two couples were led to the bridal chamber. Xiao Ge'er still lived in the courtyard of the South Courtyard. The Yu Shu Courtyard built specifically for Chao Ge'er was also completed. The group finally settled down after much fanfare. The banquet with a hundred tables in the central hall was also held, and it was very lively.

Zhan Xue waited for nearly two hours with her veil on, but Wang Chaozong still didn't come, so she simply lifted her veil and walked out the door. There were two maids guarding the door, coaxing her, "Madam, the newlyweds can't go out, it's unlucky."

Zhan Xue asked, "Where is Wang Chaozong?"

The two maids looked away for a moment, "Chao Ge'er is still entertaining the guests."

Zhan Xue was not someone who could be easily fooled. She immediately reached out and pushed the two women away, "Get out of the way!"

The two maids were so panicked that they hugged Zhan Xue's waist and said, "No, this is not okay, Madam, you can't go out."

If Zhan Xue and the delicate young lady were hugged by these two women, they would probably not be able to leave. But Zhan Xue was Zhan Xue after all. She only pushed the two women away with a slight push. Zhan Xue swung the whip at her waist to the ground and asked angrily, "I ask you, where is Wang Chaozong?"

The two women were so frightened that they told the truth, "Brother, brother is in the room of Miss Green Waist in the side yard."

Zhan Xue seemed to be struck by thunder. It took her a while to recover. "Who is Green Waist?"

"Luyao is my brother's concubine..."

Zhan Xue held the whip and walked forward. The side yard was not far from the main yard. After a while, Zhan Xue saw the so-called side yard. It was a very delicate small yard with two red lanterns hanging at the door. The lanterns glowed ambiguously in the night. She frowned, retracted her half-opened foot, gently pushed the door open with her hand, and walked in.

The lights were dim and Zhan Xue saw the shadows of two people printed on the window. The man is tall and straight, and the woman is charming.

They were drinking, and Zhan Xue heard a woman's voice in her ear, "Chao Zong, today is your wedding night, but you came to my place instead. How are you going to explain this to the daughter of the Duke of Huguo?"

Wang Chaozong raised his head and took a sip of wine. "That was a marriage granted by the emperor. I didn't do it voluntarily. I don't want to marry her."

The woman covered her mouth and laughed like a silver bell. "That's true. I heard that the daughter of the Duke of

Protectorate grew up in the northwest. She was like a barbarian and had killed people. Her waist is as thick as a bucket, and her arms and legs are stronger than a man's. She can't be called a woman at all..."

Wang Chaozong frowned, "It's not as exaggerated as you said, but it's definitely not feminine."

Zhan Xue felt as if her heart was pierced by thousands of arrows when she heard these words. She never expected that the person she loved so much, the person she wanted to marry, would look at her like this and would betray her sincerity like this.

boom!

Zhan Xue kicked the door open and swung the whip in his hand. Snap! The whip hit the wine table and smashed the wine pot on the table.

Luyao had never seen such a scene before. She was so frightened that her face turned pale and she hid behind Wang Chaozong.

Wang Chaozong had a complicated expression. He looked at her and just said, "If you have anything to say, tell me. Don't hurt Lu Yao."

Zhan Xue's heart was broken, but her expression did not change at all, as if covered by a layer of frost. "Okay, Wang Chaozong, if you have anything to say, let's talk about it. Get this woman out first!"

Lu Yao ran out quickly.

Zhan Xue whipped the door, and it closed

with a snap.

Zhan Xue looked at Wang Chaozong, put the whip in her hand back to her waist, and sat down. "Why didn't you tell me that you didn't want to marry me?"

"What's the point of saying it? This is a marriage granted by the emperor. How can we change it on our own?"

Zhan Xue's hands tightly grasped her bright dress, "If you had told me, I would have called off this marriage even if I had to die."

Wang Chaozong looked up at Zhan Xue. She had taken off the phoenix crown on her head, but was still wearing her bright wedding dress. Her face was painted with formal attire, and her jet-black hair was loose, making her heroic features look softer.

Zhan Xue's nose felt sore and her tone lowered, "The night I saved you, I thought you liked me."

Wang Chaozong's eyes flickered slightly when he heard Zhan Xue say this, "That night, I didn't know you were a woman, otherwise I wouldn't have..."

"You won't sleep with me?"

Wang Chaozong nodded with difficulty.

Zhan Xue suppressed the sadness in her heart and raised her head stubbornly, "I understand, Prince Wang, it turns out that everything is a misunderstanding. But I have already married you, and it is hard to undo what has been done. But since you don't like me, let's just be a fake couple.

I won't care about you, and you don't have to care about me, that's it."
Having said that, he turned and walked out.
"Hey, wait."
Wang Chaozong called her.
She turned her head and looked at him, "What's the matter?"
Wang Chaozong took a good look at Zhan Xue for the first time. She was actually very pretty, with a heroic look in her eyes and eyebrows, which made her different from all other women. He bowed deeply to her and said, "I, Wang Fusheng, owe you a lot in my life."
Zhan Xue held back her tears, turned around, and said in a trembling voice, "You don't owe me anything. It's all my own fault."
Xiuxin always felt uneasy. Wang Fusheng was half lying on the couch in his middle clothes, watching Xiuxin walking back and forth in the bedroom with her hands clasped. "What's wrong with you? Why are you so uneasy?"
Xiu Xin said, "I always feel like something is going to happen. No, I have to go check out the new house."
"Hey." Wang Fusheng called her, "Even if Chaozong doesn't like Miss Liu, today is his wedding night. He shouldn't be so ignorant. What could go wrong?"
Xiu Xin asked, "Could it be that you forgot about Lu Yao?"
"this……"
Xiu Xin turned around, put on a piece of

clothing and walked out, "Husband, I'll just go take a look and be back soon."

When Xiu Xin arrived at the gate of Yu Shuyuan, she heard the sound of weapons hitting each other, which frightened her. She thought Zhan Xue had taken action. She pushed open the door of the courtyard and saw Zhan Xue dancing with a sword alone in the small plum blossom forest.

Yu Shuyuan was brightly lit, and dozens of red lanterns were hung in the plum blossom forest, each emitting a dim red light. The red lights reflected each other, setting off the bright red wedding dress on Zhan Xue, which was a beautiful sight.

Snapped!

Zhan Xue swung his sword, cut off a small branch of the plum tree, and a few plum petals fluttered down.

"Battle Snow."

Zhan Xue slowly turned her head, and Xiu Xin was shocked to find that her face was covered with tears.

For a moment, Xiu Xin couldn't believe her eyes, "You...you are crying?"

Zhan Xue threw away the sword in his hand and hugged Xiu Xin fiercely, "Xiu Xin... Xiu Xin... Wuu Wu... He doesn't want me anymore..."

At the same time, outside the courtyard gate, Wang Fusheng, who was holding a white goose-feather felt in his hand, looked a little dark. He was afraid that she would catch a cold, so he specially sent her

clothes. It was really pitiful for a husband to find out that his wife was having an affair with another woman...
Zhan Xue cried for a long time in Xiu Xin's arms, and Xiu Xin kept comforting her in a soft voice.
"Cough, cough." A few dry coughs were heard in the silent courtyard.
Xiu Xin turned around and asked, "Husband? Why are you here?"
Wang Fusheng raised the goose-feather blanket in his hand and said, "You are so lightly dressed. I will bring you some clothes."
Zhan Xue returned to normal in just a moment, with even the traces of tears on her face gone. She bowed to Wang Fusheng and called out, "Father."
Wang Fusheng felt a slight sense of disillusionment when he heard the word "father", but the next word that Zhan Xue said made Wang Fusheng proud.
Because Zhan Xue also bowed to Xiu Xin and called out, "Mother."
Well······
The expression on Xiuxin's face was a little stiff. This was even stranger than hearing Wang Chaozong calling her mother...
She and Zhan Xue were obviously good sisters?
However, all this is not the point; the point is to separate these two people.
Wang Fusheng carefully covered Xiuxin with a felt blanket, curled up his fist and

coughed a few times, "Okay, it's getting late, go to bed early. I'll take care of Chaozong for you."
Zhan Xue said, "Father, don't worry. His marrying me was originally a misunderstanding. He already has someone he loves, so why should I force him? Let everything take its course."
Wang Fusheng thought that although Liu Baozi looked so barbaric, his daughter was actually quite reasonable. He nodded with satisfaction, "Very good, very good."
"Embroidered Heart."
"Um?"
"Let's go."
Xiu Xin glanced at Zhan Xue, took a few steps and stopped, "Husband, I want to stay tonight."
Wang Fusheng thought he had misheard, "What?"
Xiu Xin said, "Zhan Xue looks a little strange. I'm afraid something has happened to her. I want to stay with her tonight."
Wang Fusheng's heart broke into pieces, "How can a mother-in-law abandon her husband and spend the night with her daughter-in-law?"
Xiu Xin pulled at the corner of Wang Fusheng's clothes and said coquettishly, "Just this once..."
If he didn't agree, it would seem that he was unkind, so Wang Fusheng had no choice but to nod and agree, "You said it, just this once..."

"Yeah." Xiu Xin nodded vigorously.
After washing up, Xiuxin and Zhanxue lay down to sleep. The kang was heated in the new house, and the whole house was warm. Xiuxin and Zhanxue didn't feel cold even though they were only wearing their undershirts.
"Are you really going to give up?"
Zhan Xue asked, "What else can we do?"
Xiu Xin said, "It's not like you if you give up so easily."
Zhan Xue pursed her lips, "He doesn't like me, what can I do?"
Xiu Xin said, "Even if he doesn't want to be close to you, you have to control him and prevent him from getting close to other women."
"You mean Green Waist?"
"Yeah." Xiu Xin nodded.
Zhan Xue snorted coldly, "I don't care about that kind of woman at all. I hate Wang Chaozong. I risked my life to save him. It turns out that he didn't even know I was a girl."
Xiu Xin said, "You wore men's clothes, wielded a big knife, and killed so many people with red eyes. No normal person can regard you as a girl."
Zhan Xue turned over and said, "Xiu Xin, I think you and Wang Fusheng are getting along very well. I can see that he really cares about you."
Xiu Xin blushed, "We are an old married couple..."

Zhan Xue chuckled and stretched out her hand to pinch Xiu Xin's cheek, "You, you have been married for less than a year and you have the nerve to say that you and him are an old couple.
The author has something to say: The National Day is over, and the next update will have to wait a few days.

☆, Chapter 70: Establishing Authority

Chapter 70: Establishing Authority
Zhan Xue chuckled and stretched out her hand to pinch Xiu Xin's cheek, "You, you've been married for less than a year and you have the nerve to say that you and him are an old married couple."
Xiu Xin pulled Zhan Xue's hand off and said, "Let's be serious. Now that you've married into the Wang family, you can't just wield swords and sticks all day long, and you can't wear men's clothes. The Wang family has a lot of rules. If the old lady and Duan Yi don't like you, they will make trouble for you."
Zhan Xue said, "I don't care. If they don't like me, I will just go back to the Duke of Huguo's Mansion."
Xiu Xin sighed in her heart, and at the same time felt envious. Zhan Xue could live such an easy, comfortable, free and easy life, which was something others could never envy.
The next morning, everyone knew that Wang

Chaozong had abandoned his newly married wife and was hanging out with a lowly concubine, which was like a slap in the face to the Liu family.

When the bride came home, she naturally had to offer morning tea to her mother-in-law. Princess Anyang was waiting in the main hall early, and Ma Yunyun and Wang Xiaozong came soon after. Princess Anyang looked out the door and said to herself, "It's not early anymore, why hasn't the second wife arrived yet?"

Ma Yunyun was wearing a gorgeous dress, heavy makeup, three or four gold hairpins on her head, and an eight-treasure necklace around her neck. She thought that this would show the strength of the Ma family and make people dare not underestimate them. Who knew that the next second, when Xiu Xin and Zhan Xue came in, she immediately became indignant.

Ma Yunyun was indignant not for anything else, but because she found that she had to bow respectfully to Cui Jiaxiuxin, whom she used to look down upon! Just because she was now a person of the same level as her mother-in-law!

But she had no choice but to bow respectfully with Emperor Xiaozong, "Greetings to mother, greetings to aunt."

"Get up." Anyang called quickly.

Xiu Xin glanced at Ma Yunyun indifferently, and deliberately paused for a long time before slowly uttering two words, "Get up."

Zhan Xue also bowed, "Greetings, mother, aunt."

A maid had already prepared two bowls of hot tea for the two brides, but Wang Chaozong was not there yet, so Zhan Xue couldn't be the only one to serve tea, right?

Xiu Xin frowned and said, "Go and find Chao Ge'er for me."

"Yes, Second Madam." A maid answered and hurried out.

Then, Ma Yunyun showed a smug look, pretending to be surprised, and turned to ask Zhan Xue, "Hey, Third Sister-in-law, could it be that Chao Ge'er was not with you yesterday? Why didn't he come with you?"

Zhan Xue glanced at her coldly and sneered, "You are too nosy."

Ma Yunyun was ridiculed and her face turned ugly. She pulled Wang Xiaozong's hand and shook it, saying coquettishly, "My husband." At this moment, Wang Xiaozong had no time to care about her. Earlier, he coveted Xiuxin's beauty, but it was because of Wang Fusheng that he gave up the idea. But now the one next to him is really not even a finger better than Cui Xiuxin who sat above. Look at her clothes today, she wants to wear a box of jewelry on her body.

Ma Yunyun was the wife of Princess Anyang, so Xiuxin didn't know what to say, but glanced at Anyang next to her. Anyang coughed dryly and frowned, "Yunyun, if you don't say anything, no one will think you are dumb."

Ma Yunyun never expected that her mother-in-law would be so disrespectful to her. Her face turned pale. But at this moment, she was not stupid enough to challenge her mother-in-law openly. She only responded weakly, "Yes."

The five people waited for a long time before Wang Chaozong finally arrived. When he saw Anyang and Xiuxin, he bowed and said, "Mother, aunt, I am late."

Zhan Xue looked at him from a distance, then quickly looked away and closed her eyes.

Xiu Xin was really angry and said angrily, "Brother Chao, don't you know that you have to offer tea to me today together with your new bride?"

Wang Chaozong bowed and said, "Mother, please forgive me. It is because I woke up too late today."

Xiu Xin was so angry that Wang Chaozong didn't care about Zhan Xue, but he actually humiliated her in front of so many people. How could she survive in this palace in the future? However, she was just her stepmother, so she couldn't be too harsh, so she suppressed her anger and said, "Forget it, serve tea."

After finally serving tea, everyone breathed a sigh of relief.

Wang Chaozong glanced at Zhan Xue from a distance, feeling somewhat reluctant, and

called out to her, "Zhan Xue!"
Zhan Xue stopped and turned to look at him with a calm expression, "Third Young Master, what's the matter?"
She called him like this, indicating that she wanted to draw a clear line between them. For some reason, Wang Chaozong did not feel relieved but felt a little disappointed. "Even if we are not real husband and wife, there is no need to do this, right?"
"It doesn't have to be like this?" Zhan Xue smiled faintly, "Then according to Third Young Master's opinion, what should we do?"
Wang Chaozong seemed a little embarrassed. "From tonight on, I will live on the small couch outside the main room...you..."
"Third Young Master, you are the real master of the Wang family. You can sleep wherever you like. I can't control you, and you don't have to tell me." After saying that, Zhan Xue turned and left, leaving behind only a cold and resolute back.
The days passed one by one, and in the blink of an eye, another month had passed.
As the New Year was approaching, Wang Fusheng became busier and busier, leaving early and returning late all day long. Xiuxin knew that something big had happened in the court recently, so it was natural for him to be busy. She became more gentle and accommodating, and Wang Fusheng was overwhelmed with joy and flattered. Fortunately, Zhan Xue was there to chat

with her during the day to relieve her boredom, and occasionally accompanied the old lady to worship Buddha, and chatted with Duan Yi for a few times, and the day passed quickly.

That day, Xiuxin went to look for Zhanxue as usual. When she reached the door of her room and was about to knock, she heard Zhanxue's personal maid named Xueyan hushing at her.

Xiu Xin was puzzled, "What?"

Xueyan lowered her voice and winked, "The Third Young Master is in there."

Xiu Xin suddenly understood and was very surprised at the same time, "Could it be that they...could it be that..."

Xueyan pursed her lips and smiled, then pulled Xiuxin to a secluded place to talk and told her everything that happened last night.

It turned out that Wang Chaozong had been playing finger-guessing games and drinking with Zhan Xue in the courtyard last night. Zhan Xue was very good at it, but somehow, she always lost to Chaozong that day. Before they knew it, they had drunk the whole jar of wine. Of course, Zhan Xue drank more, while Wang Chaozong only drank a few cups. Even Zhan Xue, who was good at drinking, felt dizzy after drinking a jar of wine, so she stood up unsteadily and walked around in the plum blossom forest.

Zhan Xue likes to wear red clothes. As she spins, plum blossoms fall. The woman in red

is hunting for beauty. Wang Chaozong somehow feels like he is a little drunk.
Snap.
Zhan Xue twisted her ankle and her body began to tilt, "Ah..."
Wang Chaozong rushed forward and hugged her. Zhan Xue was very drunk. She put her arms around his neck, tears streaming down her face. "Wang Chaozong, why don't you love me? Since you don't love me, let's get divorced. From now on, you go your way and I go mine. I can also... hehe... find another partner..."
The last sentence completely angered Wang Chaozong. He hugged her and pressed her against the tree. "Looking for another partner? How dare you!"
Zhan Xue laughed, her eyes blurred, "Why wouldn't I be afraid of that? Um..."
Wang Chaozong stopped her from talking without letting her finish. Xueyan watched helplessly as Chaozong lifted Zhan Xue up and carried her into the room.
As she spoke, Xueyan blushed a little, "Son-in-law is really something, in broad daylight..."
After listening to Xueyan's words, Xiuxin couldn't help but laugh, "What a pair of enemies!"
The author has something to say: There are no more than ten chapters left. It's almost over.

☆、Chapter 71 Twists and Turns

Chapter 71: Twists and Turns

The next morning, according to the palace's rules, every five days one must go to pay respects to the elders, so all the children and relatives gathered in the main hall of the west courtyard. Duan Yi sat at the head of the table, smiling at the people sitting down, "It's rare that everyone is here today." Old Lady Wang said, "That's right, it's even more lively since Xiao'er and Chao'er got married."

Everyone complimented, "Our ancestors are so lucky."

Xiu Xin glanced at Zhan Xue who was standing beside her and couldn't help but smile, "Tomorrow Zhan Xue and Yun Yun will give birth to a great-grandson for our ancestor. That will truly be five generations living under the same roof."

Zhan Xue's face didn't show any shyness, but rather some shyness and annoyance. However, she hid it so well that no one noticed.

Duan Yi laughed a few times, "That's right."

Ma Yunyun said, "Aunt, don't just point your finger at Zhan Xue and me. You are still young, and the second master only has one son, so you don't have many children."

As soon as she said this, Xiuxin's face changed, "How dare you!" Xiuxin had a miscarriage last time and her body was damaged. She was afraid that it would be difficult for her to get pregnant again. It was really cruel for her to bring it up again at this time.

Not only did Xiu Xin change color, but even her mother-in-law frowned, "Ma Yunyun, there are some things you should say and some things you shouldn't say. Don't you have any idea? How can you be a rich lady if you speak so freely?"

Madam Wang said calmly, "Okay, Yunyun is just a little restless. From tomorrow on, you should follow me to worship Buddha and relax."

Ma Yunyun had been spoiled since she was a child, and no one dared to blame her like this. But now was different from the past, no one would protect her unconditionally anymore, so she could only bite her lip and bow, "Yunyun knows she was wrong."

Through this incident, Ma Yunyun finally understood that Cui Xiuxin had completely established her foothold in the palace. Although the Cui family lost power, she did not lose the favor of her husband at all. Everyone in the palace took good care of her. From Duanyi to the maids and servants, who was not respectful to her? More importantly, she had the power of the East Courtyard tightly in her hands. It seemed that she had to avoid her limelight in this palace.

That evening, Xiuxin estimated the time and prepared several exquisite snacks early in the morning in anticipation of Wang

Fusheng's return. Lanxiang joked, "I always feel that the girl has become a different person since her serious illness."

Xiu Xin asked, "Why did you change someone?"

Lan Xiang said, "In the past, you never took your son-in-law seriously. You would go back to your room to rest after washing up. How could you care whether your son-in-law would come back or not? Even if your son-in-law came back, you would not be in a good mood."

Xiu Xin gently tapped her forehead and said, "You little devil, you are the only one who is nosy."

Lan Xiang giggled, "Did I get it right? When I look at you, young lady, you only think of me as your son-in-law."

The two were laughing and joking when they suddenly heard a voice outside announcing, "The Second Master is back."

Xiuxin's eyes lit up and she stood up to greet them. Lanxiang and the others retreated with a tactful look and considerately closed the door for the two of them. Xiuxin untied Wang Fusheng's cloak and shook off the snow stuck on it. "Why do you come home later and later recently? Has something big happened in the court?"

Wang Fusheng's face was as pale as ice, and he only uttered one sentence slowly, "The emperor is seriously ill..."

Although Xiu Xin was only a woman, she also knew the meaning of this sentence and could not help but frowned, "Then who is the person that the current emperor is interested in..."

Wang Fusheng shook his head. "I heard that a secret decree has already been drafted, but we have no way of knowing it now."

Xiu Xin said worriedly, "I'm afraid it's five..."

Wang Fusheng extended his index finger to Xiuxin's lips and said, "I know what you are going to say, but with me here and the Wang family here, no one dares to act rashly."

"Yeah." Xiu Xin nodded.

Wang Fusheng held Xiuxin in his arms and kissed her on the forehead.

Xiu Xin looked at the dark sky outside and always felt that something storm was about to come.

Knock knock.

There were several regular knocks on the door, and Lan Xiang's voice sounded outside the door, "The second master, the second wife, the third young wife and the third young master started fighting in the yard, and the third young wife even took out a whip.", no one dares to persuade."

"What?" Xiuxin was shocked, opened the door and walked outside, "Isn't it fine this morning? Why is it like this at night?"

Lan Xiang said, "The message came from Xue Yan in the third young lady's room. I don't know the specific situation."

Wang Fusheng held Xiuxin's hand and said,

"I'll go with you."

Xiuxin and Wang Fusheng looked at each other and nodded.

The two of them hurried to the gate of Wutong Garden and heard a bang, like air thunder exploding from their ears. Xiu Xin could not help but whisper softly, "Ah!"

The two men walked into the courtyard and saw Zhan Xue in a red dress, holding a long whip in her hand and whipping a bottle of daughter's red wine that had been lying beside her for more than ten years. The bottle broke with a snap.

"Liu Zhanxue! Are you going to kill your husband?"

Liu Zhanxue stood tall, with a cool heroic aura lingering around him, "What am I afraid of? You..." As he spoke, Zhanxue seemed to find it difficult to speak, "You took advantage of me, while I was drunk... watch out for the whip!"

As he said this, he swung the whip again.

Wang Fusheng was about to speak out to stop him, but Xiuxin quietly pulled his sleeve and whispered, "Hey, let's take a look first."

Wang Fusheng frowned, "But look at Zhan Xue's posture..."

Xiu Xin smiled and said, "Zhan Xue's whip is very skilled. If she really wanted to hurt Chao Ge'er, how could Chao Ge'er still be standing here intact? I think she is just making a lot of noise but bringing down the storm."

Wang Fusheng looked up and saw that the whip had hit the tree trunk again. Xiuxin could see that Zhanxue was just putting on a show, so how could Wang Chaozong not see that? When Liu Zhanxue swung the whip at him, he deliberately walked towards the direction of the whip. Zhanxue was so frightened that her face turned pale. She used her hand to change the direction of the whip, and the tip of the whip almost brushed Wang Chaozong's nose.

"Hey, you're looking for death!"

Wang Chaozong smiled, "Isn't this exactly what you want?"

"You!" Seeing that the whip was about to be thrown out again, Wang Chaozong grabbed Zhan Xue's wrist, pulled Zhan Xue into his arms, and kissed her on the lips, "Okay, stop being upset, can't I apologize to you?"

Zhan Xue's face suddenly turned red, and she stammered out three words, "You scoundrel!"

Wang Chaozong smiled softly, "You and I are husband and wife, so what I am doing is reasonable and legal."

"You, you let me go!" Zhan Xue was skilled in Kung Fu after all, so she broke free with a slight shake. Wang Chaozong, however, was indomitable, and hugged Zhan Xue from behind, picked her up horizontally, and walked into the house.

"Uh..." Xiu Xin and Wang Fusheng looked at each other for a long time before saying,

"Like father, like son..."
Wang Fusheng: "..."
The author has something to say: There is an update!! o(╯□╰)o Sorry for keeping you waiting for so long.

☆、Chapter 72 Changes

Chapter 72: Changes
Since that day, the image of Wang Chaozong, the "son" in Xiuxin's mind has been refreshed. She originally thought that he was a well-read and elegant gentleman, but he was actually the same as his father in some aspects. However, Zhanxue also had him in her heart, otherwise how could she let him succeed?
This kind of love affair between a man and a woman is nothing more than one person wanting to hit the other willing to be hit. However, now that the two of them are so close, it is very annoying for someone to be caught in the middle. Zhan Xue is not the kind of person who likes to calculate. She is open and aboveboard. Even if she cares about it, she probably won't do it. It is inevitable that Xiu Xin, as a mother-in-law, will worry about it. Xiu Xin wondered how to get rid of the girl named Lu Yao without making a fuss. Tsk, Xiu Xin thought again, after all, this is someone from the royal family of the dynasty, and it doesn't seem good for her, as a mother-in-law, to interfere...

The matter was delayed. On the other hand, Wang Chaozong and Zhan Xue's relationship improved day by day, and they seemed to have really forgotten about Lu Yao.

Just at this time, something big happened.

The little girl who served Lu Yao closely was peeking out of the door. Lan Xiang saw her and called her, "Stop! What are you doing sneaking around here?"

The little girl was only about thirteen or fourteen years old and was wearing a goose yellow dress. She knelt down when she saw Xiu Xin and said, "Second Madam, I am Feng Bi, who serves Miss Lu Yao. I came here to report to you that Miss Lu Yao came in with a poor appetite and was sleepy. I have just asked a doctor to see her. The doctor said..."

Loss of appetite... Lethargy...

Xiuxin's heart immediately rose to her throat, "What did the doctor say?"

The little girl stammered, "They said...the girl is pregnant."

"What?" Xiu Xin was stunned and held the armrest tightly with her hands. "Are you pregnant?"

"Yes, Second Madam."

Xiuxin only felt a throbbing pain in her head. It seemed like it was about to heal, so why did this happen?

After a while, Xiu Xin calmed down and said, "Since Lu Yao is pregnant, you have to take good care of her. You can bring some bird's nest and ginseng back to nourish her body."

After a pause, Xiu Xin continued, "Also, Lu Yao is still in the first three months, so don't go out easily. I will go to see her when I have time."

"Yes." The little girl bowed and walked out.

Xiu Xin said to Lan Xiang, "Keep this a secret from Zhan Xue and keep everyone under control. Don't let her know about this. Do you understand?"

As soon as he finished speaking, a clear female voice said, "I already know..."

Xiu Xin looked up and saw Zhan Xue striding in. His face was calm and expressionless.

"Zhan Xue..." Xiu Xin called her worriedly.

Zhan Xue smiled in a relaxed manner, "Isn't it normal for a wealthy family to have three wives and four concubines? Even though Princess Duanyi is from a noble family, didn't the old man of the Wang family take in two concubines? What about me?"

Xiu Xin was choked, "That's true, but..."

"Okay, don't worry about me. I'm fine." Zhan Xue stood up and said that, looking very free and easy.

Seeing her like this, Xiuxin became even more worried.

Sure enough, after nightfall, Xiu Xin heard that Zhan Xue packed up her belongings and returned to the Huguogong Mansion, leaving a letter of divorce. Xiu Xin was not very surprised, "Zhan Xue has always been very intolerant of any injustice, so it's not surprising that she would do this."

Wang Fusheng didn't take it seriously. "It's just a child throwing a tantrum. He will be back in a few days. How can we divorce him just like that? Besides, what's the big deal about how many concubines a clan member has?" After a pause, Wang Fusheng took off his boots and said, "It's just that Lu Yao's background is not right."

After Wang Fusheng finished speaking, he felt that the atmosphere was a little strange. He looked up and found that his wife was sitting at the table with a pouty mouth and sulking. Wang Fusheng's eyes turned and he immediately understood. He smiled and went over to hug her in his arms, "Are you angry already?"

Xiuxin ignored her, turned around and snorted, "That's right, it's not uncommon for the young men in your clan to have three wives and four concubines, and there are even many who keep dozens of singing girls and dancers. Compared to those people, the number of people in Chaozong's room is really pitifully small." Xiuxin paused and continued, "Not to mention Chaozong, there are only two concubines in your room, Second Master. It's really too few. Alas." Xiuxin exclaimed softly, turned her head as if she had just remembered and said, "Isn't there a girl named Hongxiu in Wutong Garden? She is also very beautiful. Why don't you take her in?" After that, she raised her head and looked at Wang Fusheng steadily.

She looked as if she would completely go crazy if Wang Fusheng dared to say a word.

Wang Fusheng pinched Xiuxin's cheek, not knowing whether to laugh or cry. "You are such a heartless little thing, you always say things to me. Since I had you, when have I ever been close to the two concubines in our house, let alone outside?"

Xiu Xin snorted, her cheeks still puffy.

Wang Fusheng looked at her under the lamp. Her eyebrows and eyes were as picturesque as a painting, her skin was as white as fat, and her lips were as red as cinnabar. He couldn't help but have an idea. He bent down slightly and covered her bright red lips.

After a while of lingering, Xiu Xin felt weak all over. She stretched out her fist and looked at Wang Fu's hard chest like cotton. "I'm still angry. You always bully me."

Wang Fusheng pinched her little nose and said, "If I don't bully you, who else can I bully?"

Xiuxin snuggled into his arms. The familiar smell mixed with a slight smell of sweat rushed into her nose, and suddenly she couldn't hold back her tears. "Second Master..." Her voice was a little hoarse, and her left arm tightly hugged his waist. "I……"

Wang Fusheng knew what she was going to say, and gently pressed his index finger against her lips. "Stop talking, don't say anything, you don't have to care about these. I already have Chaozong, so my bloodline has been continued. Why should you still be bothered by that incident?"

"That being said..." Xiu Xin put her hand on her belly, "But...but, I also want to be a mother and give birth to children for you."

Wang Fusheng sighed softly and held her in his arms.

The next day, when Xiuxin woke up, Wang Fusheng had naturally gone to the court. After washing up, Xiuxin opened the door and was shocked to find her "son" Wang Chaozong kneeling at the door. Although Wang Chaozong was dressed neatly, he had two scratches on his forehead and chin, some stains on his body, two dark shadows under his eyes, and a short stubble on his chin...

It's easy to guess who caused the injuries on his body...

Xiu Xin looked at Wang Chaozong's appearance and inexplicably felt a bit of envy. Even if she had ten thousand courages, she would not dare to hit Wang Fusheng. Zhan Xue was indeed very tough!

"Mother!" Wang Chaozong said as he kowtowed, "I only regret that I was possessed by evil spirits and made a big mistake. Now Zhan Xue left in anger, and I am heartbroken. But now, the big mistake has been made and it is irreversible. Now, I can only ask you, mother, to persuade Zhan Xue to change her mind!"

Xiu Xin raised her eyebrows, "Do you think my persuasion will be useful?"

Wang Chaozong said, "Aren't mother and Zhan Xue close friends? She will listen to mother's words, right?"

Xiu Xin shook her head. "How can you be so confused? The crux of the problem is not with me, nor with the child, but with you."

"On me?"

Xiu Xin nodded, "It's up to you. Zhan Xue is a person who can't tolerate any sand in her eyes, but Lu Yao already has your child. No matter what, this is an established fact. There will always be a stain between you and Zhan Xue, and Zhan Xue will never be able to get over it in her heart."

Wang Chaozong was a man who understood things quickly. He understood immediately, "Indeed, a person as passionate as her, how could she tolerate three wives and four concubines?"

Xiu Xin bent down and said, "Okay, stop kneeling. You should know what to do."

Wang Chaozong nodded, "I understand, thank you mother."

Looking at Wang Chaozong's back, Xiu Xin sighed, "These two enemies."

Lu Yao was soon sent to the Wang family's courtyard in the suburbs, under the pretext of nurturing her pregnancy, and Hong Xiu from Wutong Garden was also sent away. Wang Chaozong was the one who decided the former,

and Xiu Xin casually added a sentence to the latter, "I see that Miss Hong Xiu and Miss Lu Yao have a close relationship, so why not let Miss Hong Xiu go with them, so that they can keep each other company."
Everyone agreed, and in a few seconds, they drove Hong Xiu and her baggage onto the carriage.
Xiu Xin was not very clear about what happened afterwards, but more than a month later, Zhan Xue came back with a nearly two-month-old fetus in her belly.
Zhan Xue is pregnant, and everyone in the mansion is filled with joy. Duan Yi is especially happy, with a smile on her face, "I never thought that an old woman like me would be so blessed to see my great-grandson."
Princess Anyang said, "That's right, old ancestor, your blessing is still to come."
Xiu Xin was also very happy for Zhan Xue. She put her hand on Zhan Xue's belly and said tenderly, "How wonderful."
Zhan Xue knew Xiu Xin's worries, so she couldn't help but comfort her, "Xiu Xin, you are still young. As long as you take good care of yourself, you will get better."
Xiu Xin's lips curled up into a slight smile, "I hope so."
After everyone left, Duan Yi called out to Xiu Xin, "Xiu Xin, please stay for a moment."
Xiu Xin suddenly had a bad feeling, and her

body became stiff as she turned around.
"Yes, grandma, what do you want to say to your granddaughter-in-law?"
Duanyi looked at Xiuxin and said with emotion, "Xiuxin girl, you have been in my Wang family for more than a year, right?"
Xiu Xin lowered her head and said, "Yes."
Duan Yi continued, "I know Fu Sheng loves you. Although you two had quarrels several times before, he never approached the two concubines in his room."
Xiuxin looked at Duanyi in surprise, "Grandma..." She actually knew everything?
Duan Yi smiled and said, "Don't think that I don't know anything just because I'm old. Is there anything in this palace that I don't know? Loving your wife is the most legitimate thing, but loving too much is not a good thing. Fusheng is not an ordinary person. He is the pillar of the Wang family and the prime minister of the current dynasty. Do you understand?"
Xiuxin's heart grew colder and colder. It turned out that Duanyi's favor towards her was conditional. It was her indulgence towards me on the premise that I did not hinder Wang Fusheng.
"Grandson's wife understands."
"The emperor is seriously ill and the whole court is in a panic. Judging from the current situation, the fifth prince was previously the most favored by the emperor, but because of you, my entire Wang family has become enemies with the fifth prince.

Do you know how much pressure Fusheng is under? The Cui family is relying on the fifth prince and is in the limelight, while our Wang family is declining. Now the only way is to unite with the Xie family to add a protective talisman to my Wang family in this precarious situation."

At this point, Xiu Xin understood everything in her heart, and her heart sank, "Mother means... marriage?"

Duan Yi glanced at Xiu Xin, who was looking pale, and felt a little reluctant. She had always loved this child, but now she had to sacrifice her. "The Xie family has a daughter named Yu Lan, who is the best candidate for the mistress of my Wang family."

Xiu Xin's eyes widened. "Xie Yulan? Didn't she become a nun?"

Duan Yi's expression did not change. "After becoming a nun, can't she return to secular life? Her appearance and talent are outstanding among the noble ladies today."

Xiu Xin felt that she was about to lose the strength to stand and almost collapsed to the ground. She finally squeezed out a sentence from between her teeth, "Then grandma, how are you going to arrange for your granddaughter-in-law?"

The author has something to say: There will be an update tomorrow.

☆, Chapter 73: Heartless

Chapter 73: Heartless

Duan Yi showed a trace of pity, "Now that things have come to this, I can only let you down, kid."

Xiu Xin tried hard to hold back the tears in her eyes and took a few steps back, with a hint of sarcasm in her eyes, "Oh, grandma, are you planning to make me leave the house and give up my position? I wonder if grandma is planning to let the second master divorce me directly, or to give me face and write a letter of divorce?"

Duan Yi kept silent.

Xiu Xin chuckled a few times instead, "Does Second Master know?"

Duan Yi looked at her and nodded silently.

Xiuxin originally thought that there would not be a greater harm than this moment, but Duanyi nodded gently, shattering Xiuxin's last fantasy. It turned out that he knew it long ago, long ago, long ago! It was a pity that she was still fantasizing before that he knew nothing. This decision was made by Duanyi alone. He would not be willing to give up on her, no!

Her heart seemed to have a hole in it, and a cold wind was blowing through it.

"Grandma, you lied to me, you lied to me, right? He wouldn't treat me like that, he wouldn't." Xiuxin's voice was low, like a whisper.

Duanyi felt something was wrong, so he walked down and wanted to hold Xiuxin's hand, but Xiuxin had already turned around and ran out.

"Girl Xiu Xin!" Duan Yi was so flustered that he hurriedly chased after her for a few steps, but Xiu Xin ran so fast, like a gust of wind, that she disappeared in a moment.

Duan Yi hurriedly called around, "Quick, follow her!"

"Yes." A boy hurriedly followed Xiuxin and Xiuxin and ran out.

Duan Yi said again and again, "Go and inform the Second Master, go quickly!"

Xiu Xin ran out like this. Before anyone could react, Xiu Xin had already flown out like an arrow. The young man in blue standing at the door stopped him slightly, "Second Madam, you Where are you going?"

Xiuxin paused for a moment, and even had a faint smile on her face, "I'm going to find the second master."

The boy replied, "Second Madam, would you like a carriage?"

Xiu Xin shook her head, "No, I'll go on my way. I'll go on my way."

The servant saw that Xiuxin looked unwell and asked worriedly, "Second Madam, are you okay? Hey, Second Madam..."

As Xiu Xin walked away like a whirlwind, the servant behind her caught up with her and asked, "Have you seen the Second Madam?"

The blue-clothed servant scratched his head in confusion, "It seems to be going that way."

It started to snow and the sky was covered with dark clouds.

The vermilion Lama Palace was majestic and grand. Xiuxin was still dressed the same way as when she went to pay her respects to Duanyi in the morning, wearing a light green double-breasted fox fur jacket, a plush pleated skirt of the same color, and a white felt blanket draped over her outer clothes.

She stood quietly in the snow, with snow falling on her hat, her dark eyebrows, and her lips, feeling very cold. But she did not even blink her eyelashes, and just stared at the direction of the palace gate quietly and steadily, like a statue.

The peddlers and hawkers passing by saw this and said to each other, "Hey, maybe this is another concubine abandoned by some nobleman?"

"That's right, why would we stand at the palace gate in such a cold weather?"

Xiu Xin turned a deaf ear to all this and just stood there quietly, as if she had escaped from this noisy world. Finally, with a creaking sound, the heavy palace door opened.

Finally, the court was dismissed, and people in official robes came out of the palace gate one after another. After a while, Xiuxin saw Wang Fusheng and a man in crimson official uniform walking out, talking and laughing. Xiuxin also recognized the man, who was the current head of the Xie family and Concubine Xie's brother Xie Yunqing.

Xiuxin neither went forward nor walked away, but just stood there firmly.

Wang Fusheng saw Xiu Xin standing far away and froze immediately. He bowed to Xie Yunqing and said, "Brother Xie, I have some urgent matters at home, so I may have to leave first."

Xie Yunqing said, "Please do as you wish."

Wang Fusheng walked a few steps to Xiuxin and asked, "Why are you here?" He touched Xiuxin's palm and said, "Why is it so cold? Be careful not to catch a cold. Why are you alone and not in a carriage? Where is Lanxiang?"

Xiu Xin smiled at him and said, "I came here alone."

Wang Fusheng took Xiuxin's hand and held her cold palm with his wide sleeves. "Let's go, get in the carriage."

The spacious carriage was covered with thick cushions, and when the curtains were lowered, the howling cold wind outside was immediately blocked out.

"Are you still cold?" Wang Fusheng rubbed Xiuxin's hands carefully.

Xiu Xin shook her head.

drive!

The driver cracked his whip and the carriage moved forward steadily.

Xiu Xin lowered her head and asked him, "Fusheng, how is everything going in the court recently?"

Wang Fusheng pondered for a while, "The emperor may die in the next few days. It is estimated that the fifth prince will succeed to the throne, and the second prince... has been placed under house arrest in the palace."

Xiu Xin asked, "Didn't His Majesty leave a will?"

Wang Fusheng laughed sarcastically, "Whoever is in power and in control of the situation can make whatever will he wants, right?"

"So how is the husband preparing?"

Wang Fusheng fell silent.

Xiu Xin clenched her hands tightly together, and spoke in a gentle tone, "My husband wants to divorce me and then marry into the Xie family, right?"

Wang Fusheng stood still as if he had been electrocuted. After a long while, he turned around and looked at Xiu Xin beside him. Wang Fusheng, who would not change his expression even if Mount Tai collapsed, said in an unstable tone, "You...where did you hear that..."

Xiu Xin smiled softly, with tears in her eyes, "So this is true?"

Wang Fusheng's heart was pounding in his chest. He wanted to argue, but finally closed his lips weakly.

When the carriage reached the moat, Xiu Xin suddenly shouted, "Stop!"

The coachman thought the Second Lady had something urgent to do, so he quickly tightened the reins and stopped the carriage.

Xiuxin lifted the curtain and walked out. Her steps were not big, but she walked very fast.

Wang Fusheng followed behind her and called her repeatedly, "Xiu Xin! Xiu Xin!"

Finally, Wang Fusheng caught up with her, grabbed her shoulders, and held her waist tightly, but for some reason, he felt like he was holding onto nothing.

"Xiu Xin, please listen to my explanation. I had no choice. When everything is over, we will be the same as before."

"I have no choice? Yes, you are the legitimate son of the Wang family, you are the prime minister of the dynasty, you are the father of Wang Chaozong, all of them are more important than me. And me? I am just one of your many women, but because I am a little favored, I become self-righteous and think that I am irreplaceable. Haha, I am so stupid."

Wang Fusheng frowned tightly, feeling extremely heartbroken. "Xiu Xin, it's not like that, it's not like that. Why do you have to slander yourself like that?"

Xiu Xin fiercely shook off his hand and took a few steps back. "I am not slandering myself. I have always overestimated myself. Wang Fusheng, do you still remember the question I asked you before we got married? Since I am not the only one, why did you marry me?"

Xiu Xin raised her hand to wipe away the tears that were welling up in her eyes. She stepped back as she spoke, "I forgot that the powerful and wealthy like you are always good at playing with people's hearts. It's not just me. Aunt Chu, who was neglected by you, is an example. You dared to challenge the secular world and marry her for her. I believe you must have loved her very much at that time, right? But what about now? You just abandoned her like that? People's hearts are fickle. I am stupid."

"Xiu Xin, believe me, I didn't want to hurt you. I had my own plans. I really didn't expect that grandma would tell you, Xiu Xin..." Wang Fusheng said as he was about to hold Xiu Xin's hand.

However, Xiuxin had already fallen into extreme self-abandonment and hatred. She didn't pay any attention to what he said. She pushed Wang Fusheng hard and cried heartbreakingly, "Why did you force someone like you to marry me in the first place? If it weren't for you, I would have married Li Yuzhi long ago!"

"Yuzhi? Li Yuzhi?" His student? Frames after frames flashed through his mind. Her rejection, indifference and resistance to him at the beginning were all because of Li Yuzhi? "You...you and Li Yuzhi...had an affair before marriage?" Wang Fusheng said word by word, as if it was extremely difficult.

"Yes!" Xiu Xin raised her head triumphantly,

"From the beginning to the end, the one I wanted to marry was him! It was always him!"

"No wonder, no wonder you resisted me so much in the beginning? It turns out you already had someone in your heart."

Jealousy and resentment surged into Wang Fusheng's heart. It seemed as if his heart was being gnawed by millions of ants, devouring his reason. "You had an affair with a man before marriage. Do you still have any shame?"

Xiu Xin smiled sadly, "Yes, I am shameless, stupid and foolish, I deserve to be divorced by you..."

Wang Fusheng forced himself to calm down. He thought that arguing like this would only make things worse, so he stopped talking and turned away.

It was this turn that made Wang Fusheng regret for the rest of his life.

Because, the moment he turned around, Xiu Xin's right foot slipped and she fell into the icy moat, "Ah..."

Wang Fusheng turned around in shock and jumped into the water, "Xiu Xin!"

Two servants ran over, shouting, "Second Master! Second Madam!"

Xiuxin opened her eyes in the water. Her vision was blurry. She vaguely saw a man in red clothes swimming towards her eagerly. He called her name anxiously, over and over again, so eagerly and affectionately.

She smiled dreamily and wanted to reach out

her hand.
But the water around was really cold, cold to the bone.
It's so cold… Really so cold…
In a trance, she felt something rapidly flowing out of her body. Her hand slowly moved to her lower abdomen. It was going to leave again. Was it going to leave again?
child……
The author has something to say: There will be an update tomorrow.

☆、Chapter 74

Chapter 74: Serious Illness
In a trance, she felt something rapidly flowing out of her body. Her hand slowly moved to her lower abdomen. It was going to leave again. Was it going to leave again?
child……
She shed a tear in the water. Why do you always leave me before I even realize your existence?
Palace, East Courtyard.
"How is she?" Zhan Xue stared at Chen Yuyi with eyes like knives, as if she would eat him alive if he dared to say anything bad.
Chen Yuyi shrank his neck in fear, "This... this... The second wife had a miscarriage and was injured. She was soaked in ice water for such a long time. The cold penetrated into her bones, so she has a high fever. If she can't survive tonight, I'm afraid..."

After hearing this, Zhan Xue immediately became furious. She grabbed Chen Yuyi's collar and lifted him up like a chicken, "Did you treat me properly? You quack! Someone, get me a new doctor!"

"Zhanxue..." Wang Chaozong said in embarrassment, "Imperial Physician Chen is already the best doctor."

Zhan Xue then sat down dejectedly, holding Xiu Xin's hand, tears streaming down her face, "Xiu Xin, Xiu Xin, you must hold on, Xiu Xin... Wang Fusheng abandoned you, but you still have me, and you still have your father and mother, huh? Wake up, please wake up?"

Wang Chaozong sighed and sat next to Zhan Xue. "Should we inform the Cui family?"

"Yes, that's right. Quickly, send someone to pick up Madam Cui. Maybe Madam Cui can be of use." Zhan Xue pushed him and said, "Go and get Madam Cui. I'll stay here with her."

After Wang Chaozong left, Zhan Xue stayed by Xiu Xin's side without blinking.

There were soft footsteps, and Zhan Xue thought it was Wang Chaozong who came back, but when she turned around, she found it was Wang Fusheng.

He also jumped into the water. He caught a cold and was obviously still sick. His face was pale, his cheeks were thin, and there was no trace of blood. He coughed a few times and said hoarsely, "How is Xiuxin?"

"How is Xiuxin?" Zhan Xue stood up, not

caring about his father-in-law status at all, pointing at his nose and scolding, "How dare you ask how Xiuxin is doing? When you cruelly abandoned Xiuxin and planned to marry someone else, why didn't you think about how Xiuxin is doing? You come to ask how Xiuxin is doing now? Are you qualified?"

Wang Fusheng seemed extremely weak, and coughed several times in succession. His body was as thin as a piece of paper, which would tear apart in a short while. He pulled the corners of his mouth with difficulty, as if he was very contemptuous, "Yes, I don't deserve it, I don't deserve it..." His eyes were fixed on Xiu Xin, "I don't deserve it..."

"Go away, go away! Xiu Xin doesn't want to see you! Do you know that she is pregnant? Ah? Do you know? Are you still human?" Zhan Xue pushed him away unable to bear it any longer.

Zhan Xue originally just wanted to push him out of the door gently, but he was so weak, like a piece of thin paper, that he staggered and fell into the dirty snow.

Zhan Xue snorted and slammed the door shut. Wang Fusheng fell in the snow, but his eyes were still fixed on Xiuxin's direction, as if he could see Xiuxin through the door. "This is the second time, the second time... Xiuxin, why can't I protect our child? Why? Why..."

"Help the Second Master up." Princess Duan

Yi's majestic voice came from behind.

A servant came over, bent down, and tried to help him stand up, but Wang Fusheng shook his hand off and struggled to stand up crookedly. He gave a hastily curt greeting to his grandmother with a strange smile on his face, "Yes... it's grandma, grandson, I'm paying my respects to you."

Duan Yi's face turned cold, and after a while he sighed softly, "You are blaming me."

The strange smile on Wang Fusheng's face grew even bigger. "How dare I, grandson! You are Princess Duanyi of my Hua Dynasty, the ancestor of the Wang family. How dare I, grandson?"

Duan Yi felt a trace of anger in her heart, and said angrily, "Wang Fusheng! Look at how half dead you are now! She is just a woman! Even if you like her, she is just a woman! Like a precious object! You can pamper her! You can love her! But you must not let a woman affect the overall situation!"

"The overall situation?" Wang Fusheng sneered, and staggered into the snow again. The dirty snow water stained a large area of his clothes. "My grandson is tired. I don't want the overall situation. I only want Xiuxin and our child…"

"Snapped!"

A loud slap landed on Wang Fusheng's face, causing numbness and pain.

"Are you still my grandson? Are you still

the head of the Wang family? You are destroying yourself like this for a woman? For a woman! You are destroying yourself like this!"

Wang Fusheng tilted his head and coughed violently a few times. "Grandma, you know how much I love her. Even at the critical moment of our family's survival, I don't want her to be hurt. I planned it well, I planned it well, why did you break it? Why?"

"Too much love is a burden and a handle. Fusheng, you have always been involved in official circles, so you should understand this principle better than me."

"So, so you're going to take my life like this?" Wang Fusheng's tears flowed down his thin cheeks, drop by drop, and fell into the dirty snow water.

Duan Yi held Wang Fusheng's face and finally shed tears. "Fusheng, I have an extremely precious Tianshan Snow Lotus here, which was left to me by the late emperor. It should be able to save her. But you have to promise grandma, promise grandma, if Xiuxin survives tonight, you will never see each other again. Can you do it?"

Wang Fusheng choked with sobs and remained silent.

Duan Yi asked again, "Can you do it?"

Wang Fusheng raised his head and asked her, "Will she be okay?"

Duan Yi said, "Yes, she will be fine, and you should be fine too."

Wang Fusheng lowered his eyes and responded softly, "Okay, I promise you."

Xiuxin had a very long dream. She dreamed that many, many years ago, when she was only five or six years old, she held her mother Jiang's hand and went to Huguo Temple to burn incense. The abbot was an old man with white eyebrows and a white beard. She was not afraid of strangers at all, and smiled and wanted to pull the abbot's long white eyebrows.

Her mother stopped her, "Xiu Xin, don't move."

"Abbot, what does the fortune say?"

The old man with white beard looked at me with a smile, "Your daughter has noble bones and beautiful features. You are a very blessed person."

Jiang thanked him repeatedly, bid farewell to the abbot, and walked out with her hand.

Jiang was very happy to receive the abbot's comments. She hugged her and said, "My Xiuxin is a very lucky person."

I smiled sweetly at my mother.

At this time, a young man walked in from outside the door. He was wearing a moon-white robe, with black hair tied behind his head with a hairpin, hanging softly on his shoulders. His face was as beautiful as jade and his complexion was as beautiful as spring flowers, just like a banished immortal. Xiu Xin stared at him steadily, with a glimmer in her almond-shaped eyes, "Where did this immortal come from?"

Jiang covered her mouth and said, "Don't talk nonsense." She bowed to the man and stepped aside.

The man stopped, his eyes fell on her, and he smiled brightly, "What a beautiful girl. May I know who your wife is?"

Jiang replied, "My name is Cui Jiang."

The man bowed and smiled, "Nice to meet you, I am Wang Fusheng."

The camera turned, and she dreamed that she was lying on the snow with her eyes open. She wanted to move, but her limbs were frozen, and she could almost feel her blood gradually stopping flowing. Then she heard a steady sound of footsteps, the sound of stepping on the snow, crunch, crunch, crunch...

Her heartbeat suddenly accelerated, closer and closer, and a pair of boots stopped in front of him.

It was a pair of beautiful boots, made of golden satin with dragon patterns embroidered on them, and a few grains of snow on the toes. She wanted to call for help, but she found that she couldn't speak. She could only fix her eyes on the man's face as if asking for help. She looked at him pitifully, saving me, saving me, please save me...

But the man just looked at her indifferently, with a hint of sarcasm on his face. "Who do you think you are? Why should I save you?"

After saying that, the man walked away.

No, help me... help me...
"Xiuxin, Xiuxin, I'm here, I'm here." A familiar voice sounded in my ears.
Xiu Xin slowly opened her eyes.
"Zhan Xue..." The voice was so hoarse and unpleasant.
"Are you thirsty? Want some water?"
"Yeah." Xiu Xin nodded.
Zhan Xue poured her a glass of water and served her with a small spoon, then sighed, "You cried all night."
Xiu Xin looked at the ceiling, "Zhan Xue, I had so many dreams..."
"Don't let your imagination run wild..."
Perhaps because the high fever had just subsided, Xiu Xin's eyes looked very lifeless, and she just stared blankly at the void in the distance, "Zhan Xue, why don't you light the lamp?"
Zhan Xue's heart skipped a beat. She looked around. The Wang family was a wealthy family. Not to mention at this time, even on normal days the lights were on all night long.
"Ah... I was afraid that the light would disturb you, so I asked someone to turn off the light..." Zhan Xue lied with difficulty, reaching out to wipe away the tears from the corners of her eyes, and holding back a small sob, "Your fever has just subsided, do you want to sleep a little longer?"
But it was Zhan Xue's small sobs that betrayed her. Xiu Xin immediately realized something and said, "Light the lamp."

"Embroidered Heart..."
"Light the lights! I said light the lights!" Xiuxin became excited.
"Xiu Xin!" Zhan Xue hugged Xiu Xin and cried, "Don't be like this, don't be like this... It will be fine, everything will be fine."
Xiu Xin's tears flowed from her sunken eye sockets, "No, it won't get better..."
The author has something to say: There will be updates tomorrow.

☆, Chapter 75: Divorce

Chapter 75: Divorce
Xiu Xin's tears flowed from her sunken eye sockets, "No, it won't get better..."
The next morning, Jiang led the servants to the Wang Mansion and said that they wanted to take Xiuxin back to the Cui family. Old Madam Wang said calmly, "Madam, what are you talking about? Xiuxin is now the daughter-in-law of my Wang family. Madam Cui, what right do you have to take Xiuxin back to the Cui Mansion?"
Jiang's eyes were red in an instant, "My precious daughter is almost dying of illness in your Wang family, and you still ask me why? Madam Wang, although my Cui family is not as good as before, it is not so bad that it can be bullied like this. I will take Xiuxin back today. Whether you agree or not, I will not leave without bringing Xiuxin back today!"

Madam Wang said, "Madam Cui, please be careful."

Jiang didn't care about all this and turned around and walked towards Xiuxin's east courtyard.

Pushing open the heavy door, the East Courtyard looked unusually desolate at the moment. No one had cleared the snow in the yard, and the heavy snow was almost breaking the plum blossom branches. The door to the master bedroom was tightly closed, as if it was also covered with a layer of frost.

"Embroidered Heart..."

"Embroidered Heart!"

Jiang took a few steps and pushed open the door.

Squeak...

Xiu Xin turned towards the source of the sound, but her eyes were still empty.

"Who is it?" she asked.

In just a moment, the expression on Jiang's face was completely frozen. Stiff, painful, and unbelievable, she called out, "Xiu Xin..."

Embroidered Heart...

How did her Xiu Xin become like this? She was as thin as a piece of white paper, bloodless, with sunken eyes and blind!

"Xiu Xin!"

"Mother?"

The next second, Xiuxin was hugged tightly by Jiang, "Xiuxin!" Then there was a suppressed cry, "Daughter, my daughter..."

At this moment, Jiang found sadly that her previous worries had come true. She was not optimistic about this marriage because she was worried that Wang Fusheng, a man at the top, would not be devoted to Xiuxin and marrying him would only cause her heartbreak. She was also worried that the Wang family was powerful and influential. If Xiuxin was wronged in her husband's family, the Cui family would not be able to help her at all.

Now, this is indeed the case.

But, what can we do now?

Not to mention that the Cui family is not as powerful as before, even in the past, what could they do to the Wang family which is so deeply rooted?

Jiang hugged Xiuxin and cried uncontrollably for a long time. Zhan Xue said a few words to her and she gradually stopped crying.

"Come, Xiuxin, I'll take you home." Jiang hugged Xiuxin.

Xiuxin's hands groped around Jiang's neck, "No, mother, I can't go back with you now."

"Could it be that even now you still can't let go of Wang Fusheng?"

Xiu Xin shook her head, "Mother, you have to think about it. No matter what, I am still a member of the Wang family. It is not reasonable for me to go back with you."

"Then how long do we have to wait?"

"You don't have to wait too long, mother. I believe that in a few days, Wang Fusheng will write the divorce letter to me. Mother just needs to wait quietly at home." Xiu Xin said calmly.

However, the divorce letter that Xiuxin was waiting for never arrived.

The weather was getting colder and colder, the snow outside was getting heavier, and the air was filled with a chill of despair. Seeing how sick Xiuxin was, how she had lost favor, and how she was about to be divorced, the maids and servants in Xiuxin's room lost their patience to serve her, and either did things perfunctorily or looked for another master. After a few days, Lanxiang was the only one serving Xiuxin.

"Where are Qinxiang and the others?"

"Oh, they... they are busy with other things." Lanxiang's tone was evasive.

Xiu Xin smiled and said, "Don't hide it from me. It's normal for them to find another way out in my current situation. Why should I be so demanding? It's just an injustice for you to serve me."

Lanxiang's tears immediately overflowed from her eyes, and she cried, "What kind of nonsense are you talking about, young lady? To be disrespectful, I grew up with you since childhood, and I have long regarded you as my own sister. Now that you are in trouble, how can I, Lanxiang, be such an ungrateful person?"

"Lanxiang..." Xiuxin smiled weakly, "Luckily I have you."

"Girl..." Tears slowly flowed from

Lanxiang's eyes, "No matter what, I will always be with you, always with you."

"Girl, you are tired, do you want to take a rest?" Xiu Xin looked outside blankly, "Is it day or night now?"

"It's getting dark."

"It's time to take a rest." Xiu Xin said and closed her eyes.

For the past ten days, Xiuxin has been like this, lying in bed in a daze, sleeping most of the time. She is getting thinner and thinner, and her complexion is getting worse and worse, as if her weak breath will stop in the next second! Lanxiang's heart has never fallen from her throat from beginning to end.

After Xiuxin fell asleep, Lanxiang tucked the quilt for her and turned to walk out.

Whoosh…

The heavy snow had not stopped yet. Lanxiang gathered her clothes and went to Wutong Garden in the wind and snow.

Knock knock.

After a few knocks on the door, Xueyan opened it and said, "It's Sister Lanxiang. Please come in."

"Is the young lady here?"

"Yes, yes. Please wait a moment, Sister Lanxiang." Xueyan said and went towards the door.

After a while, Zhan Xue came out wearing a large felt blanket, "But what's the matter, Xiu Xin?"

Lanxiang's tears immediately flowed, "Madam,

my girl... I'm afraid my girl is not going to make it. She has been waking up for several hours every day these days. Although she hasn't had a high fever, the low fever has not subsided. I think she doesn't want to live! The most hateful thing is that group of scary people, who flatter the powerful and bully the weak, even withhold our charcoal. Now our charcoal is almost gone. Madam, you are so close to our girl, I beg you, please save her, I beg you to save her!" She was about to kneel down as she spoke.

Zhan Xue hurriedly stopped her, "No, Miss Lanxiang! Even if you don't tell me, I won't ignore Xiuxin. Why didn't you tell me earlier that you didn't have enough charcoal?" At the same time, he said anxiously, "Xueyan, what are you still standing there for? Go get some charcoal and bring some more over!"

"Come on, let's go see her together." Zhan Xue pulled Lan Xiang back to the main courtyard.

The two of them were busy, and four stoves were lit in the four corners of the main room, which was so warm that people were almost sweating. Xiuxin also woke up in this rare warmth. Zhan Xue saw Xiuxin stretched out a hand, and hurried over to hold her hand, "Are you warmer now?"

Xiu Xin said weakly, "I'm much better now. Please come and see me every day."

Zhan Xue was heartbroken as she watched Xiu

Xin getting worse day by day. She turned her head away and could not bear to watch any longer. "I will feel relieved if you get better. Xiu Xin, I know you are desperate now, but your body is your own. If something happens to you, not only will Miss Lan Xiang and I be heartbroken, how will your mother cope with it?"

"Zhan Xue, if I didn't think so, do you think I could still survive in this world?" Xiu Xin turned her head towards her and looked at her with empty eyes. "I hate that I gave my heart to the wrong person. If it were before... cough cough..." As she spoke, Xiu Xin burst into a violent cough. Lan Xiang hurried over to pat Xiu Xin's back to help her calm down.

Zhan Xue knew she was talking about Wang Fusheng, and secretly hated him for being so hard-hearted. After all, a husband and wife should be bound by love for each other for a hundred days, and Xiuxin had been pregnant with his child twice. Now that she was in such a state, he didn't even bother to look at her. It was really despicable!

"Zhanxue, I heard that your father has regained his military power?"

"Yes." Zhan Xue said, "The world is in chaos now, and foreign tribes are eyeing us covetously. Who else in the world can stop the Hu tribe except my father?"

Xiu Xin nodded, "That's great."

Zhan Xue intentionally led the topic to something interesting and said, "Do you still remember the first time we met? That was when all the flowers were blooming. When this cold winter is over, spring will come..."

The two of them talked back and forth, and Xiu Xin became tired as she was talking, and she closed her eyes and let out a steady breath. Zhan Xue stood up and exhaled softly, "This won't work, I have to go find the Second Master, I can't let Xiu Xin stay here any longer."

Lanxiang bowed and said, "Then I'll leave everything to you, young lady."

Although Wang Fusheng was Zhan Xue's father-in-law, Zhan Xue did not regard Wang Fusheng as her godfather at all. She knocked down the two servants guarding the academy and rushed into the study. She kicked the door open with a bang and pointed at Wang Fusheng's nose and cursed, "Wang Fusheng, what do you mean? If you still have Xiuxin in your heart, kneel down and beg her for forgiveness. If you want to divorce your wife and marry him, then write the divorce letter quickly. Why torture Xiuxin anymore?"

Wang Fusheng was writing on a red memorial. He only raised his eyelids when he heard this. "Zhan Xue, is this how you talk to your father?"

Zhan Xue didn't buy his nonsense, "Father? How dare you say that?" Zhan Xue kicked her foot on the table, "Wang Fusheng! Today, you have to write the divorce letter whether you want to or not!"

Wang Fusheng put down his pen, raised his head and looked at her, "What if I don't write this letter of divorce?"

"You won't write?" Zhan Xue grabbed Wang Fusheng by the collar and raised her right fist. "Will you write it or not?"

At this moment, Wang Fusheng remained calm and composed, "Zhan Xue, don't forget your identity."

Zhan Xue didn't care about that. "You're threatening me? You should be able to ask Chaozong to write a letter of divorce to divorce me! I'm not afraid of you!"

Wang Fusheng closed his eyes, and when he opened them again, Zhan Xue seemed to see an indescribable sorrow in his eyes, "Do you think I don't want to?"

Do you think he didn't want to write that letter of divorce?

Every time he picked up the pen, every time he wrote a word on paper, every time he thought that after writing this, he and Xiu Xin would no longer have any intersection, he felt heartbroken. So, he could only write and tear it up, write and tear it up again, repeating this cycle, with no end...

Zhan Xue closed her eyes and cried, "Xiu Xin is dying... If you don't write this divorce letter, she will die in this palace!"

Wang Fusheng's eyes suddenly widened, then closed dejectedly, "Xiuxin...she..."

Zhan Xuesong opened his collar and said,

"Wang Fusheng, to this day, I still don't believe that you have no sympathy for Xiuxin. You write this divorce letter, just as letting Xiuxin go and saving her life..."

The author has something to say: There will be updates tomorrow.

☆、Chapter 76

Chapter 76 Farewell

The heavy snow that had been falling for more than ten days finally stopped on January 15th. A glimmer of light appeared in the sky, the thick layer of snow began to melt, and the icicles on the eaves dripped down.

Tick, tick, one sound after another.

Amid the sound of dripping water, she heard the footsteps of a person, walking gently, slowly, and the person's shoes made a slight creaking sound on the snow that had not yet melted. Since she became blind, Xiuxin's hearing has become extremely sensitive, and even the slightest sound can alert her. She frowned slightly and held Lanxiang's hand tightly, "Lanxiang, who is coming?"

The sudden darkness made Xiuxin afraid of this world and became cautious.

Lanxiang's voice sounded a little unsteady, "Oh, young lady, it's the boy leading the horse outside who's here."

"Oh." Xiuxin didn't loosen her grip on

Lanxiang's hand, but smiled and said, "Thank you for your trouble."

The man didn't say anything, but just took a few steps forward and walked straight in front of her.

Although Xiuxin couldn't see, she knew that the man had walked very close to her, because she clearly felt an indescribable sense of threat, which was a natural feeling of a blind person.

Her brows knitted tightly together, "Young man, is there anything I can help you with?"

At this moment, Wang Fusheng raised his hands and embraced Xiuxin's body, but without any contact.

How much he wanted to hold her in his arms, but he couldn't, at least not now.

Lan Xiang said, "Young man, our girl is leaving, don't delay."

Wang Fusheng's hand finally fell down weakly, he turned around and walked out.

After walking for a while, we finally arrived at the gate of the palace.

When Xiuxin stepped out of the door, she stopped and retracted her foot. She said to Lanxiang beside her with a smile that seemed to be crying, "Lanxiang, if I am willing to be a concubine, will the Wang family give me a place to stay?"

Lan Xiang almost burst into tears when she heard this, and her heart was filled with bitterness, "Girl..."

Wang Fusheng beside her was even more

shocked, and took a few steps forward, wanting to keep Xiuxin at all costs. However, the next words Xiuxin said made him feel heartbroken.

"Look, I'm so confused that I actually had such fantasies. Haha, haha." He chuckled as he spoke. "The people of the Wang family have always valued profit above all else. Who am I..."

"Girl, stop talking, let's leave this sad place as soon as possible."

Xiuxin nodded, stepped forward and laughed again, "There is no one in our Cui family who is happy now. My eldest sister Jinxin has a tyrannical concubine and a concubine's eldest son. Her husband is partial to the concubine and is unhappy all day long. As for me, I was divorced and sent home. My eldest brother was implicated by my father and could not realize his ambitions. My second brother was even exiled to a remote county. My father has been ill since he was released from prison, and my mother's old illness has relapsed and she is getting thinner..."

Lanxiang opened the curtain of the carriage for Xiuxin and helped her get in.

Xiu Xin fumbled to grab the edge of the carriage and turned her head back. "Actually, I am the stupidest one. I expected Wang Fusheng to help turn the tide when something like this happened at home..."

Lanxiang was very worried when she saw

Xiuxin was not normal at the moment, "Girl, girl, what's wrong with you?"

Xiu Xin shook her head, with a strange smile on her lips, "Nothing, nothing, I just saw some things clearly."

Finally, Xiuxin got on the carriage. The coachman cracked the whip and spurred the horse, and the carriage started moving.

Wang Fusheng stood at the gate, looking at the dust kicked up by the carriage, and suddenly felt a chill in his heart. He felt that from this moment on, he had truly lost her, and it was probably impossible to get her back.

However, at this moment he had no other choice.

One month later, Qingming Festival, Chenzhou.

"Sister, sister, the sun is shining brightly outside, and the willows are swaying by the lake. Would you please go for a walk with me? What's the point of staying in this room all day?" Jiang Zixuan pushed the door open and came in, pulling Xiuxin and acting coquettishly.

Xiu Xin smiled and said, "You, a grown-up girl who is about to get married, are still so playful."

Jiang Zixuan has now been betrothed to the eldest son of the governor of Chenzhou, Du Chengyu. It is said that Du Chengyu is extremely talented, handsome, and proficient in music, chess, calligraphy and painting, especially painting. He is one of the four great talents in Jiangnan.

When Jiang Zixuan heard Xiuxin mention her marriage, she pouted and said, "I don't want to get married. That Du Chengyu is not as the rumors say. He is full of bad intentions..." As if she remembered something, Jiang Zixuan stopped talking silently, but two red clouds appeared on her face.

Although Xiuxin couldn't see, she could hear that Zixuan was being suppressed by the eldest son of the Du family even before she got married.

"Sister, sister, please accompany me for a walk." Zixuan shook Xiuxin's sleeve.

Xiu Xin sighed, "It's not that I don't want to, but look at me now, how can I go out and play with you?"

Zixuan smiled and said, "I will take care of you. Besides, after Dr. Zhang gave you acupuncture last time, didn't you see some blurry light?"

Xiu Xin stretched out her five fingers and waved them in front of her eyes, whispering, "It was only a moment, and now, everything is gone."

Zi Xuan comforted her, "Sister, Doctor Zhang is such a good doctor. Just give her a few more acupuncture treatments and drink more medicine, and everything will be fine."

Xiu Xin said, "I hope so."

In the end, Xiuxin couldn't persuade Zixuan, so she sat in a wheelchair and was pushed out by Zixuan. Aunt Wu was worried, so she not only had two maids with her, but also asked five or six servants to escort her. Before she left, she repeatedly reminded her, "Zixuan, you are a grown-up girl now, and your sister Xiuxin is not mobile, so you have to take better care of her, understand?"

Zixuan replied, "I know, I know, mother. I am always worried."

Half an hour later, the carriage stopped at the shore of Mingyue Lake in Chenzhou.

The servants brought the wheelchair down, and Zixuan helped Xiuxin sit on it. "You just follow behind. We two sisters need to talk in private."

"Yes, Miss." Upon hearing this, all the servants took a few steps back.

Zixuan slowly pushed Xiuxin along the lakeside and said, "Sister, today is the beginning of spring. The willows on both sides are green, and the lake is also green. It's so beautiful."

"Yeah." Xiuxin nodded. Although she couldn't see anything now, she could smell the fresh air and hear the birds singing. She imagined the beautiful scenery in her mind, and her mood unconsciously became more relaxed, and the corners of her mouth curled up slightly.

"Sister, you are so beautiful."

It was the first time that Xiu Xin was praised so directly. She blushed and said, "What's so beautiful about a blind person?"

Zixuan said, "Sister is beautiful."

A month ago, when Xiu Xin was secretly sent to Chenzhou, Jiang Yunhai was almost frightened. The person in front of him was no longer the lively niece he had been a year ago. She was yellow and thin, like a sugar cane that had been drained of water. Fortunately, she had been carefully taken care of for a month, and she gradually became white and plump. But her eyes were still not good.

"Sister, the peach blossom forest is ahead."

"Peach blossom forest?" Xiu Xin could faintly smell the fragrance of peach blossoms. She could hear the noise of tourists, including children, women, and adult men.

Xiuxin held on to the wheelchair nervously, "Zixuan, are there a lot of people here?" Since she became blind, Xiuxin had never been to a place with so many people, so she couldn't help feeling a little nervous.

"It's okay, don't worry, sister."

As soon as Zixuan finished speaking, a child pointed at Xiuxin and said, "Daddy, daddy, look, there is a cripple over there."

Xiuxin's eyes were open, and if you didn't look closely, you couldn't tell that she was blind. The child saw her sitting in a wheelchair and thought she was lame.

The child's father quickly covered the child's mouth and scolded him in a low

voice, "Don't talk nonsense."
Zi Xuan said angrily, "This kid really has no restraint in his words!"
Xiu Xin didn't mind, "Children's words are innocent."
Zi Xuan let it go after hearing Xiu Xin say that. She was about to push the wheelchair forward when a clear and gentle male voice sounded beside her, "Xiu...Xiu Xin?"
The author has something to say: There will be an update tomorrow. If I have to work overtime, I will say it in the comments.

☆、Chapter 777 Storm

Chapter 77: Storm
This call was extremely familiar, making Xiuxin feel as if she were in another world. She turned her head towards the source of the sound, thinking hard about the owner of the voice, and then a person flashed into her mind like lightning. Before Xiu Xin opened her mouth, someone had already answered for her.
"Brother Yuzhi?"
Sure enough, it was Li Yuzhi.
The Li family has a son who is a very handsome man.
Xiuxin still remembers Li Yuzhi, who was dressed in plain clothes, elegant and graceful, like a graceful jade tree, and one glance at her made people feel like the breeze was blowing on their faces. She also remembered that she had written him a

letter, asking him to come to his house to propose marriage, but due to some strange circumstances, the two were destined not to be together. Looking back, she was not yet in love at that time, and only knew how to analyze the world in terms of pros and cons. She might not have liked him, but at least, she admired him.

Xiuxin grabbed both ends of the wheelchair and struggled to stand up. Zixuan helped her stand up and walked a few steps towards Li Yuzhi. Zixuan was a heartless girl and did not notice the unusual atmosphere.

Chenzhou is far away from the capital. Li Yuzhi also heard that Wang Fusheng divorced his wife and remarried. She was heartbroken and extremely anxious. She wrote a letter to her former classmates and old friends, secretly inquiring about Xiuxin's whereabouts. Unexpectedly, they met again here.

Li Yuzhi clenched her hands excitedly. Isn't this God's will?

"Zixuan." Li Yuzhi finally calmed down and suppressed the surging emotions in her heart. She fixed her eyes on Xiuxin and pretended to ask, "Who is this?"

Xiuxin had her head down at this moment, so Li Yuzhi had not yet discovered that Xiuxin was blind.

Just as Zixuan was about to speak, Xiuxin said, "I am a poor woman, Cui."

She said Cui, and did not use her husband's surname. It seems that, teacher, no, Li

Yuzhi no longer wants to call him like this. It seems that Wang Fusheng really divorced his wife and remarried!

Xiu Xin is so good, like a treasure in his eyes, but he treats her like a worn-out shoe!

A glimmer of hatred appeared in Li Yuzhi's eyes. He hated not that Wang Fusheng married Xiuxin, but that Wang Fusheng did not cherish Xiuxin after marrying her!

"She is my cousin." Zixuan said, "Brother Yuzhi has not been to my house for a long time since he came here. My father was still talking about her yesterday."

Li Yuzhi bowed and said, "It's Yuzhi's fault. Yuzhi will definitely visit you someday."

Although Li Yuzhi was talking to Zixuan, her eyes were always on Xiuxin. Even if Zixuan was slow, she understood and smiled foolishly, "Brother Yuzhi, before you met my cousin, you only came once every few months. Why do you come so frequently after meeting my cousin? I'm afraid you have other intentions?"

Li Yuzhi blushed at these words, "Ms. Zixuan, it's better not to say such nonsense."

Zixuan touched Xiuxin's arm and said, "Sister, tell me, am I talking nonsense?"

Xiu Xin raised her head and looked directly at Li Yuzhi with empty eyes, "Sister, stop joking. How can a blind girl like me who has been divorced stand your jokes?"

Blind, female?

Li Yuzhi opened her eyes wide in shock and took a closer look. Sure enough, although Xiuxin's eyes were open, they were empty and lifeless. She knew something was wrong at a glance.

His heart seemed to be split in two, "How... could it be?"

Xiu Xin sighed, "Mr. Li, don't mention the past."

Zixuan was afraid of touching Xiuxin's scar, so she quickly changed the subject, "It's spring today, and the peach blossoms are blooming so beautifully. Why don't we go for a walk in front?"

Xiu Xin lowered her eyes, held Zi Xuan's hand and sat on the wheelchair, and said coldly, "It's late today, let's go back. If we go back too late, your uncle and aunt will scold you again."

Zi Xuan stuck out her pink tongue and said, "I know, I know. Let's go back now." She paused and bowed to Li Yuzhi who was standing stiffly, "Mr. Li, we will say goodbye now."

Li Yuzhi bowed and returned the greeting.

Zixuan pushed Xiuxin and walked further and further away. Li Yuzhi, dressed in white, watched Xiuxin's figure getting farther and farther away and murmured, "Xiuxin, I am willing to be your eyes and see all the prosperity in the world for you."

In the evening, Doctor Zhang came to the Jiang Mansion as usual to give Xiuxin acupuncture. He also opened a new pharmacy and asked Lanxiang to go to the pharmacy to get medicine.

"Miss, do you feel anything?" Doctor Zhang stretched out his hand and waved it in front of Xiu Xin's eyes. "Do you feel any light?"

Xiu Xin stared ahead with empty eyes and shook her head in disappointment, "No."

Doctor Zhang pondered for a while and said, "Don't worry, young lady. Eye diseases require patience. I'll give you acupuncture every few days. Don't lose confidence."

Xiu Xin twitched the corner of her mouth slightly, "Doctor Chen, can my eyes really be cured?"

"Of course." Doctor Zhang said, "The girl's eyes are not seriously damaged. As long as time passes, she will be able to see again."

"Thank you, Doctor Zhang." Xiu Xin shouted to the front, "Lan Xiang, please see Doctor Zhang off for me."

"It's a girl."

After a while, Xiuxin heard brisk footsteps while sitting on the edge of the bed. She knew it was Zixuan. The corners of her lips slightly raised. It was a good thing that she had Zixuan by her side these days.

Sure enough, not long after, Zixuan's clear voice rang out, "Sister, sister, mother is here to see you."

Upon hearing this, Xiu Xin quickly stood up and bowed, "Greetings, aunt."

Mrs. Wu quickly supported Xiuxin's hand and said, "We are family, why do you need to perform such a big ceremony? Please sit down, please sit down."

"Xiu Xin, are the food and daily necessities here complete? If you need anything, just tell me and I'll ask the servants to get it for you."

Xiu Xin said, "Aunt, I don't lack anything here. Besides..." Xiu Xin's tone slowed down, "I'm blind now, I don't need those things."

Wu felt sad after hearing these words. She sighed and said, "You have suffered a lot. It's a pity that you have such a bad marriage." Wu paused and said, "You can rest assured to stay at your aunt's place and take care of your eyes first."

Xiuxin thought that Wu must have something important to tell her, so she said, "Aunt, what happened outside? Please tell me directly."

Wu paused, but finally said, "Originally, I should have kept this secret from you, but now I can't. A few days ago, the second master of the Wang family married Xie Yulan, the eldest daughter of the Xie family..."

Wu secretly glanced at Xiuxin. Seeing that Xiuxin was looking straight ahead with no change in her expression, she felt relieved and continued, "Before this, Xie Yulan had been practicing in a nunnery with her hair uncut. She looked like she was a sincere convert, but she got married the next moment."

Xiu Xin's expression still looked calm. After a while, she slowly spoke, "So that's what happened. I knew it would happen sooner or later." After a pause, she smiled sarcastically, "The Wang family has had so many happy events lately."

"How is the emperor?" Xiu Xin asked.

Wu said, "Every day is getting worse. According to the news from the capital, it will be over in the next few days."

"Yeah." Xiu Xin nodded. Judging from the situation, Wang Fusheng was ready to put all his chips on the second prince. Once the emperor died, if the second prince ascended the throne, with his soft and sticky personality, wouldn't Wang Fusheng have the final say in the court? However, the fifth prince and the Cui family were not easy to deal with, not to mention that among the four major families in the capital, the attitude of the Sun family was not very clear. You know, the people of the Sun family controlled a small part of the military power and controlled nearly half of the economic lifeline of the Hua Dynasty. The power of the Sun family should not be underestimated.

However, none of this matters to her anymore, she is just a blind person now.

"Aunt, what happens outside has nothing to do with me now. I am just a blind man, and I just have to live one day at a time."

Zi Xuan interrupted, "Sister, don't say

that. I'm still young and there are many good days waiting for me."

Xiu Xin smiled faintly, "I hope so."

Wu said, "You should take a good rest. I will go back first."

Xiu Xin stood up and said, "See you off, aunt."

Zixuan smiled and said, "Sister, I will come to see you tomorrow."

The night finally fell silent.

Xiu Xin listened to the rustling of the wind outside, and for some reason she seemed to hear the sound of ritual music, and was stunned for a moment. After a long while, she came back to her senses, smiled to herself, and fell asleep.

The author has something to say: There will be updates tomorrow.

☆、Chapter 788: Visit

Chapter 78: Visit

The next day, Xiuxin slept until 15:00 as usual before she sat up lazily. She became extremely sleepy after she became blind. Not only did she get up late, but she also had to rest at noon. In total, she slept for more than six hours. Lanxiang woke up early in the morning and heard the noise, so she lifted the curtain and came in, "Miss, are you awake?"

Xiu Xin nodded, "What time is it?"

Lanxiang brought in the toiletries and said, "It's one quarter past the hour."

"Yeah." Xiu Xin nodded, took the teacup, lowered her head, took a sip of tea, and then spit it into the copper basin.

"Girl, after dinner, why don't we go out for a walk along the garden? Won't you get sick if you stay in the yard all day?"

Xiu Xin shook her head and said, "I can't see anything anyway, so what does it matter whether I go out or not?"

"After all, I moved around for a while, so it's naturally different."

Xiu Xin thought about it and agreed, "Okay."

On the other hand, after tossing and turning for several nights, Li Yuzhi finally found an excuse to go to Jiang's house. Since Li Yuzhi became the magistrate of Chenzhou, she had done several things that won the hearts of the people of Chenzhou and Jiang Yunhai's appreciation, so he invited him to visit his house. As a result, Li Yuzhi and Jiang Yunhai became close friends regardless of age, chatting about everything, playing chess and appreciating paintings, feeling very comfortable.

Jiang Yunhai had thought about marrying his only beloved daughter to Li Yuzhi, but firstly, Li Yuzhi had revealed that she was not interested in marriage for the time being, and secondly, his daughter seemed to be interested in the eldest son of the Du family. So Jiang Yunhai let the matter go.

After Li Yuzhi and Jiang Yunhai played two

games of chess, it was already noon. Then a servant came to tell them that lunch was ready. Li Yuzhi naturally stayed to eat.

While eating, Li Yuzhi was worried about Xiuxin and asked indirectly, "Uncle Jiang, what do you think about the marriage between the Wang and Xie families?"

Jiang Yunhai snorted, "That's the business of the four major families in Beijing. Let them make trouble. It has nothing to do with us."

Li Yuzhi said, "That's not entirely true. The court is ever-changing, and many things can change in an instant. As the saying goes, a small move can affect the entire body."

"My dear nephew, what you said makes sense, but it's better for us not to get involved in those matters and wait and see what happens." Jiang Yunhai tightened his grip on the wine glass, "Although our Jiang family is the number one clan in the Jiangnan area, it is still far behind the Wang family. Otherwise, I..." Jiang Yunhai paused and took back the words that were about to come out, "Come on, my dear nephew, drink a glass with me."

The two drank one cup after another and soon became drunk. Jiang Yunhai was helped by the scary man to rest in the side room. The Jiang family's servant also prepared another room for Li Yuzhi to rest. Unexpectedly, Li Yuzhi waved her hand and said, "No, I'm not drunk yet. Let's go to the lakeside and take a walk and get some fresh air. Why bother with this?"

Li Yuzhi had just walked to the entrance of the garden when he saw Jiang Zixuan, dressed in purple, walking towards him. After all, there was no clear distinction between men and women, so Li Yuzhi immediately turned around and tried to dodge. Unexpectedly, Jiang Zixuan called him, "Master Li."

Li Yuzhi frowned and turned around to say, "Miss Jiang."

Jiang Zixuan covered her lips and chuckled for a while, "Master Li, why are you so reserved every time you see me?"

Li Yuzhi was speechless. Shouldn't one be dignified when meeting an unmarried lady? Instead, should one approach and flirt with her, which is the normal behavior?

Zi Xuan laughed again, "You are such a fool. How can you win the heart of my sister Xiu Xin?"

Li Yuzhi was so frightened when she heard this that she quickly waved her hands, "Miss Jiang, be careful with your words, be careful with your words, aren't you afraid of ruining Miss Cui's reputation by talking like this?"

"Okay, okay, look how scared you are." Zi Xuan straightened her expression and said seriously, "Master Li, my sister Xiuxin is injured. I also know that you have been interested in my sister for a long time. As for me, I just want to be a matchmaker, which can not only help you but also pull my sister out of the abyss. Tell me, do you really want to marry my cousin?"

Li Yuzhi blushed after hearing Zixuan's words, but now was the time to express her determination. She coughed and said, "Since I first saw Miss Cui, I have decided to marry you."

"Good! That's straightforward!" Jiang Zixuan smiled with satisfaction. "Now, I finally persuaded my sister to go for a walk by the lake. Why don't you go?"

"Huh?" Li Yuzhi stood there in a daze, as if she hadn't reacted.

Jiang Zixuan cursed, "Are you stupid? Go now!"

Li Yuzhi then woke up as if from a dream. After hurriedly thanking Jiang Zixuan, she ran to the lake.

Jiang Zixuan looked at Li Yuzhi's back and couldn't help but smile with her hands covering her mouth, "This silly scholar..."

Jiang Zixuan was feeling proud, but when she turned around, she saw her mother, Mrs. Wu, standing not far away with a gloomy face looking at her. She was so scared that she screamed "Ah" and secretly stuck out her tongue. She was so unlucky that she was caught by her mother.

Wu came over and poked Jiang Zixuan on the forehead. "You are an unmarried girl, and you actually did such a thing. Aren't you afraid of damaging your reputation?"

Jiang Zixuan was relieved when she saw that

Wu didn't seem to be seriously angry. "I'm doing this for my cousin. Mother, don't you think they are a good match?"

Wu said, "It's not your place to worry about whether they are a good match or not. Xiuxin's affairs are naturally decided by her parents. Even if her parents are not around now, your father and I are there. Why should you be so anxious to act as a matchmaker?"

Zi Xuan shook Wu's arm and said coquettishly, "I promise, this is the first time and the last time, mother, will you forgive me this time?"

Mrs. Wu had only this one precious daughter, so she could only pinch her gently and the matter would be over.

On the other side, Xiuxin was unable to see properly, so Lanxiang helped her to a pavilion to rest. Cuixiang waited in the pavilion and boiled tea with a small stove. Lanxiang poured a small bowl of tea for Xiuxin and handed it to her, "Miss, be careful of the heat."

Xiu Xin half-supported her head, "I don't know why, but I always feel that life is very difficult. I wake up every day and can't find anything else to do except eating and drinking."

Lan Xiang felt sad when she heard this, "Girl..."

In the past, there were times when Xiuxin was bored during the day, but there were always ways to pass the time, either by reading story books or going to see a show. If not, most of the day passed by taking out an embroidery sample and learning embroidery. . Now, there is no fun at all. Fortunately, Zixuan often comes to talk with her to relieve her boredom, so she won't be so sad.

At this time, a melodious flute sound came out.

The song is very familiar to Xiuxin, it is "Looking at the Moon over the River".

A year ago, Xiu Xin pretended to be ill and escaped from marriage to Chenzhou, but was caught by him. The two of them traveled to Yanzhou, and he played this song to the water of Yanjiang River.

The past events were still vivid in her mind, only one year had passed. When Xiuxin recalled it, she felt as if she had been in another world for a long time. Now, when she listened to this song again, she felt a little emotional but her mood was calm.

However, she had been bored for a long time, and occasionally listening to the music of stringed instruments felt a sense of freshness.

"Who's playing the flute?"

Although Cuixiang did not recognize Li Yuzhi, Lanxiang had already recognized his figure among the flowers and trees. She was secretly happy and secretly moved. After a year, Master Li still had her girl in his heart. It was such a great blessing for her girl that he was so infatuated with her.

"Oh, maybe she is a musician from the Jiang Mansion." Lanxiang said. She thought that if she told the girl that it was Li Yuzhi, she would probably stay away from her.

"Oh, I see." Xiu Xin smiled faintly, "This song is so beautiful."

Lanxiang looked at Li Yuzhi playing the flute among the flowers and trees from afar, and sighed with emotion, "Yes, it's so good, so beautiful..."

The author has something to say: There will be an update tomorrow.

☆、Chapter 79: Confession

Chapter 79 Confession

The next day, after taking a nap, Xiuxin went to the pavilion in the garden. After Cuixiang had made tea, the flute sounded again. Xiuxin listened attentively, smiled and tilted her head, saying, "Today's music has changed."

"Yes, yes." Lan Xiang replied dryly, "Do you like today's song, young lady?"

Xiu Xin nodded, "The tune of 'Between Water and Clouds' is more cheerful and lively, while yesterday's 'Looking at the Moon over the River' is long and gentle. Both have their merits, but I still like today's. Listening to this song, I feel as if I am really in the stream of water and clouds."

Lan Xiang said, "The musicians are very skilled."

Xiu Xin nodded, "It is indeed rare. Even in

the palace, it is rare to find such a good musician."

Among the flowers and trees, Li Yuzhi played the flute while casting her eyes on Xiuxin, a warm feeling in her heart. He was able to make her smile for a while, and he had already accomplished his mission.

From then on, Xiuxin would sit in the garden for a while after her nap every day. Gradually, she became interested in the flute player. "Lanxiang, is the flute player a man or a woman? What does he look like? What's his name?"

"Why do you suddenly ask this, young lady?" Lanxiang poured Xiuxin a cup of Longjing tea before the rain, and the faint tea aroma lingered around her nose.

"I'm just curious. Who is playing the flute here every day? It's a good thing for me."

Lanxiang glanced at Li Yuzhi, who was surrounded by flowers and trees, and saw him gently shaking his head. Lanxiang sighed in her heart and said softly, "He is the musician of the Jiang Mansion. He comes here to practice every day. I don't know his name. If you want to know, I will go and ask him."

Xiu Xin propped up her chin and said, "Listening to the sound of the flute, it has a strong voice, so it should be a man."

Lanxiang replied, "That's right."

Xiu Xin couldn't help imagining his appearance in her mind, and murmured, "Listening to his flute, I think he must be

a handsome man. It's a pity that I am blind now and can't see him."
Lanxiang said, "If the young lady wants to see him, shall I go and call him to come and talk to her?"
"Don't, don't." Xiu Xin shook her head repeatedly, "Don't disturb him. If you talk to him so rashly, maybe he won't come again in the future. Then I won't be able to hear the flute sound anymore."
Lanxiang could only say, "What the girl said is true."
On this day, Xiu Xin woke up from her usual nap. She heard the sound of wind and rain outside. She put on her clothes, sat up and asked, "Lan Xiang, is it raining outside?"
"Yes, girl."
Xiu Xin frowned, "Why is it raining? It was fine this morning."
"Spring is like this, it often rains."
Lanxiang helped Xiuxin put on her shoes. "Miss, do you still want to go to the garden today?"
Xiu Xin groped her way to the door and said, "It's raining. He should be gone."
Lan Xiang's eyes flickered. "That's not necessarily true. I saw that the musician was very diligent. He might work hard regardless of weather conditions."
Xiuxin stretched out her hand, feeling the cold raindrops falling on her fingertips, "I really want to see what Chunri looks like."
Lanxiang remained silent, feeling sad.

"Lanxiang."

"Um?"

"Go get two umbrellas and let's go into the garden."

Lanxiang was stunned for a moment, "But, it's raining."

Xiu Xin shook her head. "What's wrong with Luo Yu? If he comes and I'm not here, wouldn't it be a waste of the great music?"

Lanxiang smiled and said, "Okay, I'll go get the umbrella now."

The two of them walked towards the garden, one step deep and one step shallow. The rain was not heavy, but the ground was very muddy. Xiuxin couldn't see and almost slipped several times, but Lanxiang held her tightly. They finally walked into the pavilion, but didn't hear the flute.

Xiu Xin couldn't help but feel a little disappointed, "He didn't come today."

Lanxiang leaned over to take a look, and sure enough, there was no sign of Li Yuzhi among the flowers and trees. She could only comfort Xiuxin, "It's raining today, so he probably wants to take a break. If it stops raining tomorrow, he'll come."

Xiu Xin nodded, feeling somewhat disappointed. "Yes, it's raining, and I'm covered in mud when I go out. It's quite inconvenient."

As soon as she finished speaking, the sound of a flute began to play slowly from behind her. Xiuxin was delighted and listened attentively. It was a cheerful song "Happy

Rain".
"The music played today is very appropriate for the occasion." Xiu Xin couldn't help but smile, but her smile soon faded and her expression became a little nervous, "Lan Xiang, why is the sound getting closer? Is he coming towards us?"
At this moment, Li Yuzhi, dressed in white, was walking slowly towards the pavilion while playing the flute.
Step by step, slowly but surely.
The raindrops fell on his body and head, wetting his clothes. His black hair was also wet with rain, but he didn't care at all, and his eyes were lingering.
Lanxiang smiled. It seemed that Mr. Li wanted to reveal his identity today.
The sound of a flute rang in front of her, and Xiu Xin slowly stood up.
After the song was over, Li Yuzhi put down the flute and put it on her waist.
Xiu Xin bowed first, "Sir, your flute playing is truly extraordinary. I have admired you for many days, please don't blame me if I forget you."
At this time, Lanxiang winked at Cuixiang, and Cuixiang understood and retreated with Lanxiang.
Li Yuzhi stood in front of Xiuxin without answering. He looked at Xiuxin boldly and wantonly. If it were in the past, he would never dare to do so. She was the daughter of a rich family, and he was just a poor student. He did not have the status to peek

at her like this. But now it was different. Even if he looked at her like this, she would not know.

"Young Master?" No one answered for a long time, so Xiu Xin asked back in confusion.

Finally, Li Yuzhi coughed dryly and answered hoarsely, "It's me."

"Ah!" Xiu Xin exclaimed in surprise and took a few steps back. "Mr. Li?"

"I'm sorry for deceiving you for so long." Li Yuzhi whispered.

Xiuxin had an embarrassed expression on her face. She turned around and wanted to walk out, but she couldn't see and didn't know there was a staircase in front of her. She stepped on empty air. "Ah!" In a flash, Li Yuzhi rushed over and hugged Xiuxin's waist. "Be careful!"

The skin contact made Xiu Xin blush with shame. She struggled to break free from his embrace and stumbled back a few steps. She stopped when her back touched the vermilion pillar. "You...you!"

Li Yuzhi took a few steps forward and approached Xiuxin, "Miss Cui, I am sorry for the offense."

Xiu Xin turned her head away, "Mr. Li, I really didn't expect you to..." She paused, "It's really not appropriate for a man and a woman like us to be in the same room together. I hope you will respect yourself."

Li Yuzhi's eyes flashed with sadness, and she whispered, "Miss Cui, today, there are some things I have to say. Since the first time I saw you, I have admired you. After many twists and turns, the heavens have mercy on me. Now you and I are still single, isn't this a marriage sent by heaven, allowing you and me to meet again?"

After hearing these words, Xiu Xin felt really troubled and her heart was full of mixed feelings. "Mr. Li, you don't understand..."

"I understand, I understand." Li Yuzhi took a step forward, her eyes burning, "I understand, I understand everything. Miss Cui, I am willing to give you some time. I'll wait for you."

"I've been married." Xiuxin's tears rolled down her eyes, "and I'm blind. Mr. Li, you're happy with the innocent Cui Xiuxin who knew no worries, not the current Cui Xiuxin who is full of scars!" Although Xiuxin has recovered in recent days and is trying hard to forget everything that happened, the past has already dealt a heavy blow to her heart, and the scar is still bleeding.

"Xiu Xin." Li Yuzhi stretched out his hand, wanting to hold Xiu Xin's hand, but he still held back and retracted his hand, his voice full of friendship, "Yuzhi's love for you has never changed from the beginning to the end. Whether in the past or now, I, Li Yuzhi, only have you in my heart."

The author has something to say: Update tomorrow.

☆, Chapter 80: Chaos

Chapter 80: A turmoil
The next afternoon, the rain had stopped and the air was filled with the faint scent of grass. Water was still dripping from the eaves, making a dripping sound.
"Miss, Miss Zixuan is here." Lanxiang opened the curtain and saw Xiuxin propping up her head, not knowing what she was thinking, so she called out again, "Miss?"
Xiu Xin suddenly came back to her senses, "Oh, what?"
Zixuan poked her head out from behind the curtain and said with a smile, "Sister Xiuxin, what are you thinking about? You are so absorbed in your thoughts."
Xiu Xin stood up and smiled, "Nothing, what kind of tea would you like to drink?"
"Chrysanthemums will do." Zixuan sat down next to Xiuxin. "Sister, you look much better these days, and you look a lot more rosy."
"Every day I just eat and sleep, how can it be bad?"
Zi Xuan asked, "Sister, why didn't you go to the garden today? Didn't you go there every day these days?"
Xiu Xin's heart was as clear as a mirror, "You know it, right?"
Zi Xuan was stunned for a moment, then laughed dryly, "Know what?"
"You are still playing dumb. Young Master

Li comes into the garden every day. How could you not know? All of you know about it and you are just trying to fool me."

Zixuan shook Xiuxin's arm and said, "Sister, Master Li is infatuated with you. I just want to help you and Master Li be together."

"You haven't even gotten married yet, and you want to be a matchmaker?" Xiu Xin frowned. "My heart is calm now, how can I have the energy to think about other things? Zi Xuan, you know that I..." Xiu Xin paused, as if it was difficult to speak, "You know that now I have nothing left except being alive."

The sadness in Xiuxin's tone made Zixuan's nose ache and she almost shed tears, "Sister..."

"Zi Xuan, it's impossible for him and I to be together. Young Master Li is both talented and handsome, and he is naturally a match for a lady from a famous family."

"But sister, your eyes will be fine, and your body has recovered, why don't you give yourself a chance?" Zixuan said, "Do you know that my father wanted to marry me to Li Yuzhi, but he found me privately and said that he already had someone he loved. I went to persuade my father, and he gave up the idea. It can be seen from this, sister, that he will not marry anyone but you."

"Zi Xuan! I've made up my mind. Don't say these words anymore."

"elder sister!"

"Okay." Xiu Xin stood up, her tone already revealing a hint of fatigue, "Zi Xuan, I'm tired..."

Zixuan looked at Xiuxin's back, sighed helplessly, turned around and walked out.

Zixuan returned to the main hall, and Jiang Yunhai and Wu both stood up and asked with concern, "How is it?" Jiang Yunhai was also troubled by Xiuxin's matter. Last year, Wang Fusheng took Xiuxin away from him, which made him feel ashamed and felt that he had failed his sister's trust. Some time ago, Xiuxin suffered such a thing again, which made him, as an uncle, feel distressed. Now, he sincerely hopes that Xiuxin can find a suitable husband again.

Zixuan slowly shook her head under the expectant gazes of Jiang Yunhai and Wu.

"No way?" Jiang Yunhai sighed heavily, "This girl is like her mother, too stubborn."

Zi Xuan said, "Sister is now completely hopeless, and I'm afraid she has never thought about having children. Besides, sister's body..."

Mrs. Wu said, "Doctor Zhang has already examined her. Xiuxin had a weak body and it was indeed difficult for her to conceive. Now she has recovered and is fine. However, Xiuxin has had two miscarriages, so she may not be able to keep the baby even if she gets pregnant."

Jiang Yunhai said, "Since Xiuxin is

unwilling, let's put this matter aside for now. I will arrange a meeting with Li Yuzhi in a few days. If he is willing to wait for Xiuxin, it would be the best. If he is unwilling, I will personally send someone to propose marriage to him and find another famous lady."

Zi Xuan said, "We should try our best to cure sister's eye disease. Doctor Zhang has been giving sister acupuncture every day, but it has not been effective. Should we find another doctor to see sister?"

Jiang Yunhai stroked his beard and pondered, "Speaking of this, I think of someone. Didn't the imperial physician Feng from the palace retire a few days ago? I had some friendship with him when I was young. Why not ask him to take a look at Xiuxin tomorrow?"

Wu said, "This is the best. Xiuxin has had such a hard life."

The next day.

After Imperial Doctor Feng carefully examined Xiuxin's eyes, he said to Jiang Yunhai, who was standing beside him in a state of anxiety, "The girl's eye disease is a bit tricky."

"How to say?"

"The girl's eyes themselves are fine. They were soaked in cold air and had a high fever for seven days, which caused blood stasis and blocked the meridians, leading to blindness. The doctor Zhang used acupuncture for a full month, and the blood stasis should have dissipated long ago, but the girl's eye disease has not improved. This is a problem." said Imperial Physician Feng.

Xiu Xin felt a chill in her heart after hearing this. "So the doctor is saying that my eyes can't be cured?"

"Not really." Imperial Physician Feng said, "I think your eyes should be almost healed, but you just lack an opportunity. I'll prescribe a prescription for you. You can use herbs to fumigate your eyes every day and see the effect."

Zi Xuan said, "Doctor Feng, are you sure you can cure my sister?"

Imperial Physician Feng said, "Only 30%. Everything still depends on you, young lady."

Xiu Xin asked, "What do you mean?"

"If the girl is in a good mood, all her illnesses will naturally go away. If the girl is depressed and worried, the illness will naturally be difficult to recover."

"I understand." Xiuxin held Lanxiang's hand and stood up, bowing to Imperial Physician Feng, "Thank you."

Jiang Yunhai welcomed Imperial Physician Feng to the front yard for tea, and then asked, "Brother Yuanzheng, you are the fifth-rank director of the Imperial Medical Bureau, and you are only sixty years old. Why do you want to retire and return home so early?" Yuanzheng is the courtesy name of Imperial Physician Feng.

Feng Yuanzheng said, "Now is a time of great trouble. If I don't withdraw now, when will I be able to withdraw?"

Jiang Yunhai understood, "I see, Brother Yuanzheng is indeed far-sighted."

Feng Yuanzheng smiled slightly, "I am not the one with foresight. I am afraid that the emperor will not survive this month. I think changes will come soon."

Jiang Yunhai said, "If the world changes, it has nothing to do with our Jiang family. The emperor is far away, so we Jiang family just need to do our own business well." The Jiang family almost monopolized the tea and mulberry silkworms in the Jiangnan area.

Feng Yuanzheng said, "That's true."

After bidding farewell to the Jiang residence, Feng Yuanzheng went to the study and wrote a letter with only a few words in it: Lord Wang, your wife is now in good health, but her eye disease has not yet healed. I will do my best to treat her. Don't worry.

After sealing the letter, Feng Yuanzheng called the servant and instructed, "Send this letter to the post house, and remember not to let anyone know."

"Yes, sir."

After the servant left, Feng Yuanzheng thought of Wang Fusheng's numerous instructions before he left, and shook his head with emotion. He could never have imagined that Lord Wang, who was as powerful as the rest of the world, was actually such a lovesick man.

On the other side, Jiang Yunhai asked Li Yuzhi to come over and explained Xiuxin's attitude to him in detail. Li Yuzhi looked sad, but finally said, "No matter how long it takes, I am willing to wait for her. I just hope that uncle can support the students."

Jiang Yunhai was a little worried. "My dear nephew, I know you are sincere to Xiuxin, but there is a difference between men and women after all, you..."

Li Yuzhi smiled and said, "Uncle, you are worrying too much. How can I not care about Miss Cui? I just hope that I can come into the mansion, look at her from a distance, play the piano and flute for her, and make her happy." Although the Hua Dynasty attaches great importance to the separation of men and women, it is very normal for unmarried ladies and gentlemen to look at each other from a distance before getting married, or even chat a few words through the screen. Li Yuzhi's behavior is really normal.

Jiang Yunhai was really moved by this. "If that's the case, how can I not agree?"

The author has something to say: There will be an update tomorrow.

☆、Chapter 811 Recovery

Chapter 81 Recovery
Three days later, the emperor passed away

and the whole country mourned.

The emperor's will passed the throne to the second prince Hua Yun. All the ministers knelt down to praise him. Three days later, the second prince ascended the throne and named Wang Fusheng as the regent. For a time, the Wang family was in power and unrivaled. At the same time, the fifth prince Hua Ling was demoted to the wild land of Luzhou and became the King of Zhennan. Cui Jinyi of the Cui family was also dismissed from office, and the Cui family was in a state of depression.

The second prince was cowardly and incompetent. At this point, it was no exaggeration to say that the entire court was in the hands of Wang Fusheng.

The main hall of the Wang family's west courtyard.

Duan Yi looked serious, "Are you really going?"

Wang Fusheng, who was standing in the hall, bowed his head and whispered, "So far, everything has been done to fulfill grandma's wish. Now I have only one wish: I want to take Xiuxin back."

Duan Yi sighed softly, "Is that girl that important to you?"

"She is my grandson's life."

Duan Yi's body trembled slightly, and he said slowly, "How do you know that girl is willing to come back with you? Even if she is willing to come back with you, have you thought about how to arrange for her?

Fusheng, don't forget that you already have a wife, and she can only be a concubine when she comes back."

Wang Fusheng raised his head, his eyes burning, "Grandma, don't forget that I can still divorce my wife."

"You!" Duan Yi was furious. "How dare you!"

Wang Fusheng's expression did not change, "My grandson nowadays can't take care of so many things."

Duan Yi clenched her hands, "You are old now, and grandma can't control you anymore, but don't forget that Yu Lan is the legitimate daughter of the head of the Xie family. You can't just divorce her."

"What about Xiuxin?" Wang Fusheng's voice suddenly became sharp, with pain in his eyes that was hard to hide. "What about Xiuxin? Xiuxin was so innocent. At that time, she was pregnant with my child!"

Duan Yi's throat seemed to be strangled by someone, "Fu Sheng..."

Wang Fusheng gasped for breath for a long time before he calmed down. He bowed and said, "Grandma, I have overstepped my bounds. I will take my leave now."

When I returned to the main room in the east courtyard, I saw Xie Yulan sitting at the desk with a book in her hand as soon as I opened the door. The daughter of the Xie family lived up to her reputation, with a kind heart, full of talent, and a temperament like an orchid in a valley. She did nothing, just sitting there quietly,

and she became a painting in her own right.
Seeing Wang Fusheng push the door open and come in, Xie Yulan put down her book, stood up and greeted him with a smile, "Husband."
Wang Fusheng raised his lips to her with difficulty, "Yulan, you haven't rested yet?"
Xie Yulan smiled and said, "My husband, you haven't come back yet, how can Yulan rest alone? My husband, would you like some tea?" As she spoke, Xie Yulan poured a cup of tea for Wang Fusheng and handed it to Wang Fusheng with both hands.
Every word and action of the Xie family girl is truly impeccable.
However, Xie Yulan seemed fake, extremely fake, like a fake person acting according to a set routine.
Wang Fusheng took the tea from her hand and took a sip. "I'm going to Chenzhou."
Xie Yulan's expression did not change, she just said calmly, "My husband is going to take sister Xiuxin back?"
Wang Fusheng raised his head and glanced at her, "Yu Lan is really a very smart person."
Xie Yulan had an illusory smile on her face, "Really? Since my husband is going to take my sister back, I'm afraid Yulan will have to retire after accomplishing her mission."
Wang Fusheng didn't say anything. He was silent for a long time before he said, "I'm sorry for putting you in such a difficult position."

Xie Yulan snorted softly, "I am just a bargaining chip for the alliance between Daddy and you. Now that the big thing has been accomplished, I should naturally retire. Why should I feel wronged?"

Wang Fusheng asked, "What are you going to do?"

Xie Yulan gently shook the teacup in her hand, and the emerald green tea floated slightly in the cup. "Of course I'm going back to my Shuiyue Temple. I originally belonged there."

Since their marriage, Xie Yulan and Wang Fusheng have been loving and respectful to each other, but in fact, Xie Yulan has been sleeping alone in bed since the wedding day, while Wang Fusheng has been sleeping on the couch with his clothes on. This is a marriage that neither of them wants. Xie Yulan, a smart woman, knew from the first day of her wedding that her marriage with Wang Fusheng would fall apart as the kingship was settled.

Seven days later, Chenzhou.

It was late spring and early summer. The weather was getting hotter. Xiuxin was already wearing very thin clothes, but she still felt a little hot in the afternoon. When she took a nap, Cuixiang fanned her.

Xiuxin rested for an hour as usual. When Cuixiang saw Xiuxin wake up, she hurriedly shouted outside, "Lanxiang, the girl is awake."

Lanxiang brought in a bowl of snow fungus

and red dates soup on a tray. "Miss, would you like some snow fungus and red dates soup?"

Xiu Xin suddenly opened her eyes and felt a hazy light shining in front of her eyes. The light was blurry, but so bright that she shouted in surprise, "Light, Lanxiang! Lanxiang, I can see a ray of light!"

Lan Xiang was delighted when she heard this, "Really? I'll ask Dr. Feng to come and take a look!"

After carefully examining Xiuxin, Imperial Physician Feng said happily, "Congratulations, young lady. Your eyes have recovered and you can see the light. I believe you will be able to see again soon. But you haven't seen the light for a long time. It's best to cover your eyes with a layer of white gauze to prevent the strong light from hurting your eyes."

"Yes, I understand." Xiuxin was overjoyed and bowed to the imperial physician Feng, "Xiuxin thanks you, Lord Feng, for your kindness in treating me."

Feng Yuanzheng was busy supporting Xiuxin, "How can I accept such a great gift from you, young lady? Please get up quickly. As long as you can recover your sight, it will be worth my long journey to Chenzhou. Now I have completed my good deed."

Xiu Xin heard something strange in Feng Yuanzheng's words and asked in confusion, "You traveled all the way to Chenzhou? Could it be that Lord Feng was entrusted by someone?"

Feng Yuanzheng knew that he had let the cat out of the bag, so he simply said, "It was Lord Wang who asked me to rush to Chenzhou to treat the girl."

Xiuxin's heart suddenly rose to her throat, and she felt the veins in her temples throbbing. "Wang... Lord Wang? Which Lord Wang?"

Feng Yuanzheng smiled, "Miss, you are asking even though you already know the answer. Of course it's Lord Wang Fusheng. Is there any other Lord Wang in the world who can make me, a fifth-rank judge, resign from my post and travel thousands of miles to Chenzhou to treat you?"

Xiu Xin's face suddenly changed, "Master Feng, I'm not feeling well. I'll take my leave now."

"girl!"

Xiu Xin turned around and said slowly, "What else do you want, sir?"

Feng Yuanzheng said, "Lord Wang loves you deeply, and he had no choice but to make that decision. Why don't you look back?"

Xiu Xin raised her lips in a cold arc, "Yes, the Wang family is rich and powerful, not to mention that he is already the regent. Now that he is willing to come back, I should naturally be grateful."

Feng Yuanzheng saw that Xiuxin's words were not very appropriate, so he felt a little embarrassed. He was silent for a while, then he bowed and said, "Feng will take his leave. Miss, please think about it carefully."

Something cold ran across her cheeks, and Xiu Xin knew it was her tears. Once upon a time, she had buried her tears for him. From the day she left the Wang family, she decided that she would never shed another tear for him.

Since I have already decided to give up, why look back now? It will only rub salt into the wound.

A soft cloth touched Xiuxin's cheek. Lanxiang put the handkerchief into her sleeve, covered Xiuxin's eyes with white gauze, and tied it behind her head. "Will the girl look back?"

Xiu Xin turned her head, a mocking arc appeared on the corner of her mouth, "What do you think, Lan Xiang?"

Outside the window, the sound of a flute slowly rose. Every afternoon after Xiu Xin finished her nap, the sound of the flute would rise, rain or shine.

However, today's song is "Looking at the Moon on the River".

This song "Looking at the Moon over the River" brought back too many memories for Xiuxin, and her mind began to become confused. She frowned slightly, held Lanxiang's hand and slowly walked out.

The author has something to say: There will be an update tomorrow.

☆, Chapter 822: Strange Road

Chapter 82: Strange Road

During this period of time, Xiuxin would be lying if she said she was not moved at all. Even if it had nothing to do with love, the fact that Li Yuzhi played the flute for her for two months regardless of the weather really filled her heart with an indescribable feeling. However, until now, Xiuxin had too many concerns that made her hesitate to move forward.

Although the doctor said that she was not seriously injured and her eyes would soon get better.

However, she still had no plans to marry someone else. However, she thought, just like Zixuan said, she should give herself a chance and give others a chance. She still remembered that the person she tried so hard to marry was Li Yuzhi.

She held Lanxiang's hand and walked towards the direction of the flute sound step by step.

Through the white gauze, Xiuxin could only sense light, and everything in front of her was blurry, but she could feel that there was someone standing in front of her, so she stopped.

The flute stopped.

Xiuxin heard a few very light footsteps, it should be him turning around.

Then she heard a very low scream, very quick and short, but as if the person was extremely frightened by something.

Xiu Xin held Lan Xiang's hand tightly and asked nervously, "What's wrong, Lan Xiang?"

"Ah, no, nothing. A bee flew over and I got startled."

Xiu Xin breathed a sigh of relief, "So that's how it is."

Lanxiang then let go of Xiuxin's hand and said in a dry voice, "Miss... your servant, your servant, I will take my leave first."

Xiuxin nodded. It was indeed inconvenient for another person to be present when she wanted to talk to Li Yuzhi.

The man seemed to take a step forward. Xiu Xin heard his shallow breathing. For some reason, she felt that such a close distance made her feel a sense of oppression. She could not help but take a step back, bowed, and called out, "Mr. Li."

The person on the other side was silent.

Xiuxin continued, "Young Master has played the flute for me for two months. I am deeply grateful for your love. But time has passed, things have changed, and I am no longer the same Xiuxin I used to be. You may not know that a year ago, I wrote a letter to you..." Xiuxin paused, seeming a little embarrassed, "But at that time, you happened to set off for Chenzhou, and the letter was not delivered to you, but was put into the stove by my mother. In the past two months, I have been thinking, if you could come to my Cui family to propose marriage earlier, or if you could receive that letter, would everything be different?

Thank you for not abandoning me and waiting for me. I really have no way to repay you..."

The breathing of the person opposite him gradually became heavier, as if he was forcibly suppressing his anger, or as if he was suppressing his great sadness.

Xiu Xin was a little confused, "Mr. Li?"

The person opposite was still silent. Suddenly, a cool breeze blew past and a hand grabbed his neck!

The force was not strong, but it immediately made it difficult for her to breathe.

She immediately knew that the person in front of her was not Li Yuzhi at all! She had never been like that from the beginning. Li Yuzhi would not have such an overwhelming aura! Li Yuzhi was such a gentle, elegant, and graceful person, how could she make her feel oppressed?

She instinctively used both hands to pry apart the iron hand that was clasped around her neck, but she had just recovered from a serious illness and had no strength left, it was like an ant trying to shake a tree!

Who is it? Who could it be? Who wants to kill her? Who dares to kill her in Jiang's house! Then, Xiu Xin heard a suppressed, low, hoarse male voice with infinite resentment:

"A fickle woman!"

Wang Fusheng!

It turned out to be Wang Fusheng!

He's back, and he's going to kill her as soon as he comes back!

Xiu Xin calmed down at this time, and said with difficulty, "Wang Fusheng, what's the matter? I didn't die last time, so you had to come and strangle me to death?"

The strength in his hands gradually loosened, but he still didn't let her go. His voice was heavy and filled with bloody resentment, "It's only been three months, and you're ready to leave Pipa and return to the arms of your old lover? Hmm? You can't repay me?" Wang Fusheng laughed softly, as if mocking her, "Why, are you ready to pledge yourself to me?"

A lot of fresh air entered Xiuxin's throat, which made her speak fluently. At the same time, something else was accumulating in her chest, which made her wish she could grow thorns of hatred all over her body and pierce into the other person's heart. So she smiled coldly, "Yes, I am ready to pledge my love to him. I am also worried that Li Lang will despise me. After all, I am no longer clean and unworthy of him."

"Not clean anymore?" Wang Fusheng was so angry that he laughed out loud, "Why, you feel you are dirty now that you have slept with me." He lowered his head suddenly and bit her lip like crazy, They ravaged fiercely, as if a wild animal was tearing apart its prey, and soon, a strong smell of blood spread between their lips and teeth.

Xiuxin's lip was bitten by Wang Fusheng,

and drops of blood were dripping out.

His rough fingers ravaged Xiu Xin's lips, and his voice was horribly low, "What should I do? Your place is not clean." Then his fingers roughly opened Xiu Xin's short placket, covered hers, and forcefully After ravaging her for a while, he whispered in her ear, like a devil's whisper, "You're not clean here either... Is there any part of your body that I haven't tasted? Huh? Do you think Li Yuzhi will Do you want shabby shoes like yours?"

Xiu Xin's face turned red with anger, and her whole body was shaking. It was early summer, but she felt so cold. She was powerless to resist, but she always had a way to maximize his anger. "Mr. Li is so affectionate, how could he mind such a small detail? Lord Wang, you are worrying too much."

"Cui, Xiu, Xin!" The words came out one by one, as if they were popping out from between his teeth. The strength in his hands gradually tightened, making Xiu Xin's breathing difficult again.

Before coming, he had already prepared himself mentally. Xiuxin might find it difficult to forgive him, but he was willing to wait for her to change her mind. After all, he was the one who failed her first. He had thought it through. Even if she said something hurtful, even if she never wanted to look at him again, he would put aside all his self-esteem and ask for her forgiveness. He played a song "Looking at the River Moon" for her. This song was the starting point for the easing of their relationship.

However, he had not expected or anticipated that she would come towards him with a smile and call out another person's name! The flame of jealousy instantly burned all his rationality.

Xiuxin smiled at him and even said that she could never repay him, and lamented that fate was cruel and made them miss each other!

What a long-lasting love! It's so touching!

"Lord Wang wants to kill me... Hehe..." Xiu Xin actually laughed and said intermittently, "Earlier, Xiu Xin didn't die in your hands, Lord Wang, you must be unwilling, right? Would you please trouble Lord Wang to come here from afar to strangle a little girl to death?"

Xiu Xin's words made Wang Fusheng regain his sanity for a moment. He completely let go of her hand.

What on earth was he doing? His hands drooped weakly, and his whole body seemed to be exhausted, kneeling on the ground. What on earth was he doing? Didn't he come to Chenzhou to get Xiu Xin back at all costs? What on earth was he doing now?

Xiuxin slowly pulled away the white veil covering her eyes. The dazzling light rushed into her eyes, causing tears to flow from her sore eyes. But she still struggled to open her eyes, because at this moment, she really wanted to see his expression.

But through the rolling tears, she could only see a blurry shadow slumped on the ground.

"Girl!" Lanxiang rushed out from the house, "Girl, how can you take off the white veil? Don't you want your eyes?" She wrapped the white veil for her again, and held Xiuxin's hand and walked back step by step, "Girl, let's go, let's go back to the house, back to the house..."

The author has something to say: There will be an update tomorrow.

☆, Chapter 83 Heart-wrenching

Chapter 83 Heartbroken

Since that day, Wang Fusheng had not appeared in front of Xiuxin for several days. However, everyone in the Jiang Mansion knew that the powerful regent had bought a large house next to the Jiang family, and was going to live in Chenzhou permanently. In the past few days, the maids and servants in the house carried all kinds of rare things into the house, and it was very lively. The maids of the Jiang family gathered together and whispered, "As expected of the regent, he is very generous. Did you see that? Everything he carried in is worth a thousand gold coins."

"Miss... I heard..." Lan Xiang hesitated for a long time, and finally spoke, "I heard that Lord Wang has divorced Xie Yulan, and Xie Yulan has returned to Shuiyue Temple and is cultivating with her hair uncut... Because of this incident, the whole government was shocked."

However, Xiu Xin didn't even raise her eyebrows, and after a long while she smiled faintly, "What does the divorce between Lord Wang and the daughter of the Xie family have to do with me?"

Lanxiang wanted to say something else, but seeing Xiuxin like this, she had to keep silent.

At the same time, in the main hall of Jiang Mansion.

"Sir Wang, you took Xiu Xin away from my family before. This time, Sir Wang has become the regent and has tremendous power! Do you want to do the same thing again? I tell you, this time, unless you wipe out my entire Jiang family, forget it!" Jiang Yunhai slammed the teacup in his hand on the table, "Someone, show the guests away!"

Wang Fusheng remained calm and gently put down the tea in his hand. "Master Jiang, why are you so excited? I didn't say I would take your niece away by force. I came here today just to visit you, Master Jiang, and I have no other intentions."

Jiang Yunhai was still furious. "Lord Wang, let's not beat around the bush. You, the regent, have come all the way to my small Chenzhou. You wouldn't have come all the way here just to visit an old man like me, right?"

Wang Fusheng drank his tea slowly, "Lord Jiang, the scenery in the south of the Yangtze River is unique. It won't be a problem for me to come here to rest for a while, right?"

Jiang Yunhai snorted, "I have no right to interfere with where Lord Wang wants to go. But please stop harassing Xiuxin! She just escaped from the gates of hell. After all, you are husband and wife, even if you have no feelings for her, you should at least give her some leeway."

"We were husband and wife..." Wang Fusheng's expression became somewhat lost, as if he was trapped in some kind of situation. "We were husband and wife...why would she be willing to give me a chance?"

Jiang Yunhai was a little surprised to see his expression. In his impression, Wang Fusheng was always a smooth-talking person, and he would never show such an expression in front of others, as if he was too sad to control himself.

"Master Jiang." Wang Fusheng stood up and bowed to Jiang Yunhai, saying, "I came here not for anything else but to win back Xiuxin. I hope Master Jiang will help me." He bowed deeply. You know, Wang Fusheng had never bowed to anyone else except for the emperor and elders. Jiang Yunhai was the first one.

Jiang Yunhai was shocked. It took him a long time to calm down. He snorted and said,

"If I had known this would happen, I wouldn't have done it in the first place. Now that it's done, it's hard to undo it. Although Xiuxin is my niece, she's grown up. I can't control your relationship with her..."

Jiang Yunhai's attitude was very clear this time. He would neither interfere with him nor help him. Wang Fusheng knew that this was the maximum Jiang Yunhai could do, so he stopped forcing him and bowed again, "Wang will take his leave."

Jiang Yunhai returned the greeting, "Farewell, Prince Regent."

On the second day after Wang Fusheng arrived in Chenzhou, Li Yuzhi handed in a visiting card to the Wang Mansion. Wang Fusheng glanced at it briefly and threw it aside. Mo Yan didn't understand the reason and asked hesitantly, "Master, this..."

"Just leave it there." Wang Fusheng said indifferently.

"Um... yes, master." Li Yuzhi has always been Wang Fusheng's favorite student. Mo Yan, this shrewd man, was a little confused by his master's sudden change.

The visiting cards were sent for three consecutive days. On the fourth day, Wang Fusheng finally gave in and said, "Go, invite him in."

Li Yuzhi was led in. When she looked up, she saw her former mentor sitting on the armchair with an unpredictable expression on his face. Li Yuzhi bowed deeply to Wang

Fusheng and said, "Greetings, teacher."

Wang Fusheng drank a sip of tea slowly, and then said, "Yuzhi, you are my most valued disciple. It has been almost a year since we last met, right?"

Li Yuzhi said, "Yes, it's been more than a year. How is your health recently, teacher?"

Wang Fusheng stood up and approached Li Yuzhi step by step, his eyes sharp as a cheetah, "Yuzhi, you have sent me visiting cards again and again, it can't be just to reminisce about the past, right?"

Li Yuzhi raised her head, with a neither humble nor arrogant attitude, "I am a student here and do have a few words to say to you, teacher."

You are quite courageous! The corners of Wang Fusheng's mouth sank slightly, and his whole body began to exude an oppressive aura, "Why don't you tell me about it."

Li Yuzhi looked calm, as if she was not affected at all. She cupped her hands and spoke slowly, "As the saying goes, a teacher is a father for life. I will never forget the teacher's kindness. But, about Xiu Xin..." Li Yuzhi paused, raised her head, and looked directly into Wang Fusheng's eyes, "I missed Xiu Xin once a year ago. This time, I will never give in, even if I die."

Wang Fusheng was furious, but his voice was still elegant and pleasant, even with a hint of advice from a teacher, "Yuzhi, have

you thought it through? Aren't you afraid?"
Li Yuzhi smiled slightly, "Teacher, if you want to deal with me, it's as easy as crushing an ant. It's just that Yuzhi's mother died of illness a few days ago. Now she is alone and isolated from the world. If you want Yuzhi's life, just take it."

"You have thought it through clearly." Wang Fusheng smiled slightly. Although his expression was gentle, it made Mo Yan, who was standing beside him with his head down, shiver inexplicably.

Li Yuzhi seemed unaffected. "Teacher is the head of the civil officials. You must know the old saying that the past cannot be retrieved and the human heart cannot be restored."

Wang Fusheng's hands, hidden in his wide sleeves, slowly clenched, making a clattering sound. With his current power, killing Li Yuzhi, let alone one, would be as easy as killing ten or a hundred Li Yuzhi. But, so what? What if I kill him? Can Xiuxin return to him? She will just hate him more.

If he loses power, he can use tricks and tyranny to get it back, but if he loses the hearts of the people, what can he use to get them back?

Xiuxin, what can I do to win back your heart?

"Student, take your leave." Li Yuzhi bowed and turned to leave.

As soon as Li Yuzhi left, Mo Yan heard a

series of loud bangs, which frightened him so much that he trembled all over.

Looking up, Wang Fusheng saw broken porcelain all over the floor, and some tea leaves on his shoes.

Mo Yan was standing nearby. Seeing his master's face was really ugly, he couldn't help but call out worriedly, "Second Master... Imperial Physician Feng just sent someone to pass on a message, saying that he wants to take off the white veil covering the eyes of Second Madam, oh, no, Miss Cui."

Wang Fusheng was silent for a while before he said, "Let's go to Jiang's house."

"Yes, master." Mo Yan hurriedly followed Wang Fusheng out the door.

The author has something to say: There will be updates tomorrow.

☆, Chapter 84 Awakening from a Dream

Chapter 84: Awakening

Jiang Yunhai, Wu, Zixuan, Lanxiang and others in the room all stared at Feng Yuyi's hand in silence, while Feng Yuyi was untying the white gauze covering Xiuxin's eyes circle by circle.

When the last circle of white yarn was untied, Xiu Xin suddenly shouted briefly, "Wait."

Imperial Physician Feng paused, startled. "What's wrong, Miss Cui?"

Xiu Xin's hands were twisted nervously,

"Doctor Feng, do you think... my eyes... can be healed?"
Imperial Physician Feng laughed, "Miss Cui, don't worry, your eyes must be completely healed."
At this moment, Xiuxin heard a very light sound of footsteps. Xiuxin raised her head and asked, "Who's coming?"
Zixuan smiled gently, "Sister Xiuxin, who's here? Just look for yourself."
Imperial Physician Feng couldn't help laughing and lifted the last layer of white veil.
A burst of burning light pierced into Xiuxin's eyes, and tears immediately rolled down her eyes. But through the tears, a blurry scene came into her sight.
Lanxiang used a brocade handkerchief to wipe the tears from Xiuxin's cheeks, "Girl, girl, did you see it?"
"Yeah." Xiu Xin couldn't help but let out a big smile, "I saw it... I saw it. I saw it!"
Xiu Xin's eyes first fixed on Jiang Yunhai, and she smiled and called out "Uncle". Jiang Yunhai happily responded.
"aunt."
Mrs. Wu smiled and nodded.
"Zixuan." Xiuxin stood up and shook Zixuan's hand, "Zixuan."
Zixuan wiped her tears and hugged Xiuxin, "Sister, it's okay, everything is okay."
After letting go of Zixuan's hand, Xiuxin fixed her sight on a man. She smiled

faintly and bent her knees slightly towards the man, "Mr. Li."

"Miss Cui." Li Yuzhi returned the greeting.

"Ahem." Jiang Zixuan coughed a few times and made a face at Lanxiang and her mother. Wu said hurriedly, "Oh, Xiuxin's eyes have recovered. This is a great event. We have to celebrate tonight. I'll go and make some preparations." Zixuan said hurriedly, "Mom, I'll go with you." Zixuan paused and took Lanxiang's arm again, "Mom is short of help. Sister Lanxiang, can you go with me?"

How could Lanxiang disagree? "Okay."

Imperial Physician Feng saw everyone's attitude and knew that they were trying to bring Li Yuzhi and Cui Xiuxin together. He sighed for Wang Fusheng in his heart. Even if he owned the whole world, he couldn't win back a woman's heart after all his efforts...

Seeing that Imperial Physician Feng was standing there, Wu turned around and said, "Doctor Feng, our Xiuxin's eyesight is all dependent on you. Please go to the front hall for a cup of tea, how about that?"

Imperial Physician Feng glanced at Xiuxin and Li Yuzhi and sighed again, "Thank you, Madam Jiang, for your hospitality."

After a while, everyone in the room left, leaving Cui Xiuxin and Li Yuzhi staring at each other. Li Yuzhi was shy and her cheeks turned slightly red. Xiuxin was also a little embarrassed, "Mr. Li, would you like a cup of tea?"

Li Yuzhi smiled slightly, "Thank you, young lady."

The two sat opposite each other. Xiu Xin picked up the boiling water on the small copper stove and scalded the teacup and teapot. Then, she took a handful of tea leaves and put them in the small teapot, and finally sifted the boiling water into it. The green tea leaves rolled up and down, and the tea water slowly turned clear green. This was the top-grade pre-rain Longjing tea of the Jiang family. Not only was the tea color good, but the tea fragrance was also overflowing.

However, what attracted Li Yuzhi's attention was not the tea, but Xiuxin's hands.

The white hands holding the sky-blue teacup looked even whiter than bone china and more delicate than jade.

"Mr. Li, please have some."

Li Yuzhi picked up the teacup and took a sip, the sweet taste overflowing between her lips and teeth, "I didn't expect that the girl's tea art is so outstanding."

Xiu Xin smiled gently, "It's not that my tea art is good, it's that this tea is good. The Jiang family only produces ten kilograms of Rain Dragon Well tea a year, and half of it is sent to the palace, so only five kilograms are left. This Rain Dragon Well tea can be sold outside for the price of two taels of gold for one tael of tea leaves."

Li Yuzhi said, "Lord Jiang really loves you."

Xiu Xin smiled slightly and lowered her head to take a sip of tea.

"I heard from my uncle that you will be transferred back to the capital soon? Congratulations, Mr. Li, you are on your way to a higher position."

"A few days ago, the imperial court did issue a transfer order." Li Yuzhi paused, "Who is in charge of the Hua Dynasty now? Even a three-year-old child knows it. Who issued the transfer order? I'm sure you know it too, young lady."

"Of course I know that." Xiu Xin raised a sarcastic arc at the corner of her lips, "What else can he do besides using his power to oppress others?" Xiu Xin put down the teacup, raised her head and looked at Li Yuzhi, "What is Master Li going to do?"

"If I go, it will be his wish. If I don't go, it will be a capital crime." Li Yuzhi paused and said, "Rong Yuzhi, I'm sorry to say this. Miss, are you willing to go back to Beijing with me?"

Xiu Xin's lips curled up slightly, "Mr. Li, do you know what your words mean?"

Li Yuzhi said, "What does it mean? It means that I will become an enemy of the powerful regent."

"Mr. Li, you will regret this."

"In your heart, Yuzhi is such a cowardly person?"

Xiu Xin was shocked, and after a long

silence, she said, "Xiu Xin is not worthy of you doing this for me."

"It's worth it. There is no one in the world who is more worthy of me than you." Li Yuzhi said, "A few days ago, I received a letter from your mother. I realized what I missed a year ago. It was all Yuzhi's fault."

"Let's not talk about the past anymore."

"So what about now?" Li Yuzhi boldly held Xiuxin's hand, her eyes burning, "Miss, are you still willing to give me a chance to make amends now?"

Xiuxin was about to speak when she heard a bang in her ears. She was startled and turned around to see Wang Fusheng, dressed in a purple robe and with a sullen face, standing at the door. His brows were deeply furrowed, and he was staring viciously at Xiuxin and Li Yuzhi's clasped hands.

"Cui, Xiu, Xin!"

Xiu Xin slowly pulled her hand out, her expression unchanged, "Regent, what brings you here this time?"

Wang Fusheng suppressed his rage and said, "Li Yuzhi, get out of here."

Li Yuzhi stood up and bowed, "Master Wang, this is Miss Cui's place. It seems that you, Master Wang, don't have the right to make decisions, right?"

Wang Fusheng snorted coldly, "Li Yuzhi, are you really not afraid of death?"

"Li is all alone, why should he fear death?"

"Good, good!" Wang Fusheng laughed in anger, "You are really very nice! Someone come here!"

"Here!" In an instant, two guards with swords appeared from nowhere and stood behind Wang Fusheng, staring at Li Yuzhi ready to attack.

"Wait." Xiu Xin said.

Wang Fusheng waved his hand to stop the two men's actions.

Xiu Xin said to Li Yuzhi, "Mr. Li, I have something to say to Lord Wang. Could you please step aside for a moment?"

"Embroidered Heart!"

Xiu Xin said, "Sir, please go back."

Li Yuzhi glanced at Xiuxin worriedly and whispered, "Take care of yourself."

After Li Yuzhi left, Xiu Xin smiled faintly and waved her hand, "Sir Wang, would you like to come into my humble abode for a cup of tea?"

The author has something to say: There will be updates tomorrow.

☆、Chapter 85 Retreat 8

Chapter 85: Retreat

Xiuxin boiled a pot of water again, picked up a handful of wild chrysanthemums and put them into the pot. The wrinkled chrysanthemums slowly stretched out in the water, becoming light and full. Xiuxin took another blue and white cup and poured a cup of tea for Wang Fusheng, "Please have it."

Wang Fusheng saw the clear green tea that Li Yuzhi had just used, snorted, and smiled coldly, "What you gave Li Yuzhi was the precious Rain Dragon Well tea, but what you gave me was wild chrysanthemum tea."

Xiu Xin poured herself a cup of tea. "This wild chrysanthemum tea is what I usually use. But how can I use such cheap tea to entertain the prince? I am really guilty."

When Wang Fusheng heard that this was the tea she drank daily, the depression in his stomach disappeared instantly and the expression on his face relaxed a little.

"Xiu Xin, you should know why I came to Chenzhou this time?"

Xiu Xin smiled slightly, "Of course I know. When will the prince leave? I will pack my luggage."

Wang Fusheng was so excited that he couldn't even finish his words, "Xiu...Xin, Xiu Xin, are you willing to go with me? Have you forgiven me?"

"Your Majesty." Xiu Xin raised her eyes and glanced at him calmly. "A year ago, when you were still the Prime Minister, my Cui family was like an ant in front of you. Now, you are the regent, with great power in the court. How could I have the courage to compete with you, Your Majesty?"

Wang Fusheng's smile froze for a moment, and the corners of his mouth slowly slid down. He smiled bitterly, "Xiu Xin, why do you have to say that? You know clearly that I won't force you."

"You are already forcing me!" Xiu Xin's expression suddenly turned cold. "Wang Fusheng, we have already divorced. There is no relationship between us anymore. You own the whole world, and you have all kinds of beauties. Why do you want to go back to me?"

"I only want you." He said it firmly, as if he was swearing.

Xiu Xin sneered a few times, "No, Your Majesty, maybe you really want me, but what you really care about is power. If you still have a little affection for me, you shouldn't force me anymore. If you still force me, I will die."

"Xiu Xin!" Wang Fusheng clenched his hands tightly. He wanted to say something but couldn't. Finally, he took a deep breath and whispered, "Your father has been reinstated, and your two brothers have returned to the capital. Your home is in the capital, so why do you have to hide in Chenzhou because of me? If you don't want to see me, I won't show up in front of you."

"Your Highness, a promise is worth a thousand gold." Xiu Xin stood up and bowed to him.

Wang Fusheng looked at her and said, "Xiu Xin, I know I'm sorry for you, but sometimes, there are things that I just can't choose."

"Farewell, Your Majesty."

A tear slowly overflowed from Xiuxin's eye

socket and slowly slid down her smooth cheek.

Cui Xiuxin, now that things have come to this, could it be that you still have him in your heart?

Ridiculous, so ridiculous.

After an unknown amount of time, Jiang Zixuan gently pushed the door open and came in, "Sister..."

"Zi Xuan……"

"Sister, what's wrong with you?"

"nothing."

Zi Xuan had just heard intermittent crying outside the door and thought that Wang Fusheng had bullied her. She asked worriedly, "Sister, what exactly is the Regent going to do?"

"Zixuan." Xiuxin wiped her tears, "Send a servant to give a message to Lord Li Yuzhi, and tell him that I have something to say to him."

Zixuan thought Xiuxin had made her choice, and said with a smile, "Okay, okay, I'll go right away. So, sister, are you planning to go back to the capital with Lord Li?"

Xiu Xin paused and said, "My father and mother are in the capital after all, I have to go back. He has already followed me here, and hiding is no use."

Zi Xuan asked, "Sister, when are you going to leave? Why not wait until I get married?"

Jiang Zixuan and the young master of the Du family's wedding date is set for next month, which is only about ten days away if you count carefully.

"Of course. How can I be absent from Sister Zixuan's wedding?"

The next evening, Xiuxin and Li Yuzhi met in the pavilion in the back garden.

"Embroidered Heart."

"Mr. Li." Xiu Xin bowed to him, "I asked you to come here today to meet me because I really have something to say to you."

Li Yuzhi looked at Xiuxin's expression and knew what she was going to say. She felt cold in her heart and said with difficulty, "Miss, have you thought it through?"

"I've thought it through." Xiuxin's feelings for Li Yuzhi were complicated. At first, she did have a little affection for him and even wanted to marry him. But that was just because she thought he was right for her. Later, after marrying Wang Fusheng... Xiuxin laughed at herself. She hardly thought of him. And then it was now... It's not that she hadn't thought about accepting him. After all, being with him was always easy. But that man left too many things on her. Whether it was joy or scars, her whole body was already covered with his traces. She couldn't break free at all.

"Sir, some things are missed once they are missed. Although it has only been a short year, things have already changed. I cannot bear your kindness, and I have no way to repay you."

"Is it because of him, because he's back?" Xiu Xin said, "No, it has nothing to do with him. It's just that Xiu Xin can't turn back..."

"I understand..." Li Yuzhi's eyes were filled with pain, and she almost couldn't stand steadily, but a smile gradually appeared on his face. He even bent down deeply and clasped his hands, saying, "Yuzhi is unlucky. From now on, I wish you everything goes well and you live a long and safe life."

When Li Yuzhi was about to turn around, Xiuxin called him, "Mr. Li."

"You and I are not destined to be together. Young Master will surely find a beautiful woman who is worthy of you in the future."

The next day, Li Yuzhi took four or five servants and two carriages to the capital to take up the post of Minister of Personnel. Before leaving, Zixuan and Xiuxin stood in the distance to see him off. Li Yuzhi also bowed to the two of them from a distance.

Xiu Xin smiled slightly and returned the greeting.

Mr. Li, the road ahead is long, so we will say goodbye now.

Since Li Yuzhi left, Wang Fusheng began to visit Jiang's house from time to time, without caring whether Jiang Yunhai was happy or not, showing his true ruffian nature.

"Master Jiang, how about we play a game of

chess?"

Jiang Yunhai said coldly, "My chess skills are not good, I am afraid that I have ruined your fun, Lord Wang."

"Haha, since Master Jiang is not good at chess, he should practice more. Come, let me put the chessboard on the table first." He then said to the stunned servant in the Jiang Mansion, "What are you still standing there for? Do you have any sense? Didn't you see that your master wants to play chess? Why don't you bring the chess pieces and chessboard?"

Jiang Yunhai: "…"

Whose house is this? This is... the guest has become the host.

Since Wang Fusheng came to Jiang's house every day, it was not to play chess with Jiang Yunhai. He played chess with Jiang Yunhai in the morning, so he naturally had lunch in Jiang's house at noon, and then after lunch, he naturally went to the yard to walk a few steps to digest the food... The so-called drunkard's intention is not to drink, nothing more than this.

However, the devil is always one step ahead of you.

That day Wang Fusheng went to the garden as usual. Although he hadn't seen Xiuxin in the past few days, at least he could stand in front of her door and be closer to her.

But what about this wall that appeared out of nowhere today? Wang Fusheng's face turned completely black.

Jiang Yunhai smiled naturally, "Lord Wang, this is the backyard where my wife and daughter are. I think it would be better to separate the front yard from the backyard to avoid being criticized."

Haha, you are really quick, Lord Jiang, to build a wall overnight.

"Master Jiang, I remember that I have some unfinished business, so I'll leave first."

Jiang Yunhai said with a fake smile, "Lord Wang is very busy, and state affairs are of course the most important. Jiang will see you off."

Wang Fusheng turned around and looked at the wall grimly, and snorted in his heart, "Jiang Fox, just wait and see, a mere wall can stop me? You underestimate me too much."

The author has something to say: There will be an update tomorrow.

☆, Chapter 86 Missing

Chapter 86: Disappearance

Even if Xiuxin never leaves her house, it is impossible for her to stay in the inner courtyard all the time and spend her days reading some idle books. Zixuan, however, cannot stay there. In the past, there was no place in the Jiang Mansion that she dared not go. Now, the wall has been built and it is useless to Zixuan. Because she quickly got the key from Jiang Yunhai.

"Sister, let's go out for a walk. There's a

temple fair today. It's going to be very lively."

Xiu Xin looked at her lazily, "You are going to get married, and you are still making a fuss like this."

"Sister, you spend all day eating and sleeping, don't you feel bored at all?"

Xiu Xin shook her head, "I want to fatten myself up so that my mother will be happy to see me."

Zixuan smiled and said, "Sister... accompany me for a walk. I won't get thinner if I go out for a walk, okay?"

Xiu Xin still shook her head.

"Sister... go ahead..." Zixuan said coquettishly while shaking Xiuxin's arm.

"Okay, okay, I'm afraid of you..." Xiu Xin sighed, "But we have to agree on three rules."

"Ah?" Zi Xuan pouted, "Which three chapters?"

"First, you are not allowed to run around alone."

"good."

"Second, we must wear veils when we go out and not reveal our identities."

"good."

"Third, we have to bring a few guards with us to prevent any accidents."

"Ah? Sister, it's so boring to bring them along." Zixuan said with a bitter face.

"What if something unexpected happens? You have to bring them along. If you think they're in the way, why not just let them

move away from the election?"
"Okay." Zi Xuan said, "I'll listen to you, sister."
The temple fair was as lively as imagined. People dressed in all kinds of strange costumes carried clay sculptures of various Bodhisattvas and gods and walked along the street with music. On both sides of the road stood all kinds of small stalls, selling sugar people, clay sculptures, wontons, red hairpins and other utensils.
Zixuan was so excited that she pulled Xiuxin's hand and ran around, squeezing into the crowd.
"Ah, slow down, slow down." Xiuxin was dragged into a crowd of people. Inside, a burly man was playing with a monkey. The monkey was quirky, jumping up and down, and even standing and waving to the tourists, just like a little adult. Then, the monkey held a gong and walked around in circles asking for money. Some people gave him a few copper coins.
Zi Xuan was amazed at what she saw, "Wow, so smart."
As he was talking, the monkey came up to Zixuan holding a tray. Zixuan reached into her sleeve and threw a small ingot of silver into the gong with a clang.
The monkey trainer glanced at Zixuan and a strange look flashed in his eyes.
Seeing this, Xiu Xin hurriedly pulled Zi Xuan out of the crowd and said, "Zi Xuan, when you go out, you must avoid showing off

your talents. The two taels of silver just now are indeed nothing to us, but in this market, I am afraid it will easily cause trouble."

Zi Xuan said, "Chenzhou is now well governed, what could possibly happen? Besides, didn't we bring a lot of guards with us?"

Xiu Xin said, "That's true, but it's always better to be careful."

"Ah, it seems like someone is performing acrobatics over there. Sister, sister, let's go over and take a look." Zixuan's attention had long been attracted by other things.

Xiuxin had no choice but to follow Zixuan and walk forward.

But Zixuan was very agile and full of energy. She twisted and turned and soon squeezed into the crowd and disappeared. Xiuxin guessed that she must have squeezed to the front, so she simply waited for her outside the crowd.

At this time, Xiuxin vaguely heard someone calling her name, and turned around suddenly. Sure enough, it was Wang Fusheng. He was wearing a purple robe and holding a white jade fan in his hand, looking very noble.

"Your Highness." Xiu Xin restrained the expression on her face and bowed to him solemnly.

Wang Fusheng frowned and said, "Even if we are not husband and wife anymore, there is no need to be so distant, right? You are showing such a great courtesy to me when you see me."

Xiu Xin just said calmly, "Etiquette cannot be abolished."

Wang Fusheng said helplessly, "Okay, whatever you want."

At this moment, Mo Yan, who was behind Wang Fusheng, came over and looked at Xiu Xin with tears in his eyes, "Madam...Madam, it's me, Mo Yan."

Xiu Xin asked, "Mo Yan, I haven't seen you for a few months. Are you okay?"

Mo Yan said, "Thank you for your concern, Mo Yan is doing well."

Xiu Xin said, "Mo Yan, I am not your master now, so it is better not to use this title carelessly."

Mo Yan had no choice but to respond, "Yes, master. Oh, no, Miss Cui." After saying that, he glanced at his second master.

Wang Fusheng had no other expression, and slowly fanned the folding fan in his hand, "Since we are so predestined, why don't we go to this temple fair together?"

Xiu Xin said, "There is a difference between men and women, I'm afraid it's not appropriate?"

Wang Fusheng was speechless after hearing this sentence. He wanted to ask, what kind of relationship do we have? We have done so many intimate things, why are we afraid of such a small thing now? But at this moment, he couldn't say it, so he had to hold back the words that were about to come out, "In this case, Wang will not bother you anymore."

Wang Fusheng was determined to win Xiuxin's heart again, but his previous methods of force and dominance would only make Xiuxin's heart colder, so now he could only go along with Xiuxin and try to please her.

Xiu Xin looked at him suspiciously as he turned and walked in the opposite direction. She felt relieved. In fact, until now, she felt a thorn in her heart that hurt slightly when she faced Wang Fusheng. She tried hard to ignore the pain and the waves in her heart when she faced him.

She turned around and scanned the crowd for Jiang Zixuan's figure.

Why hasn't it come out after so long?

Xiu Xin was puzzled and squeezed into the crowd to take a look. She saw two big men stacked high together, forming a triangle, and everyone was cheering. Xiu Xin looked around at everyone and her heart skipped a beat. Oh no! Where is Zi Xuan?

"Zixuan? Zixuan?" Xiuxin called out anxiously, but there was no response. She called out again anxiously, "Zixuan!" Still no response. Xiuxin's cold sweat broke out. Nothing will happen, right? Did Zixuan show off her talent in front of others just now? Could she have been captured by some bad guys?

The more she thought about it, the scarier it became. Xiu Xin quickly left the crowd

and asked, "Zi Xuan, Zi Xuan?"
"Cousin, what's the matter?" Several guards from the Jiang residence came forward.
"Have you seen the lady?"
The guards all showed horrified expressions on their faces, "The young lady is missing?"
"Just now I saw her squeeze in to watch the circus by herself, but when I followed her in a moment later, she had disappeared."
One of the guards waved his hand and said, "You go back and report to the master, and the rest of you follow me!" With that, four or five people started to chase after him.
Xiu Xin was also frightened and at a loss of her wits. She had never encountered such a situation before, and she blamed herself and was afraid. Suddenly she remembered someone, ran forward a few steps, and a figure in purple came into her sight.
Xiuxin didn't even think about it and grabbed the man, "Wang Fusheng!"
The man turned around, but it was a strange face, with a hint of impatience, "Who are you?"
Xiu Xin let go of her hand and said, "Sorry, I got the wrong person."
"Are you looking for me?" At this moment, Xiuxin heard a man's voice behind her.
Xiu Xin turned around suddenly and grabbed Wang Fusheng's sleeve as if she had found a treasure, "Wang Fusheng, Zixuan is missing! Send someone to save Zixuan!"
The author has something to say: This is

the second update today. Is Manman diligent? There will be an update tomorrow.

☆, Chapter 87: Assassination

Chapter 87: Assassination
Wang Fusheng was startled. "Zi Xuan? The daughter of the Jiang family? When did she disappear?"
Xiu Xin said, "Just now, in the blink of an eye, but now the person is gone!"
Wang Fusheng pondered for a moment and clapped his hands. In an instant, dozens of people stood behind Wang Fusheng. These dozens of people were dressed in cloth and looked like ordinary people, but they were all tall and strong, with bright eyes, and they were obviously masters of the palace.
Wang Fusheng asked, "Xiu Xin, what is she wearing today?"
Xiu Xin said, "She was wearing a light yellow double-breasted short jacket and a pink skirt."
"You go find Miss Jiang." Wang Fusheng said in a deep voice.
"Yes, Your Highness!" Everyone bowed and said in unison, with an awe-inspiring aura.
Mo Yan said worriedly, "Master, should we leave a few guards behind? I am worried about your safety."
Wang Fusheng hesitated for a moment and said, "No need. Let them all go. What can happen?"
Wang Fusheng saw Xiu Xin frowning, and

couldn't help but comfort her, "It's okay, it's okay, the people around me are all top-notch experts, they will definitely find it."

Xiuxin nodded, but she was still very worried. It was all my fault for not watching her. She was playful and playful all day long, so why did I let her walk into the crowd alone? "

Wang Fusheng held Xiuxin's shoulders and said, "Don't think like that. Even if you, a weak woman, stay with Miss Jiang, it will be useless. You might even be kidnapped."

Mo Yan said, "Master, Miss Cui, let's find a teahouse and wait for news. I have just sent someone back to the mansion, and someone will come over soon."

Xiu Xin thought about it and nodded, "This is the only way."

The group walked around the crowd and headed for a teahouse not far away. Wang Fusheng followed Xiuxin to a teahouse with the words "Xingsheng Teahouse" written on the plaque. After Xiuxin and Mo Yan entered the teahouse, they saw that Wang Fusheng had not followed them in, so they turned around and looked at him in confusion, "Why don't you come in?"

Wang Fusheng nodded and walked in.

There were men and women sitting in the teahouse, not too crowded. A waiter came over and asked, "What would you like, my dear guests?"

Wang Fusheng said, "I want a private room."

The waiter smiled and replied, "Oh, what a bad luck. The private room is full today. Could you please sit in the lobby now?"

Wang Fusheng looked around and nodded.

After Wang Fusheng and Xiuxin sat down, the waiter asked, "What kind of tea would you like?"

Wang Fusheng said, "A pot of Longjing."

"Okay, please wait a moment, gentlemen."

After a while, the tea was served. Mo Yan poured two cups of tea for Wang Fusheng and Xiu Xin respectively, "Master, please enjoy your meal."

Xiu Xin picked up the teacup, and Wang Fusheng stopped her, saying, "Wait."

"What's wrong?"

"Mo Yan, try using a silver needle."

Mo Yan dipped a silver needle into the tea, but the needle did not change color at all.

Xiu Xin asked, "Are you afraid someone will poison you?"

"It's always better to be careful."

Xiu Xin glanced at him and thought to herself, now that the new emperor has ascended the throne, the court is not stable, and the power of the Fifth Prince Hua Ling and the Cui family has not been eliminated. There are indeed many people who want to kill him.

Mo Yan interrupted, "I encountered an assassination attempt on my way here. Fortunately, I brought a lot of secret guards with me, otherwise the consequences would be disastrous."

Xiu Xin said, "The court is not stable right now, and you just came to Chenzhou like this. Aren't you afraid that the Cui family and the fifth prince will revive and make a comeback?"

Wang Fusheng stared at her with his eyes as black as black jade. "Don't you know why I gave up everything and came to Chenzhou?"

Xiu Xin avoided his gaze and said, "Wang Fusheng, do you know that when you throw away something, it is extremely difficult to find it again later?"

"I know it's hard as climbing to heaven..." Wang Fusheng said, "I didn't expect you to come back to me so soon. As long as you don't hate me so much, I will be satisfied."

Suddenly, a cold light flashed before Xiuxin's eyes. She was startled and shouted, "Be careful!"

Wang Fusheng quickly stood up, protecting Xiuxin behind him, and looked around. All the guests drinking tea had swords in their hands. The waiter who had received them at the beginning quickly closed the door and came in.

Xiuxin's cold sweat quickly wet her back. The doors and windows were all closed. It seemed that this assassination was planned for a long time. She felt like she couldn't escape even if she had wings.

"Lure the tiger away from the mountain." Wang Fusheng sneered, "You really put in a lot of effort this time." First they kidnapped Jiang Zixuan, mobilized Wang Fusheng's secret guards, and then caught the turtle in the jar.

"Of course. How can I kill you, Lord Wang, without putting in some effort?" The door to the private room on the second floor opened, and a man in a blue robe walked out with an extremely cold smile on his face. "Lord Wang, long time no see."

Yes, the fifth prince Hua Ling!

Wang Fusheng smiled slightly, "Your Highness the Fifth Prince, I am flattered that you gave me such a big gift upon meeting me."

Hua Ling said, "Guess what, if you died here today, would that idiot Second in the court still be able to keep his throne?"

"You have a good plan, but don't forget that I am not the only male in the Wang family."

"There are indeed more than one person in the Wang family, but you are the one who makes the decision. If we kill you, the Wang family will be seriously injured." The fifth prince showed a cold smile on his face, "Everyone listen to me, kill Wang Fusheng." After a pause, he said, "You must not hurt the beauty next to you, do it!"

In an instant, Wang Fusheng pressed Xiu Xin under the table and said urgently, "Hide well! They are coming for me this time, it has nothing to do with you!"

Mo Yan randomly picked up a soup spoon from the table and tremblingly stood in front of

Wang Fusheng, "Master, I'll block it. Master, take the second wife and leave quickly."

Wang Fusheng patted Mo Yan on the forehead and said, "What's the point of holding a soup spoon?"

Mo Yan was so scared that he almost cried, "But Master, I don't have a knife..."

The assassins knew that Wang Fusheng was just a scholar, and that killing him would be easier than killing a chicken. Seeing this, they laughed a few times and approached Wang Fusheng step by step, "Don't struggle, just accept your death."

"How stupid!" Wang Fusheng cursed, took out a small knife inlaid with gems from his sleeve, threw away the scabbard, and the blade flashed with cold light.

A slender hand snatched the knife from Wang Fusheng's hand and took a posture to meet the enemy, "I'll do it!"

"Embroidered Heart!"

Xiu Xin's eyes were filled with determination, "They don't dare to hurt me, so I'll delay it as long as possible."

"Don't be so stubborn, this is none of your business."

Xiu Xin used her hands to block Wang Fusheng behind her, "Although there is no friendship between us anymore, I can't watch you die."

Wang Fusheng said excitedly, "Xiu Xin! You still have me in your heart, don't you?"

The fifth prince on the second floor

snorted coldly, "It's already this late and you're still being sentimental. Hurry up and do it!"

"Yes! Your Highness!" Everyone rushed forward.

Although Xiu Xin had learned some basic skills from the female martial arts master since she was young, those were just fancy moves to strengthen her body. Facing so many people, Xiu Xin's hands immediately broke out in sweat. When a knife came over, Xiu Xin looked back at Wang Fusheng. She would never let him die!

Ding!

The small knife actually blocked the big knife.

The man was stunned. He never expected that such a fragile woman could block his attack. Xiu Xin took advantage of the moment when he was stunned and stabbed the man in the heart with a knife, then kicked him hard in the abdomen. These actions were done in one go, as if they had been practiced many times.

Wang Fusheng was stunned watching from the side. He had always thought his wife was a little rabbit, but he never thought that the little rabbit would become a tiger one day.

Because the Fifth Prince had instructed beforehand not to hurt Xiu Xin, those people were very cautious and restricted their moves. After a few times, Xiu Xin blocked several attacks. The assassins

became anxious and slashed at Xiu Xin's abdomen without any hesitation.
Xiu Xin was fighting with someone at the time, and the other party was unable to dodge.
At that moment, Xiu Xin closed her eyes and secretly laughed at herself. She was such a loser. He had abandoned her so cruelly, but she was still willing to die for him...
"No! Xiuxin!" In a trance, Xiuxin heard someone calling her name, so miserably...
When she lowered her head, she saw Wang Fusheng lying on the ground with a deep wound on his abdomen. Blood was gushing out and soon all over the ground.
Xiuxin's eyes suddenly became blurry. She rubbed her eyes, as if she couldn't believe it. She squatted down, covered his wound tightly with her hands, and screamed, "Husband!"
The author has something to say: There will be updates tomorrow unless there are special circumstances. The so-called special circumstances refer to overtime.

☆, Chapter 88: Dying

Chapter 88: Dying
One day later, Jiang Mansion, Chenzhou.
Zixuan opened the curtain, came in with a tray, put a few side dishes and rice on the small table, and said to Xiuxin, "Sister, please have some rice."
Xiuxin stared at Wang Fusheng, who was

lying unconscious on the bed, and replied hoarsely, "I'm not hungry."
"Sister!" Zi Xuan said anxiously, "You will collapse if you continue like this. If Lord Wang wakes up and something happens to you, he will be very worried..."
"Zi Xuan······"
"Um?"
"He'll be fine, right?" Xiuxin held his hand tightly, fearing that she would lose him completely if she let go. He was bleeding a lot, and she couldn't even imagine how a person could bleed so much.
"Imperial Physician Jiang said that the prince will be fine and he will wake up soon." Zi Xuan saw Xiu Xin crying and was so flustered that she started crying too. "Sister, it's all my fault. I was too playful. If it weren't for me, you wouldn't have fallen into such a dangerous situation."
Xiu Xin said tiredly, "It's none of your business. If you don't leave, they might tie you and me up together."
Xiu Xin took the towel from Wang Fusheng's forehead, put the warm towel back into the basin, wrung it out, and applied it to his forehead, "It's still so hot..."
"Miss, Imperial Doctor Zhang is here."
"Please ask him to come in."
Zhan Xue also came in with Imperial Physician Zhang. It was Zhan Xue who arrived in time yesterday to save everyone. The fifth prince was captured and sent to

the capital, and the rebels were also imprisoned. Everything seemed to be over.
Imperial Physician Zhang first felt Wang Fusheng's pulse, then slowly unbuttoned his clothes and carefully removed the layers of blood-stained gauze wrapped around his waist.
All the gauze was taken off, and Xiuxin clearly saw a long, deep, hideous wound that was still oozing blood! She held her hands to her chest, feeling so heartbroken that she could hardly breathe.
Imperial Physician Zhang carefully applied the prepared medicine on his wound, and then slowly re-bandaged the wound with clean gauze.
"Doctor Zhang, when will he wake up?"
"I don't know. The prince was seriously injured, lost too much blood, and had a high fever. I really can't give you a definite answer..."
"Okay, I understand." Xiu Xin's voice was so tight that it seemed like it would break at the slightest touch.
Zhan Xue held Xiu Xin's shoulders and said, "Xiu Xin, don't worry too much. He will get through it. Because of you..."
Zhan Xue's eyes fell on the untouched food on the small table. Zi Xuan shook her head at Zhan Xue. Zhan Xue waved her hand, "Take away all the food and make a bowl of ginseng tea."
"Yes." Cuixiang replied.
After a while, Cuixiang brought a bowl of

hot ginseng tea over. Zhanxue took the bowl, scooped a spoonful with a spoon and handed it to Xiuxin's mouth, "Take a sip. You look so ugly. You have been going without food, water or sleep since yesterday. How can you bear it?"

Xiu Xin still shook her head, "How can I drink it?"

"You have to drink it even if you don't want to." Zhan Xue said firmly, "Open your mouth."

After half-forcing Xiu Xin to drink a whole night of ginseng soup, Zhan Xue finally breathed a sigh of relief and glanced at Wang Fusheng. "My father has been fighting on the battlefield for many years and was seriously injured in his early years. He met a monk who gave my father a packet of medicine. After applying it, not only did the fever go down, but the wound also healed quickly. My father has sent people to look for that person. When he is found, the prince will be fine."

"Zhanxue!" Xiuxin held Zhanxue's hand, "Zhanxue...you must hurry up, hurry up, I'm afraid of him...I'm afraid of him..."

"Don't worry, don't worry, everything will be fine." Zhan Xue hugged Zhan Xue and patted her back gently, "Everything will be fine, Xiu Xin..."

Another night passed.

Xiu Xin woke up from the nightmare, wiped the cold sweat from her forehead with her hand, and reached out to wipe the temperature of Wang Fusheng's forehead. The temperature on his forehead was even hotter. That temperature made her heart clenched tightly, "Husband? Husband!"

Wang Fusheng lay on the bed with his eyes tightly closed, his lips cracked and his face pale.

"Imperial Physician Zhang, Imperial Physician Zhang!" Xiu Xin stood up suddenly and screamed, "Imperial Physician Zhang! Come quickly, come and see him!"

After a while, Imperial Physician Zhang hurried over and put his hand on Wang Fusheng's wrist. Slowly, his brows became more and more furrowed.

"Why is his body so hot? What should I do? What should I do..." Xiuxin's tears flowed down and her speech became incoherent.

Imperial Physician Zhang shook his head grimly.

"Zhang... Imperial Doctor Zhang, you shake your head...what do you mean?"

"My Lord, I'm afraid he is..."

"Fear...what...is..." Xiu Xin's eyes opened wide.

"I'm afraid I can't hold on any longer..."

"Ah! Girl! Girl!" Lanxiang hurriedly hugged Xiuxin, "Girl!"

Imperial Physician Zhang felt Xiuxin's pulse and said, "Miss Cui has not rested for the past few days, and has neither eaten nor drunk. She is already weak, and is recovering from a serious illness. Now she is overly sad... I'm afraid she won't wake up for a few days. But fortunately, it's not a serious illness."

Zhan Xue on the side breathed a sigh of relief and asked, "Is the prince really beyond saving?"

Imperial Physician Zhang sighed, "The wound has become infected. The cut was too deep. There is really no way to save it."

Zhan Xue's face darkened when she heard this. "How could it be... How could it be..."

The author has something to say: There will be an update tomorrow. If I don't work overtime…

☆、Chapter 89: Complete

Chapter 89: Perfection

Three days later.

It was midnight when Xiuxin woke up. Lanxiang was sleeping beside her bed. There was a bowl of ginseng tea on the table next to her. It seemed that she had survived the past few days because of this. Xiuxin slowly got up and opened the window. The air was a little stuffy, as if a heavy rain was coming.

Sure enough, the next second, a bright flash of lightning pierced through the darkness, illuminating Xiuxin's face white. Then, thunder roared in Xiuxin's ears.

Amidst the thunder, there was a faint sound of crying that reached Xiuxin's eardrums. It was very faint, but hard to ignore.

She suddenly remembered what the imperial physician Zhang said before she fainted, "The prince... I'm afraid he can't hold on any longer..."

Bang!

Another thunder exploded, and Xiu Xin's heart seemed to break.

She didn't even bother to put on her shoes, she pushed open the door and ran out, the heavy rain poured down, soaking her whole body. It was only early summer and it was midnight, the rain should have been cold on her body, but Xiuxin didn't feel anything. She just ran desperately in the rain, running towards the source of the sound.

"ah······"

All that was visible was white, so blindingly white, so heart-wrenching. In the center of the main hall was a coffin, with people in white cloth kneeling around it, weeping.

Xiuxin's legs went weak and she almost couldn't stand. She slowly approached the coffin step by step, and she lay on the coffin, unable to suppress her sharp sobs, which made anyone who heard it feel sad and cry.

"Husband... Husband!" Xiu Xin couldn't stop crying, "You are sorry for me, you owe me! Who allowed you to leave like this! Who allowed you to leave like this!"

"Wuwu... Wuwu..." Xiuxin understood at that moment that no matter what this person did to her, his weight in her heart could not be erased. Because hating someone also requires strength.

"Xiu Xin..." A male voice sounded in my ears, familiar, low and pleasant.

Xiuxin's crying suddenly stopped, as if the surging sea and river had suddenly stopped. She slowly turned her head, her eyes were full of tears, her hair was disheveled, and her clothes were in disarray.

"Husband..." She was stunned, as if she didn't react. She even reached out and touched his face. Well, it was warm.

He was still in the mood to joke, "How come I didn't know when you became so familiar with the Fifth Prince? You cried so sadly."

The Fifth Prince was poisoned before he set out to return to the capital, so his mother was set up in Chenzhou, and the coffin would be transported back to the capital in a few days.

Xiu Xin hugged him suddenly, "You are not dead?"

He put his arm around her and patted her on the back, "I'm not dead. Good people don't live long, but bad people live a thousand years. I was so bad to you, so the King of Hell didn't take me."

"Wow..." Xiu Xin cried for a long time in Wang Fusheng's arms, "I'm so scared, so scared..."

When Xiuxin raised her head from Wang Fusheng's arms, Wang Fusheng saw Xiuxin's appearance and couldn't help but burst out laughing, "Your face has become like a little cat's." As he said that, he used his sleeve to wipe the tears and snot from Xiuxin's face.

"Okay, okay, that's enough for the two of you, right? There are so many people watching here." A female voice said with a smile.

Wang Fusheng then put on the attitude of a father-in-law, "Is this how you talk to your father?"

Zhan Xue snorted, "If my father's medicine hadn't arrived in time, would you be so lively now? You will never see Xiu Xin again!"

Xiu Xin sighed inwardly. These two people just didn't get along when they met. I really don't know how they will live under the same roof in the future...

Wang Fusheng said, "Look, you are all wet. Go back and change your clothes."

Xiu Xin nodded.

The two of them walked back into the house together. Lan Xiang came up to them in surprise. "Girl, are you awake? I just woke up and didn't see you. I was so scared."

Wang Fusheng instructed calmly, "Go prepare some hot water, and remember to add some old ginger. Xiuxin has been caught in the rain, so she needs to ward off the cold."

"Yes." Lanxiang replied and left. Soon, two maids came in with two large buckets of hot water and poured them into the bathtub. Lanxiang came in, added ginger slices and sesame oil, and placed a small dish of bath beans next to it before leaving. Xiuxin was about to reach out to unbutton her collar when she suddenly realized that someone was still in the room. She couldn't help but blush and glared at someone who didn't realize it, "Hey, get out."

Who is Wang Fusheng? His face is as thick as a city wall.

"We are husband and wife, do you need me to avoid you when you take a bath?"

Xiu Xin scooped up the hot water and poured it over him, spitting, "Who calls you husband and wife? Don't forget, we're divorced!"

Wang Fusheng approached with a playful smile, unbuttoned Xiuxin's clothes with his hands, his eyes darkened, and his breathing became heavier, "When we return to the capital, I will marry you right away."

Hey, you're taking advantage of me!

Xiu Xin pushed him hard and said, "What are you doing?"

"Ah!" Wang Fusheng's face suddenly changed and he bent over, holding his abdomen.

Xiu Xin was startled. "What happened to you? Did I touch your wound? Does it hurt? Is it okay? Do you want to call Imperial Doctor Zhang?"

Wang Fusheng endured the great pain and said, "Xiu Xin, I just saved my life, but my wounds are not healed yet."

"I...I didn't mean it..." Xiu Xin blamed herself very much.

Wang Fusheng smiled slyly, "So, it doesn't

matter if I watch you bathing next to you. I can't do anything."

Xiu Xin: "..."

Ever since Wang Fusheng saved his life, he became more and more arrogant, relying on his injuries and Xiuxin's pity for him. Not only did he stay in Xiuxin's boudoir all day, but he also took advantage of no one to touch her and steal her body. However, Xiuxin was afraid of his injuries and did not dare to push him hard. He became more and more proud, hugged Xiuxin tightly, and kissed her.

After being bullied several times, Xiu Xin felt that she couldn't let it go on like this. She put her hands on her hips and said fiercely, "Wang Fusheng, I'm telling you, we've already divorced. It doesn't matter anymore! You're flirting with decent women by touching them like this!"

Wang Fusheng said innocently, "But you have me in your heart. If you have me in your heart, then we are in love with each other. How can you say that I am flirting with you?"

Xiu Xin said stubbornly, "Who said I have you in my heart? Stop being so self-indulgent!"

Wang Fusheng asked, "You don't have me in your heart? If you don't have me in your heart, why would you stand in front of me in such a critical situation? Why would you lie on the coffin and cry heartbrokenly?"

"You..." Xiu Xin was speechless, but her

ears turned red.

Wang Fusheng smiled proudly again and kissed Xiuxin's lips.

Facts have proved that Xiu Xin is still too young and cannot defeat the wily and scheming Wang.

Wang Fusheng chuckled and lay down lazily, "Actually, I should really thank the Fifth Prince. Without him, there wouldn't be such a good time today."

Xiu Xin said, "Don't talk nonsense."

Wang Fusheng reached out and pulled Xiuxin to lie on his chest. Xiuxin carefully avoided his wounds, closed her eyes, and felt his strong heartbeat.

"Embroidered Heart..."

"Hmm?" Xiu Xin responded softly.

Wang Fusheng's hand stroked her back slowly. "Actually... I originally planned to send you to the border to hide. My uncle is there, it's absolutely safe, and there's no news. You stay with him for half a year, and when you come back, everything will be over, and we'll still be fine."

"Hmm..." Xiuxin's nose suddenly felt a little sour.

"Xiu Xin, you have to know that in my heart you are much more important than power, but there are some things I don't have the right to choose."

"Hmm..." Xiu Xin responded softly, tears already flowing out.

"Embroidered Heart."

"Um······"

"Have you forgiven me?"

Xiu Xin's tears suddenly burst out. She buried her head in his chest and replied muffledly, "I don't know."

Xiuxin didn't dare to say that she forgave him, because the wound in her heart had not healed yet and was even bleeding. But she couldn't let herself leave him, even though it hurt.

Wang Fusheng sighed deeply, "I will make you forgive me."

After Wang Fusheng had been lingering at the Jiang family for more than half a month, he finally set off after the emperor's repeated urging. Of course, Xiu Xin and Zhan Xue also followed him back to Beijing.

Xiuxin was originally in the same carriage with Zhanxue, but later Wang tricked Xiuxin into his carriage with the poor excuse of a relapse of her wound. Xiuxin believed it, asked about her health, served her medicine, and then flirted with her in various ways.

On a dark and windy night, Lord Wang took everyone to the best inn in Yanzhou under the pretext of recuperation, and squeezed into Xiuxin's room under the pretext that he had no one to take care of him at night.

"You sleep on the floor."

"How can you bear to let me, who is still seriously injured and has not recovered, sleep on the ground?" A pitiful expression.

Xiu Xin sighed and got out of bed holding a quilt, "Is it okay for me to sleep on the floor?"

"Hey..." Wang Fusheng hugged her from behind, lowered his head and gently kissed the delicate skin on Xiuxin's neck, and called softly, "Xiuxin..."

"Don't move, your injury isn't fully healed yet."

"It's all healed, really!" As if to prove that someone's injury was really healed, Wang Fusheng carried Xiuxin and her quilt to the bed, then pressed his whole body on her, proving with his own actions that his injury was really healed.

Of course, the next day, the wound on his waist split open mercilessly, oozing a little blood. A certain unscrupulous imperial doctor ambiguously went back and forth between Wang Fusheng and Xiu Xin, and earnestly warned, "Your Majesty, you have not fully recovered yet, and some intense exercises are not suitable for you at this time."

This sentence made Xiuxin blush, and Wang Fusheng was so thick-skinned that he even said, "How can I resist when I see such a beautiful woman?"

"Cough cough." Imperial Physician Zhang coughed a few times, completely defeated by Wang Fusheng's shamelessness.

Five days later, they finally arrived in the capital. The carriage from the palace went straight to the Wang family.

Xiu Xin lifted the car curtain and said, "Stop the car!"

Wang Fusheng hugged Xiuxin, "What's wrong?

Baby."

Xiu Xin said seriously, "You and I have already divorced, so I should naturally return to my Cui family."

Wang Fusheng really wanted to stay with her for a moment, but Xiuxin's words made sense, so he had to take a step back and said, "I will send someone to propose marriage right away."

Xiu Xin ignored him, got off the carriage and got on another carriage, and told the driver, "Let's go back to Cui Mansion."

After Xiuxin went back, Wang Fusheng could no longer meet her. Although he sent a matchmaker to her house the next day, he was rejected by Cui Zhengkai. A few days later, Wang Fusheng sent another matchmaker to her house. He was rejected again.

Wang Fusheng was a little anxious this time. He was still unsure whether Xiuxin had forgiven him. Could it be that she didn't want to marry him? What should he do? Could he ask His Majesty to grant him a marriage? Of course, it would be too easy for Wang Fusheng to ask His Majesty to grant him a marriage, but he didn't want to force her anymore.

So I had no choice but to visit them again and again. But without exception, I was always turned away and received many cold stares.

Wang Fusheng had never suffered such a humiliating insult in his life, but there was nothing he could do about it. Who could have told him that he loved the other person's daughter?

So Wang Fusheng flattered Cui Zhengkai in every way in the court. Outside the court, he chased after Cui Zhengkai and sent all kinds of rare treasures to Cui's mansion.

Finally one day, the door opened in the face of Mrs. Cui Jiang's cold face.

Wang Fusheng was overjoyed, "Mother, you are finally willing to let me see Xiuxin!"

Jiang snorted coldly, "You are lucky! If Xiuxin wasn't pregnant, you wouldn't even think about entering my house!"

"Yes, yes, yes." Wang Fusheng agreed habitually. He only realized what was happening halfway through his words. Then he let out an "ah" and froze.

"Mother, mother, you just said Xiuxin... is pregnant!"

"Ah." Jiang responded calmly.

The smile on Wang Fusheng's face slowly spread outward from the corners of his mouth, all the way to his ears. He jumped and ran to the inner courtyard with a smile on his face, like a child who had received candy, "Xiu Xin! Xiu Xin! We have a child!"

The author has something to say: Dear friends, this "What is House Fighting" has been serialized for half a year, and today is finally the end! There will be no extra chapters for this article, so you can imagine your life in the future.

During the writing process, I encountered many difficulties. It was the most difficult novel I had written in the past three years. For example, I had to work overtime, lost my train of thought, and received various attacks from the comments below. There was a time when I was really tired and didn't want to write anymore, but I still persisted because I felt that no matter what, I had to do my best to be worthy of the readers who paid to read it. Okay, I won't say any more nonsense. Thank you all for your support for so long. Especially those who have invested in minefields. I will fill in the gaps in my current works. It will probably take a week. Then I will start a new article! I hope you will continue to support me! Muah! If you want to know when my new article will be published, please bookmark Manman! Muah!

Printed in Great Britain
by Amazon